AA

TOWN&COUNTRY AUCTIONS IN·BRITAIN

·THE BARGAIN HUNTERS HANDBOOK·

·Eric Geen·

Produced by the Publishing Division of The Automobile Association

Written by Eric Geen

Printed and bound in Great Britain by William Clowes Limited, Beccles and London

Produced by the Publishing Division of The Automobile Association

The information in this book is believed correct at the time of printing. However, changes may have occurred or may occur during the currency of the publication. Whilst the Publisher endeavours to ensure that the information is as accurate as possible, it makes no guarantee in this regard. In particular the Publisher cannot accept responsibility for any transaction entered into by any person or body as a result of the information contained in this publication. The opinions expressed in this book are not necessarily those of The Automobile Association.

Published by The Automobile Association, Fanum House, Basing View, Basingstoke RG21 2EA

ISBN: 0 7495 0186 3

A CIP catalogue record for this book is available from the British Library.

· CONTENTS ·

• INTRODUCTION •

This book is about auctions. It lists over 400 salerooms holding regular auctions that will be of interest to the casual browser, interested amateur, bargain hunter, serious collector, or professional dealer. Some of the auctions are specialist sales, devoted to an area of particular interest to collectors. Most are general sales, though, and include a mixture of household goods and antiques. You can find all sorts of things at these auctions - a Victorian pewter teapot perhaps, or a box of old crockery; a Regency sideboard or a pre-war butcher's delivery bicycle. The best auctions are those at which everything and anything can turn up, from the essential to the ridiculous.

I discovered auctions when furniture and equipment were needed for a small cottage my wife and I had bought in Norfolk. We visited a sale held in Swaffham one Saturday, and were so excited by it that we could barely stop ourselves from bidding for everything. By the end of that day, we had all we needed, including lounge and bedroom furniture, a cooker and a refrigerator, and much that we didn't need at all.

One doesn't have to go to Norfolk, however. Most towns have at least one auction house holding regular sales, and many villages have auctions too.

Any auction-goer will know the excitement of arriving at an auction, never being sure what they are going to find, discovering perhaps an old photograph album or a piece of well-crafted furniture, and enjoying the constant surprises and changes that an auction offers. There can be few better ways of passing a morning than browsing around an auction and listening to an entertaining auctioneer. As someone who earns a living writing comedy, I've often been impressed by the spontaneous wit and ad-libbing skills displayed at the rostrum.

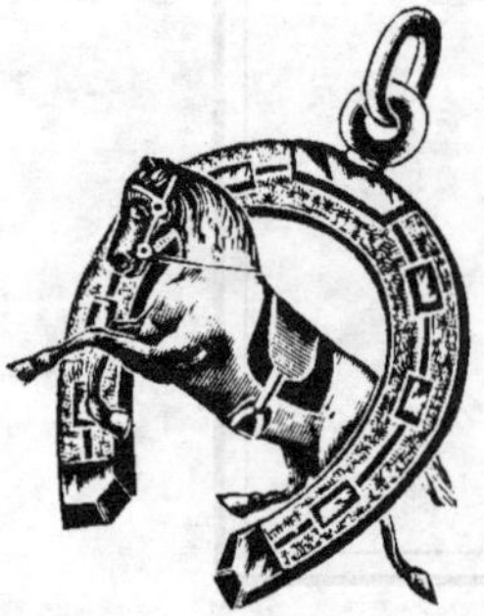

This book is a product of that excitement and enjoyment, and in particular of my attempts to explain my enthusiasm to family and friends who have joined me at sales. Auctions are rare things — endlessly varied and exciting, but poignant too, with fragments of the past in the furniture, pictures and bric-à-brac, all of which must have stories to tell.

Before the Swaffham auction, my only knowledge (like most people's, I suspect) of the auction scene had been reading now and then of the millions of pounds paid in London salerooms for famous paintings. Since then I have attended auctions in every part of Britain, from the Shetland Islands to the Cornish coast. It doesn't take long to become an avid auction-goer.

Venues

The traditional country auction is held out in the open, perhaps in the market square of a country town. Following the custom of generations, vendors set out their goods on the ground, and the auctioneer walks along the rows, taking bids for each lot as he comes to it. Cash changes hands on completion of each successful bid.

Such auctions are a delight, but they're not the whole story. Auction venues vary, so a wide range is included here — open air, cattle pens and sheds, purpose-built salerooms or specially rented halls, and some grand settings like Sotheby's

Summers Place – a magnificent mansion with 37 acres of gardens and fields, in Billingshurst, West Sussex.

Where appropriate, the information in the entries also mentions surroundings. An auction can make an entertaining family day out, but remember that it is always advisable to check sales and viewing details with the auctioneers before setting off.

Children

Auctions make a good day out for all the family, and children particularly enjoy the country ones, where there is so much to see, including, very often, animals. However, auctions are also a place of business, so make sure that children have due respect for the proceedings.

Auctioneers

Auctioneers can be eccentric. There are some who will stop a sale, and like a teacher in a classroom, refuse to continue until everyone is quiet. I know one who becomes increasingly irritated when things are sold for what he considers give-away prices. He will tut, snarl and sulk — even throw down his gavel after failing to elicit a higher bid for a lot, and, with a face red with rage, lecture the audience about the modern-day cost of things, and the price of goods in the High Street. One suspects an unspoken conspiracy among the regulars, who seem intent on not bidding for certain lots in order to provoke these Basil Fawlty-style ravings.

Another auctioneer (of whom I was very fond, and whose sales I looked forward to with some relish) enjoyed a drink. He would often consume a liquid lunch before the afternoon session. His speech became slurred and difficult to understand, and he often forgot what stage he was at with the bidding. On occasion he would even fall asleep standing up while taking bids!

The message is, don't mind some quirky behaviour — it's all part of the show.

Dealers

When auctions are mentioned, the majority of people will make a face and say 'Oh, but aren't they full of dealers?'

The answer is yes, antique dealers and second-hand dealers do attend auctions: that is how they get most of the stock that fills their shops. But a private buyer can always outbid a dealer. Going to the sale is part of the dealer's business, so time and expenses have to be added to the price he pays for any lots. A dealer has to increase the price of an item bought at an auction quite considerably in order to resell it at a profit. Indeed, it is the dealers who are nervous when too many private buyers attend a sale, because they fear they may drive prices up.

Viewing

Viewing times are often quite generous, so you have plenty of time to decide how much you want to bid. I prefer to view just before the sale. Most of the excitement is in the spontaneity of finding something and deciding how much it is worth to you.

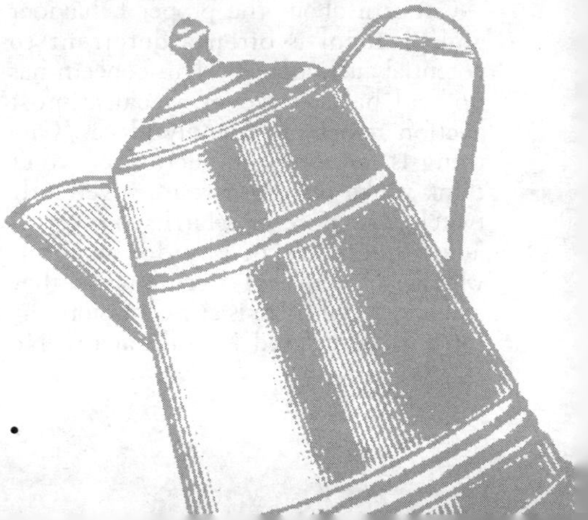

However, making a successful bid never seems such a matter of life and death after a night's sleep, no matter how much you like the thing that is on offer.

How high to bid

Deciding your maximum bidding price is the most skilful part of buying at auction. The value of anything is only what someone is prepared to pay for it. If you have your eye on something special, though, look at prices for comparable items in shops. Most objects sold at auction are likely to become less plentiful in future, so they may increase in value. This isn't inevitable however, and nothing should be bought purely as an investment.

Once you've decided your price, stick to it and don't bid higher. It is easy to get carried away. Remember, too, that you should take account of the buyer's premium, which will be added on to the successful bidding ('hammer') price by the auctioneers after the sale. This varies from nothing at all to 10 per cent or more, depending on which auction house you are at. Many auctioneers will also charge VAT on the buyer's premium, so it is important to check their policy before the sale, when you are deciding how high you can afford to bid.

Bidding and paying

Concern about the proper behaviour and protocol is often a deterrent to potential auction-goers. This concern has no real basis however, because most auction rooms are friendly places. One thing is for sure: the auctioneer won't think you're bidding if you inadvertently twitch your nose or scratch your ear. If auctioneers are in any doubt about whether or not a bid is being made, they will ask, and if there is any confusion, the lot will be offered for sale again. No

Bidding and paying—four important things to know:

1. Bidding increments

These are the stages by which bidding advances. Auctioneers always announce them at the start of the sale. If you don't know them, you may find yourself paying much more than you expected. Typical increments would be 25p or 50p for bids up to £5, £1 for bids up to £20, and then at intervals of £2 and £3 - for example £22, £25, £27, £30. Bids from £30 to £100 are usually increased by £5 and thereafter by £10. Over £1,000, bids are usually increased by £50.

2. Starting and stopping bidding

If you want to join in the bidding, you must make a clear gesture, like raising your arm. Once the auctioneer knows you're interested, your bid will be invited again. If you want to stop bidding, shake your head firmly. If your bid is successful and the auctioneer doesn't know your name, shout it out to him across the saleroom.

3. 'Paddle' bidding

This method is used in all the main auctions and is increasingly common in smaller ones. It entails registering your name and address on arrival at the saleroom, and receiving in return a card or plastic 'paddle', with a number written on it. The auctioneer asks for this to be shown at the completion of every successful bid.

4. Cash sales

Payment at traditional open-air sales is often made in cash, on the spot. Even at indoor salerooms, the auctioneers may want cash rather than cheques from people they don't know. Find out what is acceptable — unless you're happy to brazen it out.

auctioneer is going to sell to someone who doesn't want to buy.

It is always wise to register and have a 'paddle' number, even if you don't intend to bid. Registering costs nothing and does not oblige you to bid or buy, and you may regret not having registered if something catches your eye during the sale. Now that many salerooms are computerised, the 'paddle' system is supposed to speed up the process of paying, although the wait for paperwork to be completed after a successful bid rarely takes longer than 10 minutes in any sale.

I like the old system in which you hear the successful bidder's name — it helps to focus irritation if you know who is outbidding you. Shouting names across the saleroom can cause confusion, however. I remember one Norfolk auction where the auctioneer was constantly trying to increase the bids by shouting what sounded like 'Five pounds Shirley!' or 'Twenty pounds Shirley!' It wasn't until I'd visited the auction a few times and become used to the Norfolk accent that I realised what he was shouting was 'Five pounds, surely!'

Bidding is something that worries people, but it shouldn't. Bidding is fun and exciting. Once you have got over the initial embarrassment of waving your hand at the auctioneer, it becomes second nature. The problem then is to stop yourself from bidding for everything in sight!

Prices

Prices for similar lots can vary greatly, even at the same sale. You may be the only person bidding for a particular lot in one auction; another week, there may be another buyer who is determined to have whatever it is you want, at any price. I have tried to avoid quoting prices for specific items for this reason, although at some sales I have mentioned some figures to give you a better idea of what happens during the proceedings. You would normally expect to pay more for antiques than for modern items. Even in the best auctions, there are usually lots which sell for only a few pounds. It is the very flukiness of prices at auctions which makes them so fascinating to attend.

Practicalities: storing, transporting and shipping your goods

You should check what the auctioneers' policy is on these matters before bidding - although most auctioneers do not insist that goods are moved immediately after their sales. They usually allow the buyer two or three days before starting to charge for storage. There are professional removers at most sales, but if not, the *Storage*, *Transportation* and *Shipping* details given with each entry in this book show you whether the auctioneer is willing to *advise* you of suitable companies.

If these services are available, you can turn up at a sale on a bicycle and bid for a large piece of furniture. Remember the possible costs of storing and transporting goods when you're deciding how much to bid, however.

I must confess that my motto is 'buy first and worry later'. I once bought two three-piece upholstered lounge suites at one sale — the first because it was so cheap and it seemed impossible to let such a bargain pass, the second because it was of even better quality and an even better bargain. This did present some difficulty, as we had a perfectly good three-piece suite at home, and no need of another. However we sorted things out by giving one of the new suites away and putting the old one up for auction. So everyone was happy, and I had two marvellous days: one buying, and one watching my old suite being sold.

Junk or treasure?

None of the above will necessarily seem relevant at some country auctions. Vendors bring along goods which have no obvious worth, but may be just what someone else was looking for all the same. So these auctions can be a good place to sell odds and ends which it seems pointless to keep, but wasteful to throw away.

Selling at auction

This book is mostly about buying, but auctions can be an excellent way of selling something, too. At an auction, the whole of the sale price goes to the vendor (except a percentage which the vendor must pay the auctioneer in commission). A friend of mine called in a dealer to give her a price for the contents of a house. When I heard about this I talked her into selling at auction. The auctioneer found small items such as lace handkerchiefs and linen which could be sold separately, and which the dealer had included in his total price. Two items in the auction fetched more than the dealer had offered for the entire contents of the house!

If you are considering selling in this way, be careful. If you choose the wrong auction your valuable goods may be sold for a fraction of their true worth, because no one has realised their value. One way of safeguarding yourself is to put a 'reserve' price on a lot. This is a price below which an item may not be sold. This may turn out to be expensive if your item is not sold, though, because you will have to pay the auctioneer commission whatever happens. Another way is to choose an auctioneer whose policy is to keep better items back for special sales. For specialist items, always go to a specialist auction firm.

It is also wise to have your goods valued before you sell them. Most auctioneers carry out valuations free of charge, although they may charge you expenses if they have to travel to your home, etc.

. . . and finally

I do not know if there is an entry in the *Guinness Book of Records* for the number of auctions visited by one person, but if there is, I must be a serious contender. Even so, there must be many auctions I have missed. I would be grateful to hear from any member of the public, or indeed any auctioneers, who would like to recommend a sale to me, and there is a form at the end of this book for readers to use if they wish to.

May all your bids be bargains.

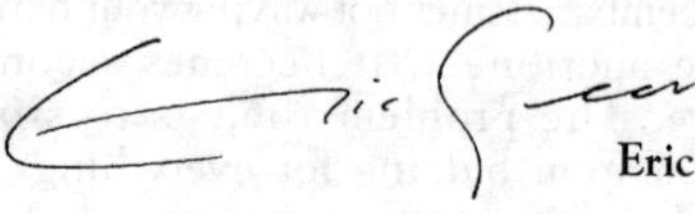

Eric Geen

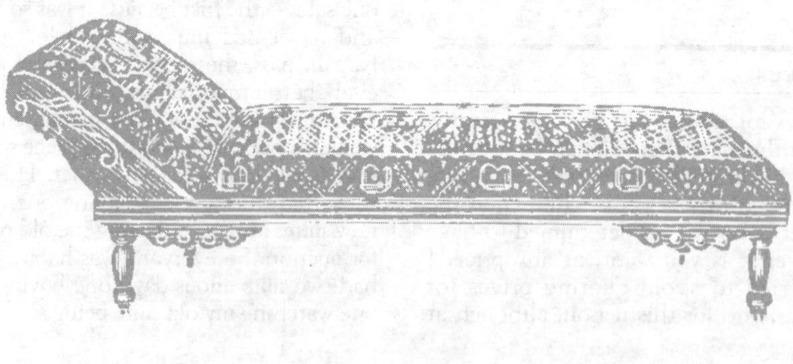

• HOW TO USE THIS BOOK •

The sales in this book are listed in sections under England, Wales and Scotland; then alphabetically by county and then place. London auctioneers may be found in alphabetical order at the end of the section on England.

EXAMPLE OF AN ENTRY

DERBYSHIRE

Clay Cross — Place name or nearest town

JB'S AUCTIONS — Name of establishment

130a King Street
Tel: (0246) 866452

400-500 lots. — Approximate number of lots in a sale, which may vary. Most auctioneers sell between 80-100 lots an hour, so this figure can be used as a rough guide to the duration of a sale. Be careful,though. Sometimes an auctioneer will sell more than 100 lots an hour, if there are fewer bids. At some auctions in Scotland, all the items brought to a sale by one vendor may be given the same lot number. Each item will be sold separately, so it is important to look at items being sold, and not just to listen for lot numbers, during the bidding.

The saleroom is in the town's main shopping street at the rear of JB's café, which is owned and run by the family responsible for the auction. JB's also offer bed and breakfast, useful for those overcome by the excitement of bidding.
This is a popular weekly sale and a regular meeting place for local people. The selling is brisk and businesslike, however. Too much talking between customers, and the auctioneer is likely to stop the proceedings and remind those responsible that 'this is a place of business'. Antique and shipping furniture is set out in a large saleroom, with modern furniture, general household effects and gardening equipment. There is usually a fair amount of domestic and ornamental china of all periods, plus silver and jewellery, bric-à-brac, toys, books and an assortment of miscellaneous items. — Description of entry

BUYER'S PREMIUM: 10%	The commission charged by auctioneers to successful bidders. It is a percentage of the 'hammer' price, and varies from auction to auction. VAT may also be charged on the buyer's premium. Always read auction catalogues thoroughly before a sale, especially the small print. If you are in any doubt, consult the auctioneers before deciding how high to bid.
SALES: Weekly on Thu at 6.30pm. VIEWING: All week 10.00am-5.00pm.	Although every effort has been made to ensure accuracy, these details may be subject to change at short notice. Always confirm details with the auctioneers before setting out on a journey.
REFRESHMENTS: Own café.	The establishments listed in this book are not necessarily AA inspected. However, the AA is always pleased to hear of any reader's recommendations.(See the form at the end of this book.)
PARKING: Own car park.	Details of NCP or other car parks in the area are given where necessary.
STORAGE: Yes TRANSPORTATION: Yes SHIPPING: Yes	'Yes' indicates that the auctioneers are willing to *advise* bidders of suitable services; it does not mean that the auctioneers offer these services themselves.

The auctions described in this book have been selected by the author personally. No financial transactions have been entered into with regard to choice of establishments. The opinions given in each entry are the author's own personal view, and are not necessarily shared by The Automobile Association. The AA cannot accept any responsibility for the future quality and range of goods at these auctions, or for any financial transactions entered into by readers. It is always advisable to read the small print in auctioneers' catalogues, and to confirm sale details with them, before making firm plans to attend an auction.

• ENGLAND •

AVON

ALDRIDGES OF BATH

Bath

The Auction Galleries, 130-132 Walcot Street.
Tel: (0225) 462830

400-500 lots. This is a long established, independently run sale situated about half a mile from the centre of the attractive city of Bath.

The sale is held in a converted old school with four salerooms, one for paintings, one for porcelain and china, one for the general sale and the other used as needed. Auctions are held weekly on Tuesday, with a fortnightly general sale of household furniture and effects, alternating with classified sales in the other weeks. The latter are for special categories of antiques, which usually go in rotation. The categories cover items like clocks and carpets, silver and porcelain, paintings, drawings and prints, collectables and many other specialities. All the sales are interesting and well attended.

BUYER'S PREMIUM: *10%*
SALES: *General: fortnightly on Tue at 10.00am. Antiques (different specialities): fortnightly on Tue at 10.00am (alternate weeks to general).*
VIEWING: *Sat 9.00am-12.00 noon, Mon 9.00am-5.00pm.*
REFRESHMENTS: *Own café.*
PARKING: *Own car park.*
STORAGE: *Yes*
TRANSPORTATION: *Yes*
SHIPPING: *Yes*

BLACK HORSE AGENCIES/ALDER KING

Bath

The Auction Rooms, Old Malthouse, Comfortable Place, Upper Bristol Road. Tel: (0225) 447933

400-600 lots. Usually there are two sales per month, although in some months there can be as many as four. 'Victoriana and Later Furnishings' is the name given to the general sale, held on the last or penultimate Thursday of the month. This can include up to 200 lots of electrical items such as televisions and audio systems, plus unredeemed pawnbroker pledges like cameras and compact disc players. The jewellery sale is held on the Wednesday before and also includes unredeemed pledges, such as gold, silver and antique jewellery. Prices vary from a few pounds to a few thousand pounds. Four times a year, this sale becomes a special sale of antique jewellery, silver and plate.

Also four times a year, the general sale is replaced by one of antique furniture and works of art. There are special sales of musical instruments three times a year, when instruments of all ages and types can be found here. 'Garden Pots' is another speciality sale, and takes places twice a year, in spring and late summer. New pots for the sale are imported from such places as Thailand and Malaysia. Other speciality sales are held periodically, including popular categories such as books and model railways.

BUYER'S PREMIUM: *10%*
SALES: *General: monthly on last or second-to-last Thu of month at 10.30am (replaced by antiques and works of art four times a year in Feb, May, Sep and Nov). Jewellery: monthly on last or second-to-last Wed of month at 12.00 noon. Musical instruments: three times a year in Apr/May, Sep and Dec on Fri at 2.00pm. Garden pots: twice a year in Apr and Aug/Sep on Sat at 10.30am.*
VIEWING: *General: Tue prior 12.00 noon-6.00pm, Wed prior 9.00am-6.00pm. Jewellery: Tue prior 12.00 noon-6.00pm, morning of sale. Musical instruments: day prior, 4.00pm-8.00pm. Garden pots: day prior 9.00am-5.00pm. All: morning of sale from 9.00am.*
REFRESHMENTS: *Own café.*
PARKING: *Charlotte Street public car park.*
STORAGE: *Yes*
TRANSPORTATION: *Yes*
SHIPPING: *Yes*

Bath

BUYER'S PREMIUM: *10%*
SALES: *Weekly on Mon at 11.00am.*
VIEWING: *Fri 9.00am-5.00pm, Sat 9.00am-1.00pm, morning of sale from 8.30am.*
REFRESHMENTS: *None available on the premises.*
PARKING: *Own car park.*
STORAGE: *Yes*
TRANSPORTATION: *Yes*
SHIPPING: *Yes*

PHILLIPS

1 Old Street. Tel: (0225) 310609

150-500 lots. The saleroom is in a large old building with blue painted doors by the rear entrance to Jolly's Department Store — about a mile from the abbey church, Pump Room and Roman Baths. Like all Phillips auctions, this one is at the upper end of the market. Sales are held most Mondays in various specialist categories. There are often two sales per month under the heading 'Victorian, Edwardian and Reproduction'. Other categories are 'English and Continental Furniture, Clocks and Works of Art', 'Oriental and European Ceramics and Glass', 'Fine Jewellery', 'Oil Paintings, Watercolours and Prints', 'Silver and Silver Plate', 'Collectors' Items', and 'Antiquarian Books'.

Bristol

BUYER'S PREMIUM: *10%*
SALES: *Household and Commercial: fortnightly on Tue at 10.30am. Antique and Decorative: about eight times a year on Tue at 10.30am. Antique and Modern (Wells): monthly on Wed at 1.30pm.*
VIEWING: *Household and Commercial: day prior 12.00 noon-5.00pm. Antiques and Decorative: Sat prior 9.30am-1.00pm, Mon prior 9.30am-7.00pm. Antique and Modern (Wells): day prior 1.00pm-5.00pm, day of sale from 9.00am.*
REFRESHMENTS: *Bristol: own café. Wells: none available on the premises.*
PARKING: *Own car parks.*
STORAGE: *Yes*
TRANSPORTATION: *Yes*
SHIPPING: *Yes*

OSMOND TRICKS WITH ALLEN AND HARRIS

Regent Street Auction Rooms, St John's Place, Apsley Road, Clifton. Tel: (0272) 737201

400-500 lots. The saleroom lies about two miles from the Clifton Suspension Bridge over the River Avon. The company is a member of Royal Life Estates, and associated companies have sales in Wiltshire, Dorset, Hampshire and Somerset, with another Avon sale at Weston-Super-Mare. Auctions are held two or three times per month in Bristol. A fortnightly general sale goes under the heading 'Household and Commercial', and there are 'Antique and Decorative' sales about eight times a year. The auctioneer conducting this sale is also responsible for the monthly 'Antique and Modern' sales about 20 miles away at Wells. The address is 66-68 Southover, and you will find a predominance of antiques.

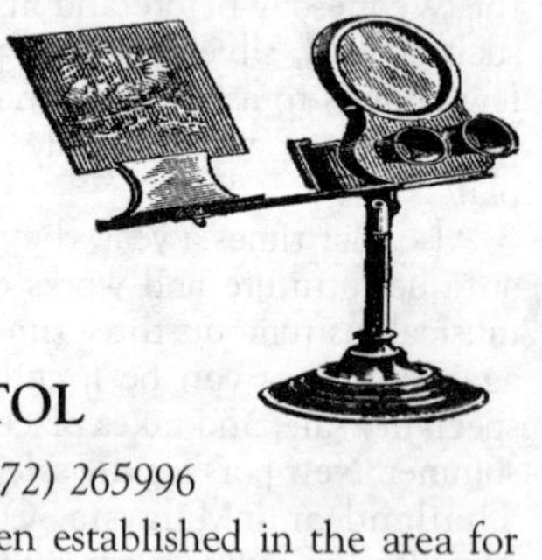

Bristol

BUYER'S PREMIUM: *10%*
SALES: *General: weekly on Fri at 12.00 noon. Special categories: fortnightly on Thu at 12.00 noon. Bristol pictures etc.:*

TAVINER'S OF BRISTOL

Prewett Street, Redcliffe. Tel: (0272) 265996

300-400 lots. Taviner's have been established in the area for over 20 years, and hold a general sale every Friday (except Good Friday and at Christmas). This includes complete house contents, office effects and stock, with a variety of bric-à-brac and other items. Every fortnight on Thursdays Taviner's also have sales in special categories in rotation. 'Antique and Quality Furniture' includes clocks, rugs, boxes and table furniture; 'Ceramics and Collectables' includes glass, metals, silver, jewellery, toys and dolls, medals, coins, scientific and musical instruments, textiles and weapons; 'Postcards' includes cigarette and trade cards, stamps, photographs, albums and ephemera. 'Printed Books and Pictures' includes antiquarian and secondhand books and literary properties, together with paintings, drawings, maps, prints and frames. A sale of Bristol pictures, maps and books is held twice a year.

twice a year in Nov and Jun at 6.00pm.
VIEWING: *General: morning of sale from 9.00am. All others: day prior 10.00am-7.00pm, morning of sale.*
REFRESHMENTS: *None available on the premises.*
PARKING: *None available on the premises.*
STORAGE: *Yes*
TRANSPORTATION: *Yes*
SHIPPING: *Yes*

Farrington Gurney

WICKS & PIERCE

The Old Parsonage. Tel: (0761) 413060

400-500 lots. The Old Parsonage is one of the oldest and most attractive houses in this pretty little village. It is situated just off the main road where the A37 and A39 meet. The easy access from Bristol, Bath and the coast may be one reason why the sales are so well attended, and another attraction is the beautiful surrounding countryside. The saleroom atmosphere is good too. Sales occur on average every four to six weeks, but may be less frequent in the winter months. This auction is at the more up-market end of the country auction scene. Included are general antiques, Victorian and Edwardian furniture, pine, good quality shipping furniture, good quality china, porcelain, silver, silver plate, metalware, collectables, bygones of various types, oil paintings, watercolour drawings, prints and so on.

BUYER'S PREMIUM: *Nil*
SALES: *About every four to six weeks on Sat at 11.00am.*
VIEWING: *Day prior 2.00pm- 6.00pm.*
REFRESHMENTS: *Own café.*
PARKING: *Own car park.*
STORAGE: *Yes*
TRANSPORTATION: *Yes*
SHIPPING: *Yes*

Weston-Super-Mare

WOODSPRING AUCTION ROOMS

Churchill Road. Tel: (0934) 628419

500-600 lots. Churchill Road is a turning off Locking Road, the main route through this seaside resort. The very large premises are used by two auctioneering companies. Woodspring Auctions hold excellent fortnightly sales of general household furniture and effects, plus periodic special sales of antiques. About once a month, again on a Thursday, the premises are used in association with Osmond Tricks for commercial auctions. These alternate between sales of catering and office furniture, and plant machinery and equipment.

The number attending the general sale noticeably increases during the summer months. There are plenty of other attractions around here, but many visitors enjoy the out-of-the-ordinary atmosphere of a sale. The excitement of bidding for a fine old Royal Doulton tea cup beats walking into a souvenir shop, too.

BUYER'S PREMIUM: *10%*
SALES: *General: fortnightly on Thu at 10.00am. Commercial: monthly on Thu at 11.00am.*
VIEWING: *General: day prior 2.00pm-6.00pm, day of sale from 9.00am. Commercial: 10.00am-4.00pm, day of sale from 9.00am.*
REFRESHMENTS: *None available on premises.*
PARKING: *None available on premises.*
STORAGE: *Yes*
TRANSPORTATION: *Yes*
SHIPPING: *Yes*

BEDFORDSHIRE

Bedford

BUYER'S PREMIUM: *10%*
SALES: *General: weekly on Sat at 9.30am. Antiques: monthly on first Fri of the month at 10.45am.*
VIEWING: *Day prior 8.30am-8.00pm.*
REFRESHMENTS: *Own café.*
PARKING: *None available on the premises.*
STORAGE: *No*
TRANSPORTATION: *Yes*
SHIPPING: *Yes*

WILSON PEACOCK

26 Newnham Street. Tel: (0234) 266366

1,000-1,500 lots. Visiting Wilson Peacock's Saturday sale could be an enjoyable and rewarding day out for the whole family. Almost certainly there will be something to interest everyone. Eggs are sold at 9.30am, followed by bicycles, plants, and general household furniture and effects. More unusual is the sale of motor vehicles, which takes place at the same time outside. Office furniture and heavy goods — windows, doors and lawn mowers — are sold at 11.00am, followed by ornaments, books, magazines, lamps and general electrical goods. The day's bidding is usually over by 3.30pm.

Luton

BUYER'S PREMIUM: *Nil*
SALES: *Weekly on Wed at 7.00pm.*
VIEWING: *Day of sale from 10.00am-5.30pm.*
REFRESHMENTS: *Own café.*
PARKING: *Own car park.*
STORAGE: *Yes*
TRANSPORTATION: *Yes*
SHIPPING: *Yes*

ADELAIDE AUCTION ROOM

Stuart Place, off Adelaide Street. Tel: (0582) 423809

300-400 lots. The saleroom is situated at the rear of 82 Wellington Street and next door to the Driving Test Centre. There are excellent sales here, which normally include bargains in all categories of household furniture and effects and miscellaneous items. The lots are of all ages, and in all kinds of condition, from 'perfect' to 'in need of attention'. There are often good buys among the antique, modern and reproduction furniture, and also among the electrical goods, paintings and prints, china and gardening items. Boxes of miscellanea are always worth inspection — they might contain anything from china and postcards to books and toys. Many local people attend regularly, not necessarily to buy but purely to enjoy the occasion.

Luton

BUYER'S PREMIUM: *50p per lot.*
SALES: *Weekly on Thu at 7.00pm; Slip End: first Sun of the month at 5.30pm.*
VIEWING: *All week from 10.00am-5.00pm (10.00am-9.00pm Wed); Slip End: day of sale from 2.00pm.*
REFRESHMENTS: *Own café.*

LUTON MULTI AUCTIONS

37 John Street. Tel: (0582) 405281

300-500 lots. This evening auction is a well-known local event and a focal point for those looking for bargains. The saleroom is also used as an antique centre six days a week, from 10.00am to 5.00pm. Many people just pop in on their way home from work, or while they are on a shopping trip in Luton (the saleroom is opposite the Arndale Shopping Centre in the middle of the town) to look at antiques which can be bought or are on view for a forthcoming auction.

This is a family-run business, and the proprietors, Frank and

Shirley Horn, are also responsible for the long-established and very popular regular Sunday antiques auctions at the Village Sports Hall, Slip End. These offer a good day's entertainment for the whole family because in addition to the auctions in the Sports Hall, which begin at 5.30pm, there is usually an antiques fair with more than 30 stalls at the Village Hall near by. This is open from 10.00am onwards.

PARKING: *Own car park.*
STORAGE: *Yes*
TRANSPORTATION: *Yes*
SHIPPING: *Yes*

DOWNER ROSS

Woburn

Old Town Hall. Tel: (0525) 290502 or (0908) 679900

350-450 lots. Woburn's Old Town Hall is difficult to miss. It is an attractive old building in the town centre, standing alone, almost in an island surrounded by roads. Woburn Abbey, the historic home of the Duke of Bedford, with its magnificent collection of furniture and art treasures, is only about three miles away. Woburn Abbey Antiques Centre is one of the largest in the country, with more than 40 independently-run shops under one roof. Combining a trip to the abbey with a visit to an auction makes a very pleasant and interesting day out for the family.

The lots on offer at Downer Ross's auctions are usually of high quality, and cover all sorts of fields: antique, period and later furniture, pictures, prints, ceramics and metalware, ornamental items, silver and glass, and much more besides. The saleroom is attractively set out and there is plenty of room for people to view the lots before the auction. This is conducted in a friendly, efficient manner, which puts people at their ease — despite the fact that some lots fetch five-figure sums. Others are sold for as little as five pounds, so there is something here to suit most people.

BUYER'S PREMIUM: *5%*
SALES: *Usually monthly on last Thu of the month at 11.00am.*
VIEWING: *Day prior, 9.00am-7.30pm.*
REFRESHMENTS: *Café 100 yards away.*
PARKING: *Public car park is 50 yards away.*
STORAGE: *Yes*
TRANSPORTATION: *Yes*
SHIPPING: *Yes*

BERKSHIRE

DREWEATT NEATE

Donnington

Donnington Priory, near Newbury.
Tel: (0635) 31234 Fax (0635) 528195

400-500 lots. Donnington Priory is an attractive Georgian building set in beautiful grounds, which are well worth visiting in their own right. Dreweatt Neate, established in 1759, have held sales at the Priory for ten years, and before that they operated from premises in Newbury. There are three or four auctions a month to tempt prospective buyers to the Priory; a fortnightly auction, consisting of general household furniture and effects, lesser antiques and Victoriana is held on Tuesdays

BUYER'S PREMIUM: *10%*
SALES: *General: fortnightly on Tue at 10.00am. Specialist: monthly on Wed at 10.30am.*
VIEWING: *General: Sat prior, 9.30am-12.00 noon, day prior, 9.30am-4.00pm; Specialist: Sat prior, 9.30am-12.00 noon, Mon and Tue prior, 9.30am-4.00pm.*

REFRESHMENTS: *On sale days.*
PARKING: *Own car park.*
STORAGE: *Yes (limited period).*
TRANSPORTATION: *Yes*
SHIPPING: *Yes*

in Saleroom IV, but there is also a specialist Wednesday sale once or twice a month in the other three salerooms. The latter is usually devoted to one of the following areas: antiques (including clocks and instruments, furniture, rugs, textiles, collectors' items and old toys); silver and jewellery; paintings, books and ceramics. Illustrated catalogues are available for the specialist sales.

Reading

THIMBLEBY & SHORLAND

31 Great Knollys Street. Tel: (0734) 508611

BUYER'S PREMIUM: *Nil*
SALES: *General: monthly on Sat at 10.00am.*
Saddlery: first Fri of the month, at 10.30am.
VIEWING: *General: day prior, 12.00 noon-4.00pm and day of sale from 9.00am;*
Saddlery: day of sale from 9.00am.
REFRESHMENTS: *Own café.*
PARKING: *Available on the premises.*
STORAGE: *Yes*
TRANSPORTATION: *Yes*
SHIPPING: *Yes*

1,500-2,000 lots. Once a month, in the same sheds which are used every week for livestock auctions, Thimbleby & Shorland hold massive auctions of antique and modern furniture, household effects, and office furniture. Regularly among the lots are items to be sold by Order of H M Customs and Excise, H M Collector of Taxes, the County Courts, the Official Receiver, other liquidators and the High Sheriff of Berkshire. The proceedings are divided into three separate auctions in order to get through the number of items for sale. Here it is quite possible to end up buying such varied items as brass stair rods, fire surrounds, modern furniture, Victorian coal scuttles, violins, electronic components, packets of biscuits, beds and bedding, and telephone answering machines all in the course of one day. The auctioneers also hold monthly sales of horses and saddlery here, with some 30 horses and 800 lots of harnesses, vehicles, trailers, jumps and so on. Machinery and contractors' sales are also held.

'Paddle' bidding is the order of the day, which means that prospective buyers must register with the auctioneer before the sale so that they can be given a number.

Winkfield Row

ROBIN ELLIOTT (incorporating CHANCELLOR'S FINE ART)

Charlotte Pratt Memorial Hall, Chavey Down Road. Tel: (0990) 872588

BUYER'S PREMIUM: *10%*
SALES: *Monthly on Mon at 10.00am.*
VIEWING: *Sat prior, 10.00am-5.00pm.*
REFRESHMENTS: *None available on the premises.*
PARKING: *Some on the premises.*
STORAGE: *No*
TRANSPORTATION: *Yes*
SHIPPING: *Yes*

500-700 lots. Chavey Down Road is a very long, quiet country road, and the Charlotte Pratt Memorial Hall is not very well signed. This makes it somewhat difficult to find if you are a stranger to the area. The venue is close to the White Horse public house, and if there is time it is a good idea for first-time bidders to call in at Robin Elliott's 32 High Street, Ascot office in order to pick up a sale catalogue and obtain clear directions. The goods at the Winkfield Row sales reflect, on the whole, the tone of the neighbourhood; the saleroom is close to the

Royal Berkshire Polo Club and Royal Ascot Racecourse.

General antiques and good modern furniture are included in these auctions, which are, however, memorable for the range of smaller items that they offer: china, glass, ornaments, silver, jewellery, pictures and so on. Once every three months the auctioneers have a special section in their auctions devoted to small items of superior quality.

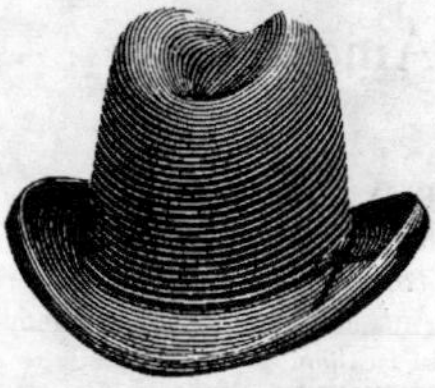

MARTIN & POLE (inc. WATTS & SON)

The Auction Galleries, 12 Milton Road. Tel: (0734) 790460

500-600 lots. Martin & Pole were established in 1846 and have been conducting auctions at this saleroom, just off Wokingham's busy main shopping street, for more than 30 years. Visitors should note that street parking outside the saleroom is limited to two hours only. Despite this difficulty, Martin & Pole's sales have gained quite a large following over the years and they now attract bidders from all over the country. The saleroom is often overflowing on sale days. There are two main auctions a month: the Saturday sale of general household furniture, kitchenalia, electrical appliances, gardening tools and miscellanea; and the Wednesday antique sale, which includes better quality lots of furniture, silver and plate, porcelain, pictures, carpets and rugs.

Wokingham

BUYER'S PREMIUM: *Nil*
SALES: *General sale: once a month on Sat at 10am. Antiques sale: once a month, usually on third Wed of the month at 10.00am.*
VIEWING: *General: morning of sale from 8.30am; antique: Sat prior, 9.00am-1.00pm, Mon and Tue prior, 9.00am-5.00pm.*
REFRESHMENTS: *None available on the premises.*
PARKING: *None on the premises.*
STORAGE: *No*
TRANSPORTATION: *Yes*
SHIPPING: *Yes*

BUCKINGHAMSHIRE

NATIONWIDE ANGLIA

The Amersham Auction Rooms, 125 Station Road.
Tel: (0494) 729292

400-500 lots. The saleroom is a few hundred yards from the railway station, and is a charming single-storey building which at one time was a theatre. It comes complete with resident ghost.

The weekly auction is of antiques and collectables on the first Thursday of the month, but in other weeks this is a general sale. The antiques sale includes better quality items of English and European glass and china, antique and modern silver and jewellery, clocks, watches, barometers, scientific instruments, oil paintings, engravings, prints, furniture and so on. The other auctions are good general household sales. As well as a wide range of furniture, there will probably be all types of electrical equipment, gardening tools, kitchen items and assorted bric-à-brac to browse through.

Amersham

BUYER'S PREMIUM: *10%*
SALES: *Weekly on Thu at 10.30am (includes antiques sale on first Thu of every month).*
VIEWING: *Day prior 9.30am-7.00pm.*
REFRESHMENTS: *None available on the premises.*
PARKING: *Own car park.*
STORAGE: *Yes*
TRANSPORTATION: *Yes*
SHIPPING: *Yes*

Amersham

BUYER'S PREMIUM: *10%*
SALES: *General: twice monthly on Sat at 1.00pm. Antiques: third Sat of the month at 1.00pm.*
VIEWING: *General: day prior, 7.00pm-10.30pm, morning of sale from 9.00am-12.00 noon. Antiques: Thu prior, 6.00pm-10.00pm, Fri prior, 10.00am-10.00pm, morning of sale from 9.00am-12.00 noon.*
REFRESHMENTS: *Own café.*
PARKING: *None available on the premises.*
STORAGE: *Yes*
TRANSPORTATION: *Yes*
SHIPPING: *Yes*

SOUTH BUCKS AUCTIONS

British Legion Hall, Whieldon Street. Tel: (0494) 722758

500-600 lots. South Bucks Auctions hold three sales a month in Amersham, a charming old town. All of these are very much looked-forward-to local events, especially as they take place on Saturdays. Twice a month there are sales of general household furniture and effects and miscellanea at the British Legion Hall, but on the third Saturday of the month there is a special antiques auction. The latter takes place at the Conservative Centre in Church Street. Both venues can become quite crowded at times.

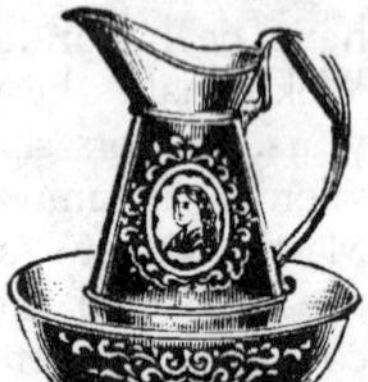

Winslow

BUYER'S PREMIUM: *Nil*
SALES: *Monthly on last Fri of month at 10.00am.*
VIEWING: *Day prior 9.00am-12.00 noon, 2.00pm-4.00pm, day of sale from 9.00am.*
REFRESHMENTS: *Own café.*
PARKING: *Ample parking near by.*
STORAGE: *Yes*
TRANSPORTATION: *Yes*
SHIPPING: *Yes*

GEO WIGLEY & SONS

12 Market Square. Tel: (0296) 712717

600-700 lots. Winslow is a quiet little town with neat thatched cottages and an attractive market square surrounded by Georgian buildings. This is where you will find Geo Wigley & Son's estate agency, and the saleroom is just behind that. This is a good general sale which offers the possibility of picking up some bargains. It takes place on the last Friday of each month, and is of general household furniture and effects, including antiques. There are three salerooms. The auction starts in the one with the better quality items. The more run-of-the-mill goods and larger pieces of furniture such as wardrobes and dressers are in the biggest saleroom. The third saleroom is for bric-à-brac and smaller miscellanea.

CAMBRIDGESHIRE

Cambridge

BUYER'S PREMIUM: *10%*
SALES: *Weekly on Thu at 11.00am (includes specialist sales on alternate weeks).*
VIEWING: *Day prior 2.00pm-7.00pm, morning of*

CHEFFINS, GRAIN & COMINS

Cambridge Sale Rooms, 2 Clifton Road. Tel: (0223) 213343

300-400 lots. Cheffins, Grain & Comins are old-established auctioneers dating back to 1825. Every week on Thursday there is a sale here, alternating between general household furniture and effects one week, and specialist sales the next.

Household furniture and effects normally include bric-à-brac, quality second-hand furniture, and china and glass. The specialist sales deal with collectors' items, Victoriana, and period furniture. Three times a year there are also sales on a Saturday of domestic and rural bygones, which may include anything from old kitchen equipment to disused farming implements and steam engines. Dates for each type of sale are arranged one year in advance and are available from the auctioneers on request.

sale from 9.00am.
REFRESHMENTS: *On day of sale only.*
PARKING: *Available in old cattle market near by.*
STORAGE: *Yes*
TRANSPORTATION: *Yes*
SHIPPING: *Yes*

HAMMOND & CO

Cambridge

Cambridge Place. Tel: (0223) 356067

200-400 lots. Mr and Mrs Seymour of Hammond & Co have ample experience in all aspects of the antiques trade. Mr Seymour was in the business for 30 years, and Mrs Seymour (now in charge of the mounds of office work involved in running a busy weekly auction) is especially knowledgeable on jewellery. The sale includes Edwardian, Victorian and antique furniture and effects along with a wide range of general furniture, cutlery, linen, china, silver and brass, paintings, pictures, books and other items. The auction is an ideal change of occupation for those a little weary from looking at the great architecture of Cambridge, and increasing numbers of overseas visitors are finding their way to it, their presence adding colour and excitement to the proceedings. The sale finishes at around 1.00pm. Cambridge Place is a small turning off Hills Road, which is the main road between the railway station and the city centre.

BUYER'S PREMIUM: *10%*
SALES: *Weekly on Fri at 10.00am.*
VIEWING: *Thu 10.00am-5.00pm, morning of sale from 9.00am.*
REFRESHMENTS: *None available on the premises.*
PARKING: *None available on the premises.*
STORAGE: *No*
TRANSPORTATION: *Yes*
SHIPPING: *No*

CHEFFINS, GRAIN & COMINS

Ely

25 Market Place. Tel: (0353) 662265

850-1,000 lots. Ely rises on a hill, or as much of a hill as you are likely to see in East Anglia, with Ely Cathedral clearly visible for miles across the surrounding countryside. The auction is close to the cathedral, just off the busy main market square. It is reached by walking down Brays Lane (beside Tesco), and is held in and around a large brick building which used to be part of the old cattle market. This is a typical country auction, colourful and noisy, with garden produce and poultry as well as general items being auctioned. Two separate sales begin at 11.00am. Outside the saleroom is the sale of 'deadstock' — a term often used in this part of England to describe such lots as bundles of timber, paving stones, rolls of wire netting, gardening tools, and perhaps window frames or doors. At the same time, produce and poultry are auctioned in a smaller

BUYER'S PREMIUM: *Nil*
SALES: *Weekly on Thu at 11.00am.*
VIEWING: *Day of sale from 9.00am.*
REFRESHMENTS: *Van selling snacks.*
PARKING: *Public car parks in town centre.*
STORAGE: *No*
TRANSPORTATION: *Yes*
SHIPPING: *Yes*

undercover area. The auctioneer of the sale that finishes first will then start selling the lots in the general sale, which does not usually begin until around 12.30pm.

March

BUYER'S PREMIUM: *5%*
SALES: *Weekly on Wed at 10.00am.*
VIEWING: *Tue 2.00pm-5.00pm.*
REFRESHMENTS: *Tea bar in hall.*
PARKING: *None available on the premises.*
STORAGE: *Yes*
TRANSPORTATION: *Yes*
SHIPPING: *Yes*

COLLINGWOODS

The March Weekly Auctions, Palace Hall Auction Rooms, Broad Street. Tel: (0354) 52488

200-300 lots. Established in 1884, this is a very popular and always interesting general auction, held in an attractive former cinema. It is in the middle of March, just off the High Street. The sale day is Wednesday, which is also market day, and the market stalls are just five minutes away. All types of good quality household furniture are sold, including antique, period and modern, together with various collectables, bygones, and a wide range of other items. There are usually some of the oddities that make country auctions so endearing: a bundle of bicycle mudguards perhaps, or a quantity of old tools including a scythe, or a horsedrawn cart jack and a pair of blacksmith's bellows from around 1878. At a typical sale, 20 bicycles were sold 'by order of Cambridgeshire Constabulary', at well below shop prices. Garden produce is sold first, including bulbs, shrubs and other plants. The main part of the auction begins at around 11.00am and takes about two hours. Payment is made on the spot: whereas at most auctions there is usually a short delay, here you should be prepared to hand over the cash as soon as a successful bid is made.

March

BUYER'S PREMIUM: *5%*
SALES: *Monthly on Tue at 12.00 noon.*
VIEWING: *Morning of sale from 10.00am-12.00 noon.*
REFRESHMENTS: *None available on the premises.*
PARKING: *None available on the premises.*
STORAGE: *Yes*
TRANSPORTATION: *Yes*
SHIPPING: *Yes*

GROUNDS

Cattle Market, Elwyn Road. Tel: (0354) 52502

300-400 lots. The motto of Grounds' auctioneer, Richard Barnwell, is to accept all sorts of goods for sale, even those that others might reject. Being a collector himself, he is aware that some people will make a collection out of the most unlikely objects. One of his satisfied customers was a collector of cardboard milk bottle tops showing the dairy's name, which were used after the Second World War.

Much has been written about the luck of buyers coming across bargains at auctions, but less is heard about the luck of the vendor. On one occasion a glass bowl was put up for sale at Grounds. It was valued at around £15, but the bidding started at £20, and the price went up...and up...and up...and up...until a bemused auctioneer found himself knocking it down for £13,700. Two London dealers were attending the auction and both had spotted its true value.

L SHAW & SON

75 New Street. Tel: (0480) 72097 and 74550

250-500 lots. The auction is carried out with a great deal of gusto and friendly banter, and is ideal for those new to auction-going. The prices usually stay within reach of most pockets, and it would be difficult not to find something to bid for in one of the lots of bric-à-brac, furniture, china, pottery, bicycles, television sets, pots and pans, garden ornaments and furniture, boxes of books, beds, paintings and so on. The saleyard is on the outskirts of town, near the common.

Selling starts with fruit and vegetables at 11.00am, followed by eggs and poultry at 12.00 noon and flowers at 12.30pm. The furniture and general sale begins at around 1.00 to 1.30pm.

On Mondays and Fridays there are special fruit and vegetable sales beginning at around 2.00pm. Sales finish at around 3.30pm, leaving plenty of time to take a walk down to the river to see the old paper mill, which first produced machine-made paper in 1798.

St Neots

BUYER'S PREMIUM: *Nil*
SALES: *Weekly on Thu at 11.00am.*
VIEWING: *Wed prior 4.00pm-5.00pm.*
REFRESHMENTS: *Van selling snacks.*
PARKING: *Room for a few cars in the saleyard, or park on the common.*
STORAGE: *No*
TRANSPORTATION: *Yes*
SHIPPING: *No*

MAXEY & SON

Cattle Market. Tel: (0945) 584609

500-2,000 lots. Maxey & Son has been established for over 130 years, and two members of the Maxey family plus two other partners now run one of the largest auctions in this area. It is situated just off the busy Chapel Road, where on Wednesdays and Saturdays there is always an interesting range of good antique, period and modern furniture on offer, in addition to other household effects, china, glassware, jewellery, pictures, implements, machinery and so on.

The lots often include collectables, such as locally found old bottles and old woodworking tools. Wisbech was built as a port, and as well as seeing some large coasters lying alongside the quays, you will often find articles connected with boating and fishing among the lots. There are also daily auctions of fruit, vegetables and flowers at 5.00pm and twice weekly sales of nursery stock, bulbs and plants, on Wednesday and Saturday at 10.00am.

Auctions of fruit, vegetables and flowers are held nearby at The Chase Auction Hall, Chapel Road, by Clifford F Cross (Wisbech) Ltd, Horticultural Auctioneers, tel: (0945) 583398, on Monday, Wednesday and Thursday at 4.00pm. Nursery stock is auctioned on Wednesday and Saturday at 10.00am.

Wisbech

BUYER'S PREMIUM: *5%*
SALES: *Weekly on Wed and Sat at 10.00am.*
VIEWING: *Day prior 2.00pm-5.00pm, morning of sale.*
REFRESHMENTS: *Saturday only, van selling snacks.*
PARKING: *Own car park.*
STORAGE: *Yes*
TRANSPORTATION: *Yes*
SHIPPING: *Yes*

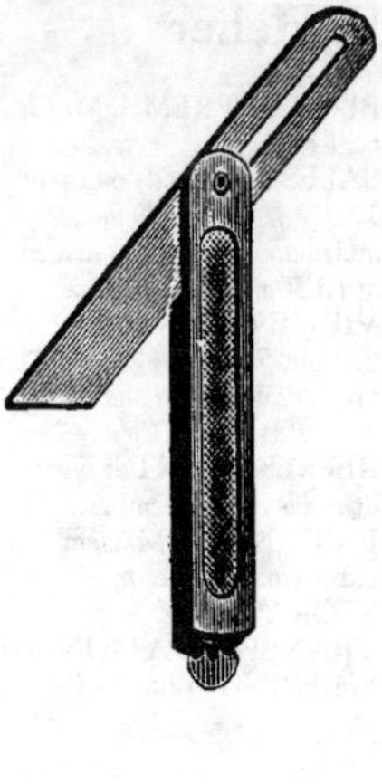

CHANNEL ISLANDS

GUERNSEY
St Peter Port

ALLEN'S ESTATE AGENCY & AUCTION CENTRE LTD

Les Amballes. Tel: (0481) 24526

250-300 lots. St Peter Port is the capital of Guernsey. It has plenty to offer visitors, but it is also well worth putting an hour or two aside from sight-seeing to sample some of the local auctions. Allen's is a short distance away from the shopping centre, and offers pleasant, unhurried auctions of general household furniture and effects, antiques and innumerable miscellaneous items.

Anything from a stamp to a car can be sold here, and 'island bygones', ideal for holiday souvenir hunters, are a speciality. Smaller items are usually kept back and sold towards the end of the auction.

BUYER'S PREMIUM: *Nil*
SALES: *Weekly on Thu at 2.00pm.*
VIEWING: *Tue and Wed, 9.00am-12.00 noon and 2.00pm-5.00pm. Morning of sale, 9.00am-12.00 noon.*
REFRESHMENTS: *None available on the premises.*
PARKING: *None on the premises.*
STORAGE: *Yes*
TRANSPORTATION: *Yes*
SHIPPING: *Yes*

St Peter Port

MARTEL MAIDES & LE PELLEY LTD

12 Allez Street. Tel: (0481) 713463

200-250 lots. The auction room, converted from an old bakehouse, is within easy reach of St Peter Port's main shopping centre. Twice yearly, usually at the beginning and end of the year, the company holds special antiques auctions in place of their fortnightly sales of general household furniture and effects (although these sales also include some antiques). The quality of lots is good, reflecting the overall standard of living in the Channel Islands.

BUYER'S PREMIUM: *5%*
SALES: *Fortnightly on Thu at 2.15pm.*
VIEWING: *Wed prior, 8.30am-4.30pm. Day of sale from 8.30am.*
REFRESHMENTS: *None available on the premises.*
PARKING: *None on the premises.*
STORAGE: *Yes*
TRANSPORTATION: *Yes*
SHIPPING: *Yes*

JERSEY
St Helier

LE GALLAIS AUCTIONS

36 Hilgrove Street. Tel: (0534) 58789

400-500 lots. Le Gallais hold well-organised, highly efficient sales. To make life easier for visitors unable to resist bidding for larger items offered in the auctions, Le Gallais have their own shipping and storage company. The auctioneers are just a few minutes away from St Helier's most famous covered market, and their premises are unusual in that they have a modern lift to help elderly and disabled clients reach the saleroom. The auctions are made up of a whole range of items, including general household furniture and effects, Victoriana and collectors' items.

The auctioneers also host quarterly fine art and antiques auctions.

BUYER'S PREMIUM: *£1 per lot.*
SALES: *Fortnightly on Fri at 10.30am. Quarterly fine art and antiques auctions on Wed at 10.30am and 2.30pm.*
VIEWING: *Day prior, 8.00am-5.00pm: Quarterly fine art sales: Mon and Tue prior, 9.00am-5.00pm.*
REFRESHMENTS: *None available on the premises.*
PARKING: *At Mindem public car park near by.*
STORAGE: *Yes*
TRANSPORTATION: *Yes*
SHIPPING: *Yes*

H W MAILLARD & SON

Glencoe. Tel: (0534) 37291

300-350 lots. Although attending an auction may not be a priority for many of Jersey's tourists, a trip to one of H W Maillard's sales (which have become almost a tradition of island life) could well turn out to be one of your holiday highlights. The auctions which take place here have a real island flavour, and many of Jersey's local characters will be found at them, together with farm workers, retired professionals and Charlie Hungerford-type millionaire immigrants. Many of those present regard the sales as social gatherings as well as opportunities to buy goods. The lots on offer range from farm equipment and livestock to vehicles, plants, and good quality furniture and household effects. The latter are sold in sheds outside the main saleroom. Once a year, on a Saturday in April, Maillard run a popular sale of boating, fishing and marine equipment.

St Lawrence

BUYER'S PREMIUM: *Nil*
SALES: *Fortnightly on Wed at 2.00pm; annual boating equipment sale in Apr on a Sat at 10.30am.*
VIEWING: *On day of sale.*
REFRESHMENTS: *Available from mobile vans.*
PARKING: *Available on the premises.*
STORAGE: *Yes*
TRANSPORTATION: *Yes*
SHIPPING: *Yes*

CHESHIRE

WRIGHT-MANLEY

Beeston Castle Sales Centre, Beeston Cattle Market. Tel: (0829) 260318

500-600 lots. The large, pleasant saleroom nestles at the foot of Beeston Castle. There is ample seating for the public and a good loudspeaker system means the auctioneer can be heard in all parts. A sale of general household furniture and effects is held fortnightly on Wednesdays. Every six weeks on Thursdays there is a sale of antiques and fine art, and excellent buys are to be had at both sales. Wright-Manley are particularly known for their 'on-site' sales: sales of the complete contents of farms and farmhouses, which take place in the house, in a marquee or partly in the house and gardens and partly in nearby fields. These sales take place at irregular intervals, but are held frequently, particularly from spring onward.

Beeston

BUYER'S PREMIUM: *Nil*
SALES: *General: twice monthly on first and third Wed of month at 10.00am. Antiques and fine art: every six weeks on Thu at 10.30am.*
VIEWING: *General: day prior 9.00am-5.00pm, morning of sale from 9.00am. Antiques: in week prior, Sun 10.00am-4.00pm, Mon 9.00am-5.00pm, Tue 9.00am-7.30pm, Wed 9.00am-12.00 noon; morning of sale by appointment.*
REFRESHMENTS: *Own café.*
PARKING: *Own car park.*
STORAGE: *No*
TRANSPORTATION: *Yes*
SHIPPING: *Yes*

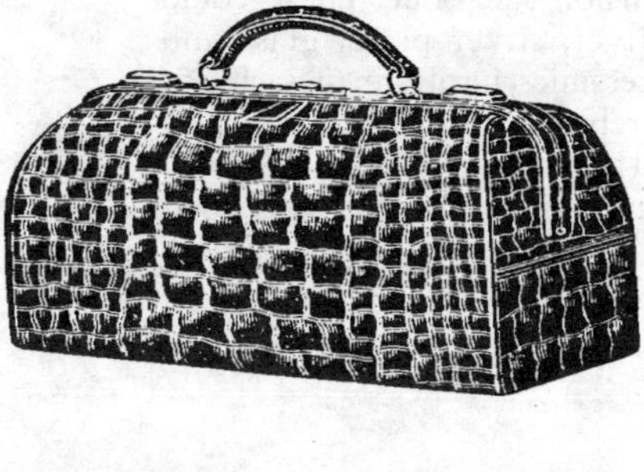

Chester

ROBERT I HEYES & ASSOCIATES

Hatton Building, Lightfoot Street, Hoole. Tel: (0244) 328941

400-500 lots. The saleroom is just behind the railway station of this most picturesque of English cities. Sales are held every Tuesday. A special antiques and fine art sale is held on the first Tuesday of the month. For the rest of the month the sale is of general household furniture and effects, and will include sitting room, dining room and bedroom suites, garden equipment, cookers, refrigerators and other electrical goods, china, porcelain, bric-à-brac and miscellaneous items. There is no particular order to the sale, except that the morning session ends with outside effects such as gardening tools and equipment. Viewing and sales times are the same for both types of sale. There is a break from around 1.00pm until 2.00pm for lunch, and the selling finishes around 4.00 to 4.30pm.

BUYER'S PREMIUM: *10%*
SALES: *General: weekly on Tue (except first Tue of month) at 10.30am. Antiques and fine art: monthly on first Tue of month at 10.30am.*
VIEWING: *Sat 9.00am-12.30pm, Mon 9.00am-5.30pm.*
REFRESHMENTS: *Not available on the premises.*
PARKING: *Ample car parking space.*
STORAGE: *Yes*
TRANSPORTATION: *Yes*
SHIPPING: *Yes*

Chester

PHILLIPS

New House, 150 Christleton Road. Tel: (0244) 313936

300-500 lots. The Phillips saleroom is about one and a half miles out of the city, heading towards Whitchurch on the A41. Two regular monthly sales are held. One, on the third or fourth Monday of the month, is of general household furniture and effects. Included will be Victorian, Edwardian, modern and reproduction furniture and various miscellaneous items, which could include ceramics and glass, tools, pictures and prints, silver and so on. On the first or second Friday of the month there are special sales in various specialist categories, which could include furniture, silver plate, silver, jewellery, collectors' items, boxes, metalware, decorative arts, ceramics and glass, dolls and toys, oriental furnishings, scientific instruments, watches, clocks, golf memorabilia and so on.

BUYER'S PREMIUM: *10%*
SALES: *General: monthly on third or fourth Mon of month at 10.30am. Specialist: monthly on first or second Fri of month at 11.30am.*
VIEWING: *General: Fri prior 10.00am-4.00pm, Sat prior 9.00am-11.30am. Specialist: day prior 10.00am-4.00pm.*
REFRESHMENTS: *None available on the premises.*
PARKING: *Own car park.*
STORAGE: *Yes*
TRANSPORTATION: *Yes*
SHIPPING: *Yes*

Chester

SOTHEBY'S

Booth Mansion, 28-30 Watergate Street. Tel: (0244) 315531

1,000-3,000 lots. Fortnightly three-day sales in various categories are held in the Booth Mansion saleroom. These could include silver, silver plate, glass and European ceramics, furniture, rugs, clocks, pocket watches, works of art, Oriental carpets and so on.

There are also periodical specialist 'Selected' sales in other categories throughout the year.

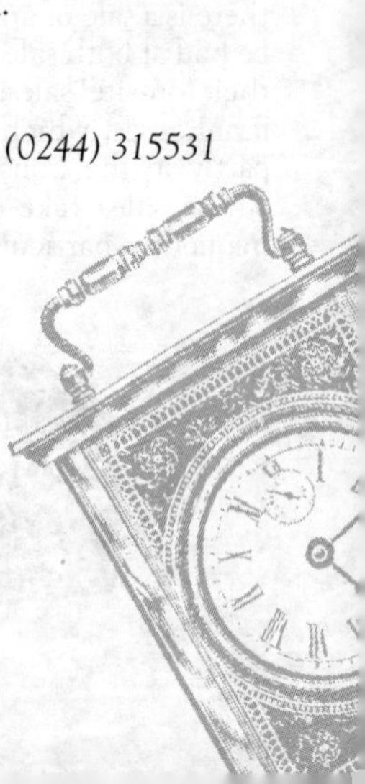

BUYER'S PREMIUM: *10%*
SALES: *Booth Mansion: fortnightly on Tue, Wed and Thu at 11.00am. Saltney: weekly on Thu at 10.00am, replaced periodically by Selected Sale starting 10.30am.*
VIEWING: *Booth Mansion and Selected: Sat prior 9.30am-12.30pm, daily in week of sale 9.30am-4.30pm (3.30pm day prior to sale of furniture). Saltney (except Selected): day prior*

Also in this area, Sotheby's have the Saltney Saleroom, which is off the High Street in Saltney, tel: (0244) 677245. The 'Arcade Auction' is held here every Thursday at 10.00am, and concentrates mainly on furniture and works of art. Periodically this sale becomes a 'Selected Sale', including 18th- and 19th-century, Victorian, Edwardian and 20th-century furniture and works of art, clocks, collectors' items and other specialist articles.

WHITTAKER & BIGGS

Macclesfield Road Saleroom. Tel: (0260) 273241

400-500 lots. Whittaker & Biggs saleroom is next to the cattle market, which they also run. The weekly sale takes place on a Friday or Saturday, and one sale in three is devoted to antiques. Otherwise this is a general sale of household furniture and effects.

Special sales of household furniture and effects take place twice a year (usually in February and September) at Knypersley Cricket Club, Knypersley, on Thursday at 10.00am with viewing the previous day from 5.00pm to 8.00pm. The firm also holds special antiques sales twice a year, at Meerbrook Village Hall, Meerbrook, Leek, Staffordshire. Four special antiques and general sales are also held at Leek each year.

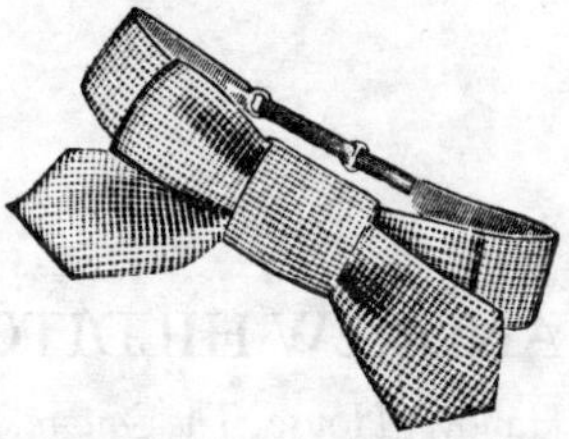

FRANK R MARSHALL

Marshall House, Church Hill. Tel: (0565) 3284

500-600 lots. The saleroom, which is close to the railway station, is a large, green-painted building which was at one time the Egerton School. Sales are held twice a month and usually alternate between general and antiques. Occasionally there is no antiques sale, in which case a second general sale is held. Both types of sale start in the first-floor saleroom with smaller items such as various collectables, silver and jewellery. At around 12.30pm the sale moves to the ground floor for the auctioning of furniture and larger items.

Six miles away at Chelford Agricultural Centre, Chelford, Frank R Marshall hold sales of another sort which are full of interest. These are more for the wholesale trade and are devoted to cut flowers and potted plants, shrubs and conifers,

9.30am-7.30pm.
REFRESHMENTS: *Booth Mansion: none available on the premises. Saltney: own café.*
PARKING: *Booth Mansion: none available on the premises. Saltney: own car park.*
STORAGE: *Yes*
TRANSPORTATION: *Yes*
SHIPPING: *Yes*

Congleton

BUYER'S PREMIUM: *10%*
SALES: *Weekly. Usually general, but antiques sale one week in three. General: Fri or Sat at 10.00am. Antiques: Fri at 5.00pm. Special antiques: twice a year (usually May and Sep) on Thu at 10.00am. Special antiques and general: four times a year in May, Jun, Sep and Oct on Sat at 10.00am.*
VIEWING: *Day prior 5.00pm-7.00pm, antiques also 3.00pm-5.00pm. Special antiques and general: day prior 5.00pm-8.00pm.*
REFRESHMENTS: *Own café.*
PARKING: *Own car park.*
STORAGE: *Yes*
TRANSPORTATION: *Yes*
SHIPPING: *Yes*

Knutsford

The following details are for Knutsford sales only:

BUYER'S PREMIUM: *General: nil. Antiques: 10%*
SALES: *Twice monthly on Wed at 10.00am (general sales usually alternate with antiques).*
VIEWING: *General: day prior 10.00am-6.30pm. Antiques: day prior 10.00am-7.00pm.*
REFRESHMENTS: *None available on the premises.*
PARKING: *Own car park.*
STORAGE: *No*
TRANSPORTATION: *Yes*
SHIPPING: *Yes*

potatoes and other vegetables, eggs, dressed poultry and the like — all in a busy day of cattle and sheep selling. Sales are weekly on Monday at 9.15am, Wednesday at 12.00 noon, and Thursday at 7.00pm. A horse and tackle sale is held on the last Friday of the month, with times as follows: saddlery and tack 10.15am; warranted horses and ponies, 12.15pm, followed by unwarranted horses; horseboxes 2.00pm. Times may change in March and September sales.

Nantwich

HENRY SPENCER & SONS

Halifax Estate Agencies Ltd, Victoria Gallery, Market Street. Tel: (0270) 623878

BUYER'S PREMIUM: *10%*
SALES: *About three times a month on Thu at 11.00am (includes Georgian sale at irregular intervals).*
VIEWING: *Day prior 10.00am-4.00pm, day of sale from 10.00am. Georgian: at least two days prior, day of sale from 10.00am.*
REFRESHMENTS: *Own café.*
PARKING: *Own car park.*
STORAGE: *Vendors only.*
TRANSPORTATION: *Yes*
SHIPPING: *No*

300-400 lots. The saleroom is a good conversion from an old school, and is near the town centre, at the rear of the bus station. About three sales are held each month, in categories including metalware, glass, ceramics, silver, clocks and barometers, or at irregular intervals, such as those of 'Georgian, Later Furniture and Works of Art'.

The auctioneers like lots to achieve a price of at least £20, and often they fetch much more.

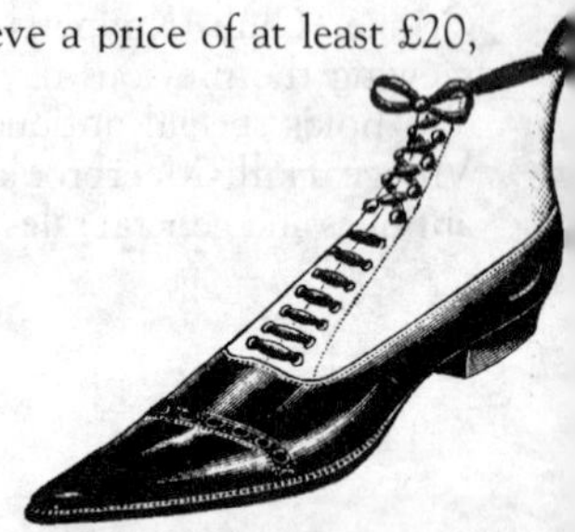

Sandbach

ANDREW HILDITCH & SON LTD

Hanover House, The Square. Tel: (0270) 767246

BUYER'S PREMIUM: *10%*
SALES: *Weekly on Wed at 10.00am (replaced quarterly by antiques and picture sale).*
VIEWING: *day prior 9.30am-4.30pm.*
REFRESHMENTS: *None available on the premises.*
PARKING: *Ample parking near by.*
STORAGE: *Yes*
TRANSPORTATION: *Yes*
SHIPPING: *Yes*

300-500 lots. The saleroom is opposite one of this quaint old town's remarkable landmarks: two Saxon crosses which stand in the market place and are said to mark a royal wedding. The proprietor of the auction is Mr Thomas Spencer Andrew, who started it as a 16-year-old 'one man band' after developing an interest in Old Master paintings. Now his hobby has grown into a thriving business with a reputation far beyond the local area. The weekly sale is of general household furniture and effects, and is replaced at quarterly intervals by special sales of pictures and antiques. There are three separate sales galleries. The general auction begins in the smaller China Room, which holds bric-à-brac, silver, china, jewellery, ornaments and other small items. The sale of general goods and furniture begins in the main gallery, always after 1.00pm. The quarterly sale is held in the first-floor gallery.

LITTONS (CHESHIRE) LTD

Guardian Street. Tel: (0925) 572199

400-500 lots. The saleroom is on the edge of the town centre, by the rear entrance of Warrington General Hospital. This is an interesting weekly sale of general household furniture and effects, which may include antiques. A special sale of antiques and collectors' items is held in place of the general sale once a quarter. There are over 10,000 sq ft of floor space, divided into two salerooms, making this one of the largest auction areas in the north of England. Only one saleroom is used at a time, while the other is prepared for the next week's sale. The general sale starts with 'white goods', such as dishwashers, refrigerators, spin driers, freezers and so on. Any motor vehicles among the lots are always sold in the middle of the sale, around lunch time. The saleroom is so large than even these are sold under cover. Better quality goods including antiques are kept for the later part of the sale.

Warrington

BUYER'S PREMIUM: *General: nil. Antiques: 10%.*
SALES: *Weekly on Thu at 10.30am (includes specialist antiques and collectors' sale once a quarter).*
VIEWING: *Day prior 10.00am-8.00pm.*
REFRESHMENTS: *Own café.*
PARKING: *Own car park.*
STORAGE: *Yes*
TRANSPORTATION: *Yes*
SHIPPING: *Yes*

CLEVELAND

HARTLEPOOL AUCTION ROOMS

Andrew Street. Tel: (0429) 275406

100-200 lots. This is a long-established general sale operated by a well-known local firm, Sanderson Removals. In addition to these two activities, the firm has a retail shop where new and second-hand furniture is sold. You go through the shop to get to the auction saleroom. The sale is held once a fortnight, and typically will offer household furniture in a variety of styles, ages and conditions, including upholstered lounge suites and easy chairs, dining room and bedroom suites, kitchen cabinets, dressers and so on. There could also be ornamental and domestic china such as teapots, cups, and porcelain plates, with candlesticks, glass, lamps, children's toys, and books, plus office furniture, hand tools, electrical tools, bicycles and other items.

Hartlepool

BUYER'S PREMIUM: *12%*
SALES: *Fortnightly on Thu at 10.00am.*
VIEWING: *Day prior 10.00am-4.00pm.*
REFRESHMENTS: *Own café.*
PARKING: *Own car park.*
STORAGE: *Yes*
TRANSPORTATION: *Yes*
SHIPPING: *Yes*

J C SIMMONS & SON

Saltburn Salerooms, Diamond Street. Tel: (0287) 22366

400-450 lots. The saleroom is in the centre of this pleasant seaside town and adjoins the fine old three-storey building which houses the firm's offices. Opposite are the equally large storerooms. The salerooms were established in the 1920s and

Saltburn-by-the-Sea

BUYER'S PREMIUM: *6%*
SALES: *Weekly on Wed at 9.30am (includes antiques and collectors' sale every six to eight weeks).*

VIEWING: *Sat prior 9.00am-4.00pm, Mon and Tue 9.00am-5.00pm.*
REFRESHMENTS: *None available on the premises but several cafés near by.*
PARKING: *Ample parking near by.*
STORAGE: *Yes*
TRANSPORTATION: *Yes*
SHIPPING: *Yes*

since 1947 have been run by the Simmons family, John Charles Simmons (now retired) and his son John. It is a very popular, well-attended auction, ideal for those wanting to furnish a house. Decorative china, ornamental items, electrical goods, bicycles, garden equipment and other household effects are sold in the morning session, which finishes at around 12.00 noon. At 1.00pm the sale continues with reproduction and quality modern furnishings, and 'shipping' goods (1930s and 1940s furniture). Every six to eight weeks the general sale is replaced by a special antiques and fine art sale.

Stockton

BUYER'S PREMIUM: *6%*
SALES: *Fortnightly on Tue at 10.00am.*
VIEWING: *Fri, Sat and Mon prior 9.30am-4.30pm.*
REFRESHMENTS: *None available on the premises.*
PARKING: *Swallow Hotel multi-storey car park.*
STORAGE: *Yes*
TRANSPORTATION: *Yes*
SHIPPING: *Yes*

STOCKTON AUCTION ROOM

17 Bridge Road. Tel: (0642) 607473

400-450 lots. Stockton is an industrial town on the bank of the tidal River Tees. The auction room is a minute's walk from the wide High Street, which has been the scene of an open-air market since 1310 (market days are Wednesday and Saturday). This is a pleasant and unintimidating sale. It is well run and has been under the proprietorship of the same family for the past 70 years. There are good buys in all categories of general household furniture and effects, including antiques. The general sale starts with 'smalls': glass, domestic and ornamental china, boxes of assorted bric-à-brac, books, children's toys and so on. A typical sale will also have craft goods and general tools of various kinds, electrical goods, gas appliances and televisions. The selling of furniture always starts at 1.00pm and usually includes some excellent 1930s and 1940s pieces, as well as modern and antique. The auctioneer ends the sale by returning to any 'smalls' that are left. A special sale of antiques and fine art replaces the general sale at irregular intervals, whenever enough lots of particularly high quality have been amassed.

Stokesley

BUYER'S PREMIUM: *10%*
SALES: *Weekly on various days at 10.30am or 12.00 noon (ring to check type of goods).*
VIEWING: *Sales starting at 10.30am: all day prior. Sales starting at 12.00 noon: day of sale.*
REFRESHMENTS: *Own café.*
PARKING: *Own car park.*
STORAGE: *No*
TRANSPORTATION: *Yes*
SHIPPING: *Yes*

LITHGOW SONS & PARTNERS

The Auction House, Station Road. Tel: (0642) 710158

600-1,000 lots. Lithgow Sons & Partners have been independent auctioneers since 1868 and are one of the largest auctioneers in the county. There is one sale per week, and although this will be well advertised locally, it is usually necessary to contact the auctioneers to find out what type of goods are to be sold. General sales of furniture and household effects are held about every four to six weeks, on Friday at 10.30am. Sales of tools and machinery, including small hand tools for the DIY enthusiast, are held every two to three weeks, on Wednesday at 10.30am. Office furniture and equipment and catering equipment sales occur monthly on average, also

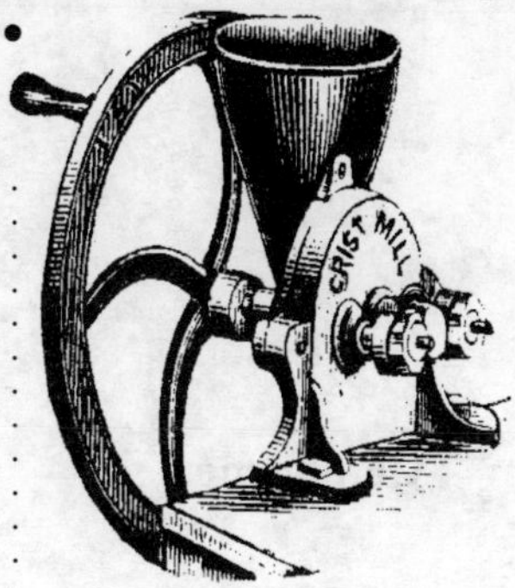

on Wednesday, but usually starting at 12.00 noon. Other sales, often of liquidated stock, are held at irregular intervals as the need arises. They usually take place in the saleroom, but occasionally will be held 'on site' — in the actual factory, office or shop which has gone into receivership. These sales could be of anything from brand new clothing to jewellery to boats, and offer excellent bargains. There are also sales of fine wines twice a year in December and June or July, on a Wednesday at 12.00 noon.

CORNWALL

KITTOWS

41 Fore Street. Tel: (0579) 83585

500-600 lots. Situated opposite Callington's imposing parish church, Kittows was established in 1850. Over the years they have gained a well-founded reputation for being a friendly but efficient saleroom: light hearted but well run, with an atmosphere that would certainly not intimidate a new auction-goer. The monthly sales offer all types of goods: antique, period and modern furniture, which includes dining suites, bedroom suites, tables, soft furnishings, bureaux and pine; electrical goods; outside effects; large amounts of bric-à-brac and miscellaneous effects, and garden and hand tools. Some lots go for as little as 50p, while in the same sale a George III mahogany bureau bookcase could fetch £2,000.

Callington

BUYER'S PREMIUM: *Nil*
SALES: *Monthly on Mon at 10.30am.*
VIEWING: *Day of sale from 8.30am.*
REFRESHMENTS: *None available on the premises.*
PARKING: *In centre of town, a few minutes walk away.*
STORAGE: *Yes*
TRANSPORTATION: *Yes*
SHIPPING: *Yes*

CHARLES STREET AUCTIONS

West Charles Street. Tel: (0209) 717570

300-400 lots. The saleroom is close to the town centre, near the library and by the statue of Richard Trevithick, the inventor of the high-pressure steam engine who was born near by. Camborne is a busy and pleasant town, and one of the few big industrial centres in Cornwall. It is the main centre for many scattered villages. The majority of the sale items for the Charles Street Auctions come from local private houses, which explains the wide difference in the value and quality of goods to be found at most sales. A typical sale will include furniture, from nearly new modern to high-quality antique, interesting pieces of china and brass, boxes of books and photographs, and so on. Many holidaymakers find a visit to the auction an interesting addition to their holiday activities. One holidaymaker from Germany recently bought an old horsehair

Camborne

BUYER'S PREMIUM: *10%*
SALES: *Fortnightly on Thu at 6.30pm.*
VIEWING: *Day of sale from 10.00am.*
REFRESHMENTS: *Own café.*
PARKING: *Public car park near by.*
STORAGE: *Yes*
TRANSPORTATION: *Yes*
SHIPPING: *Yes*

three-piece lounge suite which had been part of a house clearance. He only paid a few pounds for it and was pleased with his bargain, despite having to pay over £400 to have it shipped back to Germany.

Camborne

MGA AUCTIONS

West Charles Street. Tel: (0209) 711065

BUYER'S PREMIUM: *10%*
SALES: *General: weekly on Thu at 6.00pm. Antiques and collectors' items: about every two months on Thu at 4.00pm. Marine: twice a year in Apr and Oct on Sat at 11.00am.*
VIEWING: *Day of sale from 9.00am.*
REFRESHMENTS: *Yes.*
PARKING: *Own car park.*
STORAGE: *Yes*
TRANSPORTATION: *Yes*
SHIPPING: *Yes*

300-400 lots. MGA Auctions have been established for many years and are an excellent example of a good country auction. The atmosphere is good, and there seems no limit to the type and variety of goods. There will be good quality furniture, paintings, cutlery, crockery and electrical goods, including videos, hi-fis and televisions. Roughly every two months the Thursday sale starts at 4.00pm for the sale of antiques and collectors' items, continuing at 6.00pm with the general sale. The spring and autumn sale of marine items is also popular and well attended, and offers everything to do with boats, from books about them to engines and sails.

Falmouth

PETER KEMP AUCTIONS

See PETER KEMP AUCTIONS, Truro, Cornwall

Lostwithiel

JEFFERYS

5 Fore Street. Tel: (0208) 872245

BUYER'S PREMIUM: *10%*
SALES: *Weekly, monthly and three-monthly sales all on Wed at 10.00am at either the Lostwithiel or the Wadebridge salerooms.*
VIEWING: *Lostwithiel: Tue 10.00am-1.00pm, 2.00pm-4.00pm. Wadebridge: Mon and Tue 9.00am-1.00pm, 2.00pm-5.00pm.*
REFRESHMENTS: *Tea on the premises.*
PARKING: *None available on the premises.*
STORAGE: *Yes*
TRANSPORTATION: *Yes*
SHIPPING: *Yes*

1,200 lots. Jefferys were established in 1865, and today they hold popular weekly sales of modern and Victorian household furniture and effects, and other items. Lostwithiel is a picturesque old town, which attracts visitors for its salmon and trout fishing. Jefferys also have premises at The Belmont Auction Rooms, Wadebridge, tel: (0208) 812131. The weekly sales alternate between the Lostwithiel and Wadebridge salerooms. There are sales of antique and oriental furniture, textiles, works of art and ceramics once a month, again alternating between the two premises. The Belmont Auction Rooms at Wadebridge hold three collectors' sales a year, of stamps, postcards and cigarette cards. Wadebridge itself is a clean, bright town, worth visiting for its river scenery and bridge.

Newquay

PETER KEMP AUCTIONS

See PETER KEMP AUCTIONS, Truro, Cornwall

W H LANE & SON

Penzance

65 Morrab Road. Tel: (0736) 61447

More than 1,500 lots. The saleroom is just a few minutes' walk from the promenade and sea front, and is easily recognisable as an ex-Victorian school. A large L-shaped saleroom has been created out of the ground floor, with the second floor used for storage. The sales have a reputation far beyond the borders of Cornwall. There are sales here every month, alternating between antiques and objets d'art one month and pictures and prints the next. There are also twice-yearly book sales and specialist collectors' sales, which could include Dinky toys, coins, medals, railway memorabilia, nautical artefacts and so on.

The sea around Penzance is notorious, and there are special sales of items brought up from shipwrecks, such as old coins, parts of boats and even the odd cannon. These sales go under titles such as 'Sunken Treasure' and do not occur very often, but are well worth attending. Over the years W H Lane have also built up a reputation for their sales of West Country art, including the Newlyn and St Ives' schools of painting.

BUYER'S PREMIUM: *10%*
SALES: *Antiques: alternate months at 10.30am, usually on Tue and Wed. Pictures and prints: alternate months at 10.30am, usually on Thu. Specialist collectors' items: twice a year in spring and autumn on Fri at 6.30pm and on Sat at 10.30am. Books: twice a year in spring and autumn on Fri at 6.30pm and Sat at 10.30am.*
VIEWING: *All sales: Sat prior 9.30am-12.30pm, day prior 9.00am-1.00pm, 2.00pm-7.00pm, and morning of sale from 8.30am.*
REFRESHMENTS: *Available on the premises.*
PARKING: *Unrestricted parking near by.*
STORAGE: *Yes*
TRANSPORTATION: *Yes*
SHIPPING: *Yes*

DAVID LAY

Penzance

The Penzance Auction House, Alverton. Tel: (0736) 61414

1,000-1,500 lots. The monthly Tuesday sale is of general Victorian, good quality modern and reproduction furniture, pine, and household effects. Every eight weeks there is a two-day sale of general antiques, ceramics, silver, jewellery, plated ware, rugs and commemorative ware. Even classic cars sometimes appear for sale. In the two-day sales, furniture usually starts the afternoon session at around 1.30pm on Friday. In addition to these sales there is a three-monthly sale of paintings (mainly Newlyn and St Ives schools).

Twice yearly David Lay holds special sales of collectors' items, including books, coins, stamps, post and cigarette cards, and toys. No one should ever be surprised at what can be bought at David Lay's. A recent sale included an entire late-Victorian conservatory. The conservatory was still attached to a house, and the successful purchaser was responsible for dismantling and removing it.

The saleroom holds the provincial record for a non-art lot: £230,000 for a Georgian bookcase. Not all prices are in these realms, however.

BUYER'S PREMIUM: *10%*
SALES: *General: monthly on Tue at 10.00am. Antiques: every six weeks on Thu and Fri at 10.00am. Paintings and prints: every three months on Thu at 10.00am. Collectors' items: twice a year on Tue at 10.00am.*
VIEWING: *Sat prior 11.00am-4.00pm, day prior 9.00am-7.30pm, day of sale from 8.30am.*
REFRESHMENTS: *Own café.*
PARKING: *Good parking facilities in the area.*
STORAGE: *Yes*
TRANSPORTATION: *Yes*
SHIPPING: *Yes*

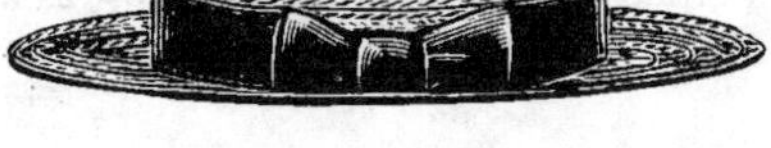

Truro

BUYER'S PREMIUM: *10%*
SALES: *General: fortnightly on Sat at 2.00pm, monthly on Thu at 7.00pm. Harness and saddlery: every three months, usually on Mon at 6.30pm.*
VIEWING: *General (Sat): morning of sale. General (Thu) and harness and saddlery: day of sale from 2.00pm.*
REFRESHMENTS: *Own café.*
PARKING: *Own car park.*
STORAGE: *No*
TRANSPORTATION: *Yes*
SHIPPING: *Yes*

PETER KEMP AUCTIONS

Parish Hall, Ladock; Ambulance Hall, Quay Hill, Falmouth; Village Hall, Quintrell Downs, near Newquay. Tel: (0326) 318975

300-400 lots. Cornwall is unusual in that many auctions do not have regular salerooms but move week by week to various parish and church halls around the county. Peter Kemp's sale is one of these — it is most often in Ladock, but check the location in the local press or by telephone. Vendors can bring in goods right up to the moment of sale, which adds to the excitement. Prices vary greatly, with one lot going for £1, the next for £1,000 and the next for £20. A typical sale will have modern, reproduction, Victorian, Edwardian, and Georgian furniture, including a notable amount of pine, plus china, jewellery, general household items and bric-à-brac. The quarterly sales of harness and saddlery include virtually everything to do with horses, from whips and saddles to brasses, books and paintings.

Truro

BUYER'S PREMIUM: *5%*
SALES: *Monthly at 11.00am.*
VIEWING: *On day of sale — times vary.*
REFRESHMENTS: *Van selling snacks.*
PARKING: *Ample near by.*
STORAGE: *No*
TRANSPORTATION: *No*
SHIPPING: *No*

LODGE & THOMAS

77 Lemon Street. Tel: (0872) 72722

300-400 lots. Truro is a cathedral city and also has a small port at the head of the river. Most of the lots at Lodge & Thomas's sales are from private sources, ensuring a wide and interesting range of goods. There is no one regular saleroom. The auctions are held at various locations in the Truro area, such as village halls which have been hired especially for the sale — the main venues are the Community Hall at Playing Place, a village near Truro, and Leedstown Village Hall, between Hayle and Helston. The sales cover the entire range of modern, Victorian, reproduction and high quality antique furniture, general household furniture and effects. Miscellaneous items, including gardening equipment and tools, china (both sets and single pieces), ornaments, glass, brass and electrical goods, are also sold. Interesting lots of bric-à-brac and collectables are also available, but many lots have sailing and fishing connections. These sales are busy and well attended.

Wadebridge

BUYER'S PREMIUM: *5%*
SALES: *Fortnightly on Mon at 11.00am (includes antiques and fine art sale five times a year, starting 12.00 noon). End of*

LAMBRAYS

Polmorla Walk. Tel: (0208) 813593

400-500 lots. Buying at auction is such a way of life in Cornwall that local people needing an item of household furniture or perhaps a gift for a friend are just as likely to visit an auction as a shop. The Lambrays auctions are particularly good for the odd little gift, because they start with perhaps 200-250 lots of trays of small miscellaneous items. There will usually be something enticing on one of the trays, such as a piece of china, a small ornament or a book. The saleroom is large, around 4,000 sq ft, and is situated in a new shopping complex in the centre of the town. Items in forthcoming sales are displayed in a large window overlooking the street (there are occasionally displays of work by local crafts people and artists here instead).

The fortnightly sale is of general household furniture and effects, including china, jewellery, paintings and many other items of all ages and values. Around five times a year this sale is devoted to antiques and fine art instead. A particularly popular sale is the 'End of the Year Sale' which is held on New Year's Eve (except when it falls at the weekend, when the sale is on the Friday or Monday). It begins at noon and covers the gambit of modern, antique, Victorian, Edwardian, pine, collectors' items, memorabilia and so on. This sale has become an annual must for locals and visitors over the years.

Year Sale: New Year's Eve (or Fri/Mon if at weekend) at 12.00 noon.
VIEWING: *General: Sat prior 9.00am-12.00 noon, morning of sale from 9.00am. Antiques and fine art: Thu prior 6.30pm-9.00pm, Fri prior 9.00am-5.00pm, morning of sale from 9.00am. End of Year Sale: morning of sale from 9.00am.*
REFRESHMENTS: *Own café.*
PARKING: *None available on the premises.*
STORAGE: *Yes*
TRANSPORTATION: *Yes*
SHIPPING: *Yes*

CUMBRIA

CUMBRIA AUCTION ROOMS

Carlisle

12 Lowther Street. Tel: (0228) 25259

500-800 lots. Carlisle is the centre for many remote villages and houses, which is one reason why there are so many excellent auctions in the area. The city is also the seat of a bishop: if time allows, take a look at the cathedral, which has stained glass to rival any at York Minster.

This sale was established in 1876 and is still held close to the original site. The present saleroom is part of an interesting building which was once the Hope & Bendle bottling factory. Past lots in the weekly general sale have included Victorian mahogany desks, wash stands, tables, chests of drawers, Edwardian bedroom suites, deal cupboards, oak bureaux and china cabinets, extending tables, Victorian day beds and cane chairs, plus electrical goods, china and glass, metalwork, silver plate, pictures and prints, carpets and soft furnishings.

About every eight to ten weeks the general sale is replaced by a catalogue sale of antiques. Items in this sale in the past have ranged from Georgian chests and William IV dining chairs, to a 1950 Sunbeam motorcycle and a reflecting telescope. Paintings, china, silver and so on can also be found at this sale.

BUYER'S PREMIUM: *General: Nil. Antiques: 10%*
SALES: *Weekly on Mon at 10.00am (includes catalogue antiques sale every eight to ten weeks).*
VIEWING: *Fri prior 9.00am-5.00pm, Sat prior 9.00am-12.00 noon.*
REFRESHMENTS: *None available on the premises.*
PARKING: *Civic Centre public car park.*
STORAGE: *Yes*
TRANSPORTATION: *Yes*
SHIPPING: *Yes*

Carlisle

The following details refer to weekly sales only:

BUYER'S PREMIUM: *Nil*
SALES: *General: weekly on Sat at 9.30am. Timber and building equipment: weekly on Fri at 1.00pm.*
VIEWING: *General: day prior 3.00pm-5.00pm, day of sale from 8.00am. Others: day of sale from 8.00am.*
REFRESHMENTS: *Van selling snacks.*
PARKING: *Tait Street public car park.*
STORAGE: *No*
TRANSPORTATION: *Yes*
SHIPPING: *Yes*

ROBERT DALTON & SONS LTD

Daltons Mart, Botchergate. Tel: (0228) 21102

600-700 lots. This auction has been established for over 100 years, and has become something of a local institution. The weekly sales generally have a wide range of goods and are enormously popular and entertaining. The Saturday sale begins with an assortment of miscellaneous items, which might include bicycles, general tools, work benches, gardening equipment and machinery, household electrical equipment such as washing machines and refrigerators, sinks, panel doors, ladders and heaters. Around lunch time, depending on the number of lots in the first section, the sale generally continues with specialist sales in various categories such as antiques, office furniture, marine objects, horse tack, vintage plant, plant and machinery, and so on. There is also a weekly Friday sale of timber and various building equipment, which might include slates, gates, boards and beams, and is ideal for the DIY enthusiast. Every two or three weeks throughout the growing season there are also Wednesday sales of bulbs and shrubs, starting at 1.00pm. Sales of dressed and oven-ready poultry are held on the Wednesday, Thursday and Friday nearest to Christmas, at 12.00 noon.

Carlisle

BUYER'S PREMIUM: *Nil*
SALES: *Weekly on Thu at 10.30am (includes periodic catalogue sale of antiques and collectors' items).*
VIEWING: *Day prior 9.00am-5.00pm.*
REFRESHMENTS: *Own café.*
PARKING: *Own car park.*
STORAGE: *Yes*
TRANSPORTATION: *Yes*
SHIPPING: *Yes*

HARRISON & HETHERINGTON LTD

Borderway Mart, Rosehill. Tel: (0228) 26292

300-400 lots. The weekly sale takes place in the Rosehill Furniture Hall within the Borderway Mart, a very large complex which houses livestock sales during the week. It is outside the city centre, close to Junction 43 of the M6. This is a good location for an auction, and a good auction is what it is. The popular and well-run general sale offers a wide and varied range of modern household furniture and effects, which may include 1930s and 1940s pieces, cottage furniture, reproductions, curios and bygones, china, ornaments and so on. Periodically the general sale is replaced by special catalogue sales of antiques, curios and collectors' items.

Cartmel

BUYER'S PREMIUM: *£1 per lot.*
SALES: *Monthly on Fri at 10.00am.*
VIEWING: *Day prior 2.00pm-5.00pm.*

HACKNEY & LEIGH

The Village Hall. Tel: (05395) 33316

400-500 lots. Hackney & Leigh is one of the largest independent auctioneers in the area, holding periodic sales in various Lake District locations but principally at Cartmel. Cartmel is two miles west of Grange-over-Sands, and is rather like a cathedral city in miniature, with a fine old priory church.

The village hall is a couple of minutes' walk away. Plenty of china and porcelain, glass, bric-à-brac, good quality household items and a selection of antiques are included in most sales. Typical sales in the past have included antiques and period furniture, collections of pictures, china, porcelain and cut glass, brass lamps and horse brasses, chairs, clocks, books, jewellers' silver and gold, electrical equipment, garden tools and furniture, carpets and so on. Sales of shop and hotel contents and other specialities are held regularly.

REFRESHMENTS: *None available on the premises.*
PARKING: *Ample parking near by.*
STORAGE: *No*
TRANSPORTATION: *Yes*
SHIPPING: *Yes*

MITCHELLS

Cockermouth

The Furniture and Fine Art Hall, Station Street.
Tel: (0900) 822016

500-600 lots. Cockermouth is famous as the birthplace of William Wordsworth, and the house in which he was born is kept by the National Trust as a place of literary pilgrimage. The saleroom is an impressive Victorian building in the centre of the town, directly opposite the cattle market. The same firm is also responsible for livestock sales, which are held on Monday and Wednesday. Within the saleroom an octagonal sale ring displays 'smalls' such as china, porcelain, glass, silver and plated ware. Larger items in the general sale might include dining room and bedroom suites, wardrobes, occasional tables, and three-piece suites. Also to be found are paintings and other pictures, mirrors, bed and table linen and other soft goods, carpets, rugs, electrical goods, kitchen utensils and gardening tools. There will usually be some antiques, but particularly good items are kept back for the special antiques sales which replace the general sale about every six to eight weeks.

BUYER'S PREMIUM: *Antiques: 10%. Others: nil*
SALES: *Weekly on Thu at 10.30am.*
VIEWING: *Day prior 2.30pm-4.30pm, morning of sale from 9.00am.*
REFRESHMENTS: *Own café.*
PARKING: *Public car park near by.*
STORAGE: *Yes*
TRANSPORTATION: *Yes*
SHIPPING: *Yes*

JAMES THOMPSON

Kirkby Lonsdale

64 Main Street. Tel: (0468) 71555

1,300-1,400 lots. There are two James Thompson sales in the town. The monthly two-day antiques and fine art sale takes place in a clearly marked saleroom behind the post office. The sale of pictures is held every two months, in the Royal Barn in New Road. Both rooms are well-known local landmarks and the sales attract buyers from a wide area, including many from Scotland.

The antiques sale is usually on the first Wednesday and Thursday of the month. Up for auction on the first day are silver and plate, jewellery, brass, copper and other metalware, glass and china. The second day is devoted to books, prints, rugs, furniture and miscellaneous items, which can include almost anything that is old: musical instruments, cameras,

BUYER'S PREMIUM: *Nil*
SALES: *Antiques: monthly on first Wed and Thu of month at 9.30am. Pictures: every two months on Wed at 9.30am.*
VIEWING: *Day prior 9.30am-3.00pm.*
REFRESHMENTS: *None available on the premises.*
PARKING: *Ample parking near by.*
STORAGE: *No*
TRANSPORTATION: *Yes*
SHIPPING: *Yes*

telescopes, tinplate toys, old games and dolls. Clocks of all types, including grandfather clocks, are always sold at 1.30pm.

The picture sale is also held on a Wednesday but is usually towards the end of the month. There may be some 300 lots of paintings and other pictures in this sale.

Millom

HARRISON COWARD

St George's Hall, Lapstone Road. Tel: (0229) 772314

BUYER'S PREMIUM: *Nil*
SALES: *Millom: every six weeks on Wed. Ulverston: monthly on Tue. Broughton in Furness: Tue or Wed. All at 10.30am.*
VIEWING: *Millom: day prior 2.00pm-7.00pm. Ulverston: 10.00am-4.00pm. Broughton in Furness: 2.00pm-5.00pm.*
REFRESHMENTS: *Millom: own café. Others: none available on the premises.*
PARKING: *Ample parking available.*
STORAGE: *Yes*
TRANSPORTATION: *Yes*
SHIPPING: *Yes*

200-300 lots. St George's Hall, which is hired for the sale, is just down the road from the company's office at 24 Lapstone Road, and next door to an infants' school. There are numerous old country houses in the area, and the sale often has good country furniture, including antiques and various interesting household and personal effects such as photograph albums, old toys, dolls and so on.

In addition to the Millom sale, Harrison Coward also hold monthly general sales at the County Auction Rooms, County Square, Ulverston, tel: (0229) 52056, and at Victory Hall, Broughton in Furness (same telephone number). The Ulverston sale tends to involve the contents of complete house clearances, while individual vendors are more likely to bring items to the Broughton in Furness sale. All the goods put in for auction by one vendor are given the same number, which makes it difficult to judge how many individual lots are for sale. However, it is a system which keeps buyers on their toes during the proceedings.

Penrith

PENRITH FARMERS & KIDDS PLC

The Castlegate Saleroom, Castlegate. Tel: (0768) 62131

BUYER'S PREMIUM: *Nil*
SALES: *Weekly on Wed at 9.30am (includes monthly collective sale of antiques).*
VIEWING: *Day prior 3.30pm-6.00pm.*
REFRESHMENTS: *Available near by.*
PARKING: *Ample parking near by.*
STORAGE: *Yes*
TRANSPORTATION: *Yes*
SHIPPING: *Yes*

600-800 lots. The ancient town of Penrith is the gateway to the Lake District from the north, and owes much of its turbulent history to the fact that the visiting Scots were not always as friendly as they are now. Today quite a few Scots regularly find their way to these sales. The saleroom is a large Victorian building near the railway station. The weekly Wednesday sales are devoted to general household furniture and effects, such as modern furniture in all styles, cottage and reproduction furniture, jewellery, ornaments, china, toys, tools, machinery and bicycles.

Once a month this general sale is replaced by a collective sale of antiques, Victoriana and shipping goods (as well as 1930s and 1940s items). This sale can also include 18th and 19th-century and later furniture, and other articles from these periods.

MICHAEL C L HODGSON

The Memorial Hall. Tel: (0539) 721375

300-450 lots. The sale is to be found about a mile from the M6 at Junction 36. The general sale includes antique and reproduction furniture as well as good quality household furniture and effects. Items sold in past sales have included cane chairs, dining suites of various types, bedroom and lounge furniture, mirrors, china, glass, silver and plate, jewellery (including costume jewellery), various electrical goods such as vacuum cleaners, kettles and cookers, curtains, bed linen, pictures, and some collectable items like cigarette card and postcard albums.

The best items are put into special sales of antiques, which are held in place of the general sale whenever enough high quality goods have been gathered.

Preston Patrick, near Kendal

BUYER'S PREMIUM: *Nil*
SALES: *Monthly on Wed at 12.00 noon (includes periodic antiques sale).*
VIEWING: *Morning of sale from 9.00am.*
REFRESHMENTS: *None available on the premises.*
PARKING: *Ample parking available.*
STORAGE: *Yes*
TRANSPORTATION: *Yes*
SHIPPING: *Yes*

THOMSON, RODDICK & LAURIE

The Market Hall. Tel: (06973) 43348

200-300 lots. The monthly Friday sale is of general household furniture and effects. About every three months, again on a Friday, there is a sale of antiques, fine art and collectors' items. The same firm also holds general sales about every two months at The Saleroom, on the Townfoot Trading Estate, Brampton, which is about eight miles east of Carlisle on the A69. Special sales of antiquarian and other books are also held here at two-month intervals.

Special fine art sales which include oil paintings, watercolours and prints, silver, silver plate and jewellery, are held quarterly at the Swallow Hilltop Hotel, Carlisle. The hotel is on the A6 between the M6 at Junction 42 and the city centre.Thomson Roddick & Laurie hold regular auctions in Dumfries and Annan in Scotland as well.

For information on all Thomson, Roddick & Laurie's sales except those in Wigton, contact the firm's office at 24 Lowther Street, Carlisle, tel: (0228) 28939.

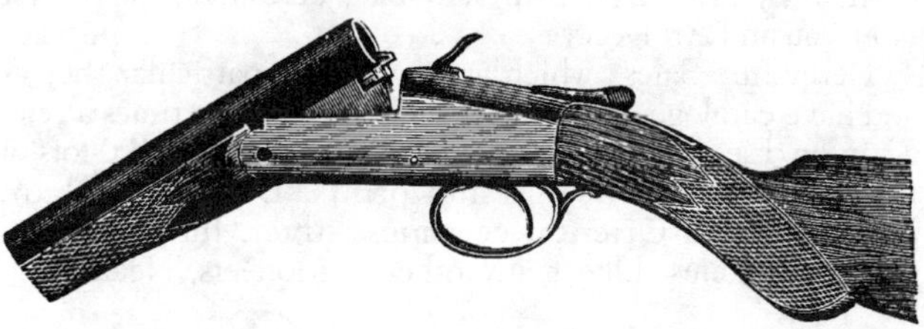

Wigton

BUYER'S PREMIUM: *10% (selected sales).*
SALES: *Wigton (general): monthly on Fri at 10.30am. Wigton (antiques): quarterly on Fri at 10.30am. Brampton (general): about every two months on Wed at 11.30am. Brampton (books): about every two months on Wed at 1.00pm. Carlisle: quarterly on Thu at 11.30am or 1.00pm.*
VIEWING: *Wigton (general): day of sale from 9.00am. Wigton (antiques): day prior 1.00pm-6.00pm. Brampton (both): day of sale from 9.00am. Carlisle: day prior 4.00pm-7.00pm, day of sale from 9.00am.*
REFRESHMENTS: *Available at all sales.*
PARKING: *Ample parking at all sales.*
STORAGE: *Yes*
TRANSPORTATION: *Yes*
SHIPPING: *Yes*

DERBYSHIRE

Clay Cross

BUYER'S PREMIUM: *10%*
SALES: *Weekly on Thu at 6.30pm.*
VIEWING: *All week 10.00am-5.00pm.*
REFRESHMENTS: *Own café.*
PARKING: *Own car park.*
STORAGE: *Yes*
TRANSPORTATION: *Yes*
SHIPPING: *Yes*

JB'S AUCTIONS

130a King Street. Tel: (0246) 866452

400-500 lots. The saleroom is in the town's main shopping street at the rear of JB's café, which is owned and run by the family responsible for the auction. JB's also offer bed and breakfast, useful for those overcome by the excitement of bidding.

This is a popular weekly sale and a regular meeting place for local people. The selling is brisk and businesslike, however. Too much talking between customers, and the auctioneer is likely to stop the proceedings and remind those responsible that 'this is a place of business'. Antique and shipping furniture is set out in the large saleroom, with modern furniture, general household effects and gardening equipment. There is usually a fair amount of domestic and ornamental china of all periods, plus silver and jewellery, bric-à-brac, toys, books and an assortment of miscellaneous items.

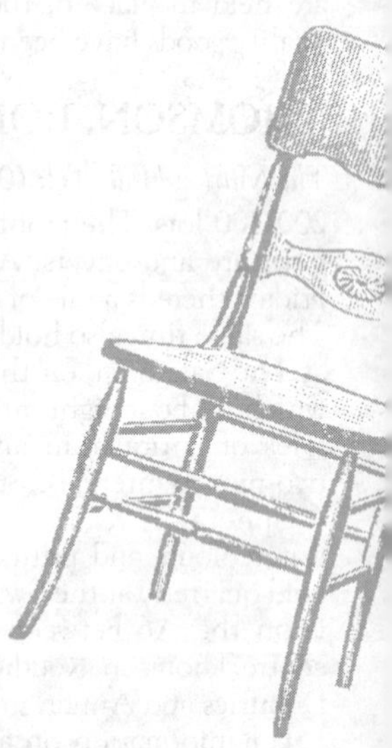

Derby

BUYER'S PREMIUM: *10%*
SALES: *General: every three weeks on Tue at 10.30am. Derbyshire Sales: at irregular intervals on Tue at 10.30am.*
VIEWING: *General: Mon prior 12.00 noon-7.00pm. Derbyshire Sales: Sat and Mon prior, times vary.*
REFRESHMENTS: *None available on the premises.*
PARKING: *NCP in Bold Lane.*
STORAGE: *Yes*
TRANSPORTATION: *Yes*
SHIPPING: *Yes*

NEALES

The Derby Salerooms, Becket Street. Tel: (0332) 43286

300-500 lots. Neales are Chartered Surveyors, Fine Art Auctioneers and Valuers founded in 1840. Their Derby saleroom is an attractive, double-fronted building in the centre of the city. Neales' three-weekly Tuesday general sales are uncatalogued and include English and Continental furniture, selected reproduction furnishings, clocks, metalwork, paintings, drawings, prints, books, ceramics, glass, Art Nouveau and Art Deco.

'Derbyshire Sales', which are devoted to particular themes and have catalogued lots, take place three or four times a year, again on Tuesdays. These sales usually include 300-400 lots of fine paintings, drawings and prints, Derby porcelain, European and Oriental ceramics, silver, furniture and collectors' items. Like many other auctioneers, Neales also organise 'Discovery Mornings' at which experts are on hand to identify and value items brought in by the public. In the Derby saleroom these are held every Wednesday, from 9.00am to 11.00am.

BURY & HILTON

Osmaston, near Ashbourne

See BURY & HILTON, Leek, Staffordshire

THE AUCTION ROOM

Staveley

Millgreen. Tel: (0246) 476012

500-600 lots. This friendly, independently run auction house is a good one for those new to bidding. There is a weekly general sale and a monthly sale of antiques and collectables. Both take place in a comfortable, single-storey, Tudor-style saleroom. The Friday sale offers a range of household furniture and effects, including televisions, electrical goods and collectables up to the 1940s. In a typical sale the lots might range from a gas iron to a gas mask, to an Edwardian printer's desk in perfect condition. There is no order of sale, so 100 lots of furniture may be sold, followed by 50 lots of collectables, followed in turn by more furniture, which keeps the buyers on their toes. The hammer comes down on bids as low as £1, or much more.

BUYER'S PREMIUM: *10%*
SALES: *General: weekly on Fri at 6.30pm. Antiques: last Sat of month at 10.00am.*
VIEWING: *General: day of sale from 10.00am. Antiques: day prior 10.00am-8.00pm.*
REFRESHMENTS: *Own café.*
PARKING: *Ample parking near by.*
STORAGE: *Yes*
TRANSPORTATION: *Yes*
SHIPPING: *Yes*

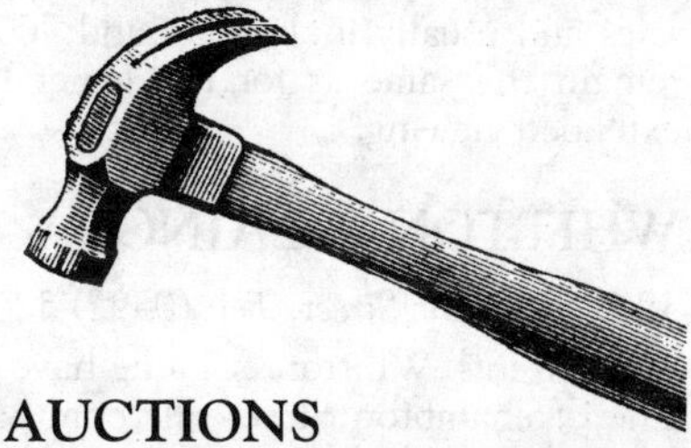

ARMSTRONG'S AUCTIONS

Swadlincote

Aults Industrial Estate, Midland Road. Tel: (0283) 550326

300-400 lots. Until recently this auction travelled around nearby villages and was held in various village halls. Then a permanent home was found in the small complex of industrial buildings in the centre of Swadlincote. John Walker, the auctioneer, has been wielding the hammer for over 20 years and the firm has been in existence for over 40. The sale has become a meeting place for old friends, and there is plenty of cheerful banter, with many of the 'audience' known to the auctioneer by Christian name. Typical lots might be galvanised corn bins, circular saws and garden urns, with the occasional piece of high-quality furniture, fine jewellery or porcelain waiting to be discovered among more run-of-the-mill lots.

BUYER'S PREMIUM: *Nil*
SALES: *Weekly on Wed at 11.00am.*
VIEWING: *Day prior 2.30pm-4.30pm, morning of sale from 9.00am.*
REFRESHMENTS: *Own café.*
PARKING: *Own car park.*
STORAGE: *Yes*
TRANSPORTATION: *Yes*
SHIPPING: *Yes*

DEVON

Dartmouth

LETCHER & SCORER WITH FULFORDS

9 South Embankment. Tel: (0803) 832223

BUYER'S PREMIUM: *5%*
SALES: *Fortnightly on Thu at 11.00am (includes antiques and collectables sale in Feb, May and Oct).*
VIEWING: *General: day prior 9.00am-5.00pm. Antiques: three days prior 9.00am-5.00pm.*
REFRESHMENTS: *None available on the premises.*
PARKING: *None available on the premises.*
STORAGE: *Yes*
TRANSPORTATION: *Yes*
SHIPPING: *Yes*

500-600 lots. Mrs Daphne Scorer has been the auctioneer in this saleroom for 30 years. She likes to keep the atmosphere light-hearted, and tries to make the sales a good day out for the would-be buyers.

The location of the saleroom is a wonderful asset: Dartmouth is one of the most picturesque towns in Britain, and the saleroom stands directly on the waterfront, close to the Harbour Master's office. Daphne Scorer sees the auctioneer's challenge as ensuring that both buyer and vendor are satisfied with the prices reached. If the sale price is too low vendors will be reluctant to place goods in future sales, but if it's too high buyers will be put off. We have a good balance here, which reflects the interests of both parties. The auctions are well attended, and usually offer plenty of interesting household furniture, effects and bric-à-brac.

Special sales of antiques and collectables are also held in October, February and May. These are larger than the general sales and usually include around 700 lots. The times of sale remain the same as for the general sale, although there is extended viewing.

Exeter

WHITTON & LAING

32 Okehampton Street. Tel: (0392) 52621

BUYER'S PREMIUM: *10%*
SALES: *Okehampton Street: general weekly on Fri at 10.30am; Specialist: fortnightly on Thu at 11.00am (antiques) or 10.00am (silver). Queens Road: fortnightly on Wed at 10.30am.*
VIEWING: *General: day prior 9.00am-5.30pm. Specialist: 2.30pm-5.30pm.*
REFRESHMENTS: *Own café.*
PARKING: *Ample parking near by.*
STORAGE: *Yes*
TRANSPORTATION: *Yes*
SHIPPING: *Yes*

400-500 lots. Whitton & Laing have two salerooms in Exeter. The Okehampton Street saleroom has weekly Friday sales of general household furniture and effects, plus two special Thursday auctions each month. One of these special sales is of antiques and the other of silver and jewellery.

Periodically throughout the year there will also be special sales of coins and medals, and of books. No general sale is held during weeks with a specialist sale.

The other saleroom is Queens Road Auctions, Queens Road, Exeter, tel: (0392) 56256, which has fortnightly sales of general household furniture and effects. These may include bankrupt stock. On a typical day the saleroom will be set out with chairs and three-piece suites, tables displaying china, bric-à-brac and so on, but the complete contents and stock of a shop or company that has gone out of business could also be up for sale.

KINGSBRIDGE AUCTIONS

Kingsbridge

Market Hall, Fore Street. Tel: (0548) 856829

600-700 lots. Kingsbridge is a busy market town at the head of the tidal estuary extending up from Salcombe. It is an ideal area for fishing, sailing and windsurfing, and many of the lots in the sale reflect these activities. Kingsbridge is also the main centre for many villages, and as most of the lots come from private vendors, this ensures there is always an interesting range of articles. The furniture will include modern, Victorian, reproduction and antique, in all conditions and of all values. There is usually a good selection of carpets, electrical goods and, best of all, miscellanea, which could include a collection of walking sticks or handbags, a box of dolls' furniture or dolls, an old Monopoly set or perhaps a camera. Twice a year, usually in March and September, special antiques and fine art sales are held in place of the general sale.

BUYER'S PREMIUM: *Nil*
SALES: *Monthly on Thu at 10.00am (includes twice-yearly antiques and fine arts sale, usually Mar and Sep).*
VIEWING: *Wed prior, 9.00am-4.30pm.*
REFRESHMENTS: *None available on the premises.*
PARKING: *None available on the premises.*
STORAGE: *Yes*
TRANSPORTATION: *Yes*
SHIPPING: *Yes*

FIELDENS CHARTERED SURVEYORS

Modbury

South Hams Auction Rooms, Poundwell Square. Tel: (0548) 830494

600-700 lots. Modbury is a small town on the main Plymouth to Kingsbridge road, the A379. There are three salerooms, in a building converted from an old factory in the centre of town, opposite the main car park. The sale usually begins in the saleroom which holds outside items, such as gardening equipment, lawn mowers and hand tools. Smaller lots such as china, ornaments, pottery, ceramics, books and so on are displayed on shelves in the central saleroom. The main saleroom has the furniture, which ranges from antique to modern. Like many other country auctioneers Fieldens also conduct outside sales, which may take place in a house, factory or store. There are no regular dates for these sales, but it is worth ringing to check if any are coming up.

BUYER'S PREMIUM: 5%
SALES: *Irregular intervals on Wed at 10.30am.*
VIEWING: *Day prior 1.00pm-7.00pm.*
REFRESHMENTS: *Own café.*
PARKING: *Public car park opposite.*
STORAGE: *Yes*
TRANSPORTATION: *Yes*
SHIPPING: *No*

CHERRY'S AUCTION ROOMS

Newton Abbot

Newton Abbot Racecourse. Tel: (0626) 56489

400-1,000 lots. Cherry's Auction Rooms hold about 30 auctions a year, mostly on Thursdays but occasionally Wednesdays. The sales are of general household furniture and effects of all periods, and often include commercial goods as well, such as the complete contents of a shop. Cherry's also hold celebrated boat auctions four times a year, usually in April and May and then again in September and October. These

BUYER'S PREMIUM: *General: 10%. Boat auctions: Nil*
SALES: *General: about 30 a year on Thu (occasionally Wed at 10.00am). Boat auctions: four times a year, usually Apr, May, Sep and Oct on Sat at 9.00am.*

VIEWING: *General: day prior 11.00am-4.00pm, morning of sale. Boat auctions: morning of sale.*
REFRESHMENTS: *Van selling snacks.*
PARKING: *Own car park.*
STORAGE: *Yes*
TRANSPORTATION: *Yes*
SHIPPING: *Yes*

sales include everything to do with boats and boating, including dinghies, engines, chandlery, trailers and so on. Two of the sales (one in the spring and one in the autumn) are held in The Racecourse, Newton Abbot, while the other two take place on Shaldon Beach, at the tip of the Teign estuary. There is a real carnival atmosphere at these sales, with the lots set out on the beach and on the pavement alongside. The auction starts at 9.00am, but it is wise to get there before 8.30am.

Paignton

AUSTINS

5 Curledge Street. Tel: (0803) 557112

BUYER'S PREMIUM: *5%*
SALES: *Fortnightly on Thu at 10.00am.*
VIEWING: *Day prior 9.30am-7.00pm.*
REFRESHMENTS: *Own café.*
PARKING: *Ample car parking near by.*
STORAGE: *Yes*
TRANSPORTATION: *Yes*
SHIPPING: *Yes*

500-600 lots. The saleroom is a large building close to the town's main bus centre. Different rooms are used for various parts of the auction. The sale is advertised as 'Victorian and Modern', and practically anything can be bought, from a grandfather clock to a box of assorted china, from a Welsh dresser to Victorian glass goblets, from a Royal Doulton baluster vase to a step ladder or bicycle. The auctions start in the upstairs saleroom with linen, bedding and bedroom suites, followed by a break at around 12.15pm for lunch. At 2.15pm the selling begins again in the yard with outside effects such as lawn mowers, gardening tools and bikes. The auctioneer and crowd then move into the Vestibule for the sale of cookers, refrigerators and general kitchen equipment. The auction ends in Saleroom B with antiques and paintings.

Paignton

D T BEESLEY

262 Torquay Road. Tel: (0803) 522222

BUYER'S PREMIUM: *10%*
SALES: *Fortnightly on Tue at 10.00am.*
VIEWING: *Day prior 9.00am-6.00pm.*
REFRESHMENTS: *None available on the premises.*
PARKING: *Public car park about 20 yards away.*
STORAGE: *Yes*
TRANSPORTATION: *Yes*
SHIPPING: *Yes*

500-600 lots. Paignton is a flourishing seaside resort, where the resident population of around 30,000 is easily doubled at the peak of the holiday season. The auction has a loyal local following, but the summer influx is easy to see at the sales. D T Beesley is a family firm, established for over 50 years, and their saleroom is in the Preston area, just out of the town centre. The sales are mixed and include both modern and antique items, with occasional reminders that the area is known for fishing and boating. There is no regular order of sale: a large and valuable item of furniture might be followed by a cheap box of china or a pile of local interest books. This haphazard method keeps prospective buyers on their toes, and some people find it helps them to focus on articles they missed during the viewing.

ERIC DISTIN & DOLTON

Plymouth

2 Bretonside. Tel: (0752) 66046

200-500 lots. The auctioneers have premises in Plymouth, but also in Saltash, Callington and Liskeard, and their weekly general Saturday sales rotate between all four salerooms. Plymouth is the main venue, though, as it has two salerooms where there are regular fortnightly sales of general furniture on Fridays (in the lower saleroom), and a monthly Saturday sale of antiques (on the first floor). The first-floor Plymouth saleroom is also the setting for a monthly Monday night collectors' sale of coins, stamps and medals. The Saltash saleroom is at 54 Fore Street, tel: (0752) 843768, while the Liskeard saleroom may be found at 18 Dean Street, by the cattle market, tel: (0579) 44366. The Callington premises, at 7 New Road, tel: (0579) 83322, are close to a public car park. All four branches attract regulars to their sales.

BUYER'S PREMIUM: *Nil*
SALES: *General: weekly on Sat at 10.30am (location varies between all four branches in Devon and Cornwall). Furniture: fortnightly on Fri at 10.30am (in lower floor Plymouth saleroom). Antiques: monthly on Sat at 10.30am. Coins, stamps and medals: monthly on Mon at 6.00pm (both in the lower floor Plymouth saleroom).*
VIEWING: *Day of sale from 9.00am, except coins, stamps and medals sales: day of sale 4.00pm-6.00pm*
REFRESHMENTS: *None available on the premises.*
PARKING: *Public car parks near each branch.*
STORAGE: *Yes*
TRANSPORTATION: *Yes*
SHIPPING: *Yes*

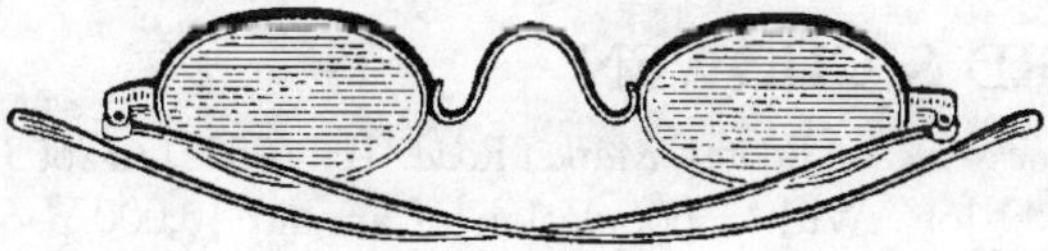

MICHAEL NEWMAN

Plymouth

The Central Auction Rooms, Kinterbury House, St Andrew's Cross. Tel: (0752) 662989

600-1,000 lots. The monthly Tuesday sale is of general furniture, antiques and later furniture and effects. Included are textiles, pictures and prints, ceramics, jewellery, silver, carpets and rugs, clocks, furniture and metals. In this saleroom, 'metals' includes more or less anything which does not fit into any other category — even such unlikely things as a document signed by Napoleon, assorted books, mahogany bellows, lacquer snuff boxes, cloisonné napkin rings, miniature brass candlesticks, wooden eggs, cotton reel holders, brass sovereign cases and table gramophones. The Wednesday sale usually deals with a different specialist area each month — perhaps militaria one month, railwayana the next and so on. When the monthly Wednesday sale is devoted to paintings and watercolours, it also includes drawings, prints and miniatures. Sales given over to the decorative arts include 19th- and 20th-century art, pottery and ceramics, as well as silver and jewellery. There is also a weekly Wednesday general sale at G S Shobrook & Co, whose premises are at 20 Western Approach, only a short distance away.

BUYER'S PREMIUM: *10%*
SALES: *General: monthly on Tue at 10.00am. Specialist: monthly on Wed at 10.00am or 2.30pm.*
VIEWING: *General: Sat prior 9.00am-12.00 noon, Mon prior 9.00am-5.00pm, day of sale from 9.00am. Specialist: Tue prior 9.00am-5.00pm, day of sale from 9.00am.*
REFRESHMENTS: *None available on the premises.*
PARKING: *Drake Circus multi-storey car park is 200 yards away.*
STORAGE: *Yes*
TRANSPORTATION: *Yes*
SHIPPING: *Yes*

Plymouth

BUYER'S PREMIUM: *Nil*
SALES: *General: weekly on Wed at 10.00am. Antiques and fine art: every two or three weeks on Wed at 1.30pm (after general sale).*
VIEWING: *Day prior 9.00am-5.00pm.*
REFRESHMENTS: *None available on the premises.*
PARKING: *None available on the premises.*
STORAGE: *Yes*
TRANSPORTATION: *Yes*
SHIPPING:*Yes*

G S SHOBROOK & CO

20 Western Approach. Tel: (0752) 663341

300-600 lots. The G S Shobrook sale is popular with locals and those travelling into town from nearby villages, with many people popping briefly into the saleroom during a day's shopping to see if there is anything they want. The weekly sale includes a fine array of general household furniture and effects, gardening tools and equipment, china of all types, brass, ornaments, bric-à-brac, kitchenalia, paintings, mirrors and so on. The sale finishes around 12.30pm as a rule, but every two or three weeks it continues after lunch with antiques and fine art. There are good bargains to be had in both sales. The saleroom is in the centre of the city in a large new complex on two floors: the ground floor is the home of the general sale, and the first floor is used for the antiques. Just across the road is an enclosed market packed with stalls selling clothes, fruit and vegetables, antiques, bric-à-brac, local crafts and so on.

Tavistock

BUYER'S PREMIUM: *10%*
SALES: *Fortnightly on Thu at 10.00am.*
VIEWING: *Wed prior 1.00pm-6.00pm.*
REFRESHMENTS: *Café adjoining saleroom.*
PARKING: *Public car parks near by.*
STORAGE: *No*
TRANSPORTATION: *Yes*
SHIPPING: *Yes*

WARD & CHOWEN

Tavistock Auction Rooms, Market Road. Tel: (0822) 612603

400-500 lots. With a population of around 10,000 people, Tavistock is an ancient market town set astride the River Tavy. Tavistock's Goose Fair, held on the second Wednesday of October, attracts visitors from afar, and so do the sales of general household furniture and effects held by Ward & Chowen in the Tavistock Auction Rooms. The saleroom, an old, attractive building that was at one time a meat warehouse, is part of the Pannier Market complex. Auctioning is a way of life for many in the West Country, and the sales provide a popular venue. They are also fascinating to visitors from other parts of the UK and abroad.

Ward & Chowen are also auctioneers at the town's cattle market. Sales are held every Friday and on the second Wednesday in every month (except December and February).

Teignmouth

BUYER'S PREMIUM: *10%*
SALES: *Fortnightly on Tue at 10.00am.*
VIEWING: *Sat prior 9.30am-1.00pm, Mon prior 9.30am-1.00pm, 2.00pm-5.00pm.*
REFRESHMENTS: *None available on the premises.*

PEPPERS SALEROOM

10 Somerset Place. Tel: (0626) 772591

400-500 lots. Teignmouth is a holiday resort with the advantage of a river aspect as well as a seafront, and holidaymakers bring a marked increase to the crowd during the summer. Peppers' auctions are a good mix of Victorian, Edwardian, antique and modern goods, in which practically anything can turn up: furniture, kitchen sinks, kitchenalia, bicycles, bric-à-brac, china, local bygones and craft items, paintings and prints, all of varying values. The sales have a relaxed light-hearted atmosphere, and are good fun to attend, especially in the summer when those new to bidding enjoy finding lots at prices they can afford.

PARKING: *Brunswick Street public car park.*
STORAGE: *Yes*
TRANSPORTATION: *Yes*
SHIPPING: *Yes*

BEARNE'S

Torquay

Rainbow, Avenue Road. Tel: (0803) 296277

500-1,000 lots. Bearne's Rainbow saleroom is off Avenue Road, between Torre Station and the seafront, less than a mile from Torquay Station.

The saleroom is in a large, imposing mansion standing in its own wooded grounds, which was converted into an auction house in 1977. Every four weeks Bearne's hold a 'Collective' sale which always includes Georgian, Victorian and Edwardian furniture. There are also either pictures, silver and jewellery or (in alternate sales) ceramics and glass, works of art and collectors' items.

Specialist sales are held monthly in one of the following categories: pictures, furniture, works of art and collectors' items, silver and jewellery, or ceramics and glass. Additional specialist sales are held throughout the year. In the past these have included Art Nouveau and Art Deco, veteran and classic cars, distinctive number plates and automobilia. There are no regular dates for these sales, but they are generally very popular and worth finding out about. Refreshments are available on sale days in the summer house next to the car park.

BUYER'S PREMIUM: *10%*
SALES: *Collective: every four weeks on Wed. Specialist (see text): approx. monthly on Wed. Starting times depend on the number of lots.*
VIEWING: *Sat prior 9.30am-12.30pm, Mon and Tue prior 9.30am-5.00pm.*
REFRESHMENTS: *Own café.*
PARKING: *Own large car park.*
STORAGE: *Yes*
TRANSPORTATION: *Yes*
SHIPPING: *Yes*

WEST OF ENGLAND AUCTIONS

Torquay

3 Warren Road. Tel: (0803) 211266

300-500 lots. The saleroom building is a short walk from Torbay Road, which is the main road along the sea front. It is also quite close the Princess Theatre and gardens. There are three sale galleries. The first floor gallery and downstairs outer gallery are used for the general sale, with the main ground floor gallery reserved for antiques. The general sale is usually held in the early part of the month, and will include some 300 lots of household furniture and effects, with another 300 lots of selected silver and jewellery. The antiques sale is at the end of the month, and has 300 to 600 lots of antiques and works of art, including pictures, clocks and other good items. This is a very busy auction, popular with both dealers and private buyers, and its reputation extends well beyond the borders of Devon.

BUYER'S PREMIUM: *10%*
SALES: *General: monthly on Mon at 11.00am. Antiques: monthly on Mon at 11.00am.*
VIEWING: *Sat prior 9.00am-12.00 noon, Sun prior 2.00pm-6.00pm, morning of sale from 9.00am.*
REFRESHMENTS: *Own refreshment area.*
PARKING: *Multi-storey car park close by in Abbey Road.*
STORAGE: *Yes*
TRANSPORTATION: *Yes*
SHIPPING: *Yes*

DORSET

Bournemouth

BUYER'S PREMIUM: *10%*
SALES: *At five-weekly intervals on Sat at 10.30am.*
VIEWING: *Sat prior 9.30am-1.30pm and 2.30pm-4.30pm, Mon-Fri prior 10.00am-1.30pm and 2.30pm-5.00pm, morning of sale 8.00am-10.00am.*
REFRESHMENTS: *Saleroom has adjoining cafeteria/restaurant.*
PARKING: *Richmond Gardens car park, in the town centre.*
STORAGE: *Yes*
TRANSPORTATION: *Postal service available.*
SHIPPING: *Postal service for small lots.*

GARNET LANGTON AUCTIONS

11 Burlington Arcade. Tel: (0202) 552352

1,000 lots. Sales take place at the Hinton Suite, Hinton Road, Bournemouth, which is part of the Charles Forte complex, but viewing is at Dalkeith Hall, 81b Old Christchurch Road. Garnet Langton's auctions are of particular interest to those who enjoy browsing and have an interest in anything nostalgic. No furniture is sold. The sales are of collectors' items and smaller antiques, including stamps, postcards, autographs, coins, cigarette cards, medals, old toys and dolls, militaria and banknotes. Mr Langton says that his sales include things that people have been throwing out for years, but which have since become valuable. A moment or two spent browsing around the lots in any sale will demonstrate that. One lot, a large box, sold by the auctioneers recently, was crammed with more than 3,700 assorted postcards.

Sales are divided into seven sessions: stamps; picture postcards (at 12.00 noon); cigarette cards, cameras, photographic and scientific instruments, coins and banknotes (at 12.30pm); military medals, pop, stage and screen memorabilia and autographs (at 2.30pm); sport, railwayana and transport collectables, toys, prints and ephemera (at 3.15pm); jewellery, ceramics, glass and other collectors' items (at 4.30pm); and finally books and manuscripts. Sales end at 6.00pm.

Bournemouth

BUYER'S PREMIUM: *10%*
SALES: *Fortnightly on Tue and Wed at 10.00am.*
VIEWING: *Mon prior 9.30am-3.30pm.*
REFRESHMENTS: *None available on the premises.*
PARKING: *Public car park near by.*
STORAGE: *Yes*
TRANSPORTATION: *Yes*
SHIPPING: *Yes*

HOUSE & SON

11/16 Lansdown House, Christchurch Road. Tel: (0202) 26232

600-800 lots. The enthusiastic auction-goer is certainly not deprived of excellent venues in Bournemouth. House & Son's premises are part of a parade, and they usually boast a long window display of lots in their forthcoming two-day sales, held fortnightly.

House & Son are a long-established firm and they enjoy an excellent reputation. In their two-day auctions you can be sure that you will find a wide range of interesting lots. The first day of such an auction usually has a morning-only sale. Any motor vehicles on offer are sold first, then come carpets and beds. These are followed by oil paintings and watercolours, books, photographs, postcards and prints, antique, Victorian and reproduction furniture, and household effects. The second day starts with pottery and porcelain, and goes on to include glass, silver and plate. Selling begins again in the afternoon at 2.15pm, when jewellery and watches, *objets d'art*, collectors' items, copper, brass, bronzes and metalware are offered.

RIDDETTS OF BOURNEMOUTH

Bournemouth

The Auction Galleries, 26 Richmond Hill, The Square. Tel: (0202) 25686

1,200-1,500 lots. There are four separate salerooms on three floors of Riddetts' tall, attractive premises. On the top floor there are sales of paintings, Persian carpets and rugs, while soft furnishings and Edwardian and modern furniture are sold on the first. On the ground floor there are sales of antiques, silver and jewellery. Outside, in the covered car park, there are also sales of general chattels, electrical goods, televisions, gardening equipment and tools.

Every fortnight there is a three-day sale, starting with small items, porcelain and pottery on Tuesday morning. The afternoon is usually taken up with antique furniture. On Wednesdays, silver, silver plate, jewellery, paintings, watercolour drawings and prints are auctioned. Finally, on Thursdays, there are sales of modern and reproduction furniture, lounge suites, bedroom suites, soft furnishings, beds, pine, televisions and electrical goods.

BUYER'S PREMIUM: *10%*
SALES: *Fortnightly on Tue, Wed and Thu at 10.00am and 2.00pm.*
VIEWING: *Mon prior 10.00am-4.00pm.*
REFRESHMENTS: *None available on the premises.*
PARKING: *Own car park.*
STORAGE: *Yes*
TRANSPORTATION: *Yes*
SHIPPING: *Yes*

WILLIAM MOREY & SONS

Bridport

St Michael's Lane. Tel: (0308) 22078

500-600 lots. Bridport lies nearly two miles from the port of West Bay, in magnificent countryside. It is a pleasant old rope-making town, with a wide street of fine, red-brick houses. The saleroom is close to the bus and coach station and was at one time part of the cattle market (now sadly defunct). The Morey family began the cattle market in 1870 and a branch of the same family is responsible for the antiques auctions that take place in the town today. The auctions are very popular events, which many local people attend purely to be entertained by the humour and chit-chat that flows back and forth between the auctioneer and the crowd. One of the auctioneers is also the Town Crier, and is a very well-known local character.

The sale is divided into two sections, which each attract different types of buyers. The first section, of cheaper outside effects, begins the auction. This is where cycles, old lawn mowers, timber and other items are offered. The second section of the sale lasts through the afternoon and is held indoors. Here there are lots of modern household furniture,

BUYER'S PREMIUM: *10%*
SALES: *Every three to five weeks on Thu at 9.30am.*
VIEWING: *Day prior 9.00am-6.00pm.*
REFRESHMENTS: *Own canteen.*
PARKING: *None available on the premises.*
STORAGE: *No*
TRANSPORTATION: *Yes*
SHIPPING: *Yes*

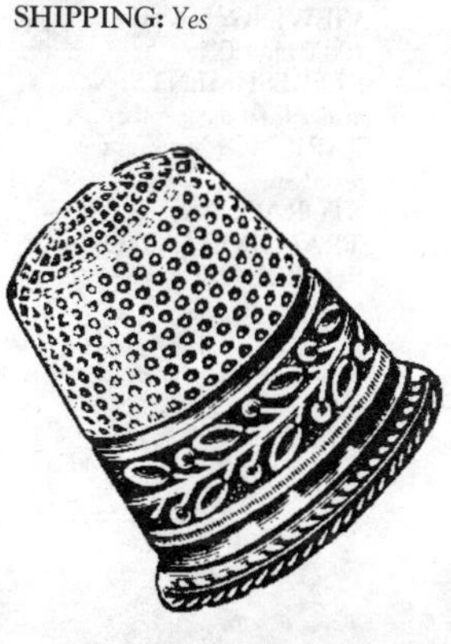

plus antiques. It used to be the custom in this area for craftsmen to visit houses to ensure that all the carving on furniture matched, and they would carry out their work *in situ*. A recent sale included an example of this work in the form of a magnificent hand-carved, five-piece oak bedroom suite. At the same sale an old RAC emergency telephone box that had been used as a garden shed for a number of years was also sold, demonstrating that these sales have a wide range of lots.

Christchurch

BUYER'S PREMIUM: *10%*
SALES: *Weekly on Wed and Thu at 10.00am (includes antiques sale twice a month on Thu).*
VIEWING: *Tue 10.00am-5.00pm.*
REFRESHMENTS: *Own café.*
PARKING: *Own car park.*
STORAGE: *Yes*
TRANSPORTATION: *Yes*
SHIPPING: *Yes*

BULSTRODES AUCTIONS

13 Stour Road. Tel: (0202) 482244

500-600 lots per day. Situated next to Christchurch railway station, Bulstrodes' premises were originally part of the railway outbuildings, but they have since been converted into modern salerooms. There are two separate salerooms, but one is used for storing the following week's sale items. Four auctioneers take it in turns to conduct the proceedings, and the sales are divided into morning and afternoon sessions.

On Wednesday mornings there are sales of outside effects, such as garden furniture and tools, plus electrical household equipment such as cookers, fridges and washing machines. The Wednesday morning sales often include dinghies, yachts and windsurfing equipment, too. The Wednesday afternoon sales are usually of modern furniture and beds.

On Thursdays there is a sale of carpets, modern and office furniture, and finally antique furniture. Twice a month, though, the Thursday sales are given over to antique furniture in the morning, with a sale of silver and other small, good quality items in the afternoon.

Dorchester

BUYER'S PREMIUM: *Nil*
SALES: *Usually every six weeks on Thu at 10.30am.*
VIEWING: *Day prior 10.00am-4.00pm.*
REFRESHMENTS: *None available on the premises.*
PARKING: *None on the premises.*
STORAGE: *Yes*
TRANSPORTATION: *Yes*
SHIPPING: *Yes*

JEFFS & SON

Northernhay Saleroom, Northernhay. Tel: (0305) 262552

200-250 lots. Dorchester is a charming old-English town on the River Frome. Jeffs & Son were established over 90 years ago and are an independently owned, family-run business. The auctions are held about every six weeks in what was a wartime dance hall. If you are hoping to furnish your house by going to one of these sales, or simply wish to collect something, you'll have fun bidding or simply browsing here. You will find almost anything and everything on sale, from china, paintings, jewellery and clocks to vacuum cleaners, beds and old brass taps.

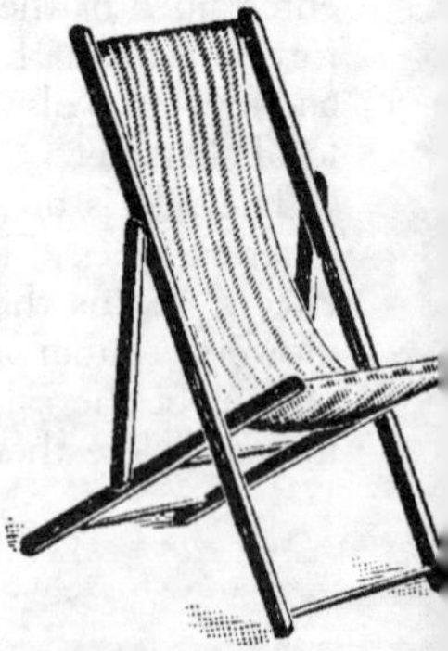

CHAPMAN, MOORE & MUGFORD

Shaftesbury

Llyons Walk Gallery. Tel: (0747) 52400

300-350 lots. The sales here are in a delightful setting. The stone building was converted about 20 years ago and has a panelled ceiling, exposed roof timbers and an attractive gallery. It lies just off the High Street, and is approached by a courtyard behind the auctioneers' offices at 9 High Street. The auctions include antique furniture, silver, jewellery, paintings and musical instruments, and the lots can be bought from a few pounds upwards. Although nothing is given away, interesting items from country homes in the area can be found at very reasonable prices. A tremendous amount can be learnt from just viewing an auction, where you may freely inspect the goods and enjoy the atmosphere, even if you are unsuccessful in the bidding.

BUYER'S PREMIUM: *Nil*
SALES: *Every six to eight weeks on Fri at 6.00pm.*
VIEWING: *Day of sale from 10.00am.*
REFRESHMENTS: *None available on the premises.*
PARKING: *Main town car park is 100 yards away.*
STORAGE: *Yes*
TRANSPORTATION: *Yes*
SHIPPING: *Yes*

COTTEES, BULLOCK & LEES

Wareham

The Market, East Street. Tel: (0929) 552826

700-800 lots. Wareham is a delightful town with broad streets and fine churches. It is also near heath, sea, and river. In the Saxon church of St Martin there is a figure of T E Lawrence in Arab attire, sculpted by Eric Kennington — unfortunately not for sale. However, there should be enough goods at Cottees busy auctions to satisfy most people who are looking for something interesting to buy.

The saleroom is about 300 yards from the only set of traffic lights in Wareham, and the proceedings begin with bidding both inside and outside the auctioneers' premises. Antique and later furniture, porcelain, silver and plate, pictures, books, carpets and rugs, collectors items and miscellanea are always included. On some Saturdays during the year Cottees also hold special sales of marine items, old agricultural equipment, and toys and childhood memorabilia.

BUYER'S PREMIUM: *10%*
SALES: *Antique and later furniture and effects fortnightly on Tue at 10.00am: for details of other sales, contact the auctioneers direct.*
VIEWING: *Day prior 2.00pm-5.00pm, and 6.00pm-8.00pm.*
REFRESHMENTS: *Own café.*
PARKING: *Own car park.*
STORAGE: *Yes*
TRANSPORTATION: *Yes*
SHIPPING: *Yes*

DURHAM

J R ADDISON

Barnard Castle

13 Galgate. Tel: (0833) 38094

900-1000 lots. Barnard Castle is an excellent centre for exploring Teesdale. It is a delightful old market town with wide streets and castle ruins which stand impressively above the river. The business was established over 110 years ago, and

BUYER'S PREMIUM: *5%*
SALES: *Fortnightly on Thu at 11.00am.*

VIEWING: *Day prior 2.00pm-4.00pm, 6.30pm-7.30pm. Day of sale from 10.30am.*
REFRESHMENTS: *None available on the premises.*
PARKING: *Ample parking near by.*
STORAGE: *Yes*
TRANSPORTATION: *Yes*
SHIPPING: *Yes*

stands in the centre of the town opposite the post office. In the summer it is packed with visitors, and during sales and viewing days the large hall has a good display of furniture and household articles. The fortnightly Thursday sale is of general household furniture, effects and miscellaneous items. Periodic sales are devoted to collectables, including high quality brass, china, glass, metalware, furniture and others. The general sales are packed with bargains, although probably as much as 90 per cent of the furniture goes to the same group of buyers. The sale starts with 'smalls' — items of china, glass and so on — and then goes on to pieces of furniture, such as chairs. Bedroom furniture is sold next, followed by dining room suites and lounge suites, with upholstered furniture completing the sale.

Bishop Auckland

DENIS EDKINS FSVA

The Auckland Auction Rooms, 58 Kingsway.
Tel: (0388) 603095

BUYER'S PREMIUM: *5%*
SALES: *Weekly on Thu at 11.00am.*
VIEWING: *Day prior 10.00am-12.00 noon, 2.00pm-5.00pm.*
REFRESHMENTS: *None available on the premises.*
PARKING: *Own car park.*
STORAGE: *Yes*
TRANSPORTATION: *Yes*
SHIPPING: *Yes*

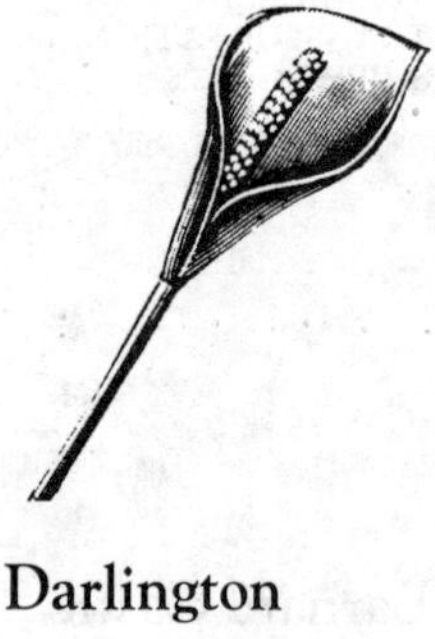

200-500 lots. The saleroom is a newish brick building at the rear of the town's main shopping centre, in the same street as the football ground. Sale day is Thursday, which is also one of the town's two market days, and there are stalls selling all sorts of interesting things in the Market Square, only a short walk from the saleroom. (The other market day is Saturday.)

The weekly sale tends to run to a theme: one week it might be of better quality household furniture and effects, the next could be for office furniture such as desks, filing cabinets, typist's chairs and so on, the next week modern furniture and effects, and then the following week plant and machinery, including small DIY hand tools. Sometimes the sales are of older furniture, which may include antiques, shipping furniture (1930s-1940s) and smaller general goods such as old china, porcelain and collectables.

All the lots put into the sale by one vendor are given the same lot number, instead of being numbered individually. This means that a wide variety of goods may share the same number, making it more important than ever to note down the specific details of items that interest you, not just the lot number.

Darlington

HUNT BROTHERS

12 King Street. Tel: (0325) 352328

BUYER'S PREMIUM: *8%*
SALES: *Weekly on Mon at 10.00am.*
VIEWING: *Fri 1.00pm-5.00pm, Sat*

300-400 lots. The saleroom is near the centre of this busy industrial and market town, which George Stephenson put on the map by opening the first passenger railway here in 1825. The No. 1 Locomotive which drew the first passenger train at a speed of 13mph is on display at Bank Top Station, south-east of the town centre. There is a wide variety of goods in Hunt Brothers' weekly sale, with something to interest most bidders. The sale starts with electrical goods such as cookers, refrigerators, freezers, televisions, video machines and so on. Next to be sold are boxes of miscellaneous items such as odd pieces of china and glass, books, pots and pans. Most sales will also include beds and carpets, modern furniture, better quality china such as Royal Doulton and other well-known makes, jewellery and antique furniture.

8.30am-5.00pm.
REFRESHMENTS: *Vending machine.*
PARKING: *Commercial Street public car park opposite.*
STORAGE: *Yes*
TRANSPORTATION: *Yes*
SHIPPING: *Yes*

THOMAS WATSON & SON

Darlington

The Gallery, Northumberland Street. Tel: (0325) 462559

300-400 lots. The saleroom is large and purpose-built, and stands within the town's inner ring road. Thomas Watson & Son are one of the oldest established auctioneers in the area, having recently celebrated their 150th anniversary. Members of the original family are still very much involved in the company, and buyers from as far away as Leeds and Newcastle regularly attend the weekly general sale. Typically this will have china, jewellery, pottery, pictures and garden equipment, as well as a variety of furniture. Once a month this sale is replaced by what the firm describes as a sale of 'semi antiques', including good quality Edwardian and Victorian furniture and effects.

BUYER'S PREMIUM: *10%*
SALES: *Weekly on Wed at 10.00am (includes 'semi antiques' sale once a month).*
VIEWING: *Sat, Mon, and Tue prior 9.00am-5.00pm.*
REFRESHMENTS: *Vending machine.*
PARKING: *Town centre car park.*
STORAGE: *No*
TRANSPORTATION: *Yes*
SHIPPING: *Yes*

LANGLEY MOOR AUCTION ROOMS

Langley Moor

Little Burn Lane. Tel: (091) 378 2009

400-600 lots. This is an excellent weekly general auction. The auctioneers can boast that they have helped to furnish and equip many homes in the neighbourhood, and that they have helped many young collectors with their hobbies. The general hustle and bustle of the saleroom adds to the excitement of the day's events at these auctions. Smaller items such as china, ornaments and knick-knacks are laid out on tables and usually receive a great deal of attention at the start of the sales. Paintings, prints and 'boxed lots' are sold off afterwards. The boxed lots consist of a whole assortment of items — and invariably there will be some rubbish among them. It is usually worthwhile spending some time checking them out, though, in case there is something hidden of particular value or interest. All types of general household furniture, including a large number of electrical goods, are sold during the afternoon. There are some excellent buys to be had, even for those of modest means.

BUYER'S PREMIUM: *10%*
SALES: *Weekly on Tue at 10.00am.*
VIEWING: *Sat 9.00am-1.00pm, Mon 9.00am-4.00pm.*
REFRESHMENTS: *None available on the premises.*
PARKING: *Yes*
STORAGE: *Yes*
TRANSPORTATION: *Yes*
SHIPPING: *Yes*

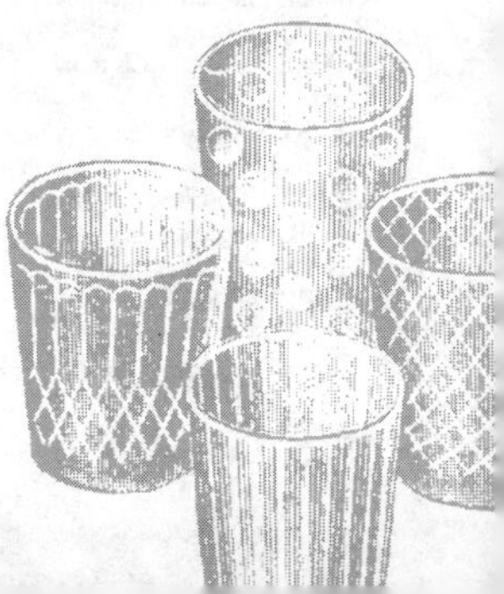

Station Town, near Wingate

BUYER'S PREMIUM: *5%*
SALES: *Weekly on Wed at 6.00pm.*
VIEWING: *Day of sale from 9.00am.*
REFRESHMENTS: *Own café.*
PARKING: *Ample parking near by.*
STORAGE: *Yes*
TRANSPORTATION: *Yes*
SHIPPING: *Yes*

SOUTH HETTON & WINGATE AUCTIONS

Station Lane. Tel: (0429) 837245

300-350 lots. This is a busy evening sale, popular with local people. Many of the lots come from houses in the nearby villages, and there is usually a great deal of furniture which has been well looked after. Vendors also bring in unwanted knick-knacks and ornaments.

The selling starts with a very popular section: perhaps 100 lots of 'smalls' such as assorted china, boxes of mixed ornaments, and various items of kitchen equipment. Next to be sold is jewellery, and there are usually some valuable hallmarked gold and silver pieces such as watches, pendants, rings and brooches. The auctioning of pictures, including prints, oils and watercolours, is followed by a return to the 'smalls' table for the better quality china, porcelain, glass and so on. Furniture completes the sale, with the entire proceedings finishing around 8.30 to 9.00pm.

EAST SUSSEX

Battle

BUYER'S PREMIUM: *Abbey Auction Galleries: 5%. Granary: nil*
SALES: *Abbey Auction Galleries: furniture, monthly on Wed at 11.00am, paintings monthly on Wed one week after furniture sale at 6.30pm. Granary: furniture, monthly on Wed at 10.30am, tools monthly on Sat at 1.00pm.*
VIEWING: *Abbey Auction Galleries: furniture, day prior 9.00am-8.00pm, paintings, day of sale 9.00am-6.30pm. Granary: furniture, day prior 9.00am-1.00pm, 2.00pm-7.00pm, tools morning of sale.*
REFRESHMENTS: *Vending machine.*
PARKING: *Own car park.*
STORAGE: *Yes*
TRANSPORTATION: *Yes*
SHIPPING: *Yes*

BURSTOW & HEWETT

Abbey Auction Galleries, Lower Lake. Tel: (04246) 2374

700-800 lots. Burstow & Hewett are a busy firm holding four sales a month in two salerooms (both at the station end of the town). The Abbey Auction Galleries hold a monthly Wednesday sale of 'Antique and Fine Furniture, Silver, Jewellery, Ceramics and Metalware'. The following week a sale of 'Antique and Modern Oil Paintings, Watercolours, Engravings, and Postcards' takes place.

The Granary saleroom five minutes away in Station Road has a monthly Wednesday sale of 'Antique and Modern Furniture, Silver, Ceramics, Metalware and all types of Household Furnishings', and a monthly Saturday afternoon special sale of 'Gardening, Builders', Carpenters' and Mechanics' Tools and Accessories', including such equipment as mowers and rotavators.

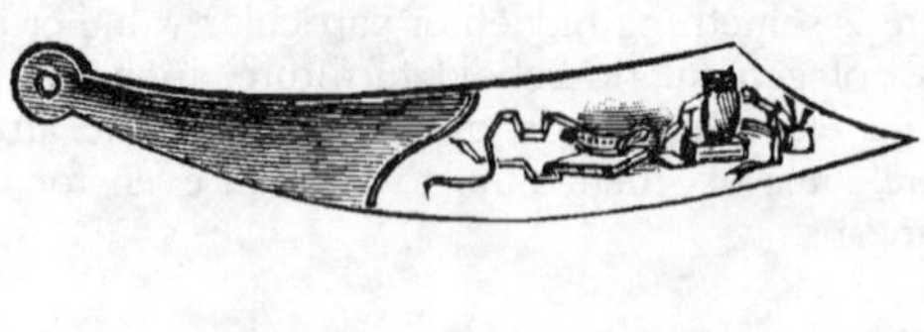

FRYER'S AUCTION GALLERIES

Bexhill-on-Sea

Terminus Road. Tel: (0424) 212994

500-600 lots. Bexhill-on-Sea is a holiday and residential town. The saleroom is an impressive ex-railway terminal with a clock tower, just west of Town Hall Square. The auctions reflect somewhat the resort's sedate reputation, and occur fortnightly on a Tuesday. In weeks with a Bank Holiday the sale is put back until Wednesday. Two auctions in every three go under the heading 'Modern Household Furniture and Effects', but the third is for special antiques. The 'Modern' sale starts at 10.00am (lunch break 1.00pm-1.45pm) and also includes good quality 1930s and Edwardian furniture, china, pottery, glass and so on. The special antiques auctions have fewer lots, perhaps 250-300, and the selling only starts at 2.15pm.

BUYER'S PREMIUM: *10%*
SALES: *Fortnightly on Tue at 10.00am (includes antiques sale every third Tue). Sales are on Wed in Bank Holiday weeks.*
VIEWING: *Day prior 9.00am-7.00pm, morning of sale from 9.00am.*
REFRESHMENTS: *Food available at Rother Arms public house, adjacent in same building.*
PARKING: *Own car park.*
STORAGE: *Yes*
TRANSPORTATION: *Yes*
SHIPPING: *Yes*

RAYMOND P INMAN

Brighton

The Auction Galleries, 35/40 Temple Street. Tel: (0273) 774777

400-500 lots. The pleasant, unintimidating atmosphere at this auction should be encouraging for new or nervous auction-goers. The reason for it is probably that this is very much a family concern. Proprietor Raymond Inman is the son of the founder, and shares the selling duties with his own son Robert, while wife Maureen Inman takes charge of the mound of office work. The sales are held on three floors in an attractive building off Western Road in the Hove direction. The lots tend to be towards the upper end of the general market, and usually include antiques and reproduction furniture, china, silver, jewellery, paintings and so on. Successful bids range from £1 to many hundreds or even thousands — the record price for a single lot here is £90,000.

BUYER'S PREMIUM: *8%*
SALES: *About every five weeks on Mon at 9.30am.*
VIEWING: *Fri and Sat prior 9.30am-4.00pm.*
REFRESHMENTS: *None available on the premises.*
PARKING: *Own small car park.*
STORAGE: *Yes*
TRANSPORTATION: *Yes*
SHIPPING: *Yes*

EASTBOURNE ANTIQUES & FINE ART AUCTIONEERS

Eastbourne

10 Cornfield Lane. Tel: (0323) 411315

700-900 lots. There are ten sales per year, at five-weekly intervals. Six or seven of the sales will be over two days, Tuesday and Wednesday. The main saleroom of this attractive building was once a showroom for vintage cars. Adjoining the main room is a large area used for storage and for selling furniture, so there is plenty of space for potential buyers to view.

The sales go under the heading 'Antiques, Works of Art and Collectables' and are at the upper end of the market: lots come from all over the world and may be bought by international

BUYER'S PREMIUM: *10%*
SALES: *Every five weeks on Tue (or Tue and Wed) at 11.00am.*
VIEWING: *Fri, Sat, and Mon prior 10.00am-4.00pm.*
REFRESHMENTS: *None available on the premises.*
PARKING: *None available on the premises.*
STORAGE: *Yes*
TRANSPORTATION: *Yes*
SHIPPING: *Yes*

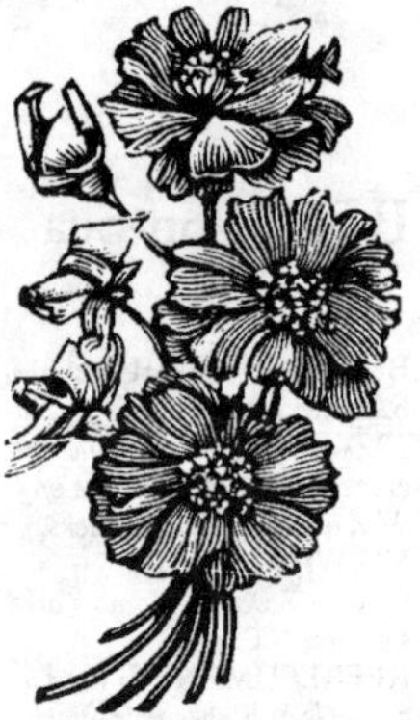

buyers. There are often telephone bids during the more important sales, which can be very exciting. The selling order is ceramics, glass and ornamental items such as clocks, bronzes and metalware, usually followed by toys such as Dinky model cars and dolls, then textiles including various costumes. Next are silver and silver plate, jewellery, prints, watercolours and oils. The furniture is sold last. Periodically there will be sections in the sale for specialist items such as books, stamps and ephemera. Vintage cars and motor bikes also appear at the auction quite frequently.

Eastbourne

PHOENIX AUCTION ROOMS

124 Pevensey Road. Tel: (0323) 645007

BUYER'S PREMIUM: *10%*
SALES: *Every three weeks on Wed at 10.00am.*
VIEWING: *Sat prior 8.30am-12.00 noon, Mon and Tue prior 8.30am-12.45pm, 2.00pm-4.00pm, day of sale.*
REFRESHMENTS: *None available on the premises.*
PARKING: *None available on the premises.*
STORAGE: *Yes*
TRANSPORTATION: *Yes*
SHIPPING: *Yes*

250-500 lots. Spend time browsing around the lots on offer at this sale. The large old Victorian saleroom is packed with assorted antiques and general household furniture and effects. Dotted about the room and sold in no particular order there will usually be plenty of domestic and ornamental china, porcelain, electrical goods, televisions, radios, outside effects like gardening equipment, furniture, collectables, and endless miscellaneous items of all ages and values. Even if you don't have time to take advantage of the three viewing days, it is permitted to wander around looking at the lots while the sale is in progress, which many people do.

The auction is close to Eastbourne's Grand Parade, and is one which summer visitors eagerly look forward to. The excitement generated between friends after a successful bid (or even an unsuccessful one) makes the noise level quite high at times. This informality is why many people like the sale.

Hailsham

SOUTH EAST MARTS

See SOUTH EAST MARTS, Guildford, Surrey

Lewes

LEWES AUCTION ROOMS (JULIAN DAWSON)

Garden Street. Tel: (0273) 478221

BUYER'S PREMIUM: *Nil*
SALES: *General: weekly on Mon at 11.00am. Antiques: about every six weeks on Thu at 10.30am.*
VIEWING: *Sat prior 9.00am-1.00pm, morning of sale. Antiques also day prior 9.00am-7.30pm.*
REFRESHMENTS: *Own café.*
PARKING: *Own car park.*

600-700 lots. The saleroom is close to the railway station and next to the cattle market. Livestock sales are on Monday, the same day as the auction, and the market is an ideal place to take children if they become bored with the bidding. With an average of 700 lots each week this is one of the largest weekly general auctions in the county, and is certainly an ideal starting place for new auction-goers — friendly and, at times, a little noisy. The variety of lots is very wide: the hammer will come down on successful bids ranging from £1 to over £1,000.

A range of goods is set out in the crowded saleroom, and includes the entire range of antique and modern furniture, general household effects and miscellanea. At roughly six-weekly intervals, Mr Dawson holds special antique sales. These take place on Thursdays.

STORAGE: *Yes*
TRANSPORTATION: *Yes*
SHIPPING: *Yes*

ASCENT AUCTION GALLERIES

St Leonards-on-Sea

11/12 East Ascent. Tel: (0424) 420275

350-600 lots. The busy general sale of furniture, household effects and miscellanea is held every two to three weeks. There is also a quarterly sale of good quality antiques. The antiques sale is always held in the East Ascent saleroom, but the general sale alternates between East Ascent and the saleroom just around the corner, the Mews Galleries at 1 Mews Road. This allows one sale to be prepared while another is in progress. Both salerooms are near the seafront and lie behind one of St Leonards-on-Sea's landmarks, the Marine Court.

Lots sell from a few pounds upwards in the general sale, and the usual selling order is carpets, linen and blankets, kitchen and garden effects, furniture, books and pictures. Next are clocks, brass, silver and silver plate, and then ornamental and domestic china and glass: there is usually a good selection in all these categories. A similar sale order is used for the antiques sale. Catalogues are available on request.

BUYER'S PREMIUM: *10%*
SALES: *General: every two to three weeks on Thu at 10.00am. Antiques: quarterly on Thu at 11.00am.*
VIEWING: *Day prior 9.00am-6.30pm.*
REFRESHMENTS: *Own café.*
PARKING: *Grand Parade public car park.*
STORAGE: *Yes*
TRANSPORTATION: *Yes*
SHIPPING: *Yes*

ESSEX

BERKELEYS OF BRENTWOOD

Brentwood

45 North Road. Tel: (0277) 224599

200-400 lots. The auctioneer is Wendy Wood, one of the few professional lady auctioneers. The general weekly sale is a mixture of everything under the sun, including household furniture, collectors' items, electrical goods, jewellery, china and the odd unexpected lot, such as a stuffed mongoose or fox. In addition to the general sales, Berkeleys hold specialist antiques sales throughout the year.

BUYER'S PREMIUM: *10%*
SALES: *Weekly on Mon at 11.00am.*
VIEWING: *Sat 10.00am-2.00pm, day of sale from 9.00am.*
REFRESHMENTS: *Own tea room.*
PARKING: *Large public car parks near by.*
STORAGE: *Yes*
TRANSPORTATION: *Yes*
SHIPPING: *Yes*

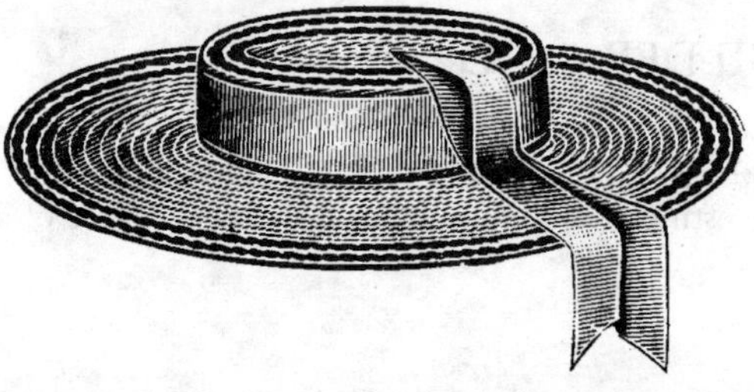

Chelmsford

BUYER'S PREMIUM: *10%*
SALES: *General: weekly on Tue at 10.00am. Outside effects: weekly on Fri at 10.00am. Antiques and fine art: every two months on Wed at 10.30am.*
VIEWING: *General and outside effects: morning of sale from 8.30am. Antiques and fine art: day prior 12.00 noon-8.00pm, morning of sale from 9.00am.*
REFRESHMENTS: *Own buffet bar.*
PARKING: *Own car park.*
STORAGE: *Yes*
TRANSPORTATION: *Yes*
SHIPPING: *Yes*

COOPER HIRST AUCTIONS

The Granary Sale Room, Victoria Road. Tel: (0245) 260535

300-400 lots. The saleroom has been well adapted from what was a factory warehouse. It is just out of the centre of Chelmsford, opposite the ice rink and about 10 minutes' walk from the railway station. The weekly Tuesday sale consists of general household furniture and effects, and might include wardrobes, dining tables, sideboards, chests of drawers and other furniture, plus cookers, refrigerators and other electrical goods. Typically there will be boxes containing interesting assortments of miscellaneous items, such as children's books, or toys, kitchen equipment and ornaments. There are usually bundles of linen and various china items, perhaps plates from an old violet-pattern dinner set, a box of assorted tea pots, a blue-and-white jug and basin, various vases, decanters and so on.

The weekly Friday sale is of what might be described as outside effects, and includes such items as bundles of timber, machinery of all types and various gardening tools and equipment. It takes place on the ground floor.

The bi-monthly antique and fine art sale takes place in a pleasant first-floor saleroom, and includes Georgian, Victorian, Edwardian and reproduction furniture of a high quality.

Chelmsford

BUYER'S PREMIUM: *Nil*
SALES: *General: fortnightly on Wed at 10.00am. Antiques and fine art: every two months on Wed at 10.00am.*
VIEWING: *General: day prior 9.00am-4.30pm, morning of sale from 9.00am. Antiques and fine art: day prior 2.00pm-8.00pm, morning of sale from 9.00am.*
REFRESHMENTS: *Own café.*
PARKING: *Own car park.*
STORAGE: *Yes*
TRANSPORTATION: *Yes*
SHIPPING: *Yes*

S H ROWLAND, CHELMSFORD AUCTIONS

42 Milmay Road. Tel: (0245) 354251

400-500 lots. The saleroom is on the London side of the city, close to the Army and Navy roundabout. Despite being only some 30 miles from London, Chelmsford is surrounded by attractive villages, including Writtle, scene of Marconi's first experiments with the wireless. It is from private houses in these villages that many of the lots on sale will have originated. Antique and fine art sales are slotted between the general sales, and while vendors are pleased with the high prices gained at auction, buyers also find that prices compare well with those in shops. Chelmsford Auctions was established in 1946 and draws vendors and buyers from a wide area. They are also the official auctioneers for the Sheriff of Essex. The sales are informal and friendly, and helpful staff are always on hand to answer any queries.

Clacton-on-Sea

BUYER'S PREMIUM: *Nil*
SALES: *Monthly on Thu at 9.30am.*

E J GILDER & CO

The Mart, High Street. Tel: (0255) 423592

250-300 lots. E J Gilder & Co was established in 1925. This is an interesting seaside sale with all the atmosphere of a good country auction. The sales include a wide range of articles, some of which may have come from house clearances. There are usually also some antiques, but best of all are the lots of miscellaneous items bundled together to give a minimum value. One successful bid could find you the proud owner of a box containing a great deal of excellent kitchen equipment, or four or five good-quality gardening tools. The sale is conducted in a very informal, friendly manner, and there is nothing to intimidate those new to auctions.

VIEWING: *All day Wed.*
REFRESHMENTS: *None available on the premises.*
PARKING: *None available on the premises.*
STORAGE: *No*
TRANSPORTATION: *Yes*
SHIPPING: *No*

WILLIAM H BROWN

Colchester

Paskells Rooms, East Hill. Tel: (0206) 868070

300-400 lots. Situated on one of the main approach roads into the town, this long-established auction room has weekly sales of antique and modern household furniture and effects. Lots include Georgian, Victorian, Edwardian and modern furniture, oil and watercolour paintings, china, porcelain and glass. Also included in the weekly sales are kitchenalia, garden tools and the like.

A monthly specialist 'cabinet' sale includes small items such as jewellery, silver, *bijouterie*, watches, figurines, pottery and glass.

BUYER'S PREMIUM: *10%*
SALES: *General: weekly on Tue at 10.00am. Cabinet sale: first Mon of month at 1.00pm.*
VIEWING: *General: Mon 9.00am-7.00pm. Cabinet sale: day of sale 9.00am-1.00pm.*
REFRESHMENTS: *None available on the premises.*
PARKING: *None available on the premises.*
STORAGE: *No*
TRANSPORTATION: *Yes*
SHIPPING: *No*

ESSEX & SUFFOLK MARKET AUCTIONS

Colchester

Wyncolls Road. Tel: (0206) 842156

2,000 lots. The sales take place in the new cattle market, close to the A12 on the London side of Colchester. This is a busy and traditional country auction, where the sale area may have as many as five separate auctions taking place at the same time.

The general weekly sale is all that a country auction should be: here are auctioned farm produce, fruit and vegetables, eggs, poultry, rabbits, timber, bicycles, cars and 'deadstock' — a term used to describe a huge range of items which cannot be classified as livestock or produce or as anything else. The sale is conducted almost entirely in the open, and starts with timber at about 9.45am, followed by bicycles at about 10.00am, and then the 'deadstock', which could include rolls of wire netting, lawn mowers, kitchen sinks, Victorian mangles, the odd piece of furniture, old tins containing somebody's store of screws or nails, boxes of boots, DIY tools, boxes of children's toys, saucepans, building equipment, lamps, assorted bric-à-brac, and so on. The sale of cars takes place at 11.00am.

On the first Saturday of the month, there is also a horse and tackle sale in the very large auction rooms. It starts at 10.00am

BUYER'S PREMIUM: *Nil*
SALES: *General: weekly on Sat at 9.45am. Horse and tackle: monthly on first Sat of month at 10.00am. Furniture: monthly on last Sat of month at 10.00am.*
VIEWING: *General: sale day only. Horse and tackle: morning of sale. Furniture: day prior 5.30pm-7.30pm.*
REFRESHMENTS: *Own café, licensed bar.*
PARKING: *Own car park.*
STORAGE: *Yes*
TRANSPORTATION: *Yes*
SHIPPING: *Yes*

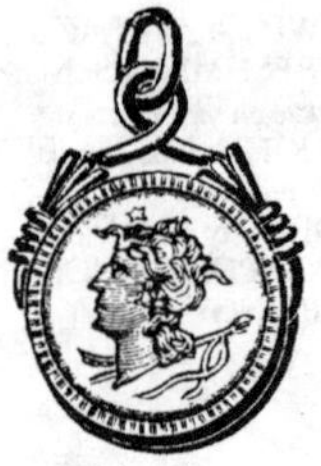

with horse tackle and other equipment, followed at 12.30pm by the sale of horses in the sale ring.

On the last Saturday of the month, again starting at 10.00am in the auction rooms, there is a sale of furniture and household effects. Lots include antique, modern, Victorian and reproduction furniture, household effects and miscellaneous items of varying value. The sales finish at around 2.30 to 3.00pm. There are also Tuesday sales of cattle, pigs and sheep, at 11.00am.

Colchester

BUYER'S PREMIUM: *10%*
SALES: *General: weekly on Wed at 10.00am. Cabinet sale: monthly on last Tue of month at 6.00pm.*
VIEWING: *General sale: Tue 9.00am-7.00pm. Cabinet sale: day of sale 9.00am-6.00pm.*
REFRESHMENTS: *Own café.*
PARKING: *St Mary's car park.*
STORAGE: *Yes*
TRANSPORTATION: *Yes*
SHIPPING: *Yes*

REEMAN, DANSIE, HOWE & SON

12 Head Gate. Tel: (0206) 574271

300-350 lots. Midweek is a busy time for auction-goers in Colchester, with this sale every Wednesday and the William H Brown sale every Tuesday at East Hill, about half a mile away. It is worth making time to look at the Norman castle and Roman wall, however. Colchester is England's oldest recorded town, and dates from the Iron Age. The first sale at Head Gate took place on 6 July 1881, and it has been a saleroom ever since.

The Wednesday auction is an excellent general sale, and includes a wide range of clean, high-quality antique, period and modern furniture, and miscellaneous effects. The lots are laid out with plenty of space for prospective buyers to study them, and the staff are helpful. There is also a monthly 'cabinet' sale of jewellery, silver, china, pottery and glass, at which you can expect to find gold and silver pendants, necklaces, brooches, rings, silver spoons, jewel and cigarette boxes, tea services, art pottery, candlesticks, decorative jars, cutlery, fountain pens and propelling pencils, pocket watches and the like.

Grays Thurrock

BUYER'S PREMIUM: *10%*
SALES: *Monthly on last Fri of month at 6.30pm.*
VIEWING: *Day prior 10.00am-6.00pm, day of sale 1.00am-6.30pm.*
REFRESHMENTS: *Own café.*
PARKING: *Free street parking.*
STORAGE: *No*
TRANSPORTATION: *Yes*
SHIPPING: *Yes*

GRAYS AUCTION ROOMS

118 William Street. Tel: (0375) 381181

300-350 lots. The saleroom is at the rear of 118 William Street, and is a little difficult to find. Only antiques are sold, but here the category includes good, clean pre-1930s items. Glass, pottery, collections of Staffordshire figures and cottages, English porcelain, Oriental ceramics and works of art, rugs, dolls, silver, pictures and many other items can be found. Regular faces turn up week after week, giving the saleroom a club-like atmosphere, and although in the past the dealers out-numbered the private buyers, it is noticeable now that the numbers have evened out.

HAMPTONS FINE ART (J M WELCH & SON)

Great Dunmow

Chequers Lane. Tel: (0371) 873014/872117

500-600 lots. The Chequers Lane saleroom has a growing reputation for collectables, which are sold on every third Wednesday of every month, together with upmarket modern and reproduction furniture and effects. There are also sales of antiques and fine art every two months.The saleroom is near Great Dunmow's police station.

BUYER'S PREMIUM: *10%*
SALES: *General furniture and collectables: monthly on third Wed of the month at 12.00 noon. Antiques and fine art: every two months on Mon at 11.00am.*
VIEWING: *General furniture and collectables: day prior 9.00am-7.00pm. Antiques and fine art: Fri and Sat prior 10.00am-4.00pm.*
REFRESHMENTS: *In saleroom at antiques and fine art sale only.*
PARKING: *Own car park; public car park opposite.*
STORAGE: *Yes*
TRANSPORTATION: *Yes*
SHIPPING: *Yes*

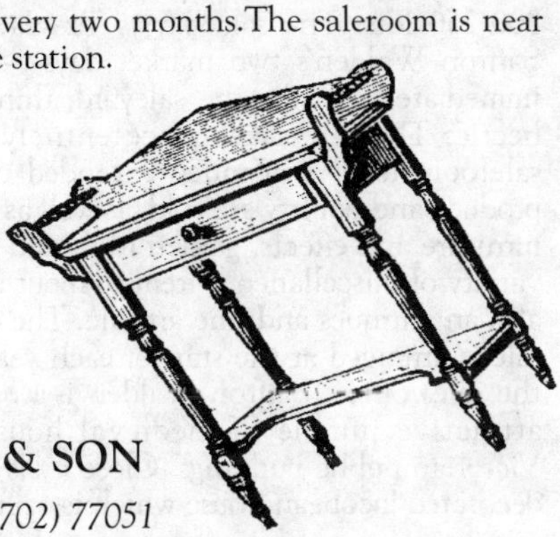

JOHN STACEY & SON

Leigh-on-Sea

86/90 Pall Mall. Tel: (0702) 77051

400-500 lots. This is a family-run firm, which has seen three generations of family involvement. The Staceys have been in the antiques trade since the 1930s. They were originally dealers, and today they are often asked to give lectures on antiques and the art of buying at auction. No modern furniture is sold at their auctions, which concentrate instead on antiques, works of art, silver, glass, jewellery, Victorian bric-à-brac, music boxes, and paintings. Very rarely, reproductions are sold. The saleroom has been in existence since 1960, and was converted from a church. There are two large floors, with plenty of room for lots to be displayed. Leigh-on-Sea is an old fishing village, which was well known long before Southend-on-Sea became popular.

BUYER'S PREMIUM: *10%*
SALES: *Fortnightly on Tue at 10.30am.*
VIEWING: *Sat and Mon prior 10.00am-4.00pm, day of sale from 9.00am.*
REFRESHMENTS: *None available on the premises.*
PARKING: *Own car park.*
STORAGE: *Yes*
TRANSPORTATION: *Yes*
SHIPPING: *Yes*

BLACK HORSE AGENCIES & AMBROSE

Loughton

Loughton Auction Room, 149 High Road. Tel: (081) 502 3951

350-400 lots. This is a monthly auction of antique and high quality furniture, gold, silver and jewellery, oil paintings, watercolours, porcelain, glass and ceramics, clocks, watches, barometers, and all collectable items and memorabilia. The sale always starts at 11.00am, ending at around 3.30-4.00pm. The sale is long established and well organised, with equal appeal to collectors, professional dealers and those looking for

BUYER'S PREMIUM: *5%*
SALES: *Monthly on last Thu of month at 11.00am.*
VIEWING: *Sat prior 9.00am-4.00pm, Mon prior 9.00am-5.00pm, Tue prior 9.00am-7.00pm.*
REFRESHMENTS: *None available on the premises.*

PARKING: *Available near by.*
STORAGE: *Yes*
TRANSPORTATION: *Yes*
SHIPPING: *Yes*

the odd handsome old piece of furniture. Potential buyers are quickly put at their ease. Loughton is on the edge of Epping Forest, with easy access from the M11 and M25 motorways.

Saffron Walden

BUYER'S PREMIUM: *10%*
SALES: *General: weekly on Tue at 10.00am. Antiques and fine art: about every six weeks on Fri at 10.30am.*
VIEWING: *General: morning of sale from 8.30am. Antiques and fine art: day prior 10.00am-5.00pm, morning of sale from 8.30am.*
REFRESHMENTS: *Antiques sale days only.*
PARKING: *None available on the premises.*
STORAGE: *No*
TRANSPORTATION: *Yes*
SHIPPING: *No*

GA PROPERTY SERVICES

Auction Sale Room, 1 Market Street. Tel: (0799) 22058

200-250 lots. The sale day is Tuesday, which is also one of Saffron Walden's two market days — and as the market is immediately outside the saleyard, things can become a little hectic. The sale takes place entirely under cover, and the saleroom itself is a much-extended old coach house. Eggs, produce and poultry are sold, as well as modern and household furniture and effects, garden tools and equipment, and a wide variety of miscellaneous items. About every six weeks there is also an antiques and fine art sale. The calendar for this Friday sale is arranged at the start of each year and is available from the sales office. Saffron Walden is worth the trip — it is an attractive jumble of medieval houses, ancient inns and Victorian public buildings. Close by is Audley End, a lavishly decorated Jacobean house which is open to the public.

Westcliff-on-Sea

BUYER'S PREMIUM: *10%*
SALES: *Fortnightly on Thu at 2.30pm.*
VIEWING: *Wed prior 2.30pm-4.30pm, day of sale 8.00am-1.00pm.*
REFRESHMENTS: *None available on the premises.*
PARKING: *Ample parking near by.*
STORAGE: *Yes*
TRANSPORTATION: *Yes*
SHIPPING: *Yes*

CHAPEL & CHAPEL

435 London Road. Tel: (0702) 347594 and 343734

200-300 lots. This is a good general auction with an excellent mixture of modern, reproduction and antique furniture, as well as china, porcelain, paintings, various collectables and so on. As most of the goods come from private houses, there will usually be some unexpected, unusual items too: perhaps a Victorian aneroid barometer or a 19th-century grained pine door, or an Italian mandolin. Lots are sold in the order in which vendors have brought them, rather than in categories. The saleroom is open for viewing at 8.00am on the day of sale but closes for lunch, so arrive early or go the day before to look round. It is usually acceptable to move about quietly while the auction is in progress.

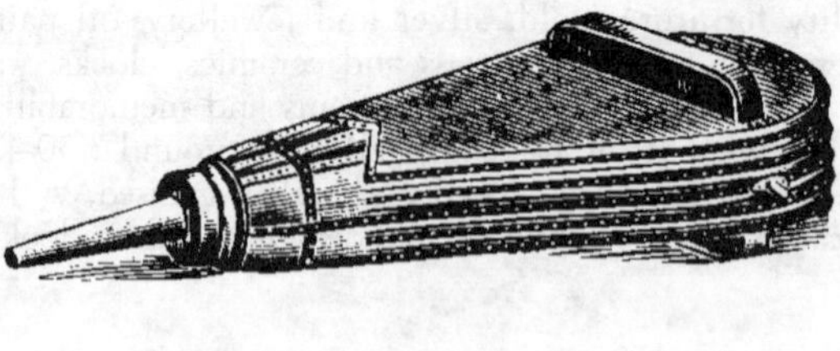

GLOUCESTERSHIRE

TAYLER & FLETCHER

The British Legion Hall, off Lansdown Road. Tel: (0451) 20913

400-500 lots. Tayler & Fletcher hold monthly sales of antique and household furniture, which take place either on a Tuesday or a Saturday. Lots may come from local houses and cottages, and include pine, Victorian and Edwardian furniture. Specialist sales are also held throughout the year. These may be devoted to sporting equipment and associated items, pictures and prints, or other subject areas.

Spring and autumn sales of nursery stock are also held by the auctioneers behind their offices at The Square, Stow-on-the-Wold, during March. The stock at this sale includes shrubs, hedging plants, ornamental trees and bedding plants.

Bourton-on-the-Water

BUYER'S PREMIUM: *Nil*
SALES: *General: monthly on Sat at 10.00am or Tue at 2.30pm. Specialist sales on Sat at 10.00am. Nursery stock: twice a year on Sat at 10.00am.*
VIEWING: *Monthly Sat sale: day prior, 4.00pm-6.00pm, and morning of sale. Monthly Tue sale: day of sale from 12.00 noon. Nursery stock: day of sale.*
REFRESHMENTS: *Yes*
PARKING: *Yes*
STORAGE: *By arrangement.*
TRANSPORTATION: *Yes*
SHIPPING: *Yes*

HOBBS & CHAMBERS

Chapel Walk. Tel: (0242) 513722

300-400 lots. Hobbs & Chambers hold fortnightly Tuesday auctions at their Chapel Walk saleroom in Cheltenham, but they also host monthly auctions on Fridays at the Bingham Hall, King Street, Cirencester. Antique, Victorian and Edwardian furniture, clocks and barometers, Oriental carpets and rugs, *objets d'art*, pottery, porcelain and glass are all regularly sold at these events. Many of the sales are organised in specialist areas, covering silver, jewellery, oil paintings, watercolours, toys, dolls and models, weapons and militaria, and other collectables. Art Deco and Art Nouveau items appear at these auctions with some regularity, as do scientific instruments, stamps, coins and medals, and post and cigarette cards.

Cheltenham

BUYER'S PREMIUM: *10%*
SALES: *Fortnightly on Tue at 11.00am (or on Wed at 11.00am in weeks when there is a Bank Holiday); monthly on Fri at 9.30am (Cirencester saleroom).*
VIEWING: *Mon prior, 10.00am-4.00pm and day of sale; Thu prior, 10.30am-8.00pm (Cirencester saleroom).*
REFRESHMENTS: *Available on the premises at Cheltenham only.*
PARKING: *None on the premises.*
STORAGE: *Yes*
TRANSPORTATION: *Yes*
SHIPPING: *Yes*

MALLAMS

See MALLAMS, Oxford, Oxfordshire

Cheltenham

SANDOES FINE ART

Wotton Auction Rooms, Tabernacle Road. Tel: (0453) 844733

900-1,000 lots. Sandoes Fine Art hold monthly antiques sales lasting two days at their main saleroom in Tabernacle Road,

Wotton-under-Edge

BUYER'S PREMIUM: *10%*
SALES: *Antiques: monthly on Tue and Wed at 10.30am.*

Tormarton: monthly on Fri at 10.30am.
VIEWING: *Antiques: Mon prior, 10.00am-6.00pm. Tormarton: morning of sale from 9.00am.*
REFRESHMENTS: *Own café.*
PARKING: *Own car park.*
STORAGE: *Yes*
TRANSPORTATION: *Yes*
SHIPPING: *Yes*

Wotton-under-Edge. The bidding is arranged so that smaller lots, such as ceramics, clocks and barometers, watches, jewellery, silver, silver plate (now much sought-after and often more expensive than solid silver items), glass, brassware, pictures and books are auctioned on the first day (Tuesday), leaving larger items of antique and quality furniture and effects to be sold on the second day (Wednesday). Sandoes also hold popular monthly sales at the Village Hall, Tormarton, Avon, two miles from Junction 18 of the M4. These always take place on Fridays and usually consist of 300-400 cheaper items of general household furniture and miscellaneous items.

GREATER MANCHESTER

Altrincham

JOHN ARNOLD & COMPANY

Arnolds Yard, Old Market Place. Tel: (061) 928 3724

BUYER'S PREMIUM: *Nil*
SALES: *Fortnightly on Wed at 10.30am.*
VIEWING: *Day prior 10.30am-4.30pm, 7.30pm-8.30pm.*
REFRESHMENTS: *None available on the premises.*
PARKING: *Own car park.*
STORAGE: *Yes*
TRANSPORTATION: *Yes*
SHIPPING: *Yes*

500-600 lots. Although Altrincham looks like a part of Greater Manchester on the map, the locals insist that it is in Cheshire. Wherever it is, the saleroom is in the oldest part of town where the roads are still cobbled, and it may be a little difficult to find for the newcomer. The best landmark is the Unicorn Hotel, a large white building. The entrance to the saleroom is along Albert Place, the small narrow road beside the hotel. Once found, the sale is packed with goods of all types, and it is a wonder that everything will be sold by the end of the day.

Starting the auction are domestic electrical appliances, refrigerators, cookers, freezers, gardening equipment, perhaps the odd garden gate, carpets, and any large item which doesn't fit into the furniture category. This part of the sale takes around one-and-a-half hours, and is followed by a 30-minute break for lunch. At 12.30pm the selling of furniture and other general household items begins, including antiques. The sale finishes with *objets d'art*.

Bury

J R PARKINSON, SON & HAMER AUCTIONS

Auction Rooms, Rochdale Road. Tel: (061) 761 1612

BUYER'S PREMIUM: *10% (vehicles 5%).*
SALES: *Often on Wed at 10.00am, but check with auctioneer.*

600-700 lots. The saleroom building is a converted church, just off Junction 2 of the M66, heading towards Bury Town. This is an interesting auction because the type of lots varies so much from week to week. The frequency of sales varies too: there are often two or three in a week, but in some weeks no sale is held. About 50 sales are held in total per year. The firm are bonded auctioneers for the county courts, Official Receiver and various liquidators, so in addition to furniture and household items you may find motor vehicles, office furniture (such as desks, typewriters and filing cabinets), or perhaps new clothing, jewellery and sewing machines. The bankrupt stock from a single company often warrants a sale of its own.

VIEWING: *Day prior 12.00 noon-7.30pm.*
REFRESHMENTS: *Own café.*
PARKING: *Own car park.*
STORAGE: *Yes*
TRANSPORTATION: *Yes*
SHIPPING: *Yes*

STEPHEN SHAWCROSS (AUCTIONEERS)

Eccles

103/105 Church Street. Tel: (061) 789 3537

250-300 lots. The auction was established in 1870 and is now a weekly sale. Local people, private buyers and dealers rush around to study the lots with the anticipatory air of excitement shown by any gold prospector shaking his sieve. You can bid for almost anything here — general household furniture and effects, electrical goods of all kinds, kitchen items, garden tools and equipment, bric-à-brac and so on. You will also find cutlery and china, jewellery and books, with bargains in all departments.

Every four weeks the general sale is replaced by a sale of antiques, including furniture, paintings, porcelain, silver and silver plate, jewellery, furniture and collectables. The variety of lots offered is as rich as in the general sale, but the goods in the antiques sale are older.

BUYER'S PREMIUM: *Nil*
SALES: *Weekly on Mon at 1.00pm (includes antiques sale every four weeks).*
VIEWING: *Day of sale from 9.30am.*
REFRESHMENTS: *None available on the premises.*
PARKING: *Own car park.*
STORAGE: *No*
TRANSPORTATION: *Yes*
SHIPPING: *Yes*

AUCTION INTERNATIONAL (MANCHESTER)

Manchester

51a Broughton Lane, Strangeways.
Tel: (061) 832 2400 Fax (061) 832 2400

300-500 lots. The majority of auctions sell antiques or at least second-hand goods, but Auction International's monthly Sunday sale is of new furniture and carpets. The lots are described as 'slight seconds' or 'end of range', and the sales are popular with those setting up home or refurbishing a house. The saleroom is to the north of the city, close to Strangeways Prison, and has a massive selling space of 10,000 sq ft.

The same firm also holds sales during the week, which are aimed at the trade rather than private buyers. If an item comes to the sale in packs of 12, then that is how it will be sold. However there are bargains to be had, even if you are a private buyer.

The fortnightly Thursday sale is of 'fancy goods', which can include clothes, toys, domestic cookware and other items. On the last Tuesday of each month except December the catering sale is held. This offers catering, baking, banqueting, canteen, restaurant and shop equipment, utensils and furnishings.

BUYER'S PREMIUM: *5%*
SALES: *Furniture: monthly on first Sun of month at 11.00am. Fancy goods: fortnightly on Thu at 11.00am. Catering Equipment: monthly on last Tue of month (except Dec) at 11.00am.*
VIEWING: *Day prior 9.00am-4.00pm.*
REFRESHMENTS: *Own café.*
PARKING: *Own car park.*
STORAGE: *No*
TRANSPORTATION: *Yes*
SHIPPING: *Yes*

Manchester

BUYER'S PREMIUM: *10%*
SALES: *General: weekly on Mon at 12.00 noon. Specialist: weekly on Tue at 12.00 noon. Gala Auctions at special venues: twice a year (usually May and Nov) at 7.30pm.*
VIEWING: *General: morning of sale from 10.00am. Specialist: day prior 10.00am-4.00pm and morning of sale from 10.00am. Gala auctions: Mon prior 10.00am-4.00pm at Capes Dunn saleroom, day of sale from 1.00pm at the venue.*
REFRESHMENTS: *None available on the premises.*
PARKING: *General and Specialist: Charles Street NCP. Gala auctions: depends on venue.*
STORAGE: *Yes*
TRANSPORTATION: *Yes*
SHIPPING: *Yes*

CAPES DUNN

The Auction Galleries, 38 Charles Street. Tel: (061) 273 1911

500-600 lots. Charles Street is off Princess Street and close to Piccadilly Railway Station. The firm was established in 1826, and holds two busy, comprehensive auctions per week. Every Monday there is a sale of Victorian and later furniture and effects, which means general household articles, often from complete house clearances. This sale is held on the ground floor. Every Tuesday on the first and second floors there are specialist sales in various categories such as ceramics and glass, fine furniture, musical instruments, oil paintings and watercolours, jewellery, silver, textiles and costume, books and prints, collectables and many others.

Twice a year in the spring and autumn (usually May and November) Capes Dunn hold Gala Auctions. These are evening sales beginning at 7.30pm, which take place in specially chosen venues such as Arley Hall near Knutsford. Only selected lots of high quality or special interest are included, and the idea is to offer private buyers a range of lots chosen for their investment quality. The dates and times for these sales are arranged well in advance and can be obtained from the sales office.

Stalybridge

BUYER'S PREMIUM: *10%*
SALES: *General: weekly on Sat at 10.00am. Antiques: every three weeks on Tue at 11.00am. Fancy goods: every three weeks on Wed at 11.00am. Oldham trade auctions: every three weeks on Thu at 11.00am.*
VIEWING: *Day of sale from 9.00am.*
REFRESHMENTS: *Own café.*
PARKING: *Own car park.*
STORAGE: *No*
TRANSPORTATION: *Yes*
SHIPPING: *Yes*

HIGHAMS

Waterloo House, Waterloo Road. Tel: (061) 338 8698

400-500 lots. Highams are a large and well-known firm holding a series of sales in Stalybridge and at Southgate Court, Southgate Street, Oldham. Although the public are welcome, the Oldham sales are mainly for trade and include plant and machinery, bankrupt or fire-damaged goods, catering equipment and so on. A fortnightly sale of private saloon cars and commercial vehicles is also held here, on Saturdays at 11.00am.

The building in Stalybridge is next door to the bus centre, and is a massive place with three separate salerooms. Saleroom 3 is where the popular weekly Saturday auctions are held, for general bric-à-brac, household sundries, furniture, televisions, electrical goods, gardening equipment and so on. The other two salerooms are used for midweek auctions, which take place every three weeks.

In saleroom 1, every third Tuesday, there is an auction of good antiques, including paintings and jewellery. In saleroom 2, every third Wednesday, the sale is of office furniture, toys and all types of fancy goods. This is mainly aimed at dealers but can be interesting for others.

A F BROCK

Stockport

269 London Road, Hazel Grove. Tel: (061) 456 5050

500-600 lots. There is no furniture in this auction, which is mainly of collectables — coins, jewellery, cigarette cards, porcelain, silver and silver plate, postage stamps, autographs, ephemera, jewellery, medals and so on, with prices ranging from a pound or two up to a couple of thousand.

The sales take place about 10 times a year at the Belgrade Hotel, Dialstone Lane, Stockport. There is always something of interest, and a visit makes an entertaining evening out for bargain hunters and collectors alike.

BUYER'S PREMIUM: *Nil*
SALES: *About 10 times a year on Wed at 6.30pm.*
VIEWING: *Day of sale from 1.00pm in hotel, or two days prior from 11.00am-4.00pm at A F Brock's premises.*
REFRESHMENTS: *Own café.*
PARKING: *Own car park.*
STORAGE: *Yes*
TRANSPORTATION: *Yes*
SHIPPING: *Yes*

PHILIP DAVIES & SONS

Stockport

The Auction Centre, Hazel Grove. Tel: (061) 483 2637

Up to 500 lots. This is another auction in Stockport which is out of the normal category but worth a visit. The regular sales are mainly of liquidated stock with an emphasis on office furniture — desks, typewriters, filing cabinets, photocopying machines, chairs, computers and so on — but almost anything can come up. Vehicles, musical instruments, wood-working machinery, tools and building materials have all featured, and one sale contained 15 full-size snooker tables. As the items are from insolvency-related cases, all lots are offered without reserve prices.

The auctioneer will advise on the types of goods to be sold, so make an enquiry before setting out on a journey. The saleroom is a large warehouse about three miles from the centre of the town. The firm also holds auctions at the premises of companies based throughout the region, on behalf of insolvency practitioners.

BUYER'S PREMIUM: *Nil*
SALES: *At frequent intervals.*
VIEWING: *Usually day prior 10.00am-3.30pm and day of sale from 9.30am, but telephone to check.*
REFRESHMENTS: *Own café.*
PARKING: *Own car park.*
STORAGE: *Yes*
TRANSPORTATION: *Yes*
SHIPPING: *Yes*

DEREK TOMMIS & SON

Stockport

15 Station Road, Cheadle Hulme. Tel: (061) 485 4729

500-600 lots. Anyone looking for a rare 78rpm record of Caruso singing, a Georgian chest of drawers, a divan bed and mattress, a silver dressing table set, a cased set of old English silver teaspoons, a pair of brass column candlesticks, a second-hand electric cooker, a 19th-century Chesterfield couch or a garden spade need go no further. The lots in Derek Tommis & Son's monthly sale are all-encompassing. The Station Road entrance to the saleroom is a small and easily missed door, but there is a more obvious way in by the loading bay in the precinct, which runs alongside the saleroom. Plenty of willing staff are on hand to give advice and assistance, and it

BUYER'S PREMIUM: *10%*
SALES: *Monthly on last Wed of month at 10.30am.*
VIEWING: *Day prior 9.30am-5.00pm, morning of sale from 9.30am.*
REFRESHMENTS: *None available on the premises.*
PARKING: *Precinct public car park.*
STORAGE: *Yes*
TRANSPORTATION: *Yes*
SHIPPING: *Yes*

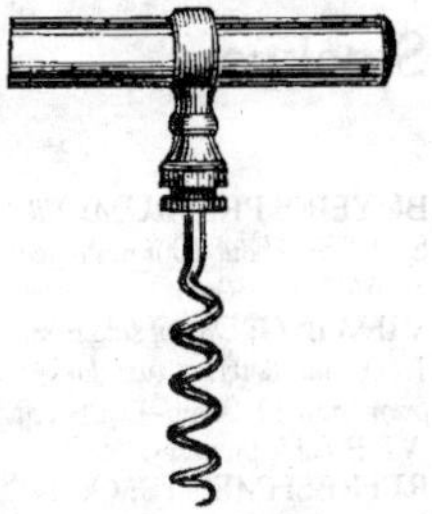

is an ideal sale for new auction-goers as well as old hands. The sales start downstairs with larger general furniture, cookers and so on, and end in the upstairs saleroom with antiques and valuable smaller items.

HAMPSHIRE

Andover

BUYER'S PREMIUM: *Nil*
SALES: *General: fortnightly on Mon at 10.00am. Jewellery, pictures, paintings and drawings: fortnightly on previous Sat at 2.30pm.*
VIEWING: *Fri prior 9.00am-9.00pm.*
REFRESHMENTS: *Own café.*
PARKING: *Public car park near by.*
STORAGE: *Yes*
TRANSPORTATION: *Yes*
SHIPPING: *Yes*

ANDOVER SALEROOM

41a London Street. Tel: (0264) 64820

700-800 lots. The fortnightly Monday sale is always a busy event at this most cheerful saleroom. Bob Herbert, the auctioneer, exchanges jokes with the crowd, many of whom he is on first-name terms with. This is an ideal place to begin for those worried by the thought of buying at auction, and there is always a wide variety of goods here. The Monday sale begins in a building outside the main saleroom and might include stripped pine furniture, beds, electrical goods, lawn mowers, gardening tools and so on. Waxed pine furniture is usually sold in the main saleroom, followed by 1930s and 1940s furniture, brass, porcelain, copper and silver. The sale finishes with antique furniture.

The fortnightly sale on the previous Saturday is of jewellery, pictures, paintings and drawings only. The sale of pictures and paintings takes place at 2.30pm, and the sale of jewellery at 4.00pm.

Andover

BUYER'S PREMIUM: *Nil*
SALES: *Monthly on third Wed of month at 11.00am.*
VIEWING: *Day prior 10.00am-4.00pm.*
REFRESHMENTS: *Own café.*
PARKING: *Own parking area.*
STORAGE: *Yes*
TRANSPORTATION: *Yes*
SHIPPING: *Yes*

MAY & SON

Penton Mewsey Village Hall, Penton Mewsey. Tel: (0264) 23417

300-400 lots. Penton Mewsey is just two miles west of Andover, in a wonderful country setting. A visit to the sale makes an ideal day out in an attractive Hampshire village, with country walks near by and excellent local pubs. The refreshments available in the hall during the sale are made in the village, and very good they are too.

The sale includes antique, period, Victorian and Edwardian furniture (English and Continental), silver, silver plate, pottery, china, porcelain, pictures, and so on. All the lots are from private sources as a matter of policy, in order to keep the sales 'fresh'. Frank May, who runs the auction with his son John, has been in the business for over 50 years, earning a well-deserved reputation over that period. The sale attracts dealers and private buyers not only from local towns such as Basingstoke, but also attracts bidders from much further afield, as well as regulars of many years' standing. Specialist sales of antique toys and textiles are also held once or twice a year, if enough lots have been accumulated.

BASINGSTOKE AUCTION ROOMS

Basingstoke

82-84 Sarum Hill. Tel: (0256) 840707

200-300 lots. There are country auctions and there are town auctions, and this is one of the latter. The auctioneers occupy an unimposing building in a part of Basingstoke that has not, as yet, been built up with office blocks. There are two small, low-ceilinged salerooms here, one of which is packed full of large items of furniture on sale days. The lots in the fortnightly Monday sale can be rather nondescript, but the sale of antiques and fine art held here every six to eight weeks is usually more interesting. Past sales have included Georgian mahogany bookcases, mahogany grand pianos, rosewood tables and fine paintings.

The Basingstoke Auction Rooms also run a monthly sale of general household furniture and effects (which sometimes includes antiques) at the Village Hall, Church Lane, Heckfield, Hampshire.

BUYER'S PREMIUM: *10% (nil at Heckfield).*
SALES: *Mon at 10.30am (fortnightly general sale); Tue at 10.30am (six to eight-weekly antiques and fine art sale); Sat at 10.30am (monthly sale, Heckfield).*
VIEWING: *Sat prior, 10.00am-3.00pm (fortnightly general sale); Fri prior, 10.00am-8.00pm, Sat prior, 10.00am-3.00pm, and Mon prior, 10.00am-5.00pm and 6.00pm-9.00pm (six or eight-weekly antiques and fine art sale).*
REFRESHMENTS: *Available on the premises at Heckfield, but not at Basingstoke.*
PARKING: *Basingstoke: 40 spaces at rear. Heckfield: ample space.*
STORAGE: *Yes*
TRANSPORTATION: *Yes*
SHIPPING: *Yes*

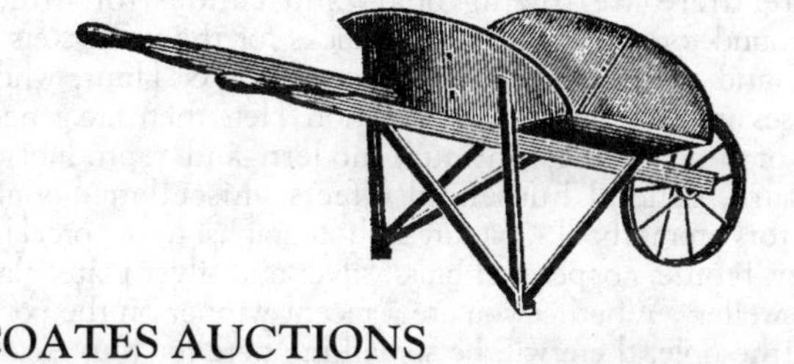

COATES AUCTIONS

Gosport

15 High Street, South Loading Road. Tel: (0705) 589418

300-400 lots. Gosport is known as 'the larder of the navy', for many stores and supply yards are based here. It is also a popular holiday area. A visit to Coates' Auctions should be high on the list of musts for locals, seasonal visitors and more experienced auction-goers alike. Converted from an old cinema, and covering two floors, this is a good, busy, well-run and long-established saleroom. The auctioneer conducts the sale from a pedestal giving a view of both floors. The general Wednesday sale is a mixture of all types of modern, Victorian, pine, reproduction and antique furniture, household effects, kitchenalia, gardening equipment, bicycles, toys, jewellery, china and glass, porcelain, photograph albums, marine artefacts, and other items. On the first Wednesday of the month, though, this sale is devoted to antiques and fine art.

BUYER'S PREMIUM: *10%*
SALES: *Weekly on Wed at 5.30pm (includes monthly antiques and fine art sale).*
VIEWING: *Day of sale from 8.30am.*
REFRESHMENTS: *Own café.*
PARKING: *Public car park near by.*
STORAGE: *Yes*
TRANSPORTATION: *Yes*
SHIPPING: *Yes*

Lymington

BUYER'S PREMIUM: *10%*
SALES: *Fortnightly on Thu at 11.00am (includes quarterly antique and fine art sale).*
VIEWING: *Day prior 12.00 noon-6.00pm.*
REFRESHMENTS: *Own café.*
PARKING: *Public car park a few minutes' walk away.*
STORAGE: *Yes*
TRANSPORTATION: *Yes*
SHIPPING: *Yes*

AUSTIN & WYATT (NATIONWIDE ANGLIA)

Emsworth Road. Tel: (0590) 677225

300-400 lots. Austin & Wyatt hold an interesting, friendly auction with an atmosphere of informality in the saleroom. The sale offers the possibility of some very good buys in the area of good quality modern, antique, Victorian and general furniture and effects. The sale may include pine kitchen dressers, mahogany sideboards, tables of all descriptions, buttoned sofas, wardrobes, dressing tables, chests of drawers, double and single divan beds, domestic and ornamental china, brass items, clocks, copper saucepans, oil paintings, watercolours and prints. At roughly quarterly intervals the general sale is replaced by a special sale of antiques and fine art. Times are the same as for the general sales.

Petersfield

BUYER'S PREMIUM: *10%*
SALES: *Every six weeks on Fri at 10.00am.*
VIEWING: *Thu prior 10.00am-6.30pm.*
REFRESHMENTS: *None available on the premises, but available near by.*
PARKING: *Public car park in town centre.*
STORAGE: *Yes*
TRANSPORTATION: *Yes*
SHIPPING: *Yes*

JACOBS & HUNT

Lavant Street. Tel: (0730) 62744

500-600 lots. Petersfield is a pleasant Georgian town. An ideal day out for the family would be a picnic at Heath and Lake (where there are rowing boats and canoes for hire, a playground for the children, and ducks for the youngsters to feed), and then a visit to a sale at Jacob & Hunt, whose premises are close to the railway station. Here there are general sales of high quality antique, modern and reproduction furniture, general household effects, miscellaneous and collectors' items, books, pictures, photographs, toys, porcelain, pottery, bronze, copper and brass, silver and silver plate, glass, and jewellery. Whether you are a recent winner on the pools, or on the dole, there will be something here for you. At one recent auction a Dutch oil painting fetched £60,000, and a wardrobe sold for just £5.

Portsmouth

BUYER'S PREMIUM: *Nil*
SALES: *Fortnightly on Tue. at 5.00pm.*
VIEWING: *Day of sale from 10.00am.*
REFRESHMENTS: *Own café.*
PARKING: *Own car park.*
STORAGE: *Yes*
TRANSPORTATION: *Yes*
SHIPPING: *Yes*

MEDLAMS

Units 5 & 6, Dragon Estate, Fitzherbert Road, Farlington.
Tel: (0705) 210110

400-500 lots. Where, other than at a good country auction, could you buy an early period lowboy, a Victorian dresser, various tiled wash-stands, various tables and display cabinets, any amount of pine furniture, plus antique and Art Deco porcelain and pottery, genuine old copper and brass, kettles, ships' lanterns and a lorry or van to take it all home in? Not even Harrods could supply all that! Medlams have a very large purpose-built saleroom which is well heated in the winter. It fills up as the evening goes on with people arriving from work. Outside are parked lorries, cars, vans and trailers, which are up for sale. They are sold from inside the saleroom at around 5.30pm. After that there is no particular order, but 'smalls' — silver and jewellery, pottery and suchlike — are always sold at the end. It is worth having a good look round, as it is possible to miss some very interesting items otherwise. A bicycle may be offered for sale among lots of furniture, and a Victorian gentleman's wardrobe may be preceded and followed by pine chests of drawers.

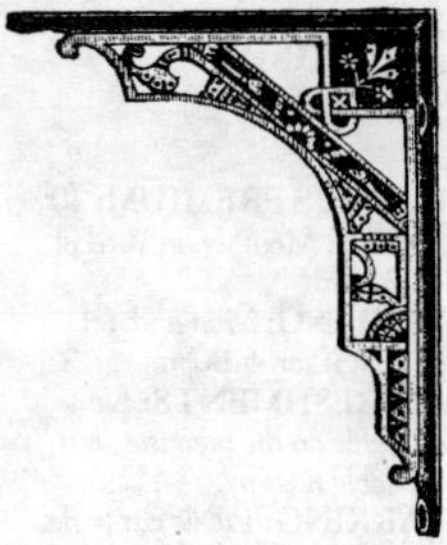

G A PROPERTY SERVICES

Romsey Auctioners, 86 The Hundred. Tel: (0794) 513331

300-400 lots. G A hold one sale of antiques a month, which usually includes Victorian and later furniture, and all manner of curiosities discovered in attics, cellars and garden sheds. The lots are fun, and many provide an excellent way to furnish a house without paying a fortune. Beds, dressers, settees, bureaux, wash-stands, tables, chairs, and other objects are up for bidding. A gas mask, a bag of razors, some brushes and chess pieces, a glass lantern and a set of scales, were all sold in one box of bric-à-brac recently, and there was no difficulty in finding a buyer. Part of the fun of attending a country auction is not only finding a bargain for yourself, but also working out just what a buyer is going to do with some of his more bizarre purchases.

Also once a month, there is a sale of silver and jewellery here. The staff are happy to help if people wish to view lots outside the official viewing times.

Romsey

BUYER'S PREMIUM: *5%*
SALES: *Antiques: monthly sale on Tue at 11.00am. Silver and jewellery: monthly on Tue at 12.00 noon.*
VIEWING: *Day prior 12.00 noon-7.30pm.*
REFRESHMENTS: *None available on the premises.*
PARKING: *Own small car park.*
STORAGE: *Yes*
TRANSPORTATION: *Yes*
SHIPPING: *Yes*

MILLBANK AUCTIONEERS LTD

72 Millbank Street, Northam. Tel: (0703) 228179

400-1,000 lots. Almost anything can be bought at a Millbank auction: plant and machinery, vans, cars, office furniture, desks, typewriters, filing cabinets, antique and modern household furniture, china, pictures, paintings, and jewellery. As Southampton is a port, many lots have connections with fishing and boating. Millbank are agents for the Sheriff of Hampshire, the Official Receiver, the county courts and bailiffs, as well as private sources, and they are one of the largest auctioneers in the area. It is not unusual to find as many as 500 people attending their sales. The two-day viewing period is a great help to prospective bidders. Like most other auctioneers, Millbank are happy to make bids on your behalf, if you are unable to attend a sale in person.

Southampton

BUYER'S PREMIUM: *Nil*
SALES: *Monthly on Thu at 10.00am.*
VIEWING: *Tue and Wed prior 8.30am-5.00pm.*
REFRESHMENTS: *Own café.*
PARKING: *Own car park.*
STORAGE: *Yes*
TRANSPORTATION: *Yes*
SHIPPING: *Yes*

Southsea

BUYER'S PREMIUM: *10%*
SALES: *Monthly on Wed at 10.30am.*
VIEWING: *Mon and Tue prior 9.30am-5.00pm.*
REFRESHMENTS: *None available on the premises, but available near by.*
PARKING: *Public car parks near by.*
STORAGE: *Yes*
TRANSPORTATION: *Yes*
SHIPPING: *Yes*

D M NESBIT

7 Clarendon Road. Tel: (0705) 864321

350-600 lots. Southsea is east of Portsmouth. It is a town with many holiday attractions, but few match the sight of the constant coming and going of ships of all kinds through the harbour mouth, including submarines. The saleroom is situated just opposite the main post office, and near the sea front. As might be imagined, sales here have a definite nautical bias, and D M Nesbit have established a reputation both nationally and internationally over the years as one of the leading auction rooms in the country for the sale of marine paintings, both by local and internationally known artists. Porcelain, ceramics and glass, metalware, oil paintings, watercolour drawings, engravings, prints, china and 18th-century and later furniture are some of the main categories, but they do not appear in the same order at each sale.

HEREFORD & WORCESTER

Great Malvern

BUYER'S PREMIUM: *10%*
SALES: *Twice monthly on first and third Thu of the month at 10.30am (includes antiques and fine art sale five times a year).*
VIEWING: *General: day prior 2.00pm-4.00pm. Antiques: 12.00 noon-8.00pm.*
REFRESHMENTS: *Own café.*
PARKING: *Ample parking near by.*
STORAGE: *Yes*
TRANSPORTATION: *Yes*
SHIPPING: *Yes*

HAMPTONS FINE ART, POCOCK & LEAR

Malvern Salerooms, Barnards Green Road. Tel: (0684) 892315

300-400 lots. A sale of general household furniture and effects is held on the first and third Thursday of each month. Among the lots might be chairs, desks, cabinets, mattresses, sitting room and bedroom furnishings, such as wardrobes and dressing tables, and smaller items, such as clocks, mirrors, desk lamps, copper, china and glass, books, carpets and rugs and a number of miscellaneous items.

Five times a year a special antiques and fine art sale is held in place of one of the general sales. These special sales attract buyers from all over the country and include antique furniture, paintings and watercolours, drawings, prints and miniatures, china, porcelain, silver and plate, jewellery, collectables, ceramics, glass and other items.

Great Malvern

BUYER'S PREMIUM: *Nil*
SALES: *Monthly on Tue at 11.00am (except Dec and Aug).*

PHILIP LANEY & JOLLY

The Portland Room, Portland Road. Tel: (0684) 892322

300-350 lots. Six places bear the name Malvern, but Great Malvern is the largest of these. Portland Road is off Victoria Road, one of the main thoroughfares of the town. The purpose-built saleroom is easy to identify on sale days, because of the people heading towards it. This sale is popular and offers the possibility of bargain buys. The lots are clean and well presented, and are usually of high quality. A typical sale will include antique and reproduction furniture, porcelain, watercolours, drawings, prints, copper, brass, china (both ornamental and domestic), jewellery and so on, plus perhaps stamps, medals, coins and other collectables. There are no sales in December and August; otherwise this is a monthly event.

VIEWING: *Day prior 2.00pm-4.30pm, morning of sale from 8.30am.*
REFRESHMENTS: *None available on the premises.*
PARKING: *Ample parking near by.*
STORAGE: *Yes*
TRANSPORTATION: *Yes*
SHIPPING: *Yes*

PHIPPS & PRITCHARD

Hartlebury, near Kidderminster

Hartlebury Village Hall. Tel: (0562) 822244

700-800 lots. Hartlebury is an old village about half a mile off the A449 and roughly three miles south of Kidderminster. It has a couple of pleasant pubs where many buyers can be found waiting for their lots to come under the hammer. The sale is rather up-market for a country auction, and most of the lots are antiques, although increasing amounts of better quality 1930s furniture can be found. There will also be coins, medals, stamps and other collectors' items, plus silver, plate, china, porcelain, pewter, watercolours, oils, drawings, prints and so on. The sale starts with smaller items, but always moves on to furniture at 2.30pm. If there are any 'smalls' still to be sold, they are auctioned once the furniture sale is over.

BUYER'S PREMIUM: *£1 per lot.*
SALES: *Monthly on third Sat of month at 11.00am.*
VIEWING: *Day prior 3.30pm-6.00pm, morning of sale from 8.30am.*
REFRESHMENTS: *Own café.*
PARKING: *Own car park.*
STORAGE: *Yes*
TRANSPORTATION: *No*
SHIPPING: *Yes*

KIDDERMINSTER MARKET AUCTION

Kidderminster

Comberton Place. Tel: (0562) 741303

800-1000 lots. This auction makes a good day out for the entire family. In the same market area as the sale there are stalls selling local crafts, clothes, antiques and general bric-à-brac. At the sale itself, it is possible to spend a few pounds or a few hundred pounds bidding for anything from a bag of potatoes to a piece of Royal Doulton china.

The auction starts at 10.30am with 20 or 30 bicycles, in an assortment of conditions and styles. These are followed by 'smalls' — bric-à-brac, china and the like. At 11.00am another auctioneer begins the outside sale of lesser-value furniture and outdoor items, such as garden tools and mowers. As might be expected in a town famous for carpet manufacturing, there is a separate sale for carpets, which begins inside at the same time.

In yet another area, 11.00am also sees the start of the sale of shrubs and farm produce, where around 500 lots are offered at the height of the season. The sale of better quality furniture begins at around 1.30pm in the main saleroom, and may include modern, reproduction and antique items.

BUYER'S PREMIUM: *7% (not furniture).*
SALES: *Weekly on Thu at 10.30am.*
VIEWING: *Day prior 3.00pm-6.00pm.*
REFRESHMENTS: *Café and licensed premises.*
PARKING: *Own car park.*
STORAGE: *Yes*
TRANSPORTATION: *Yes*
SHIPPING: *Yes*

Leominster

BUYER'S PREMIUM: *Nil*
SALES: *Weekly on Wed at 6.00pm.*
VIEWING: *Day of sale from 2.00pm.*
REFRESHMENTS: *Own café.*
PARKING: *Own car park.*
STORAGE: *No*
TRANSPORTATION: *Yes*
SHIPPING: *Yes*

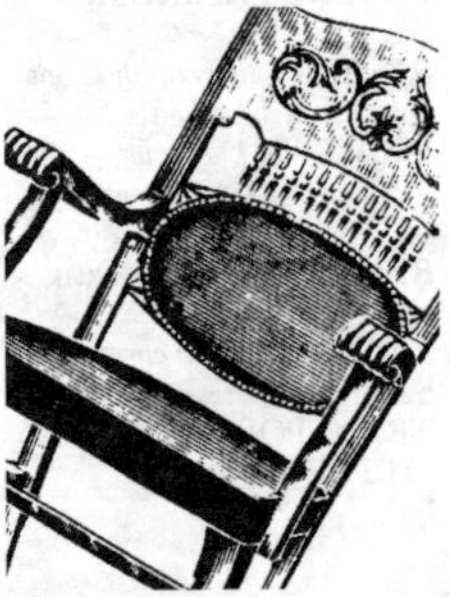

KINGSLAND AUCTION SERVICE LTD

Shirl Heath, Kingsland. Tel: (0568 81) 564

1,000-1,200 lots. The saleroom is a little off the beaten track: take the A44 out of Leominster towards Kington, then at Shirl Heath take the A4110. The premises are also used for weekly car auctions, however, so most local people will be able to point you in the right direction. The general sale is massive, and for many it makes as much an entertaining night out as a place to pick up bargains. Anything from front doors to the entire contents of a house have been sold at one time or another at these sales.

In order to finish sales at a reasonable time, auctioning takes place simultaneously in different parts of the premises. Articles sold in the large warehouse might include timber, car parts, odd pieces of copper piping, earthenware sinks, baths, toilet bowls and the like. Meanwhile, the main sale takes place in the adjoining saleroom. Behind the auctioneer's area there is a small room set out with tables laden with china, ornaments, antiquarian books, silver, bygones, postcards, cigarette cards, toys and other collector's items. Also here is a locked cabinet where the most valuable small articles are kept. Furniture, ranging from antique to the nearly new, is displayed in front of the auctioneer's stand. Everything has to be sold by the end of the evening.

Pershore

BUYER'S PREMIUM: *Nil*
SALES: *Every five to six weeks on Sat at 11.00am.*
VIEWING: *Day of sale from 9.00am.*
REFRESHMENTS: *Own café.*
PARKING: *Large public car park very close.*
STORAGE: *No*
TRANSPORTATION: *Yes*
SHIPPING: *Yes*

RICHARD WILLIAMS

2 High Street. Tel: (0386) 554031

500-600 lots. Pershore is an attractive Georgian town in the heart of fruit-growing country. If you are waiting between lots, you could look at the 14th-century bridge, which crosses the River Avon to the south of the town, or the remains of Pershore Abbey to the west. The sale occurs every five to six weeks, and is very much a social event for many of the locals. It is also a good general auction, with opportunities for bargains in the form of furniture of all ages and conditions — not only everyday chairs, tables and bedroom suites, but also unusual items, such as a Victorian mahogany-cased organ, or an enormous serpentine-fronted sideboard with a back mirror. Most sales have plenty of jewellery and china (domestic and ornamental), and other household effects as well.

Redditch

BUYER'S PREMIUM: *10%*
SALES: *General: fortnightly on Wed at 6.00pm.*

ARROW AUCTIONS (REDDITCH)

Arrow Road North. Tel: (0527) 66393

400-500 lots. The saleroom is in the Lakeside area of the town, about 50 yards from the lake itself, which is open to the public for boating. This helps to make the sale a pleasant day out, particularly for children. The popular general sale is held once a fortnight on a Wednesday, in the upstairs auction room. This sale may include police lost property, goods sold under instruction from bailiffs, or liquidated stock. These items are sold in addition to general household furniture and effects, including antiques. Also once a fortnight, but on alternate weeks to the general sale, a 'commercial sale' takes place. This is on Thursdays, beginning at 11.00am, and is devoted to a particular category of goods, for example office furniture and equipment, catering or garage equipment, or vehicles, plant and machinery. The commercial sale takes place in two sheds in the saleyard.

Commercial: fortnightly on Thu at 11.00am (alternate weeks to general sale).
VIEWING: *Day of sale from 9.00am.*
REFRESHMENTS: *Own café.*
PARKING: *Own car park.*
STORAGE: *Yes*
TRANSPORTATION: *Yes*
SHIPPING: *Yes*

SPENCERS, incorporating COLES KNAPP

Ross-on-Wye

The Georgian Rooms, Old Gloucester Road. Tel: (0989) 762227

300-500 lots. This is part of Henry Spencer & Sons, whose principal saleroom is in Retford. The Georgian Rooms is a tall, impressive building a short walk from the centre of this attractive Wye Valley town. The sale takes place on two floors. Shipping and later furniture is sold in the basement saleroom, with better quality items being sold in the main ground-floor room.

Two types of sales are held. The first is a monthly sale of Victorian and later furniture, ceramics, prints, toys and dolls, and other collectable items. The other sale is every two months and includes period furniture, Georgian items, English and Continental ceramics and glass, paintings, silver, silver plate and decorative arts.

Part of the same group is John Francis, Curiosity Saleroom, 19 King Street, Carmarthen, Dyfed, tel: (0267) 233456. A sale is held here on average every five to six weeks, always on a Tuesday at 11.00am. It offers good quality period and later furniture, pictures, ceramics and metalware, ornamental items and jewellery, and may include fishing tackle, textiles, memorabilia and other collectables.

BUYER'S PREMIUM: *10%*
SALES: *Ross, Victorian etc: monthly on first or second Wed of month at 10.30am. Ross, Georgian etc: every two months on second or third Wed of month at 10.30am. Carmarthen: on average every five to six weeks on Tue at 11.00am.*
VIEWING: *Ross: day prior 10.00am-7.00pm, day of sale from 9.15am. Carmarthen: day prior 3.00pm-6.00pm, day of sale from 9.15am.*
REFRESHMENTS: *Ross: sale day only. Carmarthen: none available on the premises but available near by.*
PARKING: *Ross: own car park. Carmarthen: public car park near by.*
STORAGE: *Yes (limited).*
TRANSPORTATION: *Yes*
SHIPPING: *Yes*

HERTFORDSHIRE

BEDMOND AUCTIONS

Bedmond

Bedmond Village Hall, High Street. Tel: (0727) 875142

300-400 lots. The proprietor is Joanne Vinton, daughter of the proprietors of the Pamela and Barry Auction at nearby Sandridge. Joanne Vinton moved this auction from Friday to Saturday in order to attract the private buyer, and it is a good

BUYER'S PREMIUM: *50p per lot.*
SALES: *Monthly on Sat at 3.30pm.*

VIEWING: *Day of sale from 2.30pm.*
REFRESHMENTS: *Own café.*
PARKING: *Own car park.*
STORAGE: *Yes*
TRANSPORTATION: *Yes*
SHIPPING: *No*

sale for those made uneasy by the thought of bidding. The proprietor conducts the sales herself in a friendly, helpful, chatty manner which should put even the most nervous at ease. Vendors can bring their goods into the hall on the sale day itself, so no one knows what the sale will hold until just before it starts. Usually there is a wide range of furniture from antique to modern, with kitchen items, pictures, prints, decorative objects, china, brass, silver, books, toys, gardening tools and equipment, and other useful or decorative goods.

Berkhampsted

BUYER'S PREMIUM: *5%*
SALES: *Fortnightly on Wed at 10.00am.*
VIEWING: *Day prior 10.00am-8.00pm, morning of sale from 8.00am.*
REFRESHMENTS: *Own café.*
PARKING: *None available on the premises.*
STORAGE: *Yes*
TRANSPORTATION: *Yes*
SHIPPING: *Yes*

G A PROPERTY SERVICES

Middle Road. Tel: (0442) 865169

400-500 lots. The saleroom is just off Cross Oak Road and to the rear of the large Nissan showroom and garage in the High Street. If you see something you want to bid for, you must give reception your name and address in return for a numbered card. Whenever you want to bid, hold up the card so the auctioneer can see it. This is a good country-style auction with modern furniture and effects, and the lots can vary in price from £1 to £1,000. Lots are sold in the order in which they arrive at the saleroom, so a three-piece suite could be followed by a small china ornament or a set of cutlery. Paintings and prints are displayed at one end of the room on a rack. Outdoor items, such as bicycles and lawn mowers, can be viewed in the yard outside, although they are sold in the saleroom.

Bishops Stortford

BUYER'S PREMIUM: *10%*
SALES: *General: weekly on Thu at 11.00am. Antiques and fine art: monthly on Tue at 10.30am. Specialist: twice yearly in May and Nov.*
VIEWING: *General: day of sale from 9.00am. Antiques and fine art: Sat prior 10.00am-12.00.00 noon, Mon prior 10.00am-4.00pm, day of sale from 9.00am. Specialist: day of sale 10.00am-4.00pm.*
REFRESHMENTS: *None available on the premises, but available near by.*
PARKING: *Available near by.*
STORAGE: *Yes*
TRANSPORTATION: *Yes*
SHIPPING: *Yes*

G E SWORDER & CO

Bishops Stortford Salerooms, 15 Northgate End. Tel: (0279) 651388

300-400 lots. G E Sworder & Co are very much part of the Bishops Stortford scene, and they have a reputation which spreads much further afield. Anything can be bought at their weekly sale of general household furniture and effects. This typically includes paintings, porcelain, china, jewellery, ornaments, carpets and much else. At one sale a cabinet full of dentures and pre-war artificial limbs was sold. The latter were made of wood and had complicated pulleys. A box of bric-à-brac might contain books, teacups, packets of playing cards and a saucepan or two, with the odd article of real interest among the rest. The furniture varies in quality and value, but most sales include dressers, dining chairs, tables, bedroom suites and so on.

In addition, there are monthly sales of antiques and fine art, and twice-yearly specialist sales of toys and collectors' items, which are also well worth visiting.

HARPENDEN AUCTION ROOMS

Harpenden

The Harpenden Public Hall, Southdown Road. Tel: (058285) 4544

350-400 lots. The Harpenden Public Hall is in the centre of the town, close to the High Street. An auction is held every month, but the day depends on the availability of the hall, which is used for other activities. Sale dates are booked well in advance though, and a list can be obtained by ringing Harpenden Auctions. The sale has been established for over 30 years, and is run by husband and wife Martin and Jean Brunning. Lots include a wide range of general household furniture and effects, but there is an emphasis on antiques.

BUYER'S PREMIUM: *£1 per lot.*
SALES: *Monthly at 10.30am (no regular day).*
VIEWING: *Day prior 9.00am-5.30pm, morning of sale from 9.00am.*
REFRESHMENTS: *Own café.*
PARKING: *Own car park.*
STORAGE: *Yes*
TRANSPORTATION: *Yes*
SHIPPING: *Yes*

NORRIS & DUVAL

Hertford

106 Fore Street. Tel: (0992) 501421

Hundreds of varied lots every Monday; 800 lots at the monthly antiques sale. Norris & Duval are furniture, fine art, agricultural and livestock auctioneers and valuers, established in 1814. Their Monday sale of household furniture and miscellaneous items takes place at Hertford cattle market on Caxton Hill, and cattle, sheep, pigs, fruit, vegetables, game and poultry are also sold. Vendors bring their goods from 8.30am onwards, and lay them out in rows. Sometimes the lots also include engineering, farming and horticultural equipment. The auctioneer walks along the rows, selling the lots in turn. Purchases must be made in cash only.

The monthly antiques sale of furniture and general effects is a grander affair at Castle Hall, a modern building in the grounds of Hertford Castle. The centrally heated saleroom is spacious, with cloakrooms, licensed bar and buffet. The sale is divided into collectors' items, carpets, furniture, mirrors, prints, oils and watercolours; and other items, such as silver, silver plate, brass and copper, European and Oriental china, glass, jewellery and so on.

BUYER'S PREMIUM: *Nil*
SALES: *General: weekly on Mon at 11.00am. Antiques: monthly on Thu at 9.30am.*
VIEWING: *General: morning of sale. Antiques: day prior 12.00 noon-7.00pm, and morning of sale.*
REFRESHMENTS: *Good facilities at both sales.*
PARKING: *Own car park for Mon sale; public car park in St Andrew's Street for Castle Hall sale.*
STORAGE: *Yes*
TRANSPORTATION: *Yes*
SHIPPING: *Yes*

NEWGATE STREET AUCTIONS

Newgate Street, near Hertford

Newgate Street Village Hall.
Tel: (0707) 54028 and (081) 4407584

200-300 lots. Vanessa Bennet is the proprietor, auctioneer and general factotum at this sale. She started the auction having become bored with selling on stalls, and recalls that her grandfather was a great auction-goer at a time when most sales were conducted in houses. 'People are fed up with modern furniture that collapses as soon as you get it home', she says, 'and as I love attending auctions, I decided to start one of my

BUYER'S PREMIUM: *50p per lot.*
SALES: *Monthly on first or last Fri of month at 7.00pm.*
VIEWING: *Day of sale from 5.00pm.*
REFRESHMENTS: *Own café.*
PARKING: *Own car park.*

STORAGE: *Yes*
TRANSPORTATION: *Yes*
SHIPPING: *No*

own.' The sale is friendly and Mrs Bennet often stops the selling to exchange a friendly word with a buyer. Among the lots will be general furniture and effects, including antique items, jewellery, china, silver and other 'smalls', pictures, and collectors' items such as stamps and postcards — something for everyone in fact. This is a pleasant, small auction.

Sandridge, near St Albans

BUYER'S PREMIUM: *50p per lot.*
SALES: *Fortnightly on first and third Tue of month at 7.00pm.*
VIEWING: *Day of sale from 3.00pm.*
REFRESHMENTS: *Own café.*
PARKING: *Own car park.*
STORAGE: *Yes*
TRANSPORTATION: *Yes*
SHIPPING: *No*

PAMELA & BARRY AUCTIONS

The Village Hall. Tel: (0727) 861180

350-400 lots. This popular fortnightly auction includes mostly antiques, collectables and small items. There are very few items of large furniture here, and certainly no modern or reproduction. A typical sale might include jewellery of all types, silver and silver plate, china (both domestic and ornamental), porcelain, copper, brass, linen, postcards, books, dolls, paintings, prints and all types of collectors' items. In the latter category there are usually a number of 1950s toys, model railway stock, military medals and the like. A catalogue is always available on the sale day. Payment can be made and the goods removed while the sale is in progress.

Tring

BUYER'S PREMIUM: *5%*
SALES: *General: fortnightly on Sat at 10.00am. Special antiques: monthly on third or fourth Fri of month at 11.00am.*
VIEWING: *General: 2.00pm-6.00pm. Special antiques: day prior 2.00pm-8.30pm.*
REFRESHMENTS: *Own café.*
PARKING: *Own car park.*
STORAGE: *Yes*
TRANSPORTATION: *Yes*
SHIPPING: *Yes*

BROWN & MERRY

Tring Market Auctions, Brook Street. Tel: (044282) 6446

1,500-1,600 lots. The sale is on a Saturday, so it is often packed with couples searching for bargains, or with people who are 'just looking' and out to enjoy the excitement of an auction. Good quality furniture, paintings, china, porcelain, gardening equipment, garden plants and other items are sold. The general sale begins at 10.00am and offers around 1,000 lots of antique furniture, restoration pieces, modern furniture, gardening equipment, general household effects and miscellaneous items. At 11.00am, while this sale is still going on, the sale of antiques and better quality items begins in another part of the complex. A small part of the premises is used on Mondays for livestock sales, which adds to the atmosphere of this friendly and informal, but efficient, auction house.

Once a month, on either the third or fourth Friday, there are special sales of antiques, with quality furniture, porcelain, pottery, silver and silver plate, paintings and prints.

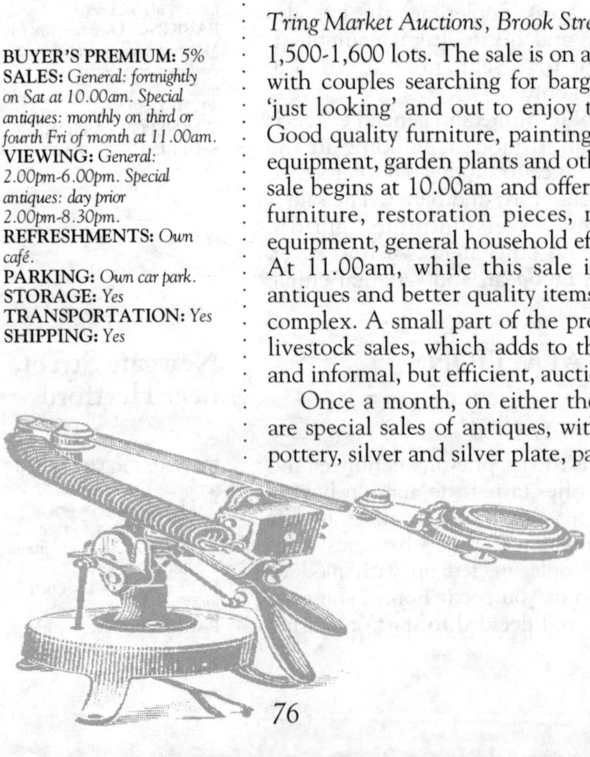

HUMBERSIDE

DICKINSON, DAVY & MARKHAM

Brigg

The Old Congregational Church, Wrawby St. Tel: (0652) 53666

700 lots. This is one of the largest auction houses in the East Midlands. The fortnightly Saturday sale is of good quality furniture, and will include pine, Victoriana, shipping furniture (which usually means 1930s and 1940s furniture), household effects of all kinds, bric-à-brac, carpets and so on. There is also a catalogued monthly sale of antiques and fine art, which in the past has included Royal Doulton tea and dinner services, Royal Worcester, Victorian inkwells, wine decanters, silver and gold pocket watches, sapphire and diamond cluster rings, a George III one-third guinea from 1808, a collection of 11 various albums of Wills cigarette cards, a quantity of damask table cloths, teddy bears, Armand Marseille bisque head dolls, sporting guns, rugs and carpets, clocks and barometers, and furniture — all of the quality you would expect in a catalogued sale.

The system of bidding at this saleroom involves 'buyer's numbers': would-be bidders should register with the auctioneer, who will give them a numbered card. This must be shown to the auctioneer at the completion of each successful bid. The same firm also holds general auctions at Alford, Lincolnshire.

BUYER'S PREMIUM: *5%*
SALES: *General: fortnightly on Sat at 10.00am. Antiques and fine art: every six weeks on Wed at 10.00am.*
VIEWING: *Day prior 2.00pm-7.00pm, morning of sale from 8.30am.*
REFRESHMENTS: *Own café.*
PARKING: *Own car park.*
STORAGE: *Yes*
TRANSPORTATION: *Yes*
SHIPPING: *Yes*

G A DEE & ATKINSON

Great Driffield

The Exchange, Exchange Street. Tel: (0377) 43152

350-900 lots. Driffield is a busy, attractive town on the edge of the Wolds, with a population of under ten thousand which increases noticeably on sale days. The Exchange is a large old building, close to the town's only set of traffic lights. The saleroom stands apart from the main building across a small courtyard. General household sales are held about twice a month on a Saturday, and include a wide variety of practical furniture, bric-à-brac, shipping lots, electrical and sundry items, averaging about 350 lots.

Every two months on a Friday and Monday G A Dee & Atkinson hold their widely advertised two-day sale of antiques and fine art, which is interesting for experts and non-experts alike (average 900 lots). On the Friday the lots include furniture, brass, books, albums, ceramics, carpets and rugs, collectors' items, guns, prints, paintings and so on. The Monday sale concentrates mainly on plated items, silver and jewellery.

BUYER'S PREMIUM: *10%*
SALES: *General: fortnightly on Sat at 9.30am. Antiques: every two months on Fri and Mon at 10.30am.*
VIEWING: *General: Thu prior 10.00am-7.00pm, Fri prior 10.00am-4.00pm. Antiques: Wed prior 10.00am-7.00pm, Thu prior 10.00am-4.00pm.*
REFRESHMENTS: *None available on the premises.*
PARKING: *Ample parking near by.*
STORAGE: *Yes*
TRANSPORTATION: *Yes*
SHIPPING: *Yes*

Grimsby

BUYER'S PREMIUM: *7½%*
SALES: *General: weekly on Wed at 9.15am. Antiques and collector's: occasional on Sat at 10.30am.*
VIEWING: *General: day prior 2.30pm-7.00pm. Antiques and collector's: day of sale from 9.00am.*
REFRESHMENTS: *None available on the premises.*
PARKING: *Public car park opposite.*
STORAGE: *No*
TRANSPORTATION: *Local deliveries can be arranged.*
SHIPPING: *No*

JACKSON GREEN & PRESTON

Auction Centre, 1a New Cartergate. Tel: (0472) 355195

400-500 lots. Jackson Green & Preston have been auctioneers since 1920. The sales have a relaxed and friendly atmosphere, and some of those attending seem to have come for the entertainment as well as to buy. The weekly general sale of household furniture and effects is divided into morning and afternoon sessions, with 'smalls' sold in the morning and furniture in the afternoon, starting at 2.00pm. Private vendors can bring in goods for the sale on Thursday and Friday. Typical past lots have included superb lounge suites (some apparently unused), 1930s bedroom suites, wardrobes, bureaux, pine chests of drawers, Edwardian plant stands, pedestal brass jardinières, wall plaques, blue and white ware, various Victorian and collector's items, and a range of cookers, washing machines and fridges. Light fittings, adaptors, switches and other electrical items have appeared, thanks to loss adjusters, as have a quantity of cuddly toys, toy cars, novelties and fun hats.

In addition to the general sale, there are occasional special antiques and collectors' sales, which contain many lots kept back from the general sale because their quality merits special attention.

Laxton, near Howden

BUYER'S PREMIUM: *Nil*
SALES: *Every six to eight weeks on Sat at 11.00am.*
VIEWING: *Day of sale from 9.00am.*
REFRESHMENTS: *Own café.*
PARKING: *Ample parking near by.*
STORAGE: *Yes*
TRANSPORTATION: *Yes*
SHIPPING: *Yes*

ROBIN SCREETON

The Victory Hall. Tel: (0430) 431201

400-500 lots. The general sales take place every six to eight weeks, and are much looked forward to. The area around the quiet and picturesque village has plenty of 'Robin Screeton Sale' signposts to direct you to the village hall, which is hired especially for the auction. An excellent array of home-made refreshments is provided, and many people come from nearby villages to meet friends, as well as to bid. There is usually a fine selection of lots crowded into the hall: antiques, Victoriana, silver, brass, general household furniture and effects, including interesting period pieces from private house clearances. Robin Screeton is also known for agricultural sales and on-site auctions, which take place periodically throughout the year. He established the firm over 25 years ago, and his son Ian now takes responsibility for the general sales.

Scunthorpe

BUYER'S PREMIUM: *5%*
SALES: *Weekly on Thu at*

CANTER & FRANCIS

8 Doncaster Road. Tel: (0724) 858855

300-500 lots. In a good week at Canter & Francis you will find everything needed to set up a home, including beds, bedding, furniture of all sorts and values, cups, mugs and plates, electrical goods, rugs, carpets, and so on — and even DIY equipment. There is a good family feeling at the sale. Jokes are exchanged between the crowd and the auctioneer, and proceedings go forward entertainingly, in an atmosphere that would put the most timid bidder at ease. The sale begins with smaller table items such as jewellery, china, glass, books, lamps and other electrical equipment. The main furniture sale begins at around 1.00pm to 1.30pm and finishes at around 3.30pm.

Twice a year in the spring and autumn, Canter & Francis hold special antiques and fine art sales. These take the place of the normal weekly sale, and the sales and viewing times are the same.

12.00 noon (includes twice-yearly antiques and fine art sale).
VIEWING: *Day prior 2.00pm-4.30pm and 7.00pm-9.00pm.*
REFRESHMENTS: *None available on the premises.*
PARKING: *Own car park.*
STORAGE: *No*
TRANSPORTATION: *Yes*
SHIPPING: *Yes*

A E DOWSE & SON

Scunthorpe

89 Mary Street. Tel: (0724) 842569/842039

500-600 lots. Two different salerooms are used for the three sales. The monthly Wednesday sale is of general household furniture and effects, and takes place at St Mark's Church Hall, Ashby Road, Scunthorpe. Saturday sales are held at the Forresters Hall, High Street, Barrow upon Humber. The monthly Saturday sale includes antique furniture, pictures, jewellery, silver, brass, copper, porcelain, glass and collector's items.

The quarterly Saturday antiques and fine art sale includes similar items, but they are usually of higher value and quality. The Wednesday general sales have furniture of all types, including bedroom, dining and lounge suites, electrical goods, china (ornamental and domestic), boxes of bric-à-brac (always worth a rummage for the good items beneath the books, pots and pans), and a variety of other goods. There are usually bargains to be had.

BUYER'S PREMIUM: *12%*
SALES: *General: monthly on Wed at 2.00pm. Antiques: monthly on Sat at 11.30am. Antiques and fine art: quarterly on Sat at 12.00 noon.*
VIEWING: *General: day of sale from 12.00 noon. Monthly antiques: day prior 2.30pm-7.00pm, morning of sale from 9.30am. Quarterly antiques and fine art: day prior from 2.30pm-7.00pm and day of sale from 9.30am-12.00 noon.*
REFRESHMENTS: *Own café.*
PARKING: *Own car park.*
STORAGE: *Yes*
TRANSPORTATION: *Yes*
SHIPPING: *Yes*

ISLE OF MAN

CHRYSTALS AUCTIONS

Ramsey

Bowring Road. Tel: (0624) 812236

350-450 lots. Ramsey is the second largest town on the Isle of Man, and although it is much quieter than Douglas, it is a popular resort. In May and November/December every year Chrystals hold special antiques auctions in Ramsey.

Chrystals also hold general auctions, which alternate weekly between the Bowring Road saleroom in Ramsey and the Majestic Hotel in Douglas. The general auctions are popular with the islanders, and many bidders from the mainland are also attracted to them.

BUYER'S PREMIUM: *Nil*
SALES: *General: alternating weekly between Ramsey on Fri at 10.00am and Douglas on Sat at 10.00am.*
VIEWING: *Day prior 1.00pm-6.00pm.*
REFRESHMENTS: *None available on the premises.*
PARKING: *Own car park.*
STORAGE: *Yes*
TRANSPORTATION: *Yes*
SHIPPING: *Yes*

ISLE OF WIGHT

Ryde

WAYS

Garfield Road. Tel: (0983) 62255

BUYER'S PREMIUM: *Nil*
SALES: *Every five weeks on Thu at 10.30am.*
VIEWING: *Day prior from 10.00am-6.00pm.*
REFRESHMENTS: *Own café.*
PARKING: *Own car park.*
STORAGE: *Yes*
TRANSPORTATION: *Yes*
SHIPPING: *Yes*

500-700 lots. Having been established as long ago as 1815, Ways can probably boast that they are the oldest auctioneers on the Isle of Wight. Their saleroom, with its sign swinging prominently outside, was once an old Victorian coach house with three stables. The auctions are mainly of 'antique and modern' furnishings, although they also include plenty of smaller lots such as silver and silver plate, jewellery, china, and objets d'art, all of which make good holiday souvenirs. There may also be some tempting larger items of furniture. Ways' auctions are packed with good-quality items, and they are well-attended by buyers who regularly make the journey over from the mainland.

Shanklin

WATSON, BULL & PORTER (NATIONWIDE ANGLIA)

79 Regent Street. Tel: (0983) 863441

BUYER'S PREMIUM: *10%*
SALES: *Antiques: monthly on Tue at 11.00am. General: monthly on Wed at 11.00am.*
VIEWING: *Day prior, 10.00am-4.00pm, 5.30pm-7.30pm.*
REFRESHMENTS: *None available on the premises.*
PARKING: *None on the premises.*
STORAGE: *Yes*
TRANSPORTATION: *Yes*
SHIPPING: *Yes*

300-400 lots. Watson, Bull & Porter occupy a saleroom in the town centre, close to the railway station. Their monthly auctions have proved extremely popular, perhaps because the auctioneers are very selective in the quality of the lots that they sell. Here there is also a wide range of items available, from antique to modern. There are salerooms on two floors; the first-floor saleroom is the setting for the Tuesday sale of antiques, while the ground-floor room tends to be used on Wednesdays for the general sale of modern household furniture, china, brass, and electrical goods.

KENT

Ashford

HOBBS PARKER

Romney House, Ashford Market, Elwick Road. Tel: (0233) 622222

BUYER'S PREMIUM: *Nil*
SALES: *Antiques: eight times per year on Thu at 10.00am (times vary): Household furniture: monthly on Wed at 12.00 noon: Horses and*

400-500 lots. Hobbs Parker, established in 1850, are based in the Ashford Market complex, which is the largest in the south-east — stock sales are held every Tuesday and Wednesday, and seasonally on Thursday and Friday. There are 20 sales a year, which means that the auctioneers have a full calendar. In addition to their general auctions, Hobbs Parker hold a variety of other sales on a regular basis. These may be of livestock, cars and commercial vehicles, or farm machinery. Every month there are sales of household furniture and effects, and eight times a year there are more up-market auctions of antiques and fine art. The latter take place at Amos Hall, Ashford Market, and include selected furniture, ceramics, glass, silver and jewellery, among other things.

A more unusual note is struck by the sales of horses, ponies, saddlery and boxes, which are usually well attended. Held in March, May, July, August and November, these sales usually include 50 to 70 horses, as well as trailers, lorries, and about 1,700 lots of saddlery, harnesses and riding outfits.

saddlery: Mar, May, Jul, Aug and Nov, Thu at 10.00am. General (livestock, farm equipment etc.): Tue at 10.15am, Wed, at 10.30am, other days 10.00am.
VIEWING: *Day of sale only.*
REFRESHMENTS: Own café.
PARKING: *Own car park.*
STORAGE: Yes
TRANSPORTATION: Yes
SHIPPING: Yes

GA PROPERTY SERVICES

The Auction Galleries, 40 Station Road West.
Tel: (0227) 763337

400-500 lots. This saleroom is conveniently situated only about 100 yards away from Canterbury West railway station. On the first Saturday of each month there are well-supported sales of Victorian, Edwardian and quality modern household furniture and effects. Specialist antiques auctions are held every second month on Tuesday, and include antique furniture, pictures, ceramics, silver, jewellery, books, bygones and collectors' items, clocks, carpets and rugs.

Canterbury

BUYER'S PREMIUM: 5%
SALES: *General sales: first Sat of the month at 10.00am; antiques and collectors' sales: every second month on Tue at 10.30am.*
VIEWING: *General sales: Fri prior 4.00pm-8.00pm; antiques and collectors' sales: Mon prior 10.00am-7.00pm.*
REFRESHMENTS: *None available on the premises.*
PARKING: *Public car park opposite.*
STORAGE: Yes
TRANSPORTATION: Yes
SHIPPING: Yes

HERNE BAY AUCTIONS

Hanover Square, William Street. Tel: (0277) 369448

400-600 lots. William Street is one of the principal thoroughfares in Herne Bay, and near its south end lies the 16-acre Memorial Park, with boating lake, bowling green, tennis courts and cricket ground. Herne Bay Auctions hold regular sales of antiques and collectables, at which good quality items of furniture, paintings, china and so on are regularly sold. However, the sales here are best known for their gold and silver jewellery sections, which are conducted by the proprietor, Mrs Beryl Cook (no relation of the famous artist with the same name). Visitors to the town obviously swell numbers in the saleroom during summer months, but it is usually quite full at other times of the year, too. Some buyers regularly come over to these sales from the Continent.

Herne Bay

BUYER'S PREMIUM: 6%
SALES: *Weekly (except following Bank Holidays) on Wed at 11.00am.*
VIEWING: *Day prior, 4.00pm-6.00pm, and morning of sale from 9.00am.*
REFRESHMENTS: *Own café.*
PARKING: *None available on the premises.*
STORAGE: Yes
TRANSPORTATION: Yes
SHIPPING: Yes

Lyminge

BUYER'S PREMIUM: *Nil*
SALES: *General sales: Sun at 9.30am (Barham on Sat at 9.30am); plant sales: Sat at 11.00am.*
VIEWING: *Day prior, 1.00pm-6.00pm (all sales).*
REFRESHMENTS: *Own café at each location.*
PARKING: *Available on the premises.*
STORAGE: *Yes*
TRANSPORTATION: *Yes*
SHIPPING: *Yes*

VALLEY AUCTIONS

Claygate, Brady Road. Tel: (0303) 862134

400-500 lots. 'Have gavel will travel' is the motto of Mr Edwin Hall, who over the past 15 years has regularly conducted auctions at each of three locations in the area. Six or eight times a year he holds auctions at Lyminge Village Hall; auctions also take place under his aegis at the village halls in Barham and Denton.

All the sales contain a broad mixture of general household furniture and effects, including antiques and bric-à-brac, and they are held on Sundays (unless the venue is Barham, where they are held on Saturdays). The atmosphere at these auctions is friendly, and they are often attended by entire families. In March, May, June and October, Mr Hall also holds auctions of 1,000 lots of plants, shrubs, bedding plants and bulbs (depending on the season) at Lyminge Village Hall.

Maidstone

BUYER'S PREMIUM: *Nil*
SALES: Weekly on Thu at 10.00am.
VIEWING: Day of sale from 8.00am.
REFRESHMENTS: *Café on premises.*
PARKING: *Own car park.*
STORAGE: *Yes*
TRANSPORTATION: *Yes*
SHIPPING: *Yes*

THE AGRICULTURAL HALL

Maidstone Market, Barker Road. Tel: (0622) 758705

1,500-2,000 lots. Every Thursday there are auctions here, held on alternate weeks by two companies, P S Williams & Co and B J Norris. Both companies are alike in that they hold sales of antique and modern furniture and effects, together with china, glass, silver, books, pictures and so on.

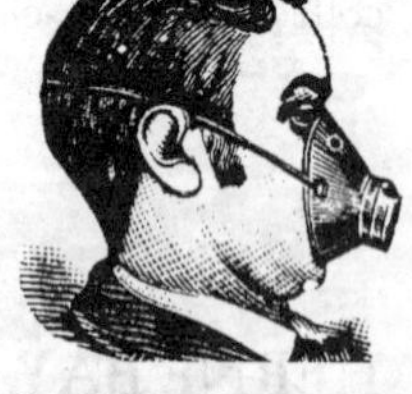

Margate

BUYER'S PREMIUM: 5%
SALES: *Monthly on Thu at 10.00am.*
VIEWING: *Day prior 7.00am-7.00pm.*
REFRESHEMENTS: *Café on the premises.*
PARKING: *Own car park.*
STORAGE: *Yes*
TRANSPORTATION: *Yes*
SHIPPING: *Yes*

GRANGE AUCTIONS LTD.

Salmestone Grange, Nash Road. Tel: (0843) 226909

150-200 lots. This is a small auction, often completed in less than a couple of hours. The specially selected lots are valued at around £30 each and upwards, and anyone wishing to buy a piece of furniture, some jewellery or china will find the sales here a good hunting-ground. The 'paddle' or 'number' bidding system is followed here. This means that those interested in bidding are required to register at the office when they arrive at the saleroom. In return, they are given a number, which must be held up and shown to the auctioneer after every successful bid.

The saleroom is part of a beautiful 13th-century farm building with magnificent stained-glass Art Nouveau windows, which are in themselves well worth a visit. Art and craft exhibitions are held in this building regularly, and once a month on a Sunday there is also an antiques and craft fair.

COUNTY GROUP

102 High Street. Tel: (05806) 2083

400-500 lots. Tenterden is an attractive town with many old buildings and an unusually wide main street. The saleroom is opposite the war memorial in the High Street. County Group were first established in 1830, and apart from auctions they also hold livestock sales at Maidstone and Rye, and what are known as 'on farm' dispersal sales of fruit and other goods. The auctions at Tenterden are friendly and comprehensive, and they are supervised by Mrs Pauline Chalk, who has more than 40 years' experience of the antiques market. Fine art, antique furniture, pottery and porcelain, glass, silver, jewellery, and clocks and watches appear in these sales regularly.

Tenterden

BUYER'S PREMIUM: *Nil*
SALES: *Monthly on Thu at 9.30am (4.30pm in Mar, Jun, Sep and Dec).*
VIEWING: *Tue prior 9.30am-4.00pm (also 2.30pm on day of sale when sales begin at 4.30pm).*
REFRESHMENTS: *None available on the premises.*
PARKING: *None on the premises.*
STORAGE: *Yes*
TRANSPORTATION: *Yes*
SHIPPING: *Yes*

BRACKETTS

27 High Street. Tel: (0892)) 33733

300-400 lots. This saleroom is situated just behind Tunbridge Wells' famous colonnaded street, the Pantiles, which is a centre for antiques shops. Bracketts' weekly sales of fine art and general household furniture and effects are in themselves a tourist attraction. The modern, glass-roofed saleroom is often full of foreign tourists who come here to browse. Coachloads of pensioners have been known to unload outside the saleroom on sale days ... and why not? A visit to an auction can make a day trip to this busy old spa town a memorable one. An abundance of china, glass, silver and porcelain, pictures, jewellery, furniture and bric-à-brac is up for bidding, as well as 'outside effects', such as lawn mowers, which are auctioned at the end of the sale. There should be something to interest everyone here, and the auctioneer's gavel comes down on bids ranging from one pound to thousands. Once every two months on average, the auction is arranged into specialist categories of antiques and collectables.

Tunbridge Wells

BUYER'S PREMIUM: *Nil*
SALES: *Weekly on Fri at 10.00am.*
VIEWING: *Day prior 9.00am-4.30pm. Day of sale from 9.00am.*
REFRESHMENTS: *None available on the premises.*
PARKING: *Own car park.*
STORAGE: *Yes*
TRANSPORTATION: *Yes*
SHIPPING: *Yes*

WESTGATE AUCTIONS

70 St Mildreds Road. Tel: (0843) 31376

300-400 lots. Westgate auctions can be found directly behind the main post office, which is one of Westgate on Sea's best landmarks. Husband and wife Colin and Shahla Langston began these auctions over 10 years ago, and they have increased in popularity ever since. The saleroom is divided into two parts and is usually packed with bidders, particularly during summer. Bidding usually begins in the part of the room

Westgate on Sea

BUYER'S PREMIUM: *Nil*
SALES: *Every two or three weeks, on Sat at 10.00am.*
VIEWING: *Day prior 9.30am-5.00pm, and morning of sale.*
REFRESHMENTS: *Own café.*

PARKING: *None available on the premises.*
STORAGE: *Yes*
TRANSPORTATION: *Yes*
SHIPPING: *Yes*

that contains inexpensive items. Here you can often find electrical gadgets, including kitchen equipment such as cookers and fridges. The other part of the saleroom is given over to good quality furniture and antiques. It is the jewellery, especially items of gold and silver, that appears to attract the most attention, however.

LANCASHIRE

Accrington

ACCRINGTON AUCTIONS

St James House, St James Street. Tel: (0254) 381739

BUYER'S PREMIUM: *Nil*
SALES: *Weekly on Thu at 5.30pm.*
VIEWING: *Day of sale from 10.00am.*
REFRESHMENTS: *Own café.*
PARKING: *Own car park.*
STORAGE: *Yes*
TRANSPORTATION: *Yes*
SHIPPING: *Yes*

500-600 lots. One of the delights of attending an auction you've never been to before is that you never know what sort of building to expect (or indeed whether there will be any building at all). Accrington Auctions take place in an ex-Salvation Army church. The weekly Thursday evening sale attracts a great deal of attention from all over the area, and includes not only the general run-of-the-mill goods which appear in most sales, but also unexpected items of antique furniture, china, silver and so on. This is an evening sale with plenty of regular visitors. For many of them the sale is a meeting place as much as a place to browse and bid.

Blackburn

FRANK CHARLES & CO

The Salerooms, Islington. Tel: (0254) 54133

BUYER'S PREMIUM: *Nil*
SALES: *Weekly on Wed at 10.30am and 1.30pm.*
VIEWING: *Day prior 1.30pm-5.00pm, morning of sale from 9.00am.*
REFRESHMENTS: *Van selling snacks.*
PARKING: *Own car park.*
STORAGE: *Yes*
TRANSPORTATION: *Yes*
SHIPPING: *No*

600-700 lots. Blackburn used to be the world centre of cotton weaving, and its Lewis Textile Museum traces the development of the spinning and weaving industry. The saleroom, a newish single-storey building, is off Canterbury Street near the centre of the town. The sales are of general household furniture and effects of all ages and periods, and may include antiques. There are two separate sessions. The morning sale, beginning at 10.30am, is for the lesser quality goods. It starts with boxes of miscellaneous bric-à-brac such as china, books, pots and pans, and continues with electrical goods and then furniture. The afternoon auction, beginning at 1.30pm, has similar lots but of higher quality. Items like china are more carefully displayed in this part of the sale, and may be set out on trays or sold as individual pieces.

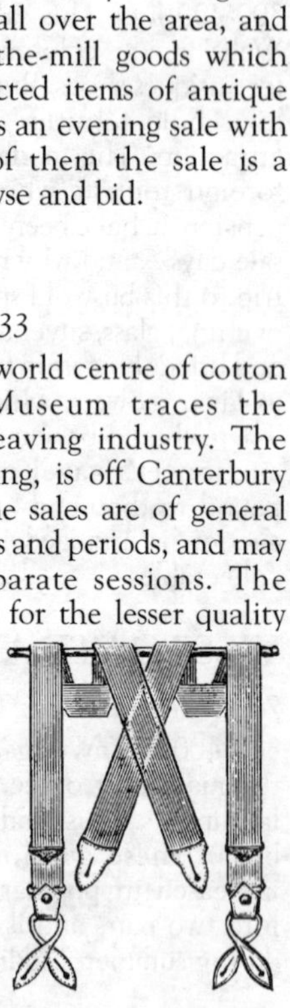

W CHARLES FORD AUCTIONS

Blackpool

Royal Oak Building, Waterloo Road. Tel: (0253) 45458

200-300 lots. The saleroom is close to the South Shore railway station and during the summer, particularly on wet days, wise holidaymakers can be found sitting in the saleroom, enjoying the proceedings as part of a day out. The informality of the sale often tempts people to bid who might otherwise be too shy. The lots include general household furniture and run-of-the-mill miscellaneous items, but it is always worth having a look for bargains. Attractive pieces of antique furniture can be found, as can good pieces of china — perhaps the odd Royal Doulton cup and saucer or even complete tea and dinner sets. It is always exciting to rummage through the bottom of a box of miscellaneous kitchen utensils and find something of value or interest.

BUYER'S PREMIUM: *Nil*
SALES: *Weekly on Thu at 10.30am.*
VIEWING: *Day prior 9.00am-5.00pm.*
REFRESHMENTS: *None available on the premises.*
PARKING: *Ample parking near by.*
STORAGE: *Yes*
TRANSPORTATION: *Yes*
SHIPPING: *No*

E GORDON ROUND FSVA

Blackpool

4 Bloomfield Road. Tel: (0253) 43588

300-400 lots. The auction was established over 35 years ago by Mr E Gordon Round, who is still actively involved in the sales but is now assisted by his son Stephen. The saleroom is near Blackpool's football ground and within easy walking distance of the Golden Mile, but it never gets too full, even in the peak summer months. There are some excellent buys to be found at most of the sales. The lots are clean and well presented, and there is ample space for viewing. An old-fashioned charm pervades the proceedings, with selling conducted at a not-too-hectic pace.

The sale is held every three or four weeks on average, and is alternately devoted to furniture and small items. The sale of household furniture and effects includes some better quality modern furniture, but on the whole the emphasis is on 'shipping furniture' and antiques, and the better bargains are in these categories. The separate sales for smaller goods include items such as china, pottery, glass, brass, silver and silver plate, crockery, collectables and so on. These sales have a good reputation.

BUYER'S PREMIUM: *10%*
SALES: *Every three to four weeks on Thu at 1.30pm.*
VIEWING: *Day prior 10.00am-4.00pm.*
REFRESHMENTS: *None available on the premises.*
PARKING: *Bloomfield Road public car park.*
STORAGE: *Yes*
TRANSPORTATION: *Yes*
SHIPPING: *Yes*

WATERHOUSES

Blackpool

Exchange Auction Rooms, Caunce Street. Tel: (0253) 22919

300-400 lots. This weekly sale is very popular with summer visitors. Some are so pleased with their buys that they regularly spend more in carriage charges to get an article home than it cost to buy, which shows the excellent bargains to be had. This

BUYER'S PREMIUM: *Nil*
SALES: *Weekly on Wed at 10.30am.*
VIEWING: *Every weekday from 9.00am-5.30pm.*

REFRESHMENTS: *None available on the premises.*
PARKING: *Ample parking near by.*
STORAGE: *Yes*
TRANSPORTATION: *Yes*
SHIPPING: *Yes*

sale is one of the longest-established in the area, and was started over 60 years ago by the father of the present proprietors, Lindsey Adcock and her husband Robert.

The saleroom is near the Winter Gardens, and the public are invited to pop in for viewing any day of the week from 9.00am to 5.30pm. The nearer it is to sale day, the greater the number of lots there will be on show. In among the general household equipment, furniture, electrical goods, gardening equipment and so on, there are often goods which are being auctioned off on the instructions of bailiffs or liquidators.

Cleveleys

SMYTHE SON & WALKER

174 Victoria Road West. Tel: (0253) 852184

BUYER'S PREMIUM: *Nil*
SALES: *General: weekly on Tue at 10.00am. Antiques: every six weeks on Wed at 11.00am.*
VIEWING: *General: day prior 8.30am-5.00pm. Antiques: Sat, Mon and Tue prior 10.00am-5.00pm, morning of sale.*
REFRESHMENTS: *None available on the premises.*
PARKING: *Ample parking near by.*
STORAGE: *Yes*
TRANSPORTATION: *Yes*
SHIPPING: *Yes*

300-400 lots. This independently run saleroom was established over 70 years ago, and members of the Smythe family are still involved. The saleroom is in the centre of Cleveleys, which is about five miles north of Blackpool and has its own promenade and sandy beach. The premises are open every day of the week for viewing, but the best time to see the lots set out for the weekly Tuesday sale will be Monday.

This sale offers excellent buys in every conceivable category of furniture, general household effects, kitchen utensils, china, ornaments, jewellery, books, bric-à-brac and so on. Every six weeks on a Wednesday there are special sales of antiques and fine art. These also contain excellent bargains, although the prices will naturally be higher because the lots have been chosen for their quality. They can be viewed during the Tuesday sale in a different room. Periodically throughout the year Smythe Son & Walker also carry out on-site auctions which are worth an enquiry. Past sales have included the entire contents of hotels and amusement arcades.

Colne

LANCASTRIAN P P (AUCTIONS)

Princess House, Linden Road. Tel: (0282) 864228

BUYER'S PREMIUM: *Nil*
SALES: *Monthly on Wed at 6.30pm.*
VIEWING: *Day of sale 10.00am-4.30pm.*
REFRESHMENTS: *None available on the premises.*
PARKING: *Own car park.*
STORAGE: *Yes*
TRANSPORTATION: *Yes*
SHIPPING: *Yes*

200-250 lots. Colne is a market town close to the Yorkshire border. The saleroom is a large Victorian building, just a little out from the centre of the main shopping area. There are several small villages near by, and it is from these as well as from houses in the town that the majority of the lots come. As might be imagined, the lots vary considerably in age and quality. Among the nondescript everyday items of furniture, china, ornaments and so on you may well find much better pieces. There is no order of sale. Perhaps 20 or 30 items might be sold from the table to begin with. Then small items and bric-à-brac, which are laid out on the floor, will be auctioned.

The auctioneer has to work quite hard on occasions to get a bid, so you may find some bargains if you are prepared to rummage through the lots.

JOHN E PINDER & SON

Grimsargh

Grimsargh Village Hall. Tel: (0772) 782282

400-500 lots. Grimsargh is an attractive, quiet village which becomes much busier when the sale takes over the village hall. The sale occurs every two to three months, and has an excellent reputation — it is ideal for those looking for something with that extra bit of quality at an affordable price. Described as a sale of antiques and furniture, it also includes an array of Victorian and later ornamental items, collectables, ceramics (vases, jugs, teapots and so on), glass (including cut and moulded glass), silver and plate, brass and pictures of all sorts.

BUYER'S PREMIUM: *Nil*
SALES: *Every two to three months on Thu at 10.00am.*
VIEWING: *Day prior 10.00am-7.00pm.*
REFRESHMENTS: *Own café.*
PARKING: *Own car park.*
STORAGE: *No*
TRANSPORTATION: *Yes*
SHIPPING: *Yes*

WARREN & WIGNALL LTD

Leyland, near Preston

The Mill, Earnshaw Bridge, Leyland Lane.
Tel: (0772) 451430 and 435252

800-900 lots. The saleroom is about a mile from the town centre, at the junction of Golden Hill and Leyland Lane. It is an old mill which has been pebble-dashed and painted cream. Mr Philip Warren, who started the firm towards the end of the 1960s, now shares the running of this busy and successful weekly auction with his son Peter.

Every third week the sale is devoted to antiques and collectors' items. In other weeks this is a sale of general household furniture and effects, including silver, china, jewellery and so on. The antiques sales have gained a particularly good reputation, and many regular buyers travel a long way to attend. The sales are conducted at a fast pace, with two auctioneers doing about an hour each at the rostrum. In the general sale lots are sold at roughly 150 per hour. The antiques sale is a little slower, and you can usually count on around 120 lots per hour.

BUYER'S PREMIUM: *General: nil. Antiques sale: 5%*
SALES: *Weekly on Wed at 10.00am (includes antiques and collectors' sale every third week).*
VIEWING: *Day prior 9.00am-7.00pm.*
REFRESHMENTS: *Van selling snacks.*
PARKING: *Own car park.*
STORAGE: *No*
TRANSPORTATION: *Yes*
SHIPPING: *Yes*

HENRY HOLDEN & SON

Longridge

Central Salerooms, Towneley Road. Tel: (0772) 783274

400-500 lots. Henry Holden & Son have recently celebrated their centenary year, and the company is still owned and run by members of the Holden family. The sale is a typical Lancashire rural auction — a fortnightly pilgrimage for people from outlying areas, who use it not only to look for bargains,

BUYER'S PREMIUM: *Nil*
SALES: *Fortnightly on Sat at 10.00am.*
VIEWING: *Day prior 10.00am-8.00pm.*
REFRESHMENTS: *None available on the premises.*

PARKING: *Ample parking near by.*
STORAGE: *No*
TRANSPORTATION: *Yes*
SHIPPING: *No*

but also as a meeting place for a chat with old friends. As a consequence the sale is friendly and informal, but often noisy. Among the general household furniture and effects will be pieces of good quality china, jewellery, mirrors, clocks, antiques and very often works of art. There is no break for lunch, but the sale is divided roughly into two parts. The early part is for more run-of-the-mill items such as household utensils, gardening tools and plainer furniture, and the second part (from about 1.00pm onwards) for better quality lots.

Newton

BUYER'S PREMIUM: *Nil*
SALES: *About monthly on Wed at 11.00am, but check with auctioneers.*
VIEWING: *Day of sale from 10.00am.*
REFRESHMENTS: *Own café.*
PARKING: *Ample parking near by.*
STORAGE: *No*
TRANSPORTATION: *Yes*
SHIPPING: *No*

C SILVERWOOD

Newton Village Hall. Tel: (02006) 652

400-450 lots. Newton is within easy reach of the Forest of Bowland, an extensive area of fells and moors which has been designated an Area of Outstanding Natural Beauty. It is wise to check that the sale is taking place before travelling any distance, particularly in winter months when the weather often makes some of the smaller roads impassable. The sale was started by the father of the present proprietor, who has himself been in the firm since 1952, and it is well advertised in magazines and local newspapers. This is a quaint, often eccentric village auction, which people from nearby villages and towns look forward to with some delight. The range of lots varies considerably, since most items are the product of house clearances, or in many cases outhouse clearances.

Ormskirk

BUYER'S PREMIUM: *Nil*
SALES: *Fortnightly on Tue at 10.30am.*
VIEWING: *Day prior 2.00pm-7.00pm.*
REFRESHMENTS: *None available on the premises.*
PARKING: *Derby Street West car park (limited to two hours).*
STORAGE: *Yes*
TRANSPORTATION: *Yes*
SHIPPING: *Yes*

EDWARD ABBOTT FRICS

The Saleroom, 22 Church Street. Tel: (0695) 579104

400-600 lots. The saleroom has a large yellow board outside and is in the centre of the town, 100 yards or so from the main Derby Street West car park. The sale was established in the 1930s and is now under the proprietorship of Edward Abbott, who describes himself as a 'one-man band' — an accurate description of the way he oversees the goods arriving, values them and conducts the sale.

This is a friendly sale attended regularly by many local people, which helps create an informal atmosphere. Lots range from modern to good quality antiques, and there are usually some surprising items. The selling starts with all types of outside effects, including garden furniture and tools. All types of furniture are sold next, and the sale usually finishes with the better quality small items. Sales are often conducted for the Sheriff's Office, County Courts and liquidators.

MCKENNAS

The Village Hall. Tel: (0200) 22695

250-550 lots. Pendleton is a picturesque little village off the A59, less than a mile from Clitheroe. It makes an ideal setting for this country auction, which takes place in the village hall, next to the pub. The auction house is an independent family concern which was originally established in the 1800s.

The well-attended sales take place monthly and go under the title of 'Antique and Later Furniture and Effects'. Selling starts with 'smalls' then goes on to pictures, clocks, prints and finally furniture.

About every three months the auction becomes a catalogued sale of better quality items which have been kept back for the occasion. These sales contain all types of antiques and collectors' items, with perhaps an emphasis on pictures and paintings (an area in which the company has a growing reputation). Occasionally, but at no set intervals, there are Saturday sales of general household furniture and effects.

Pendleton

BUYER'S PREMIUM: *Nil*
SALES: *Monthly on Thu at 10.00am (includes catalogued sale about every six weeks). Occasionally also Sat at 10.00am.*
VIEWING: *Day prior 10.00am-8.00pm (Sat sales day of sale from 9.00am).*
REFRESHMENTS: *Own café.*
PARKING: *Own car park.*
STORAGE: *Yes*
TRANSPORTATION: *Yes*
SHIPPING: *Yes*

SMITH HODGKINSON MCGINTY

The Auction Centre, Preston Road. Tel: (02572) 61055

1,000-1,200 lots. This independently run sale is famous among the bargain-hunters of central Lancashire. It is held once a week on a Thursday. The sale is packed with goods, and it is hard to see how the proprietors cope with so many lots on a weekly basis. The 1.00pm sale is mainly of lesser quality items and bric-à-brac, including as many as 400 to 500 lots of china, ornaments, toys and games, pots and pans, and various pieces of household equipment such as step ladders, rubbish bins and electrical goods. The 4.30pm sale includes general furniture from antique through to modern, and around 450 lots of better quality china, porcelain, silver, brass and jewellery.

Every four weeks on a Saturday the firm holds a plant, machinery and tool sale, with lots for the commercial user and all types of tools for the DIY enthusiast or gardener.

Once a quarter there are horsedrawn carriage sales, which have a national reputation. Included are carriages, whips, harness, pictures, prints, books — in fact anything connected with horses, except for the horses themselves. Quarterly sales of architectural antiques and of vintage and collectors' cars and memorabilia are also held.

Whittle-le-Woods

BUYER'S PREMIUM: *Nil*
SALES: *General: weekly on Thu at 1.00pm. Plant, machinery and tools: every four weeks on Sat at 10.30am. Horsedrawn carriages, architectural antiques, vintage and collectors' cars: quarterly on Sat at 10.30am.*
VIEWING: *General: day of sale from 9.00am. All others: afternoon prior and day of sale from 9.00am.*
REFRESHMENTS: *Own café.*
PARKING: *Own car park.*
STORAGE: *No*
TRANSPORTATION: *Yes*
SHIPPING: *No*

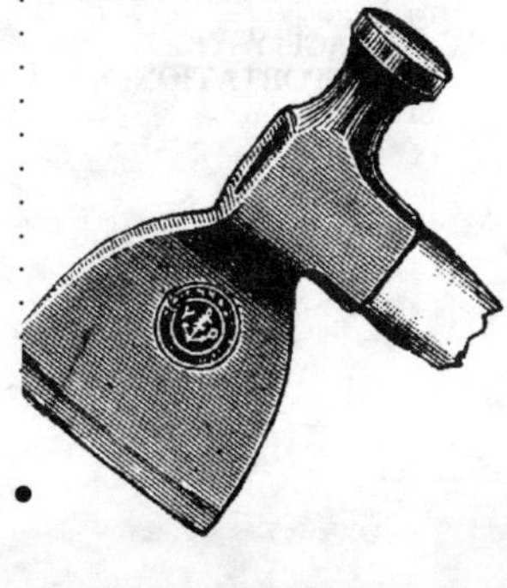

LEICESTERSHIRE

WILLIAM H BROWN

Leicester

BUYER'S PREMIUM: *10%*
SALES: *General: fortnightly on Wed at 10.00am. Better furniture: monthly on first Mon of the month at 10.00am. Antiques and fine art: quarterly on Mon and Wed.*
VIEWING: *General: morning of sale. Better furniture: Fri prior 9.00am-5.00pm, Sat prior 9.00am-12.00 noon. Antiques and fine art: Thu and Fri prior 10.00am-5.00pm, Sat prior 9.00am-12.00 noon.*
REFRESHMENTS: *None available on the premises.*
PARKING: *Large public car park within walking distance.*
STORAGE: *No*
TRANSPORTATION: *Yes*
SHIPPING: *Yes*

The Warner Auction Room, 16-18 Halford Street.
Tel: (0533) 519777

300-500 lots. Situated in the centre of Leicester (next door to British Home Stores), this sale is part of the Fine Art and Chattels division of the William H Brown Group, who run major auctions in Great Yarmouth, Colchester, Doncaster, Grantham (the headquarters) and Sudbury, in addition to various smaller auctions in this part of the country.

The fortnightly sale is a good general auction, and includes furniture and household effects, television sets, fridges, cookers, a kitchen sink or so, garden furniture and garden equipment, such as ladders and wheelbarrows. There will also be the inevitable boxes of interesting miscellaneous items to search through in the hope of finding perhaps a silver teaspoon or a copper jelly mould.

The monthly sale is of Victorian, reproduction and better quality modern furniture, mirrors and so on, and there are many bargains to be found here.

The quarterly sale is of specially selected fine furniture, antiques and fine art, including oil paintings, watercolours, prints, engravings, and miniatures. This is a two-day sale, with furniture, paintings and the like on the Monday, and silver and plate, jewellery and *bijouterie*, watches and other smaller items on the Wednesday.

CHURCHGATE AUCTIONS

Leicester

BUYER'S PREMIUM: *5%*
SALES: *Weekly on Tue and Fri at 11.00am.*
VIEWING: *Afternoon prior and morning of sale.*
REFRESHMENTS: *None available on the premises.*
PARKING: *None available on the premises.*
STORAGE: *Yes*
TRANSPORTATION: *Yes*
SHIPPING: *Yes*

Churchgate. Tel: (0533) 621416

300-400 lots. Find the centre of the city and the clock tower, and you have found the auction. It is held on the ground floor of a Grade 2 listed Victorian building with pine beams across the ceiling. On two floors of the same building there is a large permanent antique market, which is packed with stalls and ideal to wander around while resting between bids. This is a good general auction, where sales often include the complete contents of houses, perhaps from one of the grander properties abounding in nearby villages. Sometimes, though, these sales comprise single items offered by individual vendors. There is no set order of sale, and lots are sold mostly in the order in which they arrive. With two auctions a week, the staff are worked very hard, but they are usually willing to offer advice or help when needed.

HEATHCOTE BALL & CO

Leicester

Castle Auction Rooms, 78 St Nicholas Circle.
Tel: (0533) 536789

700-1,000 lots. In the dozen or so years since their foundation, Heathcote Ball & Co have established themselves as one of the leading provincial auction firms of antiques and fine art. Their Thursday sale includes furniture, porcelain, silver, *objets d'art*, pictures, collectors' items such as silhouettes and miniatures, bronzes and statuary, toys and games, antique jewellery, samplers, linen, lace and costumes, musical instruments, postcards and albums, coins and medals, pill and snuff boxes, paperweights, arms and weaponry, tribal art, fans and ephemera, and so on.

Antiquarian and collectors' book sales are held about twice a year — there is no fixed date for these sales, but they are always on a Friday. 'Outside sales', consisting of the entire contents of houses, are also held periodically throughout the year. These sales are either held in the house itself, or in a marquee in the grounds, and are often worth attending.

BUYER'S PREMIUM: *7½%; outside sales 10%*
SALES: *Antiques and fine art: every four to six weeks on Thu at 11.00am. Antiquarian and other books: twice yearly on Fri at 10.00am.*
VIEWING: *Day prior 10.00am-4.00pm.*
REFRESHMENTS: *Own café.*
PARKING: *None available on the premises.*
STORAGE: *No*
TRANSPORTATION: *Yes*
SHIPPING: *Yes*

FRECKELTONS

Loughborough

1 Leicester Road. Tel: (0509) 214564

250 lots. As might be imagined in a university city, there are usually a great number of bicycles on sale at this friendly and well-organised auction. The saleroom is prominently situated just off the A6 and is in the town centre. The auctions are held on the ground floor of a large Victorian building that was once a house of detention.

This is a family-owned business with two generations of the family now involved. As well as the bicycles there will generally be good furniture of all types and values — modern, reproduction and antique — plus kitchenalia, paintings, silver, jewellery, pottery, porcelain, plenty of china and all sorts of collectors' items and bygones. Prices vary from £5 to five-figure sums.

BUYER'S PREMIUM: *Nil*
SALES: *Monthly on Tue at 10.30am.*
VIEWING: *Sat and Mon prior 9.30am-1.00pm and 2.00pm-4.30pm.*
REFRESHMENTS: *None available on the premises.*
PARKING: *Ample off-street parking.*
STORAGE: *Yes*
TRANSPORTATION: *Yes*
SHIPPING: *Yes*

GILDINGS

Market Harborough

64 Roman Way. Tel: (0858) 410414

500-600 lots. The saleroom is a new, purpose-built single-storey building with offices and a cafeteria at the rear. It stands in the centre of the town at the rear of the church of St Dionysius, whose spire is clearly visible from almost anywhere in Market Harborough. The regular fortnightly sale is of Victoriana, pine and painted pine, with good-quality furniture and effects, including china, glass and metalware, paintings and so on.

BUYER'S PREMIUM: *5%*
SALES: *Fortnightly on Tue at 10.00am (includes antiques and fine art sale about every six weeks, and specialist sale about once every three months).*
VIEWING: *Sat prior 9.30am-12.30pm, Mon prior 10.00am-7.00pm, morning of sale from 9.00am.*

REFRESHMENTS: *Own café.*
PARKING: *Own 100-space car park.*
STORAGE: *Yes*
TRANSPORTATION: *Yes*
SHIPPING: *Yes*

About every six weeks, a sale of perhaps 400-500 lots of antiques and fine art takes the place of the regular sale. The two main sales follow roughly the same order, with smaller items at the start, followed by a lunch break at 1.00pm, and then the sale of furniture, carpets and pictures at around 1.30pm.

Roughly every three months, the sale will be devoted to specialist items, such as toys, motor memorabilia, guns and weaponry, sporting equipment, and other collectors' items.

Melton Mowbray

BUYER'S PREMIUM: *5%*
SALES: *Every three weeks on Thu at 9.30am.*
VIEWING: *Mon prior 4.00pm-7.00pm, Tue prior 2.00pm-4.45pm*
REFRESHMENTS: *Own café.*
PARKING: *Own car park in former school playground.*
STORAGE: *Yes*
TRANSPORTATION: *Yes*
SHIPPING: *Yes*

SHOULER & SON

King's Road Old School, King's Road. Tel: (0664) 60181

700-800 lots. The saleroom is on the outskirts of town, on the corner of King's Road and the main Grantham Road. It is a large old school house and difficult to miss. The sales are generally packed and friendly, and attract potential buyers with all depths of pocket: one lot might be sold for £1 and another for five figures. The first half of the sale is devoted to lesser-quality items, including furniture and effects, bygones, china, silver, pottery, paintings, ornaments, kitchenalia and various miscellaneous items. The lots in this part of the sale are laid out in six different rooms (which used to be the classrooms). The auctioneer moves from room to room, followed by the crowd, selling each lot as it is reached. At about 2.00pm and roughly from lot 500, the main room becomes the focus of the sale. It contains the better furniture and antiques, paintings, silver, brass, bronzes, china, jewellery, collectables, and many other articles. The lots are on view around the room, but they are brought up to the rostrum for show when being sold. The sale ends at around 4.30 to 5.00pm.

Oakham

BUYER'S PREMIUM: *5%*
SALES: *Fortnightly on Thu at 10.30am (includes antiques and fine art sale every other fortnight).*
VIEWING: *Tue (antiques sale only) and Wed prior 10.00am-4.00pm and 7.00pm-9.00pm.*
REFRESHMENTS: *Own small café area (antiques sale only).*
PARKING: *Not available on the premises.*
STORAGE: *Yes*
TRANSPORTATION: *Yes*
SHIPPING: *Yes*

N H NOTON & ASSOCIATES

The Sale Room, South Street. Tel: (0572) 722681

400-500 lots. The saleroom is near the centre of this pleasant, well-kept town. The sales are held every fortnight, and alternate between 'General Household Furniture and Effects', and 'Antiques and Fine Art'. The Tuesday viewing is only available for the antiques sales, as is the café. Both sales run in roughly the same order, starting off with small items of china. At the antiques sale these might include porcelain teapots, decorated vases, cheese dishes and stands, soup tureens, fruit bowls and the like. Silverware comes next, for example hallmarked silver dishes, serving spoons and ladles, followed by carpets, paintings and furniture. Boxes containing an assortment of items appear at both sales, and are always worth a look: a thorough search might reveal the odd Doulton tea cup, assorted cutlery or a quantity of Victorian ceramic door handles.

LINCOLNSHIRE

DICKINSON, DAVY & MARKHAM

Alford

111 West Street. Tel: (0507) 607781

400-500 lots. The saleroom was once a cinema, but has been completely refurbished. Selling takes place on the ground floor, with the old cinema balcony put to good use as a storage area. All lots are inside the saleroom for viewing, but the lots placed in the centre of the hall, such as bicycles, garden tools, timber, doors, wheelbarrows, ladders and so on are taken out on the sale day, to be sold in the yard at the rear of the saleroom. The auctioneer moves inside to sell smaller items such as china, ornamental and domestic crockery, cutlery, jewellery, bric-à-brac, electrical goods and other items. Next comes the furniture sale, which starts with the more modern articles, including office furniture and equipment. After these the auctioneer moves across to sell beds and carpets. At around 1.00pm the sale of the higher-value furniture begins, and the entire sale ends at around 3.00 to 4.00pm.

Alford is the home of Britain's last commercially operated windmill, which is well worth a look if you are visiting the area.

BUYER'S PREMIUM: *5%*
SALES: *Monthly on second or third Thu of month at 10.00am.*
VIEWING: *Day prior 12.00 noon-4.00pm, 6.00pm-8.00pm.*
REFRESHMENTS: *None available on the premises.*
PARKING: *None available on the premises.*
STORAGE: *Yes*
TRANSPORTATION: *Yes*
SHIPPING: *Yes*

JAMES ELEY & SON

Boston

The Green, Wide Bargate. Tel: (0205) 361687

2,000 lots. A lavatory bowl, two front doors, a quantity of timber, a wheelbarrow, an electric fire, a gas cooker, half-a-dozen tins of paint, two rolls of wire netting, a Victorian dresser, a drop-leaf table, fresh seasonal produce, eggs, caravan trailers and cars: few shops could offer such variety, but all these have been on sale at Eley's auctions. The sale starts with produce at 10.00am, followed at 12.00 noon by smaller items from the table display, such as jewellery, silver, pottery, ornaments and table lamps. Also at 10.00am, another auctioneer starts the sale of furniture, carpets, bicycles, televisions, household utensils, gardening equipment and so on, followed at 1.30pm by motor vehicles. The entire auction is held in the open and continues even in the rain, finishing at around 3.00pm.

It is a long established and well-known meeting place for locals, who come not only to buy but simply to chat and meet up with friends, although occasionally a cautious finger will be lifted to bid if one lot appears to be going cheaply. Often, if you attend the following week, you will see the same article up for

BUYER'S PREMIUM: *10%*
SALES: *Weekly on Wed at 10.00am.*
VIEWING: *Morning of sale.*
REFRESHMENTS: *Available.*
PARKING: *Own car park.*
STORAGE: *No*
TRANSPORTATION: *Yes*
SHIPPING: *No*

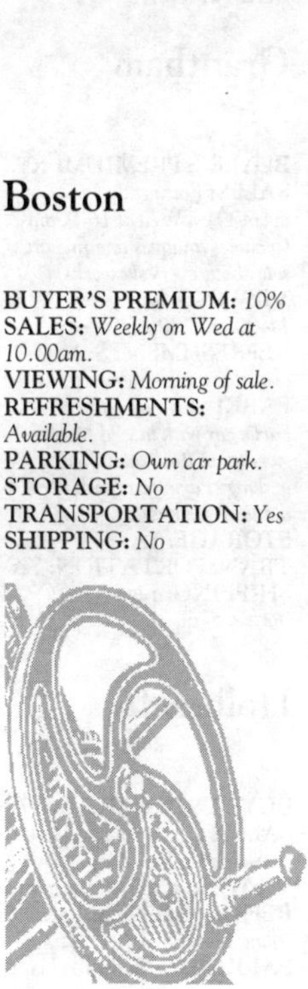

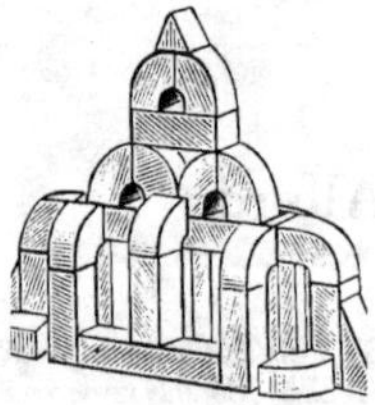

sale again, in the hope that it will fetch a better price.

Boston itself is a small but active port, handling mostly bananas and timber. The Boston stump (the 272ft tower of St Botolph Church) can be seen for miles across the surrounding fenland. The town gave its name to Boston, Massachusetts, when people sailed from here in 1630 in the wake of the Pilgrim Fathers.

Butterwick

BUYER'S PREMIUM: *10%*
SALES: *Monthly on third Sat of the month at 11.00am.*
VIEWING: *Fri prior 6.00pm-8.00pm, morning of sale from 9.00am.*
REFRESHMENTS: *Available.*
PARKING: *Own car park.*
STORAGE: *No*
TRANSPORTATION: *Yes*
SHIPPING: *No*

JAMES ELEY & SON

Butterwick Village Hall. Tel: (0205) 361687

400-450 lots. James Eley auctions and Butterwick Village Hall are well signposted on the A52. The sales include antiques and collectables of all kinds, good general furniture and household effects, silver, brass, china, books, bric-à-brac, and also many items with a shipping or fishing connection, due to the closeness of the port of Boston.

This is the same auction house responsible for weekly Wednesday auctions there.

Grantham

BUYER'S PREMIUM: *10%*
SALES: *Fortnightly (on average) on Wed at 10.00am (includes antiques and fine art sale about every six weeks).*
VIEWING: *Day prior 11.00am-4.30pm.*
REFRESHMENTS: *Not available on the premises.*
PARKING: *Not easy, but public car park in Old Market gives up to two hours' free parking. Paying car park five minutes' walk away.*
STORAGE: *Yes*
TRANSPORTATION: *Yes*
SHIPPING: *Yes*

WILLIAM H BROWN

Westgate Hall, Westgate. Tel: (0476) 68861

200-500 lots. This is one of a group of William H Brown Fine Art auction houses, which are a self-supporting part of William H Brown estate agents. Westgate Hall is just off the A1 near the town centre. It is an attractive Victorian building which used to be a dance hall, and it has a very ornate interior. The general sale usually has a good selection of collectables, plus jewellery, brass and copper. Larger pieces of furniture might include button-back leather and imitation leather lounge seats, corner units and reproduction mahogany bedroom suites, display cabinets and many other items of good-quality furniture and bric-à-brac. It is always an interesting auction, well run by Marilyn Swain, who is also secretary of the Society of Fine Art Auctioneers (SOFAA). An antiques and fine art auction takes the place of the general sale about every six weeks.

Holbeach

BUYER'S PREMIUM: *5%*
SALES: *Usually once a week on Sat at 1.30pm.*
VIEWING: *Morning of sale.*
REFRESHMENTS: *Van selling snacks.*
PARKING: *Usually roadside.*

HIX & SON

Church Street. Tel: (0406) 22777

250-300 lots. Hix & Son is a traditional firm of local auctioneers. A sale is held on most Saturday afternoons, and will probably be on the vendor's premises rather than at a saleroom. 'To the sale' signs are provided on roads in the area. The sales offer a wide range of goods, from bygone furniture and farm implements to fine art and the latest farm machinery and stock.

STORAGE: *No*
TRANSPORTATION: *No*
SHIPPING: *No*

ROBERT BELL & CO

Horncastle

The Town Hall. Tel: (0507) 52222

800-1,000 lots. This auction was established just after the Second World War, and many of the people attending now are pleased to tell you they have been picking up bargains here ever since then. 'I don't think I could have furnished my house without this auction,' one old gentleman told me, 'And when my time comes I've made arrangements for all my stuff to be put back into the sale.' The Town Hall is a very large selling area, but the acoustics are good and it is easy to hear the auctioneer. The first two hours of the auction take place outside in the area around the Town Hall. This is the sale of less valuable goods. It is always worth looking through these lots, as there are bargains to be found: perhaps a clutch of step ladders or Victorian cast-iron radiator tops (suitable for use as pot stands), an Edwardian cast-iron fire surround, crockery (of which there is a great deal), or walking sticks. The lots are not numbered and there is usually a crowd following the auctioneer as he walks from lot to lot. If you have a purchase in mind, it is wise to stand by it well before the auctioneer gets there, and to hold your ground until he arrives. At some point between 12.00 noon and 1.00pm the auction moves inside the Town Hall for the sale of better quality furniture and effects. These lots are all numbered. The proceedings usually begin with tied-up bundles of linen, which might include beautiful table cloths, embroidered afternoon tea and tray cloths, napkins and table centres. Next to be sold are silver, brass and other small items, and lastly the furniture.

Twice a year in April and October Robert Bell holds a catalogued antique sale of about 700 lots. This replaces the general sale.

BUYER'S PREMIUM: *5%*
SALES: *Monthly on last Wed of month at 10.00am (includes antiques sale twice a year in Apr and Oct).*
VIEWING: *Day prior 2.00pm-6.00pm.*
REFRESHMENTS: *Own café.*
PARKING: *Ample parking near by.*
STORAGE: *Yes*
TRANSPORTATION: *Yes*
SHIPPING: *Yes*

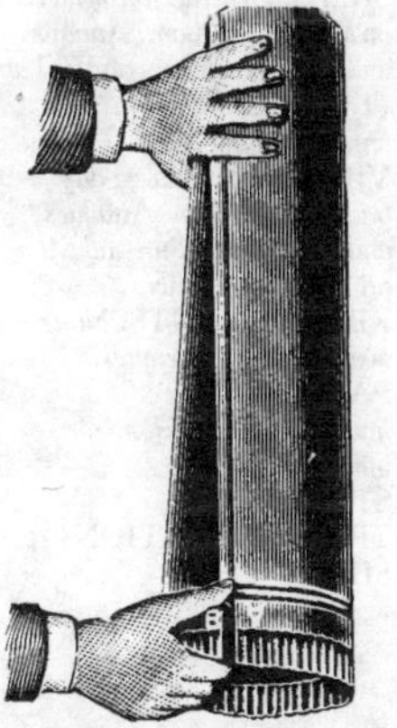

WOODROFFE WALTER, WILLIAM H BROWN

Horncastle

Town Hall, Boston Road. Tel: (0658) 22302

400-600 lots. A long-established, friendly auction which is well used by the locals, not only as a place to pick up a good bargain or to sell unwanted goods, but as a meeting place for old friends. It is noticeable that many people come to the auction chiefly to be entertained by the proceedings, making themselves comfortable by bringing their own sandwiches and flasks of drink, even though there is a good café on the

BUYER'S PREMIUM: *10%*
SALES: *Every two months on Wed at 10.00am.*
VIEWING: *Day prior 2.00pm-6.00pm.*
REFRESHMENTS: *Own café.*

PARKING: *Available in Town Hall car park and adjoining the cattle market.*
STORAGE: *Yes*
TRANSPORTATION: *Yes*
SHIPPING: *Yes*

premises. Probably they feel so much at home because the building is used for leisure activities, such as badminton and dancing, in the evenings.

The first part of the sale is devoted to 'deadstock' — step ladders, rolls of wire netting, wheelbarrows, perhaps building equipment, doors and other large, heavy goods. These are sold on the grassy area immediately outside the Town Hall. The auction then moves inside for the sale of beds, and after that smaller table items such as books, mirrors and ornaments are sold. At around 12.00 noon, there are a number of lots of good linen, china and glass. The furniture sale comes last, at about 2.00pm, and includes antique, modern, pine and reproduction items of all types.

Lincoln

THOS. MAWER & SON

63 Monks Road. Tel: (0522) 524984

BUYER'S PREMIUM: *5%*
SALES: *General: fortnightly on Wed at 11.00am. Antiques and fine art: monthly on Wed at 11.00am. Sporting guns: annually in Jan or Feb.*
VIEWING: *All sales: day prior until 4.30pm. Antiques and fine art: also Sun and Mon prior, afternoon only.*
REFRESHMENTS: *None available on the premises.*
PARKING: *Public multi-storey car park a few minutes walk away.*
STORAGE: *Yes*
TRANSPORTATION: *Yes*
SHIPPING: *Yes*

400-500 lots. Monks Road is close to the magnificent Lincoln Cathedral, which sits high on a limestone ridge overlooking the streets. Another interesting building is the Library, which has books and correspondence from the family of Alfred, Lord Tennyson. He was born near by.

Every other Wednesday, Thos Mawer has a sale of general household furniture and effects, and innumerable miscellaneous items. Once a month, slipping in between the general sales, there are special antique and fine art auctions. A sale of sporting guns is held once a year at the end of the shooting season in January or February. Anyone wishing to buy a firearm at auction must show the auctioneer a firearms certificate issued in the area in which they live. Otherwise the firearm cannot be removed from the auctioneer's custody.

Thos Mawer has a good reputation for bygones, and often there is such a section in the antiques sales. This could include kitchen, farm and garden bygones, or perhaps a variety of signs — an old roadside 'School' warning sign, an enamel advertisement for Park Drive cigarettes, a poster for PG tea, and assorted cast-iron railway plaques. One sale included over two million items, collectively weighing 50 to 60 tons, including wooden legs, a large number of dentist's extracting tools, a boar's head and a rhino's foot. These had been collected and stored by the vendor for a number of years in two chicken sheds.

Louth

BROADGATE & THOMPSON

1 Cornmarket. Tel: (0507) 603101

BUYER'S PREMIUM: *6%*
SALES: *Weekly on Wed at 10.45am.*

500-1,500 lots. Louth is a mixture of many architectural styles, from Elizabethan in the centre to Georgian at Westgate. It has a splendid 300-foot church spire, visible for miles before the town is reached. The wonderful country auction held here was established over 100 years ago and has probably changed little since. Vendors bring in goods that they wish to sell from 7.30am on the day of the sale. Buyers come for their weekly vegetables, and often leave with a piece of furniture or two as well, or perhaps a piece of jewellery or a bicycle.

The sale is in two main sections, beginning with eggs, dressed poultry and meat at 10.45am and then game (when in season) at 1.00pm. The sale of household furniture and effects is in the afternoon and usually goes on until about 3.00 or 4.00pm. The entire sale is conducted in the open, and all buying is strictly in cash only, unless you are known to the auctioneer.

VIEWING: *Morning of sale: goods arrive from 7.30am.*
REFRESHMENTS: *None available on the premises, but available near by.*
PARKING: *None available on the premises.*
STORAGE: *No*
TRANSPORTATION: *No*
SHIPPING: *No*

Louth

JOHN TAYLOR

Woolmart, Kidgate. Tel: (0507) 603648

400-500 lots. This is a traditional, family-run auction, with Mrs Laverack taking charge of all the office work, husband Jim doing the auctioning, and their two sons getting involved as well. The sale takes place in a big, three-storey auction house, and the Laveracks and staff are always on hand to answer questions. The 'smalls' are sold first, including for example silver, silver plate, jewellery, lamps, paintings, prints, glass, coins, books and photographs. These are sold on the first floor. The sale of furniture and other large items takes place next, on the ground floor, with Mr Laverack walking round and selling each item *in situ*. The lots are clean and well presented, and the furniture includes antique, Victorian, modern and reproduction. This is a good auction for those setting up home and looking for quality at an affordable price.

BUYER'S PREMIUM: 5%
SALES: *Monthly on the second Tue of the month at 11.00am.*
VIEWING: *Sun prior 2.00pm-4.00pm, Mon prior 12.00 noon-6.00pm, morning of sale from 9.00am*
REFRESHMENTS: *None available on the premises.*
PARKING: *None available on the premises.*
STORAGE: *Yes*
TRANSPORTATION: *Yes*
SHIPPING: *Yes*

Sleaford

C J DAYKIN

Northgate Saleroom, 69 Northgate. Tel: (0529) 413954

300-500 lots. The Daykin family, father and son, have been involved in the auction business for over 60 years. The saleroom and yard are just outside the town centre, close to the market (also on a Monday, with some interesting stalls). The weekly sale is a good traditional country auction, and one that children particularly enjoy. Vendors arrive with their goods from 7.00am on the day of the sale, and the lots can include anything from pheasants and rabbits to furniture (in all styles and states of repair), rolls of wire netting, boxes of books, television sets, washing machines, spin-driers, ornaments, building materials, and unwanted new toys or other presents.

BUYER'S PREMIUM: *10%*
SALES: *General: weekly on Mon at 10.00am. Better furniture etc: monthly on Thu at 10.00am.*
VIEWING: *General: morning of sale — goods arrive from 7.00am. Better furniture etc: day prior, all day.*
REFRESHMENTS: *Mobile canteen.*
PARKING: *Ample space.*
STORAGE: *Yes*
TRANSPORTATION: *Yes*
SHIPPING: *Yes*

This is a cash-only auction, and selling is fast — around 500 lots are often sold in less than two-and-a-half hours. A sale of garden produce begins at 11.00am.

Once a month in the saleroom there is a sale of better-quality items, such as antique, Victorian, Edwardian, modern and reproduction furniture, and a variety of other goods.

Spalding

AP SALES

Cattle Market. Tel: (0775) 725300

BUYER'S PREMIUM: *5%*
SALES: *General, livestock and produce: weekly on Tue at 10.00am. General only: weekly on Sat at 10.00am. Antiques and fine art: about every six weeks on Fri at 5.00pm.*
VIEWING: *General (both days): day of sale (goods arrive from 7.30am). Antiques and fine art: day of sale from 3.30pm.*
REFRESHMENTS: *Tea bar in saleyard (not antiques and fine art sale).*
PARKING: *Own car park.*
STORAGE: *Yes*
TRANSPORTATION: *Yes*
SHIPPING: *Yes*

Hundreds of lots. The very busy Tuesday auction includes livestock, eggs, fruit and vegetables, flowers, plants and other produce from local smallholders, as well as furniture, bicycles, television sets, brass and other 'deadstock' (anything which is not produce or livestock, or part of another category). The Saturday auction offers the same type of goods, but without the livestock. The 'deadstock' at these sales is quite unpredictable — one recent example was a Second World War bomb case, which fetched £5. Goods are brought in on the morning of the sale; the gates are officially open at 7.30am, but it is not unusual to see vehicles queuing up from 5.30am onwards.

Every six weeks (on average), an antiques and fine art sale is held in the Spalding Common Hall, Goodfellows Road, Spalding Common, about one mile from the Cattle Market, by AP Sales. They are the official South Lincolnshire auctioneers for the Sheriff's office and the police.

Spalding

WILLIAM H BROWN

Spalding Bulb & Produce Auction Hall, Swan Street.
Tel: (0775) 711711

BUYER'S PREMIUM: *5%*
SALES: *Every two months on Fri or Sat at 10.00am.*
VIEWING: *Day prior 5.00pm-7.00pm.*
REFRESHMENTS: *Tea bar in hall.*
PARKING: *Own car park.*
STORAGE: *Yes*
TRANSPORTATION: *No*
SHIPPING: *No*

500-600 lots. William H Brown hold sales in the Spalding Bulb & Produce Auction Hall in Swan Street, which they share with Longstaff Auctions. Richard Stimson and S Kingston, William H Brown's two chief auctioneers, conduct good general auctions here, including a wide variety of furniture and other items. A great many lots on sale are from private vendors, who are becoming increasingly aware that selling at auction is the most satisfactory way of gaining the best possible price for their goods. Other items are sold by William H Brown on behalf of executors and liquidators.

If you are new to auction-going and perhaps feel too shy to bid, it is always possible to ask one of the porters or clerks to make the bid for you. This can also be arranged if you see something you like at a viewing, but are unable to attend the actual auction in person. A telephone call to the auctioneers after the sale will confirm whether your bid has been successful or not. If you attend a sale personally, though, you will find out just how simple, but very exciting, bidding is.

LONGSTAFF

Spalding

Spalding Bulb & Produce Auction Hall, Swan Street. Tel: (0775) 766766

500-600 lots. The auction hall is just off Winfrey Avenue, by the bus station and near the town centre. The sale calendar is worked out at the start of the year, and buyers can ring Longstaff for exact future sale dates. The firm was established in 1770 and conducts interesting sales, which usually include a selection of antique, modern and period furniture. There will also usually be brass, china, silver, ornaments, paintings and other items, plus all sorts of bicycles, from the old-fashioned, sit-up-and-beg ladies' variety and butchers' delivery bicycles (which still seem to crop up in great numbers) to the most modern and up-to-date Emmelle and Dawes models. Television sets and general good-to-root-through bric-à-brac boxes are always to be found as well. Larger pieces of furniture, such as wardrobes, seem to sell for amazingly low prices, possibly because they are too large for most modern houses. Sometimes craftsmen buy these larger pieces of furniture and then make smaller pieces from them, simply because the wood is too good to destroy — the fate of unsold cumbersome items at many auction houses.

BUYER'S PREMIUM: *5%*
SALES: *Every six weeks on Fri or Sat at 9.30am.*
VIEWING: *Day prior 5.00pm-7.00pm.*
REFRESHMENTS: *Tea bar in hall.*
PARKING: *Own car park.*
STORAGE: *Yes*
TRANSPORTATION: *Yes*
SHIPPING: *Yes*

MERSEYSIDE

KINGSLEY & CO

Hoylake

3-4 The Quadrant. Tel: (051) 632 5821

350-450 lots. The saleroom is on the main road in Hoylake, by the roundabout. It has a large shop-type front, in which goods for the forthcoming sale are displayed. As might be expected in Merseyside, the atmosphere is friendly. This is a family-owned and run concern, in which Mr C L J Cadman shares the onerous duties with his daughter and son-in-law Jane and Ian McKellar. The sale is long established and has all the variation that makes going to auctions so exciting. Goods range from modern to good quality antique. The sale includes furniture and household effects, jewellery, pottery, paintings, porcelain, bicycles, televisions, videos, cookers, and many other items. Expect prices to fluctuate widely. For instance, a box of china might sell for just a few pounds, whereas some good quality items of antique furniture may well fetch five-figure sums.

BUYER'S PREMIUM: *8.7%*
SALES: *Weekly on Tue at 10.30am.*
VIEWING: *Sat prior 9.00am-12.30pm, day prior 9.00am-5.00pm.*
REFRESHMENTS: *Own café.*
PARKING: *Ample parking near by.*
STORAGE: *Yes*
TRANSPORTATION: *Yes*
SHIPPING: *Yes*

Liverpool

ABRAM & MITCHELL

32 Bedford Road, Walton. Tel: (051) 525 1718

BUYER'S PREMIUM: *Nil*
SALES: *Fortnightly on Wed at 11.00am.*
VIEWING: *Day prior 9.00am-5.00pm.*
REFRESHMENTS: *Van selling snacks usually outside.*
PARKING: *None available on the premises.*
STORAGE: *Yes*
TRANSPORTATION: *Yes*
SHIPPING: *Yes*

180-200 lots. Walton is an attractive and busy suburb of Liverpool. The saleroom is by Walton Church in the foyer of what was the old Bedford Cinema. Abram & Mitchell is a small, locally well known, independent company, who are also involved in removals and storage. The fortnightly Wednesday sale is a popular meeting place for local people, and has a reputation as a place to buy all types of good quality household furniture. Many of the lots come from house clearances, so televisions, videos, china, electrical goods and a wide variety of other items can be expected. It is worth making a thorough search for the odd good piece of furniture or china hidden among more run-of-the-mill goods. Smaller, pocket-sized items are not put out for show during viewing, but are kept locked in the office and brought out only during the sale.

Liverpool

HARTLEY & CO

12-14 Moss Street. Tel: (051) 263 6472 and 263 1865

BUYER'S PREMIUM: *5%*
SALES: *Weekly on Fri at 10.30am.*
VIEWING: *Day prior 9.00am-4.30pm.*
REFRESHMENTS: *None available on the premises.*
PARKING: *Car park facing premises.*
STORAGE: *Yes*
TRANSPORTATION: *Yes*
SHIPPING: *Yes*

300-400 lots. The saleroom is a short distance from the new Royal Hospital, which is just out from the centre of Liverpool. Hartley & Co have been established for over 120 years and their weekly Friday sales are almost as much of a landmark to some Liverpudlians as the Liver Building. The sale will include a range of goods, as is usual when many of the lots come from house clearances. Among the furniture there could be antique, reproduction or modern items, and the miscellaneous goods often include strange and unexpected pieces. There are usually plenty of small lots such as silver, china and jewellery. Outside effects will also be sold, including gardening tools, garden furniture and bicycles. The more run-of-the-mill lots are sold before 12.00 noon, when selling stops for lunch. The sale resumes at 1.00pm with antiques and better quality items, including china, silver, jewellery and any fine art.

Liverpool

OUTHWAITE & LITHERLAND

Kingsway Galleries, Fontenoy Street. Tel: (051) 236 6561

BUYER'S PREMIUM: *10%*
SALES: *General: weekly on Tue at 10.30am. Fine art and antiques: every four to six weeks on Wed at 10.30am.*
VIEWING: *General: day prior 9.00am-5.00pm, morning of sale from 9.00am. Fine art and antiques: two days prior*

300-600 lots. Outhwaite & Litherland was established in 1907, and is one of the largest independent salerooms in the north-west. The present partners are Michael Litherland, Kevin Whay and Brian Litherland. The weekly sale is held in the No 2 saleroom on Tuesdays, and is of good general household furniture and effects of all periods, including antiques. Among the lots there will usually be electrical goods, televisions, beds, dining room and lounge suites, tables, chairs, china and crockery, pictures, jewellery, gardening tools and equipment, toys, lamps and so on.

Every four to six weeks on Wednesdays there is a sale of fine art and antiques in the main gallery (called the Fine Art Saleroom).

Several times during the year, but at no regular intervals, Outhwaite & Litherland also hold specialist sales in various categories. Past examples are antiquarian and other books, musical and scientific instruments, clocks, and marine and boating collectables. These sales are worth enquiring about.

The firm also has a large restoration department, and can provide expert work on furniture, clocks, jewellery, silver, paintings, and other goods. If you see something that interests you during viewing, you can get an estimate for repairs before the sale, and take that into account when bidding. Catalogues are available for all sales.

9.00am-5.00pm, morning of sale from 9.00am.
REFRESHMENTS: *Own café.*
PARKING: *Own car park.*
STORAGE: *Yes*
TRANSPORTATION: *Yes*
SHIPPING: *Yes*

TURNER & SONS

Liverpool

28-36 Roscoe Street. Tel: (051) 709 4005

200-300 lots. Much of Liverpool seems to be in the midst of being knocked down or renovated and it is not a city where you would expect to find good quality antique furniture. However the Turner & Sons sale includes a wide variety of general household furniture and effects, and the lots range from antique through to modern. The weekly sale may also include fine art. It is the mix of quality and value that makes the sale interesting, and this is probably the reason why it is so well attended, both by local people hoping to furnish a house cheaply, and by dealers. There is plenty of Liverpudlian humour and a good atmosphere in the saleroom, although the selling is brisk — the entire proceedings are often finished by 1.00pm. The sale starts outside at 10.45am with vehicles such as cars, trailers, and perhaps plant and machinery, followed by the general goods at 11.00am. The saleroom is in the centre of Liverpool, near the imposing Anglican Cathedral.

BUYER'S PREMIUM: *Nil*
SALES: *Weekly on Thu at 11.00am.*
VIEWING: *Day prior 9.00am-5.00pm.*
REFRESHMENTS: *None available on the premises.*
PARKING: *Own car park.*
STORAGE: *No*
TRANSPORTATION: *Yes*
SHIPPING: *Yes*

ELDON E WORRALL

Liverpool

15 Seel Street. Tel: (051) 709 2950

200-300 lots. The saleroom is centrally placed with easy access to Lime Street railway station. The company's chief concern is with fine art and antiques, and Mr Eldon Worrall, the proprietor, is one of the leading authorities in the north-west on Oriental art. An antiques sale is held about once a month. The regular sale of general household furniture and effects also

BUYER'S PREMIUM: *10%*
SALES: *About every two weeks on Thu at 11.00am (alternate general and antiques).*
VIEWING: *General: day prior, 10.00am-4.00pm, morning of sale. Antiques: two*

days prior 10.00am-4.00pm, morning of sale.
REFRESHMENTS: *None available on the premises.*
PARKING: *Own car park.*
STORAGE: *Yes*
TRANSPORTATION: *Yes*
SHIPPING: *Yes*

takes place about once a month. Sales are arranged so that there is usually an auction every two weeks. The antiques sale could include collectors' items such as dolls, model trains, cars and other toys, antiquarian and other books, glass, oil paintings and watercolours, ceramics, silver, jewellery, clocks, rugs and carpets, with antique furniture finishing the sale. The general sale often includes the contents from complete house clearances, and so you may find everything from salt and pepper shakers and teapots to coal scuttles, television sets, cookers, and all types of furniture, including antiques. These sales are worthwhile for those interested in the unusual or valuable, or those who simply need to furnish and equip a house on a budget.

New Brighton

BUYER'S PREMIUM: *5%*
SALES: *Weekly on Tue at 12.00 noon (includes special antiques sale about every six weeks).*
VIEWING: *Day prior 9.00am-1.00pm, 2.00pm-5.00pm, morning of sale from 9.00am.*
REFRESHMENTS: *None available on the premises.*
PARKING: *Ample parking near by.*
STORAGE: *Yes*
TRANSPORTATION: *Yes*
SHIPPING: *Yes*

WILSON & SOUTHERN

Molyneux Drive. Tel: (051) 638 6154

200-600 lots. Molyneux Drive is 10 or 15 minutes' walk from the promenade, which stretches along the banks of the Mersey and is pleasant for a stroll. Wilson & Southern's weekly sale is a good general auction of all types of household furniture and effects, including china, porcelain, jewellery, electrical goods, televisions and videos. Outside at 1.00pm there is a sale of motor vehicles and large machinery, perhaps trailers, tractors, lifts and boats. The sale returns inside for the better quality articles. Every six weeks or so the general sales are replaced by special antiques and fine art sales. Bids can be left with the auctioneers if you are unable to attend a sale personally.

Rock Ferry

BUYER'S PREMIUM: *Nil*
SALES: *Fortnightly on Tue at 11.00am.*
VIEWING: *Sat prior 9.00am-12.30pm, day prior 9.00am-5.00pm.*
REFRESHMENTS: *None available on the premises.*
PARKING: *Ample parking near by.*
STORAGE: *Yes*
TRANSPORTATION: *Yes*
SHIPPING: *Yes*

W FLINN & CO

473/5 New Chester Road. Tel: (051) 645 1280

400-500 lots. The saleroom is a large, impressive building on the corner where Bedford Road and New Chester Road meet. It is just a few minutes' walk from Rock Ferry Station. On sale days the lots are attractively set out, with a busy team making sure that everything is clean and polished. W Flinn & Co was established in 1875 and is now owned by George Gaunt, who oversees all aspects of the sale. Mr Gaunt walks around the saleroom during the sale, stopping at various points to conduct the bidding. This brings him into closer contact with the bidders and helps to make the proceedings more informal. Many of the lots will have come from complete house clearances and may vary enormously in type, age, value and condition. Typical sales have included general household

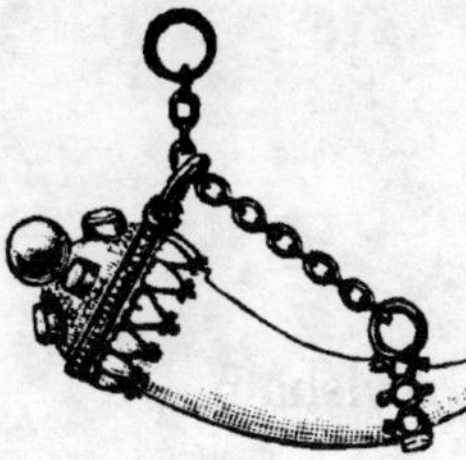

furniture, gardening tools and equipment, jewellery, china, kitchen items, photograph albums, postcards, electrical goods, lamps, cameras, general bric-à-brac, books and so on. Selling starts with the lesser quality goods; the more expensive articles are kept to the end. Something can usually be found to suit every interest and every pocket.

A J COBERN

Southport

The Grosvenor Saleroom, 93B Eastbank Street.
Tel: (0704) 500515

400-800 lots. The saleroom is about 200 yards from Lord Street, the tree-lined boulevard and main thoroughfare of this seaside resort. Sales alternate: one month an auction will be devoted to general household furniture and effects, and the next it will be given over to antiques and fine art. The general sales offer good quality modern and reproduction furniture, crockery, paintings, jewellery, electrical goods, kitchen items, boxes of bric-à-brac and so on. The antique and fine art sales have better quality goods, including pictures, silver, porcelain and furniture. Both sales are excellent for those wishing to furnish or equip a house on a budget, and they are well attended by local people and visitors. The two partners split auctioneering duties between them and conduct the sales in a manner which entices even reluctant bidders to take the plunge.

BUYER'S PREMIUM: *10%*
SALES: *Monthly on Wed at 10.00am (alternate general and antique sales).*
VIEWING: *General: Mon and Tue prior 9.00am-4.30pm. Antiques: Sat and Sun prior 11.00am-1.00pm, Mon and Tue prior 9.00am-4.30pm.*
REFRESHMENTS: *None available on the premises.*
PARKING: *Ample parking near by.*
STORAGE: *Yes*
TRANSPORTATION: *Yes*
SHIPPING: *Yes*

J KENT

Wallasey

2/6 Valkyrie Road. Tel: (051) 638 3107

400-500 lots. Wallasey is at one end of the Mersey Tunnel (the other end being just north of Liverpool's Exchange Station). It has a beach backed by sand dunes, and a pleasant shopping area. Valkyrie Road is just behind the Liscard Shopping Centre in the heart of the town. The saleroom is large, and there is plenty of room for each lot to be studied. Small items such as silver and jewellery are displayed on shelves and in cabinets. The weekly sales are of general household furniture and effects, including wardrobes, beds, dining room and lounge suites, upholstered furniture, kitchen items, jewellery, crockery, gardening tools and equipment, and linen. Every six to eight weeks the sale is devoted to antiques and collectables instead. A typewritten list giving a brief description of each lot is on view for the general sale. For the antique sales such lists are available free of charge. There are plenty of good buys to be found at both auctions, and a modern computer system means that you can pay within about 10 minutes of making a successful bid.

BUYER'S PREMIUM: *10%*
SALES: *Weekly on Wed at 10.00am.*
VIEWING: *Day prior 9.00am-6.30pm.*
REFRESHMENTS: *Tea and coffee only.*
PARKING: *None available on the premises.*
STORAGE: *Yes*
TRANSPORTATION: *Yes*
SHIPPING: *Yes*

NORFOLK

Aylsham

BUYER'S PREMIUM: *Nil*
SALES: *General: weekly on Mon at 10.00am (except Bank Holidays). Antiques and fine art: every three weeks on Tue at 10.00am. Pictures: every two months on Fri at 10.00am. Books: every two months (alternate months to picture sales) on Fri at 10.00am.*
VIEWING: *General: Sat prior 9.00am-10.30am, morning of sale from 9.00am. Antiques and fine art: day prior 2.30pm-8.30pm, day of sale from 9.00am. Pictures/books: day prior 2.30pm-8.30pm, day of sale from 9.00am.*
REFRESHMENTS: *Own tea rooms.*
PARKING: *Own large car park.*
STORAGE: *Yes*
TRANSPORTATION: *Yes*
SHIPPING: *Yes*

G A KEY

Aylsham Salerooms, Palmers Lane. Tel: (0263) 733195

1,000 lots. This is one of the largest and busiest auction room complexes in the east of England. There are eight large salerooms, and storage areas. The weekly Monday sale includes some 1,000 lots of modern second-hand furniture, second-hand motor vehicles and miscellaneous items such as garden produce, cycles and 'deadstock' —anything that doesn't count as produce or another special category. The sale starts with the produce and poultry (both at 10.00am) followed by 'deadstock' at 10.30pm, bicycles at 12.30pm and motor vehicles at 1.00pm. The furniture is sold separately in two batches. The first furniture sale starts at 11.30am in Auction Room 5, and includes a variety of antiques, collectables and better-quality items. The other furniture sale begins at about 2.00pm in Auction Room 6, and is devoted to cottage furniture.

Every three weeks there is a sale of antiques and fine art, including period, Victorian and Edwardian furniture of English and Continental design, plus porcelain, pottery, silver and plate, glass, jewellery, collectors' items and the like. Picture sales are held every other month, and have about 700 lots of watercolours, oil paintings and prints. Book and collectors' sales are held in the alternate months, with a range of topography, natural history and children's illustrated titles, first editions, and various collectables such as ephemera.

In addition, special sales are held throughout the year — these are usually sales of company assets and stock, but are sometimes devoted to vintage motor vehicles.

Burnham Market

BUYER'S PREMIUM: *Nil*
SALES: *Weekly from Jun to Sep on Mon at 1.00pm.*
VIEWING: *Morning of sale from 10.00am.*
REFRESHMENTS: *Available in village.*
PARKING: *Available in the street.*
STORAGE: *No*
TRANSPORTATION: *Yes*
SHIPPING: *Yes*

CASE & DEWING

The Green. Tel: (0362) 692004

400 lots. This auction is an attraction for the summer visitors who flock to this part of Norfolk. The setting is pleasant for browsing and buying, and gives a taste of country auctions in bygone days. The sale is held entirely in the open on the village green, which is surrounded by Georgian houses and divided by a stream. Furniture, both large and small, silver, pewter, copper and brass can be found, as well as china, ornaments, bygones, old postcards, photo albums and the like. Numerous craftsmen and women have set up workshops in this area, and many of them put their products in for auction as well. There are usually plenty of paintings, both oils and

watercolours, and various hand-made items such as jewellery, toys and furniture. The sale continues even in the rain, and bad weather has the possible advantage for the determined bidder of keeping away less hardy rivals. Mr Dewing, the auctioneer, is also responsible for the monthly auction at the Memorial Hall in East Dereham.

Diss

THOS WM GAZE & SON

Auction Rooms, Roydon Road. Tel: (0379) 650306

1,000-1,500 lots. Thos Wm Gaze & Son was established in 1867 and has been an auction house of one sort or another ever since. This is a large, busy sale where it is possible to bid for anything from eggs, vegetables and pet rabbits to tin baths, caravans, antique furniture and possibly a piece of fine art. Up to four auctions may be going on at once. Selling starts in the yard with the 'Sale Meadow' auction of items like timber, sheds, caravans, lawn mowers, rolls of wire netting, garden tools and so on. At the same time, pet rabbits, chickens and other livestock are sold in another part of the yard, with eggs, fruit, vegetables and farm produce in yet another area.

The general sale begins in Saleroom 3 at 11.00am, with modern furniture and household effects, including pots, pans and all sorts of other kitchenalia, china, paintings, prints and a wide range of miscellaneous items. At 12.00 noon the sale of antique and cottage furniture begins in Saleroom 1, with better-quality items, brass and so on. Every two months this sale is replaced by special antique and collectors' sales, which start at 12.00 noon in Saleroom 2.

BUYER'S PREMIUM: *Nil*
SALES: *General: weekly on Fri at 10.30 am. Antique and cottage furniture: weekly on Fri at 12.00 noon (replaced every two months by antiques and collectors' sale).*
VIEWING: *Day prior 2.00pm-8.00pm. Day of sale from 8.30am.*
REFRESHMENTS: *Own café.*
PARKING: *Own car park, 50p per car.*
STORAGE: *Yes*
TRANSPORTATION: *Yes*
SHIPPING: *Yes*

Downham Market

BARRY L HAWKINS

The Repository, Lynn Road. Tel: (0553) 776600

300-400 lots. The Repository is an attractive building which used to be a 28-stall stable. It is by the traffic lights — the town only has one set of lights, so it is easy to find. The pleasant town has a good selection of shops and a picturesque square with an unusual Victorian iron clock tower. If you have time between bidding, an interesting journey can be made along the Denver Road to Denver Sluice, where part of the drainage of the Fens is controlled. The auction has been going for 30 years, except for a three-year break, and usually has a good array of furniture, such as dining and lounge suites, chairs, desks and cabinets, plus brass ornaments, carpets, china, kitchenalia and a variety of outdoor effects — lathes and steam engines, tools, doors, window frames, bricks, boxes of nails and other handy items for DIY. Lots are sold at an average of about 100 per hour.

BUYER'S PREMIUM: *Nil*
SALES: *Monthly on third Wed of month at 11.00am.*
VIEWING: *Evening prior 4.30pm-7.00pm, morning of sale.*
REFRESHMENTS: *None available on the premises.*
PARKING: *Free street parking at time of writing.*
STORAGE: *Yes*
TRANSPORTATION: *Yes*
SHIPPING: *Yes*

East Dereham

BUYER'S PREMIUM: *Nil*
SALES: *About once a month on Tue at 1.00pm.*
VIEWING: *Morning of sale from 10.00am.*
REFRESHMENTS: *Splendid homemade refreshments in hall.*
PARKING: *Ample space in nearby streets.*
STORAGE: *No*
TRANSPORTATION: *Yes*
SHIPPING: *Yes*

CASE & DEWING

Memorial Hall, Norwich Street. Tel: (0362) 692004

300-400 lots. The Memorial Hall is off the market place, by the old East Dereham railway station. The sale draws most of its items from executors and private vendors from the many villages in the area, so there is a wide range of goods to suit all pockets and needs. Beautifully cared-for antique and modern furniture, brass, china and ornaments will be found, some of which have clearly been in a family for generations. In addition, there are usually gardening tools and equipment, a great deal of kitchenalia, and interesting miscellaneous items which might include old family photograph albums, or a child's collection of cigarette cards. Case & Dewing are also responsible for the fortnightly auction held in summer on the green at Burnham Market.

Fakenham

BUYER'S PREMIUM: *Nil*
SALES: *Weekly on Thu at 11.00am.*
VIEWING: *Wed 2.00pm-5.00pm.*
REFRESHMENTS: *Vans selling snacks.*
PARKING: *Town centre car parks, but very busy.*
STORAGE: *Yes*
TRANSPORTATION: *Yes*
SHIPPING: *Yes*

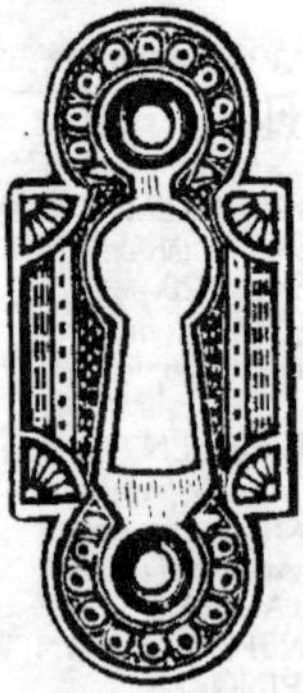

HUGH BECK AUCTIONS

The Corn Hall. Tel: (0328) 851557

600-700 lots. When Long & Beck, the previous owners of the sale, were taken over by a large public company, this auction was closed — much to the disappointment of locals and visitors alike, because it had been a focal point of Fakenham for many years. However Hugh Beck — half of the original firm — came to the rescue and started the sale up again in a brand new building on a site very near to the old auction rooms. Mr Beck, who has over 30 years experience in the art of auctioneering, said that he missed the atmosphere and the excitement of the sales. The auctioneers boast that anything from a potty to a piano can be bought here. Also to be found are furniture, washing machines, mirrors, wardrobes, bicycles, pots and pans, china, ornaments, paintings — there will usually be at least one thing you want to bid for, if not several. Also under Mr Beck's management is a flea market of around 100 stalls, immediately outside the auction rooms. More than half of the stalls are run by amateurs, and they offer anything from home-made jams to records and tapes, seeds and bulbs, antique buttons and locally hand-crafted goods.

Thursday is both auction day and market day, so the town centre is very busy then. To find the saleroom, go down Bridge Street and turn left by Finn's Fish Shop.

Great Yarmouth

BUYER'S PREMIUM: *Nil*

ALDREDS (WILLIAM H BROWN)

Kitchener Road Salerooms. Tel: (0493) 844891

300-400 lots. The firm was established in 1857 and the auction is run by the family team of Geoffrey Duffield, assisted by his father John Duffield and son Mark. The saleroom is in the centre of Great Yarmouth, off Northgate Street, by the Parish Church of St Nicholas. Yarmouth is known as the 'Blackpool of the East Coast' and has a large number of amusement arcades: an interesting feature of this auction is that quite often pinballs, various slot machines, juke boxes, snooker tables and the like come up for sale. Yarmouth's fishing industry is also reflected in the sale, which often has seafaring items such as ships' compasses and sextants. These lots will be in addition to the more usual array of antique, period and modern furniture, plus silver, glass, china, paintings and bric-à-brac that you would expect to find at all country sales. Unusually for this type of auction, Aldreds sell a catalogue describing the lots on offer.

SALES: *Fortnightly on Wed at 10.30am.*
VIEWING: *Tue prior 2.00pm-8.00pm.*
REFRESHMENTS: *Van selling snacks.*
PARKING: *On street.*
STORAGE: *Small amount available.*
TRANSPORTATION: *Yes*
SHIPPING: *Yes*

LANDLES

Blackfriars Hall, Blackfriars Street. Tel: (0553) 772816

500-600 lots. The sale includes good modern furniture, antiques and effects from local house clearances, including plenty of brass and copperware, pictures, garden tools, dinner services, tea sets and so on. The better-quality items tend to be sold at the latter end of the sale, and usually include Georgian, Victorian and Edwardian furniture. Blackfriars Street is in the centre of Kings Lynn, near the post office, public swimming pool and museum, and a few minutes from the modern shopping precinct. The sale, which is the only regular auction in the town and has been in existence since the 1890s, takes place on two floors in a large Victorian ex-school house. If possible allow time to explore the town, which has one of the finest collections of medieval merchants' combined houses and warehouses. The harbour was used as a location for the film *Revolution*.

King's Lynn

BUYER'S PREMIUM: *Nil*
SALES: *Monthly on second Wed of month at 10.00am.*
VIEWING: *Tue prior 9.00am-8.00pm.*
REFRESHMENTS: *None available on the premises, but available near by.*
PARKING: *Council car park opposite.*
STORAGE: *Yes*
TRANSPORTATION: *Yes*
SHIPPING: *Yes*

METHWOLD AUCTION MART

High Street. Tel: (0842) 827398

700-1,000 lots. This is a family business, run by George and Rosemary Reeve and their son Simon, who shares the auctioneering with his father. It is a country auction of the type that gets people hooked on attending them and wanting more.

Practically the whole village is given over to accommodating the Monday sales, especially on Bank Holiday Mondays when special antiques sales are held instead.

Vendors bring in goods for the weekly sale on Sunday and Monday morning. At 10.30am the auctioning of farm produce, plants, eggs, shrubs and so on starts in the saleyard, while the

Methwold

BUYER'S PREMIUM: *Nil*
SALES: *General: weekly on Mon at 10.30am. Antiques: Bank Holiday Mondays (never New Year's Day) at 1.00pm.*
VIEWING: *Day of sale.*
REFRESHMENTS: *Van selling snacks.*
PARKING: *Ample car parking space.*
STORAGE: *Yes*
TRANSPORTATION: *Yes*
SHIPPING: *Yes*

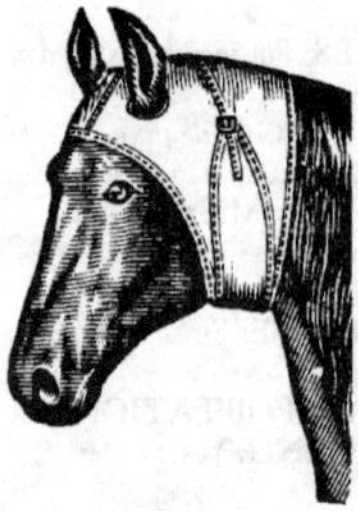

selling of household furniture and effects begins in the saleroom. The auctioneer who finishes first starts the sale of outside effects, but never before 1.00pm. This section covers lots such as bundles of timber, various building materials, gardening tools and equipment, and bygones. The sale often lasts until 5.00 or 6.00pm.

For the antique sales there is something of a carnival atmosphere in the village. Local halls take advantage of the extra visitors to hold their own jumble and bric-à-brac sales, with home-made tea and cakes. To cope with the extra numbers, St George's Hall, opposite the saleroom, is also used for the antiques auction. Furniture, paintings, china, silver, bygones and craft items may all be found at this sale.

Norwich

BUYER'S PREMIUM: *Nil*
SALES: *Weekly on Wed at 10.00am (includes antiques sale about every two months).*
VIEWING: *Tue prior 2.00pm-4.00pm (extended to 7.00pm for antiques sale).*
REFRESHMENTS: *None available on the premises.*
PARKING: *Own car park.*
STORAGE: *Yes*
TRANSPORTATION: *Yes*
SHIPPING: *Yes*

CLOWES, NASH & THURGAR

Cornhall Saleroom, Norwich Livestock Market, Hall Road. Tel: (0603) 627261/2

400-500 lots. The Cornhall auction and the livestock market moved to the present site, just outside the town, in 1960. The cattle market is one of the most up-to-date in the world, with sale rings looking rather like astronomical laboratories. It is a bonus for children, and they usually find the general sale interesting as well. This includes some antiques as well as modern furniture and effects from local house clearances, plus books, bicycles and collectables — sets of cigarette cards, comics, lead soldiers and working toys of all sorts. About every second month the general sale becomes a special antiques sale. A cannon is one of the more memorable lots sold by auctioneers Barry Martin and Chris Thurgar. In the city centre, Norwich's market is also worth a visit, with its striped awnings and interesting stalls. It is said to date back to Norman times.

Snettisham

BUYER'S PREMIUM: *5%*
SALES: *Weekly on Fri at 10.30am (includes antiques and fine art sale every two months).*
VIEWING: *Thu prior, 2.00pm-6.00pm.*
REFRESHMENTS: *Own café.*
PARKING: *Own large car park.*
STORAGE: *Yes*
TRANSPORTATION: *Yes*
SHIPPING: *Yes*

CRUSO & WILKINS

Snettisham Auction Centre, Common Road. Tel: (0485) 542656

400-500 lots. This is a good general auction selling a wide and varied range of furniture, bicycles, paintings, brass and silverware, bygones, collectables, and miscellaneous items such as garden tools, electrical appliances, bundles of wood and kitchen sinks. It would be possible to spend a day at a Cruso & Wilkins' sale and buy everything for a house, including a working television.

The saleroom is large and comfortable, and well heated in winter. The lots are laid out with generous room for viewing, and there is also plenty of seating. The sale takes place entirely under cover. It begins with wood, if there is any, then moves on to gardening equipment, electrical goods such as washing machines, cookers, vacuum cleaners, spin driers and so on, and then items of furniture. The 'table' lots come next — ornaments, china, dinner and tea sets, jewellery and other small items of value. Then the larger furniture is sold, for example lounge and bedroom suites, beds and so on, finishing up with carpets and television sets. There are ample sockets around the room for testing electrical goods, so you can plug in a television or a mower to see if it works.

Every two months the general Friday auction becomes a special auction of antiques and fine art. Snettisham is a mile from the coast and three miles from the Queen's Norfolk residence at Sandringham. Cruso & Wilkins are well signposted on the main Kings Lynn-Hunstanton road.

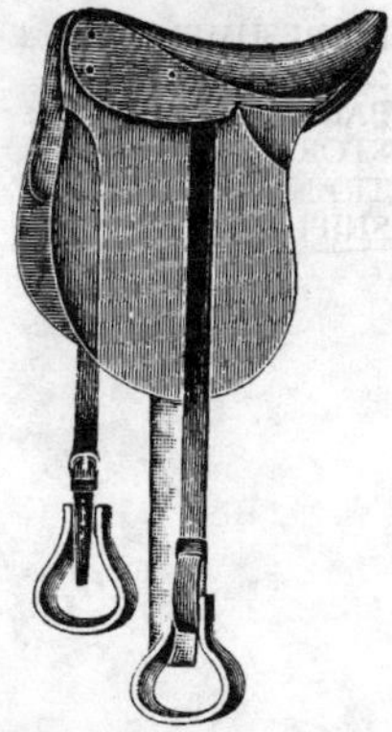

TYRONE R ROBERTS

Swaffham

The Saleyard. Tel: (0836) 723510

300-400 lots. 'Du yew open thaat owd buggar up bor. Du yew du, I du believe yew'll foind thaat'll go' ... auctioneer Tyrone Roberts offering a clock up for sale at his Swaffham Saturday auction. Unfortunately the East Anglian accent is as difficult to write as it is for a 'foreigner' (a non East Anglian) to speak, but Tyrone Roberts is one of the best and most entertaining auctioneers around. Constantly exchanging banter with the crowd, he would make most comedians green with envy. The Swaffham Saturday auction was featured in the BBC television series *In at the Deep End*, when presenter Chris Searle began his education as an auctioneer under the tutorship of Mr Roberts.

The auction is held in the open air in the market square. The lots are laid out in rows, with the auctioneer walking along and selling each lot as he comes to it. Purchases are paid for straight away, and as there is no one to check that the right buyer has the right item, it is best to grab what you have bought without delay. The goods for sale range from furniture to bicycles, and from rabbits to cars. There is always a good selection of televisions, which can be seen working and are sold under cover in the saleyard at the rear of the square, behind the Greyhound pub.

BUYER'S PREMIUM: *Nil*
SALES: *Weekly on Sat at 1.00pm.*
VIEWING: *Day of sale only.*
REFRESHMENTS: *Many cafés and pubs near by.*
PARKING: *Large council car parks, but usually very busy.*
STORAGE: *No*
TRANSPORTATION: *Yes*
SHIPPING: *Yes*

THETFORD AUCTION HOUSE

Thetford

Minstergate. Tel: (0842) 752775

600-900 lots. Conducted in a large, purpose-built, two-unit building, this is one of East Anglia's few Sunday auctions. The huge forestry area of Thetford Chase and the Neolithic mines of Grimes Graves are both in easy reach, so there is potential

BUYER'S PREMIUM: *Nil*
SALES: *Weekly on Sun at 10.00am.*
VIEWING: *Sat prior 9.00am-4.00pm.*

REFRESHMENTS: *Good café.*
PARKING: *Own car park.*
STORAGE: *Yes*
TRANSPORTATION: *Yes*
SHIPPING: *Yes*

for a varied family outing.

On both the viewing and the auction day, there is a 50-stall flea market selling bric-à-brac, handicrafts, paintings and other items. The auction attracts vendors and buyers from far afield, and at one point it had a regular attender from Sheffield. The goods on sale are typical of this type of auction, including antique, reproduction and modern furniture and effects: lounge and bedroom suites, Welsh dressers, carpets, mirrors, cookers, washing machines, ornaments, horse brasses, and the odd unusual item like the 10-foot stuffed alligator bought by someone to take back, oddly enough, to South Africa. Probably the most unusual lot was a microlight plane, which had landed in a nearby field with engine trouble and so irritated the pilot that he immediately put it up for auction. On a more serious note, to the sale is particularly good for jewellery. At the same time as the main sale, an auction of garden produce, plants, garden ornaments, bicycles, mowers, sun loungers, timber and other outside effects also takes place.

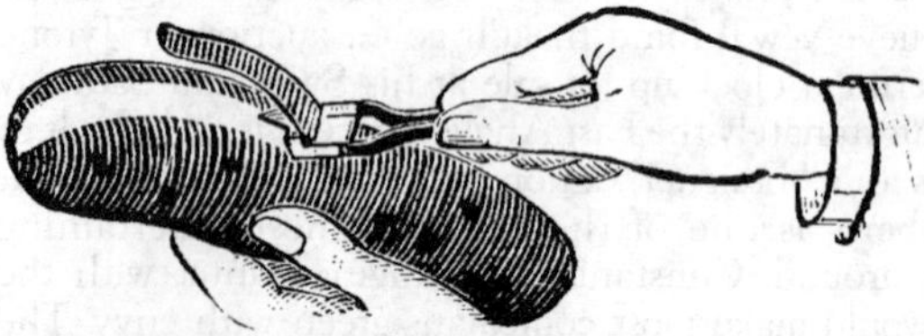

Watton

STEPHEN ROBERTS

Breckland House, Norwich Road.
Tel: (0953) 885676 and (0860) 211091

BUYER'S PREMIUM: *Nil.*
SALES: *Weekly on Tue at 10.00am.*
VIEWING: *Mon prior 4.00pm-8.00pm.*
REFRESHMENTS: *Own café.*
PARKING: *Own car park.*
STORAGE: *Yes*
TRANSPORTATION: *Yes*
SHIPPING: *Yes*

700-800 lots. This is an Aladdin's cave for the collector, connoisseur or browser. Stephen Roberts has a contract with the Ministry of Defence, so expect to see, not bombs and guns, but surplus clothing: uniforms, boots, gas masks, ski goggles, ties, socks, shirts and many, many other things, some without any obvious military connections. Carpets, furniture and gardening equipment from military family quarters are also sold. Another contract with the Norwich Union to sell their excess or redundant office furniture and equipment means that Stephen Roberts also usually have a large number of typewriters, office chairs, desks and the like for sale. Indeed, one room is entirely devoted to the sale of office equipment and furniture.

The auction starts outside with 'deadstock' — gardening equipment, mowers, timber, corrugated iron sheets, glass baths and other heavy items — then moves inside to the better quality and antique lots, arriving finally at electrical goods, office equipment, and general furniture and effects.

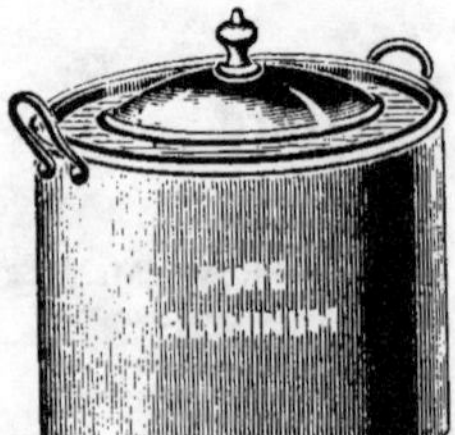

NORTHAMPTONSHIRE

SPENCERS (AUCTIONEERS)

Corby

Unit 3A, Southfold Road. Tel: (0536) 743755

500-600 lots. This is an independently run auction in the Great Oakley industrial estate, on the edge of the town. It is usually more suitable for those wanting to furnish a house on a budget than for collectors, but occasionally some good items of furniture, china or collectables do appear. The auctioneers offer the guarantee that all electrical goods sold here are 'in working order', which is unusual — most auctions prefer to emphasise that goods are sold 'as seen'. There are plenty of electric points in the saleroom so that buyers can satisfy themselves as to the condition of an article before bidding. The auction starts with 'market trading goods', which at this sale means china, porcelain, ornaments and general bric-à-brac. These are followed by domestic electrical goods, carpets, general furniture such as three-piece suites and tables, televisions, video and audio equipment, and antique and better quality furniture. Last of all come beds, bedding and bedroom furniture. Two auctioneers help to keep up the pace of the sale, which moves rapidly and finishes at around 9.00pm.

BUYER'S PREMIUM: *Nil*
SALES: *Weekly on Wed at 6.00pm.*
VIEWING: *Day of sale from 11.00am.*
REFRESHMENTS: *Own café.*
PARKING: *Own car park.*
STORAGE: *Yes*
TRANSPORTATION: *Yes*
SHIPPING: *Yes*

J M BAYES

Irthlingborough

43B High Street. Tel: (0933) 651015

300-350 lots. Irthlingborough is a small town with a big name. The saleroom is in a former Methodist chapel, about 50 yards from the post office. This is very much a local sale, offering a service to the community both as a place to sell unwanted goods and as somewhere to buy at budget prices.

Anything to furnish and equip a house may be found here, from three-piece suites and beds to cutlery, china, lamps and televisions. As in all auctions, for those who have time to search the lots thoroughly there is always the chance of exciting and unusual finds, such as rare old gramophone records, old cameras, collections of childrens' books, good ornaments, jewellery and so on. The better quality items are sold towards the end of the auction.

BUYER'S PREMIUM: *Nil*
SALES: *Every two or three weeks on Mon at 6.00pm.*
VIEWING: *Day of sale from 1.00pm.*
REFRESHMENTS: *None available on the premises.*
PARKING: *Ample parking near by.*
STORAGE: *Yes*
TRANSPORTATION: *Yes*
SHIPPING: *Yes*

SOUTHAM & SONS

Kettering

Corn Exchange Saleroom, Thrapston. Tel: (08012) 4486500

800 lots. The saleroom is centrally located in Thrapston, about eight miles east of Kettering. It is in a large building with a

BUYER'S PREMIUM: *Saturday sale 10%. Other sales nil.*

SALES: *Antiques*, objets d'art *and superior furniture: monthly on first Thu of month. General: monthly on second Sat after antiques sale at 11.00am. Sporting guns and antique arms: twice a year in Mar and Sep on Thu after general sale at 3.00pm. Sporting memorabilia: twice a year in Apr and Oct on Wed after general sale at 4.00pm.*
VIEWING: *Antiques: day prior 9.30am-8.00pm. General and others: day of sale.*
REFRESHMENTS: *None available on the premises.*
PARKING: *Council car park behind saleroom.*
STORAGE: *Yes*
TRANSPORTATION: *Yes*
SHIPPING: *Yes*

stone sheaf of corn above the main entrance. There are plenty of Southam & Sons' sale direction boards placed around the town.

The Thursday antiques sale is of catalogued lots, and usually includes Georgian, Victorian and Edwardian furniture, silver, silver plate, pottery, porcelain, pictures, prints, jewellery and collectables, such as tea caddies and cameras. The jewellery is kept in a locked cabinet, but the porters will unlock it if there is anything you wish to examine.

The uncatalogued sales, which take place on the second Saturday after the Thursday antiques sales, are of general household furniture and effects. Occasionally antiques will be found too. The furniture is placed around the walls of the saleroom; at the rear are garden chairs and benches, and tools: hammers, mowers, ladders and so on. This sale offers some very good buys. Linen of all types, such as bed linen, tablecloths, napkins and curtains, usually starts the sale. Next come carpets and rugs, then boxes of assorted items, which might include books, kitchen utensils, various pieces of china, and ornaments. Furniture is sold at the end of the day.

A sporting guns and antique arms sale takes place twice a year, and there is also a twice-yearly sale of sporting memorabilia, including fishing equipment, sporting books, prints and so on.

Northampton

HEATHCOTE BALL & CO (NORTHAMPTON) LTD

Albion Auction Rooms, Commercial Street. Tel: (0604) 22735

BUYER'S PREMIUM:
General: 10%. Antiques and fine art: 7%
SALES: *General: fortnightly on Sat at 10.00am. Antiques and fine art: about every three months on Fri at 10.30am.*
VIEWING: *General: day prior 1.00pm-4.45pm, morning of sale from 9.00am. Antiques and fine art: day prior 10.00am-4.00pm, morning of sale from 9.00am.*
REFRESHMENTS: *Own café.*
PARKING: *None available on the premises.*
STORAGE: *Yes*
TRANSPORTATION: *Yes*
SHIPPING: *Yes*

600-700 lots. Heathcote Ball & Co hold popular sales of household furniture and effects, in the attractive setting of what used to be an old brewery. It has a cobbled stone courtyard, and is one of the oldest buildings in Northampton.

The sale starts with lesser-quality furniture. At the same time, other items such as baths, sinks and bicycles are sold under a lean-to outside the saleroom. The saleroom is a large L-shaped room, and the sale tends to fall into two sections; the smaller end of the L holds smaller lots, such as boxes full of kitchenalia, sundry pieces of china and portable electrical goods like personal stereos, while the main part of the hall holds furniture, (which could include bedroom and dining room suites, single armchairs, pianos, tables, washstands and so on), and large electrical goods — photocopying machines, washing machines, dishwashers and so on. Many of these electrical goods will have come from a local warehouse, or are end-of-line or showroom items. They carry no guarantee, but it is possible to pick up

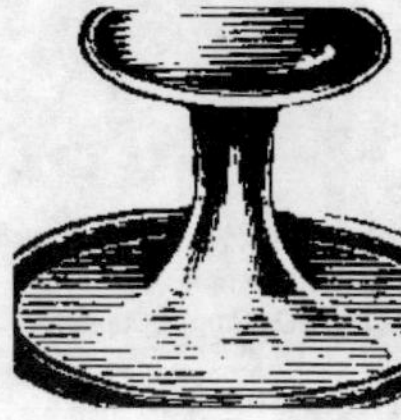

some amazing bargains in this section if you are prepared to take the risk.

Antique and fine art sales are also held, on average about once every three months.

WILFORDS

76 Midland Road. Tel: (0933) 222760

900-1,000 lots. This weekly sale attracts many regulars, and Thursdays in the saleroom are hectic. The firm was established in 1934 and is still owned by the Wilford family. The sale has a reputation for the variety of goods and the friendly, helpful service offered to both buyer and vendor. A typical sale will have electrical goods, kitchen items, modern furniture, and domestic and ornamental china. Selling starts with outside effects such as bicycles, lawn mowers and gardening tools. In among the lots there may be some good antiques. Unlike many other auctioneers, Wilfords do not keep back better quality articles for special sales.

Wellingborough

BUYER'S PREMIUM: *Nil*
SALES: *Weekly on Thu at 10.00am.*
VIEWING: *Day prior 8.00am-6.00pm.*
REFRESHMENTS: *Coffee vending machine.*
PARKING: *None available on the premises.*
STORAGE: *No*
TRANSPORTATION: *Yes*
SHIPPING: *Yes*

NORTHUMBERLAND

IAN A ROBERTSON

Narrowgate Salerooms, Narrowgate. Tel: (0665) 602725

600-700 lots. Alnwick is a delightful stone market town, set on a hill above the River Aln. The saleroom is part of the old castle — it is at the end of the castle wall, with a beautiful park to wander around during the lunch break in the sale. As might be expected in such surroundings, the selling in the auction is unhurried. The fortnightly sale is very much a local meeting place, with many people from the nearby villages arranging their regular shopping trip to coincide with the sale. The lots generally include an array of well-cared-for household furniture and effects, and interesting items of china, brass, jewellery and other goods. About twice a year, but at no set times, the auctioneers hold a special two-day catalogued sale of antiques and fine art.

Alnwick

BUYER'S PREMIUM: *5%*
SALES: *General: fortnightly on Tue at 10.00am. Special antiques sale: twice yearly on Mon and Tue at 10.00am.*
VIEWING: *General: Fri, Sat and Mon prior 10.00am-4.00pm. Special antiques sale: Thu, Fri and Sat prior, 10.00am-4.00pm.*
REFRESHMENTS: *None available on the premises.*
PARKING: *None available on the premises.*
STORAGE: *Yes*
TRANSPORTATION: *Yes*
SHIPPING: *Yes*

LOUIS JOHNSON

Oswald House, 63 Bridge Street. Tel: (0670) 513025

400-500 lots. Morpeth is an old market town in the charming wooded valley of the Wansbeck. The saleroom is part of an attractive three-storey building, which has recently been

Morpeth

BUYER'S PREMIUM: *10%*
SALES: *Monthly on Sat at 10.00am (includes sale of antiques in alternate months).*

VIEWING: *Wed, Thu and Fri prior 10.00am-4.00pm (also Thu 10.00am-7.00pm for antiques sale).*
REFRESHMENTS: *Own café.*
PARKING: *Car park opposite.*
STORAGE: *Yes*
TRANSPORTATION: *Yes*
SHIPPING: *Yes*

extended. Louis Johnson's monthly auctions alternate between general sales and sales of better quality antiques, reproduction furniture and fine art. The general sales have a typical range of household furniture and effects, and as a rule some gardening equipment as well. At the rear of the saleroom there is an area where classic cars are auctioned. Around eight to a dozen of these cars may be sold at the start of the antiques sale. There is also a craft centre opposite the saleroom, selling blown glass, dried flowers, tapestry and other locally made items.

NORTH YORKSHIRE

Bedale

BUYER'S PREMIUM: *5%*
SALES: *Every three weeks on Sat at 10.00am.*
VIEWING: *Tue, Wed and Fri 9.00am-12.00 noon. 1.00pm-4.30pm, Thu 9.00am-12.00 noon.*
REFRESHMENTS: *None available on the premises.*
PARKING: *Ample parking near by.*
STORAGE: *Yes*
TRANSPORTATION: *Yes*
SHIPPING: *Yes*

M W DARWIN & SONS

The Dale Furniture Hall, Bridge Street. Tel: (0677) 22846

400-500 lots. The saleroom is a converted chapel, and a visit is a must for many people from nearby villages, while local people will often pop in quickly during sale day just to see what is on offer.

The sale is on a Saturday, and it is a popular meeting place for many who turn up, not just to buy, but also to meet old friends and exchange local gossip. A typical sale will have general household furniture and effects, including antiques. There is usually a fair amount of china, glass, pottery, jewellery and so on, with bicycles, mowers and lesser quality items to finish the proceedings.

Within this broad range, the value of the lots varies widely. A glass ornament might be auctioned off for a couple of pounds, while a few lots later a piece of antique furniture could well fetch a three- or four-figure sum.

Harrogate

BUYER'S PREMIUM: *5%*
SALES: *General: weekly on Thu at 12.00 noon (except second Thu of month). Antiques: second Thu of month at 10.00am and 2.00pm.*
VIEWING: *General: morning of sale from 9.00am. Antiques: day prior 10.00am-4.00pm.*
REFRESHMENTS: *None available on the premises.*
PARKING: *None available on the premises.*
STORAGE: *Yes*
TRANSPORTATION: *Yes*
SHIPPING: *Yes*

MORPHETS

4 & 6 Albert Street. Tel: (0423) 530030

300-400 lots. The saleroom is a short walk from the railway station, behind the company's offices and close to the centre of this busy town. There is a general auction most Thursdays, but the second Thursday of each month is usually devoted to a catalogued sale of antiques and fine art. Lots in this sale could include period and later furniture, oil paintings and watercolours, pottery, porcelain, silver, jewellery and *objets d'art*, among other items. The other Thursday sales are just as rewarding, but they offer lesser quality goods, such as Victorian and Edwardian household furniture and effects, kitchenalia, domestic and ornamental china, various household items and some collectables.

TENNANTS OF YORKSHIRE

The Saleroom. Tel: (0969) 22411

700-800 lots. This is a Yorkshire country auction with a national reputation. The fame of Tennants' sales explains the brevity of their address. The Saturday fortnightly sale is of general household furniture and effects, with an emphasis on antiques. At most sales there will be around 400 lots of small items such as china, glass, crockery and cutlery, with some 300 lots of cottage and shipping furniture, and 200 lots of better quality furniture and antiques.

Typical lots at past sales have included Georgian mahogany tallboys, Victorian oak bookcases, chests of drawers, dining tables of all periods, writing desks, bureaux, painted and stained pine, wheelback chairs, dressing tables and pianos. In the ceramics section of the sale there is usually a quantity of English and Continental pottery and porcelain, including, very often, 18th-century items. Also to be found will be glass, silver plate, jewellery and coins, plus collectors' items and Victoriana: cigarette card albums, photograph albums, stamp albums, pictures, prints and books.

The box and tray lots of miscellaneous items are always worth looking at, as are the crochet and linen. In addition, you will probably find electrical goods such as washing machines and refrigerators, and outside effects, including tools of all types.

Note: In late 1990 Tennants were building a new saleroom complex at Harmby Road, Leyburn. This was due for completion in spring 1991. The telephone number for the saleroom was expected to remain the same.

Middleham, near Leyburn

BUYER'S PREMIUM: *10%*
SALES: *Fortnightly on Sat at 9.30am.*
VIEWING: *Day prior 10.00am-7.00pm.*
REFRESHMENTS: *Café in vicarage across the road.*
PARKING: *Own car park.*
STORAGE: *No*
TRANSPORTATION: *Yes*
SHIPPING: *Yes*

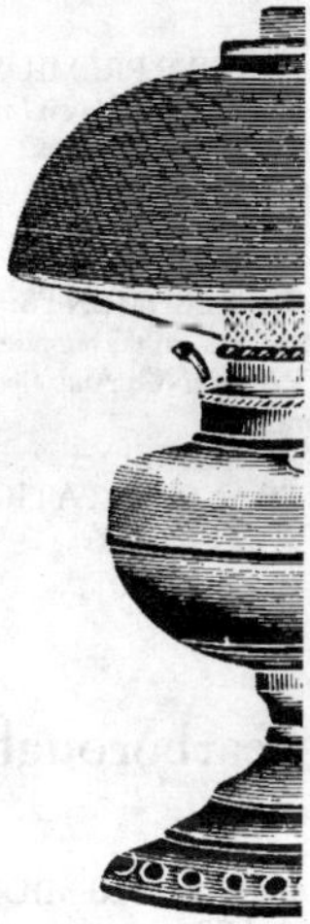

STEPHENSON & SON

The York Salerooms. Tel: (0904) 625533/489731

800-900 lots. These sales are of antiques and Victoriana, and are held usually in March, May, July, October and December. The sale calendar is arranged well in advance, and exact dates are available from the auctioneers. The lots are carefully selected and gathered over a long period, so they are generally of high quality. The range is very wide, however. Past sales have included an Aeolian pianola, brass and iron bedsteads, antique rocking chairs, antique bureaux, pictures and prints (many of local interest), silver and jewellery (including Georgian teaspoons, plated cutlery, entrée dishes, gold rings and gold watch chains), china and pottery (including Clarice Cliff, Victorian tea services and various items by Doulton, Coalport, Wedgwood and Staffordshire).

Murton, near York

BUYER'S PREMIUM: *Nil*
SALES: *Antiques and Victoriana: five times a year in Mar, May, Jul, Oct and Dec at 9.30am. Equipment and machinery: five to six times a year, from Mar to Nov on Wed at 10.00am. Horse and tack: monthly on Tue at 11.00am.*
VIEWING: *Antiques and Victoriana: day prior 2.00pm-8.00pm, day of sale. Equipment and machinery: day prior. Horse and tack: day of sale.*
REFRESHMENTS: *Own café.*

PARKING: *Ample parking available.*
STORAGE: *Yes*
TRANSPORTATION: *Yes*
SHIPPING: *Yes*

Sales of machinery and equipment are held between March and November on the same site. Among the 2,000-2,500 lots there will be second-hand timber, lawn mowers and garden tools, workshop machinery, livestock feeding equipment, tractors, combine harvesters and other vehicles.

The same firm holds monthly horse and tack auctions which are open to the public. They take place in stables at Rufforth Park, Rufforth. Saddles, blankets, spurs and other equipment are auctioned off first, followed by about 50 horses.

Ripon

BUYER'S PREMIUM: *5%*
SALES: *Weekly on Fri at 11.00am or 6.00pm.*
VIEWING: *Thu 10.00am-1.00pm and day of sale from 9.00am.*
REFRESHMENTS: *None available on the premises.*
PARKING: *Ample parking near by.*
STORAGE: *Yes*
TRANSPORTATION: *Yes*
SHIPPING: *Yes*

JOPLINGS & JOHNSTON

The Old Saleroom, Coltsgate Hill. Tel: (0765) 2614 707968

300-400 lots. Ripon is a quiet and peaceful city, with an ancient centre full of narrow streets and alleyways. The Old Saleroom is just off North Street, the main thoroughfare, and auctions have been held there since the turn of the century. The weekly sales take place on two floors, and are very much a local asset: people regularly use them for buying and selling a huge range of goods. The atmosphere is fun and there are usually many interesting lots to browse through. You will find anything from fine antiques to modern household furniture, including domestic electrical goods, gardening tools and equipment, ornaments, china, brass, books, paintings, childrens' toys, collectables and bric-à-brac.

Scarborough

BUYER'S PREMIUM: *10%*
SALES: *General: weekly on Mon at 10.00am (except weeks with antiques sale). Antiques: every four to six weeks on Tue at 10.00am.*
VIEWING: *General: Sat prior 10.00am-4.00pm. Antiques: Fri prior 4.00pm-7.00pm, Sat prior 10.00am-4.00pm, Mon prior 9.00am-12.00 noon.*
REFRESHMENTS: *None available on the premises.*
PARKING: *Own car park.*
STORAGE: *Yes*
TRANSPORTATION: *Yes*
SHIPPING: *Yes*

H C CHAPMAN & SON

The Auction Mart, North Street. Tel: (0723) 372424

200-400 lots. The weekly Monday sale was established in 1903 and is still going strong. Lots include good quality modern, reproduction and nearly-new household furniture, and a wide range of miscellaneous items, which helps to make the sale one of the most popular in Yorkshire.

Every four to six weeks there is a special sale of antiques and fine art, which is held on a Tuesday. This auction will include Georgian, Victorian and later furniture, ceramics, glass, *objets d'art*, jewellery, silver and plated items, watercolours, oil paintings and prints, and specialist categories of lots where appropriate. Sales are also held on the vendor's premises from time to time.

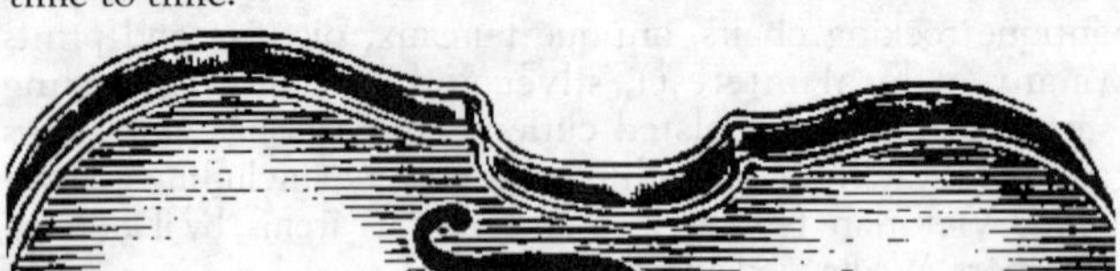

PAUL HIRST AUCTIONS

Scarthingwell Antique & Auction Centre. Tel: (093781) 7742

400-500 lots. This is a unique enterprise, a family-run concern with all members — husband, wife and children — living on the premises and helping out. The auctions are held on the first and third Monday of the month and offer an exciting and unusual day out in magnificent countryside.

The saleroom has been converted from an old barn, and stands in a group of old buildings. These house an antiques centre and a cluster of stalls selling antiques, collectables and crafts. The centre is open on weekdays and at weekends, when there are also viewings for the auctions.

Auction-goers are encouraged to bring children, who can play outside while the parents are in the saleroom or looking around the antique stalls. The delicious, home-cooked meals on offer are also worth trying. The auction itself is of general household goods, including modern, Edwardian and Georgian furniture, domestic and ornamental china, pottery, silver, brass, glass, collectables, jewellery, paintings, prints and other items.

Scarthingwell, near Tadcaster

BUYER'S PREMIUM: *10%*
SALES: *Twice monthly on first and third Mon of month at 6.00pm.*
VIEWING: *Sat and Sun prior 12.00 noon-5.00pm, day of sale from 12.00 noon.*
REFRESHMENTS: *Own café.*
PARKING: *Own car park.*
STORAGE: *Yes*
TRANSPORTATION: *Yes*
SHIPPING: *Yes*

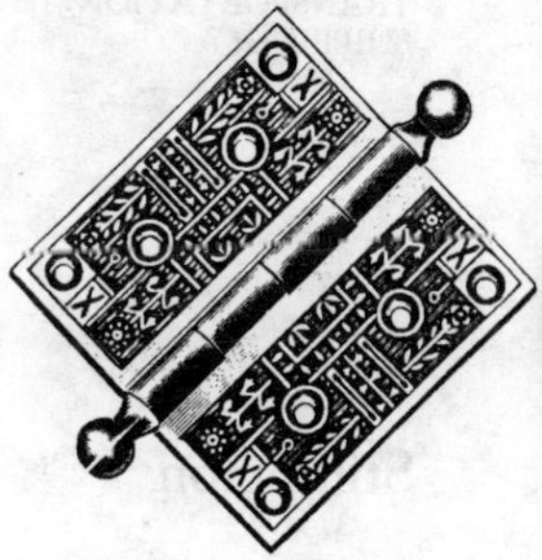

M H SKIDMORE

Victoria Hall. Tel: (0535) 275265

500-800 lots. In addition to this Wednesday afternoon sale at Settle, Mr Skidmore conducts Friday evening auctions at the Town Hall, Main Street, Cottingley (about one mile from Bingley). Both sales take place at three-weekly intervals and are similar in content, although Settle is the larger. The sales are ideal for those wishing to furnish a house cheaply, buy high quality antiques, develop a collection of one type or another, or simply browse. A typical sale might include a complete farmhouse dispersal of old furniture and general effects, as well as new and nearly new furniture, carpets and effects from modern houses.

Among the lots in past sales have been oak roll-top desks, carved rosewood chairs, marble-top washstands, oak bedding boxes, carved oak firescreens, 18th-century carved Bible boxes, books, china, silver, brass and jewellery. The selling is relaxed and there is a pleasant informal atmosphere, with a lot of country humour. Mr Skidmore travels as a livestock auctioneer when not conducting these sales, and on a Monday you may find him selling at the livestock sale at Otley.

Settle

BUYER'S PREMIUM: *Nil*
SALES: *Settle: every three weeks on Wed at 2.00pm. Cottingley: every three weeks on Fri at 6.00pm.*
VIEWING: *Settle: day of sale from 10.00am. Cottingley: day of sale from 2.00pm.*
REFRESHMENTS: *Own cafés.*
PARKING: *Own car parks.*
STORAGE: *Yes*
TRANSPORTATION: *Yes*
SHIPPING: *Yes*

Sherburn-in-Elmet (between Leeds and Selby)

BUYER'S PREMIUM: *10%*
SALES: *Monthly on last Thu of month at 6.30pm.*
VIEWING: *Day prior 12.00 noon-8.00pm, day of sale from 9.00am.*
REFRESHMENTS: *Own café.*
PARKING: *Own car park.*
STORAGE: *Yes*
TRANSPORTATION: *Yes*
SHIPPING: *Yes*

MALCOLMS NO 1

Sherburn-in-Elmet Village Hall. Tel: (0977) 684971 and 685334

300-400 lots. On both the sale day and the viewing day, the village hall is surrounded by vehicles belonging to potential buyers, so it is not hard to find. Malcolm Dowson's sales have a reputation for a good selection of antiques and collectables which sell at reasonable prices, and they attract both trade buyers and members of the public from far away. A computerised system is used to avoid long queues.

The hall is centrally heated and has seating for around 150. The sales start at 6.30pm prompt with furniture, followed by top quality antiques and collectables. Likely to be found are good quality items such as lowboys, Victorian dressers, tiled wash stands, tables, display cabinets and farmhouse pine. There is usually a selection of antique, Art Nouveau and Art Deco porcelain and pottery, which might include early Spode, Davenport, Limoges, Charlotte Rhead, Clarice Cliff, Keith Murray, Mason, Shelley, Doulton and others. Among the other lots you might find glass, old lanterns, paintings and prints, silver and quality plate, and farmhouse items.

Stillington

BUYER'S PREMIUM: *Nil*
SALES: *Every six to eight weeks on Sat at 1.00pm.*
VIEWING: *Day of sale from 10.00am.*
REFRESHMENTS: *None available on the premises.*
PARKING: *Ample parking near by.*
STORAGE: *No*
TRANSPORTATION: *Yes*
SHIPPING: *Yes*

G SUMMERSGILL

The Village Hall. Tel: (0904) 791131

300 lots. Stillington is a village about three miles from Easingwold. G Summersgill has been holding auctions in this area for over 20 years. This one is held every six to eight weeks in the village hall, which is hired for the occasion. The majority of the lots will be from house clearances, but local people will also bring in their unwanted goods. It is amazing how many pine chests, clocks, ornaments and other interesting bits and pieces farmers and others can find tucked away in their lofts or sheds. General run-of-the-mill goods mix in with well-cared-for antiques, and successful bids can range from pence to thousands of pounds. Quite apart from the possibility of picking up an unusual item, the atmosphere is pleasant, and the surrounding countryside is attractive, too.

Whitby

BUYER'S PREMIUM: *10%*
SALES: *General: twice or three times a month on Wed at 9.30am. Antiques: monthly on Wed at 9.30am.*
VIEWING: *General: day prior 9.00am-4.30pm.*

SUFFIELD WELLS CUNDALL

The Paddock. Tel: (0947) 603433

300-400 lots. Suffield Wells Cundall was established over 50 years ago, and is now part of Nationwide Anglia. The saleroom is off Skinner Street, on the West Cliff, which is the more modern area of this picturesque town. The sale is a popular meeting place for local people and holidaymakers alike. Unlike many auctions, this one includes a break for lunch, which is welcome after a morning of exciting bidding. Buyers can prepare themselves for an afternoon of hand-raised confrontation in one of the excellent pubs near by. The weekly sale usually offers a comprehensive range of general household furniture and effects, with the morning session devoted to small items and lesser quality furniture. The afternoon session is devoted to better-quality furniture, beds, linen and so on.

Once a month the general sale is replaced by an antiques and fine art sale. Due to the length of time and work involved in preparing for this catalogued sale, there is no general sale the week before.

Antiques: Sat prior 9.00am-4.00pm, Mon prior 9.00am-8.00pm, Tue prior 9.00am-4.30pm.
REFRESHMENTS: *None available on the premises.*
PARKING: *None available on the premises.*
STORAGE: *Yes*
TRANSPORTATION: *Yes*
SHIPPING: *Yes*

NOTTINGHAMSHIRE

Eastwood

J D BIRD & CO LTD

52 Nottingham Road. Tel: (0773) 760443

200-300 lots. The saleroom is opposite Victoria Street, where D H Lawrence was born in 1885. The town figures memorably as 'Bestwood' in *Sons and Lovers*, and is still a peaceful and fairly rural place. The sale concentrates on specially selected items such as pre-1930s furniture, plus silver, jewellery, pictures, ceramics, Victoriana, brass, bronzes, porcelain, linen, collectors' items, clocks, and so on. The auctioneers have a large catalogue mailing list and a regular, loyal clientele. There is a friendly atmosphere at the sales, with helpful porters always available to offer advice or take written bids should you be unable to stay for the entire auction. Bidding is relatively slow — about 60 lots an hour as opposed to the 100 per hour which is the average — so prospective buyers have a little more time to ruminate before making any bids.

BUYER'S PREMIUM: *Nil*
SALES: *Monthly on Wed at 6.30pm (except Aug).*
VIEWING: *Sat prior 9.30am-1.00pm, Sun prior 10.00am-1.00pm, Mon prior 10.30am-3.00pm, Tue prior 10.30am-3.00pm and 6.00pm-8.00pm, day of sale from 10.30am.*
REFRESHMENTS: *None available on the premises.*
PARKING: *Adequate public parking near by.*
STORAGE: *No*
TRANSPORTATION: *Yes*
SHIPPING: *Yes*

Newark-on-Trent

RICHARD WATKINSON & PARTNERS

17 North Gate. Tel: (0636) 77154

400-500 lots. Newark is a picturesque town of considerable antiquity, with many historical associations. It is also a delight for auction-goers, and this Wednesday morning sale is one that children will love. It is held on the Wharf by the side of the River Trent, just before the Trent Bridge. The first part is entirely in the open, and includes the sale of livestock such as pigeons, chickens, rabbits and peacocks, as well as fruit and vegetables, flowers and other produce. There will also be items of furniture, and boxes containing anything from books and puzzles to pots, pans and building equipment, or perhaps tins of

BUYER'S PREMIUM: *Antiques and fine art: 5%. Others: 10%*
SALES: *General: weekly on Wed at 10.30am, and Thu at 11.00am. Antiques and fine art: monthly on first Thu of month at 11.00am (replaces general Thu sale). Poultry: annual on Wed before Christmas at 2.00pm.*
VIEWING: *General (Wed): day of sale from 9.30am.*

General (Thu): day prior 9.30am-5.00pm, morning of sale from 9.00am. Antiques and fine art: day prior 9.30am-7.00pm, morning of sale from 9.00am.
REFRESHMENTS: *Vending machine.*
PARKING: *Own car park.*
STORAGE: *Yes*
TRANSPORTATION: *Yes*
SHIPPING: *Yes*

nails or electrical goods. Almost anything can turn up here. The auctioneer walks along selling each lot as it is arrived at, and payment is made in cash at the completion of each sale.

At 2.30pm the auction moves into one of the two salerooms behind the auctioneers' offices. Here 150 or so lots will be sold, mainly boxes of miscellaneous items such as china, general kitchenalia, books and ornaments. There will also be some modern household furniture and general effects. Wednesday is also market day, and the main market stalls are only a few minutes' walk away.

The Thursday sale takes place in the second saleroom, and includes some 300 lots of general household furniture (including Victorian, reproduction and modern), kitchenalia, lawn mowers, electrical equipment, tools of all sorts, brass, china, bric-à-brac and other goods.

On the first Thursday of the month this general sale is replaced by a special antiques and fine art sale, which takes place in the smaller of the two salerooms and includes Victorian and antique furniture, paintings, oils, watercolours, silver and plate, collectables and so on. There is also a yearly sale of poultry.

Nottingham

BUYER'S PREMIUM: *Nil*
SALES: *Weekly on Sat at 9.30am.*
VIEWING: *Fri 2.00pm-6.45pm.*
REFRESHMENTS: *Available.*
PARKING: *Own car park.*
STORAGE: *Yes*
TRANSPORTATION: *Yes*
SHIPPING: *Yes*

ARTHUR JOHNSON & SON

The Nottingham Auction Centre, Cattle Market, Meadow Lane. Tel: (0602) 869128

2,000 lots. This is possibly the largest weekly auction in the Midlands, if not in the whole country, with five separate sales taking place during an extremely busy morning and early afternoon. The auctions are all usually completed by 2.00pm to 2.30pm. Buyers must pay in cash, unless prior arrangements have been made, and vendors are paid on the same day, which adds to the excitement and bustle.

At 9.30am the proceedings start outside the saleroom with such things as timber, building materials, garden shrubs and produce. Inside the saleroom complex, antique and pre-1940s furniture is to be found in Saleroom 1. The smaller good quality items, for example jewellery, watches, silver, silver plate, porcelain, bronzes and brass, are sold in Saleroom 2. Modern household items such as dining room and kitchen furniture, cookers, beds and televisions, are offered for sale in a separate auction room.

In yet another saleroom, commercial goods go under the hammer. These might include filing cabinets, garden machinery and woodworking tools. General bric-à-brac is also included.

Except for those outside, all the lots are numbered, so prospective buyers can put in written bids if they are interested in lots at more than one of the sales.

NEALES

Nottingham

The Nottingham Salerooms, 192-4 Mansfield Road. Tel: (0602) 624141

1,000-1,500 lots. The four salerooms are in an imposing early 20th-century building, designed in a style which would meet the approval of Prince Charles. It occupies a prominent spot in the centre of the city.

The weekly Monday sale has general household furniture and effects, (largely Victorian, Edwardian and modern), together with secondary antique furniture and smaller items, from the 19th century and later. There are bargains to be had in all departments.

Sales of antiques and fine art are held at approximately six-weekly intervals and are spread over two days, encompassing the whole range of antique and fine art categories. The sale is divided into specialist sections, starting on the Thursday morning with silver, silver plate, jewellery, *bijouterie* and watches. These are followed at 1.00pm by European ceramics, glass, Oriental ceramics and works of art. The Friday morning begins with pictures and books, musical instruments, clocks and metalwork, followed in the afternoon by English and Continental furniture and decorative arts.

At irregular intervals three times a year, Neales also hold collectors' sales of autographs, postcards, cigarette cards, toys, dolls, stamps and other small collectables.

BUYER'S PREMIUM: *10%*
SALES: *General: weekly on Mon at 11.00am. Antiques and fine art: every six weeks on Thu and Fri at 10.30am. Collectables: three times a year (no fixed months) on Tue at 1.00pm.*
VIEWING: *General: Sat prior 9.00am-12.00 noon, morning of sale from 9.00am. Antiques and fine art: Tue prior 10.00am-8.00pm and Sun prior 2.00pm-5.00pm. Collectables: day prior 10.00am-5.00pm, morning of sale from 9.00am.*
REFRESHMENTS: *Vending machine.*
PARKING: *Own car park.*
STORAGE: *Yes*
TRANSPORTATION: *Yes*
SHIPPING: *Yes*

JOHN PYE & SON

Nottingham

The Corn Exchange, London Road. Tel: (0602) 865238

200-300 lots. The weekend is a heady time for auction *aficionados* in this part of Nottingham, with this sale on a Friday evening and the large Saturday sale held by Arthur Johnson & Sons barely 300 yards away in the Cattle Market. (The Corn Exchange is almost adjacent to Notts County football ground as well).

This Friday sale includes a good mixture of Victorian, Edwardian and reproduction furniture and effects, as well as kitchenalia, cookers, refrigerators, washing machines and televisions, plus pictures, jewellery, linen, carpets and many tempting lots of assorted items. These might include pots and pans, packets of playing cards, books, children's toys and

BUYER'S PREMIUM: *10%*
SALES: *Weekly on Fri at 6.30pm.*
VIEWING: *Day of sale from 1.00pm.*
REFRESHMENTS: *None available on the premises.*
PARKING: *Large public car park in Cattle Market.*
STORAGE: *Yes*
TRANSPORTATION: *Yes*
SHIPPING: *Yes*

puzzles, and are always worth examining.

On the second Tuesday of each month, John Pye & Son also hold a plant and machinery sale at Great Northern Close, Nottingham — useful if you need a JCB, tractor or combine-harvester, and interesting even if you don't.

Retford

HENRY SPENCER & SONS

20 The Square. Tel: (0777) 708633

BUYER'S PREMIUM: *10%*
SALES: *Victorian and later: weekly on Mon at 11.00am. Specialist: weekly on Wed at 11.00am.*
VIEWING: *Weekday prior, 10.00am-3.00pm.*
REFRESHMENTS: *None available on premises.*
PARKING: *Ample parking space.*
STORAGE: *Yes*
TRANSPORTATION: *Yes*
SHIPPING: *Yes*

400-500 lots. Established in 1840, Henry Spencer & Sons is now a part of the Halifax Building Society, but it still has the air of a family firm. It is also very up-to-date, with computerised systems in its modern complex of offices, storage areas and two salerooms. The Monday sale is of Victorian and later furniture, or fine furniture and ornamental items, which at some sales might include garden furniture and statuary, light fittings and mirrors. The Wednesday sales cover four specialist areas, with one area dealt with each week in rotation as follows. Week 1: European ceramics and glass. Week 2: silver and plate, jewellery and *bijouterie*. Week 3: Oriental ceramics, ivories, bronzes, enamels and works of art, or clocks and scientific instruments, or European works of art. Week 4: oil paintings, watercolour drawings, prints, engravings and miniatures. There are also Henry Spencer salerooms in Carmarthen, Dyfed; Nantwich, Cheshire; and Ross-on-Wye, Herefordshire.

Southwell

GASCOINES

1 Church Street. Tel: (0636) 813245

BUYER'S PREMIUM: *5%*
SALES: *Monthly on Fri at 6.00pm.*
VIEWING: *Day of sale 10.00am-5.00pm.*
REFRESHMENTS: *None available on the premises.*
PARKING: *Large public car park two minutes' walk away.*
STORAGE: *No*
TRANSPORTATION: *Yes*
SHIPPING: *No*

200-300 lots. The saleroom is in the shopping centre, just past the Minster and the Saracen's Head public house. The latter has been an inn since 1396, and Charles I stayed there for a night or two.

Southwell is also notable as the home of the Bramley apple, first raised in the garden at Bramley cottage. The entrance to Gascoines' pleasant, theatre-like auction room is up a flight of stairs. The auction is conducted from a stage at one end. Around the edge of the room are the larger lots of furniture, for example cabinets, wardrobes, dressers, bedroom suites and the like. There is more furniture in the centre, including chairs and settees, which are usually sat on by the crowd while the auction is in progress. The furniture generally includes some antiques. The paintings, prints, etchings and mirrors in the sale are displayed on the walls of the saleroom, and a wide range of brass, china, glassware, cutlery, linen, bric-à-brac, collectables and other small items is sold.

OXFORDSHIRE

HOLLOWAYS

49 Parsons Street. Tel: (0295) 253197

400-500 lots. Holloways are busy country auctioneers with a national reputation. They hold a series of sales in pleasant locations in the Thames Valley and the Cotswolds. At Banbury there are two sales per month, which alternate between 'General Antiques and Collectors' items' and 'Victorian and Other Furniture'.

The same firm has a sale every four or five weeks at the village hall in Goring, with around 400-500 lots of antiques and collectors' items. The hall is in the centre of Goring and displays Holloways' sale signs. For details of the Goring sale tel: (0491) 872318.

Every two months at the Memorial Hall, Memorial Avenue, Shiplake, Holloways hold sales of antiques and collectors' items. This auction is similar to the one at Goring and has around 500-600 lots (although the refreshments are by no means as good). The telephone number of the office dealing with the Shiplake sale is (0734) 589502.

Banbury

BUYER'S PREMIUM: *7%*
SALES: *Banbury: fortnightly on Tue at 10.30am. Goring: every four or five weeks on Wed at 10.30am. Shiplake: every two months on Thu at 10.00am.*
VIEWING: *Banbury: Sat prior 9.00am-12.00 noon, Mon prior 10.00am-6.00pm. Goring: day prior 2.30pm-6.30pm. Shiplake: day prior 12.00 noon-6.00pm. All: morning of sale from 9.00am.*
REFRESHMENTS: *Banbury: available next door. Goring: own café. Shiplake: van selling snacks.*
PARKING: *Banbury: Castle Street multi-storey. Goring: available near by. Shiplake: own car park.*
STORAGE: *By request at Banbury only.*
TRANSPORTATION: *Yes*
SHIPPING: *Yes*

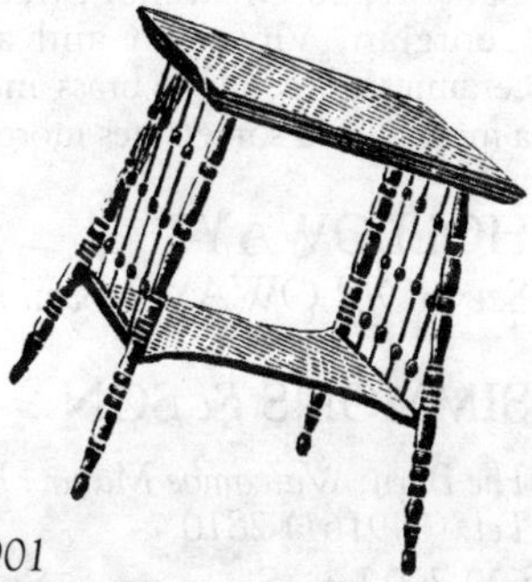

MESSENGERS AUCTION ROOMS

27 Sheep Street. Tel: (0869) 252901

400-500 lots. Bicester is an old-fashioned town with an attractive market square. The Messengers Auction Rooms are close to the Manorsfield car park, at the rear of the company's estate agency office. The saleroom is usually full on sale days. The majority of the items in the general sale are sold on behalf of private vendors and are mostly in a good or fair condition, including antique, Victorian and Edwardian furniture and household effects, domestic and ornamental china, pictures, silver, jewellery and so on.

At irregular intervals Messengers hold specialist sales of old tools for collectors of hand tools and restorers of antiques. Country pursuits sales are also held from time to time, and

Bicester

BUYER'S PREMIUM: *7½%*
SALES: *General: every six weeks (none in Aug) on Thu at 10.30am. Tools and country pursuits: at irregular intervals.*
VIEWING: *Day prior 8.30am-5.00pm, morning of sale.*
REFRESHMENTS: *At some sales, or available near by.*
PARKING: *Manorsfield public car park.*
STORAGE: *Yes*
TRANSPORTATION: *Yes*
SHIPPING: *Yes*

include odd items like coat racks made of horse shoes, as well as the more predictable old golf clubs, fishing rods, suitcases, hunting prints, shooting sticks and so on.

Goring

HOLLOWAYS

See HOLLOWAYS, Banbury, Oxfordshire

Oxford

MALLAMS

Bocardo House, St Michael's Street. Tel: (0865) 241358

BUYER'S PREMIUM: *10%*
SALES: *Oxford: three (occasionally four) times a month on Wed at 11.00am. Cheltenham: about once a month on Thu at 11.00am.*
VIEWING: *Oxford: Sat prior 9.00am-1.00pm, Mon and Tue prior 9.00am-5.00pm. Cheltenham: Tue and Wed prior 9.00am-5.00pm.*
REFRESHMENTS: *Available near by.*
PARKING: *Public car parks near by.*
STORAGE: *Yes*
TRANSPORTATION: *Yes*
SHIPPING: *Yes*

150-600 lots. Mallams are an independent auctioneering firm who have been established since 1788. At their Oxford saleroom, close to the Oxford Union Debating Hall, they hold three, or occasionally four, sales per month of high quality, carefully selected items. Three categories of sale take place on a rotating basis. One week the sale will include ceramics, glass, oil paintings, watercolours, collectors' items and other small lots. The following week the sale will be of Victorian and later furniture, and the sale after that will be of fine antique furniture and works of art, including as a rule a large number of clocks.

Mallams also hold a sale in Cheltenham, at the Grosvenor Galleries, 26 Grosvenor Street, tel: (0242) 235712. This is of Georgian, Victorian and antique furniture and effects, ceramics, glass, silver, brass and so on. It takes place about once a month, and sometimes more often.

Shiplake

HOLLOWAYS

See HOLLOWAYS, Banbury, Oxfordshire

Watlington

SIMMONS & SON

The Barn, Watcombe Manor, Ingham Lane.
Tel: (049161) 2810

BUYER'S PREMIUM: *10%*
SALES: *Monthly (except Jan, Apr, Aug and Nov) on Fri at 10.30am.*
VIEWING: *Day prior 10.00am-5.00pm.*
REFRESHMENTS: *Own café!*
PARKING: *Own car park.*
STORAGE: *Yes*
TRANSPORTATION: *Yes*

600-700 lots. Simmons & Son hold a general auction once a month, except in January, April, August and November. The Barn is part of a light industrial complex on the Watlington to Henley road. Its entrance looks like the way into a farmyard, which is what the area once was. The well attended auctions usually have a variety of furniture, household effects and bric-à-brac of all periods, from antique right through to modern. Each sale also has special sections for silver, porcelain, cutlery, glass, ceramics, textiles, paintings, watercolours, prints and collectors' items. Outside effects such as lawn mowers and other machinery are on display outside the saleroom, and the sale finishes with these items.

SHROPSHIRE

PERRY & PHILLIPS

Bridgnorth

New Market Building, Listley Street. Tel: (0746) 762248

400-500 lots. Bridgnorth is split in two, with the High Town perched 200ft up on the right bank of the Severn, and the Low Town on the opposite side of the gorge. There are interesting strolls to be had through the narrow lanes and up and down the steps connecting the two. The Perry & Phillips saleroom is a listed building in the High Town and has been described as the 'largest, ugliest building in Shropshire' and 'a cross between a Victorian Railway Station and a Public Lavatory'. It has been the home of Perry & Phillips' auctions since 1853 however, so most locals are well used to it now.

The weekly auction here is popular and friendly. It offers a typical mix of household furniture and smaller articles, including some attractive and interesting pieces. High value lots are kept back for the special sale of antiques which occurs on the first Thursday of each month.

BUYER'S PREMIUM: *General: 50p per lot. Antiques: £1 per lot.*
SALES: *General: weekly on Thu at 11.00am. Antiques: monthly on first Thu of month at 11.00am.*
VIEWING: *Day prior 9.00am-8.30pm.*
REFRESHMENTS: *Own café.*
PARKING: *Public car park 200 yards away.*
STORAGE: *Yes*
TRANSPORTATION: *Yes*
SHIPPING: *Yes*

LUDLOW ANTIQUE AUCTIONS LTD

Ludlow

29 Corve Street. Tel: (0584) 875157/873496

400-600 lots. The word 'antique' may suggest that this saleroom deals only in pricey items, but in fact it is possible to buy an attractive lot here for as little as £10 — although another lot in the same sale might fetch £25,000. The saleroom is very comfortable, carpeted and well heated. A window display on Corve Street shows articles which are to be sold in forthcoming auctions. Typical past sales have included Victorian and 18th-century furniture, silver plated tea sets, Worcester jugs, Japanese vases, pewter candlesticks and other metalware, and plenty of collectables — an African leather drum, a 19th-century musical box, cases of mounted fish, a magic lantern, clocks, barometers, pictures and many more.

BUYER'S PREMIUM: *10%*
SALES: *Every six weeks on Tue at 11.00am.*
VIEWING: *Sat prior 10.00am-4.00pm, Mon prior 9.30am-5.00pm, morning of sale.*
REFRESHMENTS: *Drinks vending machine.*
PARKING: *Public car park 500 yards away.*
STORAGE: *Yes*
TRANSPORTATION: *Yes*
SHIPPING: *Yes*

TIMOTHY MEAR & CO

Ludlow

Temeside Salerooms, Ludford Bridge Trading Estate. Tel: (0584) 876081

400-500 lots. A classic country auction will sell some of its lots outside, and there will be at least one old tin bath in the sale. Another requirement is that it contains enough goods to furnish a house completely, down to the cutlery, brooms, buckets and bowls. Timothy Mear's is just such a sale. It starts

BUYER'S PREMIUM: *Nil*
SALES: *Fortnightly on Wed at 11.00am.*
VIEWING: *Apr-Oct: day prior 10.00am-8.00pm. Oct-Apr 10.00am-7.00pm.*

REFRESHMENTS: *Own café.*
PARKING: *Ample car parking space.*
STORAGE: *Yes*
TRANSPORTATION: *Yes*
SHIPPING: *Yes*

with outside effects such as gardening tools and equipment, garden seats and general bric-à-brac. Inside the saleroom, the 'smalls' are sold first, including china (domestic and ornamental), silver, glassware, lamps, cutlery, paintings and innumerable miscellaneous items. The furniture section varies just as much as the others in quality, value and age: one sale might include antique, Victorian, reproduction, modern and nearly new lots, selling for anything between £2 and £2,000. There is something in most sales to suit all pockets and needs. Mr Mear runs the show alone, but brings to it the expertise of 20 years in the antique and auctioneering business, including experience with Sotheby's Fine Art Auctioneers.

Newport

NEWPORT SALEROOM

16 Stafford Street. Tel: (0952) 814759

BUYER'S PREMIUM: *50p per lot.*
SALES: *Weekly on Fri at 6.30pm.*
VIEWING: *Mon-Fri 9.00am-5.00pm.*
REFRESHMENTS: *Own café.*
PARKING: *Own car park.*
STORAGE: *Yes*
TRANSPORTATION: *Yes*
SHIPPING: *Yes*

350-500 lots. The saleroom is opposite the cattle market, where livestock sales take place every Monday. The Friday sale is all a good country auction should be. Its informality is shown by the fact that the saleroom is open every weekday from 9.00am until 5.00pm, with members of the public welcome to wander in to view the lots. Mr Jo Costello shares the auctioneering with an assistant, and is constantly exchanging jokes with the public during the sale, ensuring that the evening is entertaining as well as (ideally) profitable for all parties. Almost anything can be bought, and at bargain prices. Typical lots include almost new and antique furniture, domestic and ornamental china, gardening equipment, building equipment, bygones, craft items and so on, with the occasional motor car or motorbike.

Telford

TELFORD AUCTIONS

Rookery Road, St Georges. Tel: (0952) 610033

BUYER'S PREMIUM: *Nil*
SALES: *Weekly on Tue at 6.30pm.*
VIEWING: *Day of sale from 9.00am.*
REFRESHMENTS: *Own café.*
PARKING: *Own car park.*
STORAGE: *Yes*
TRANSPORTATION: *Yes*
SHIPPING: *Yes*

300-400 lots. The saleroom is in the Oaken Gate area of Telford, and tends to be full of local people chatting while the sale is in progress, something which may be frowned upon at other auctions. A typical scene is of the auctioneer smilingly soliciting a bid of £40 for a teaset which will be knocked down for £4, while an anxious customer asks the porter for a catalogue, finds there isn't one, but goes home happy with several soup plates, a milk jug and dessert bowl, and two porcelain flower bouquets, all in different designs and from different lots. Down the centre of the room are the tables containing the 'smalls' — china, silver, glass, clocks and watches, books, lamps and so on, which are sold first. Next to come under the hammer are the bicycles, electrical equipment, carpets, blankets and linen, and then at 8.00pm attention is focused on the furniture, which is placed around the room and may be almost new. By the end of the evening virtually everything will have been sold, and two days later many of the crowd will return to watch an auction of motor vehicles which is also held here.

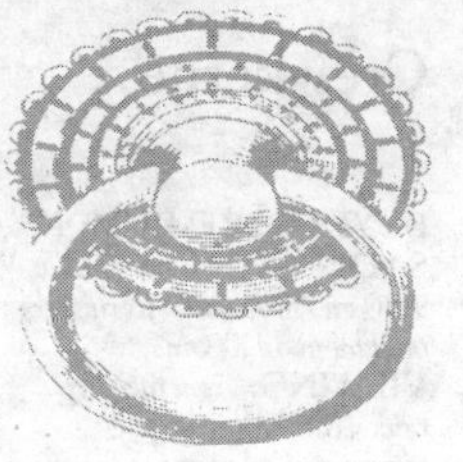

SOMERSET

Bridgwater

TAMLYN & SON

The Saleroom, Market Street. Tel: (0278) 458241

900-1,000 lots. The sales take place about once a month on Tuesday, but there is no sale in August or the early part of January. The saleroom is a three-storey brick building, purpose built in 1890. It lies west of the town centre, about 100 yards from the cinema.

This is an Aladdin's cave of an auction, where almost every type of object imaginable is offered, and buyers are kept on their toes by the hammer coming down on prices ranging from £1 to many thousands. Outside effects are the first to be sold, before attention moves on to modern furniture, such as three-piece suites, dining room furniture, beds and bedroom furniture, upholstered chairs and so on. Antiques and general bric-à-brac are not usually reached until 1.00pm. This is a genuine, independent auction, and lots are sold without a reserve price. Buyers range from local people to dealers from far afield. Many call in regularly in the hope that rare or interesting items will turn up, but they may only bid five or six times a year.

BUYER'S PREMIUM: *10%*
SALES: *Monthly on Tue at 10.00am (except Dec and early Jan)*
VIEWING: *Day prior 3.00pm-6.00pm.*
REFRESHMENTS: *Own café.*
PARKING: *Ample parking near by.*
STORAGE: *Yes*
TRANSPORTATION: *Yes*
SHIPPING: *Yes*

Burnham-on-Sea

J H PALMER & SONS

Bank Chambers, 75 High Street. Tel: (0278) 782326

250-350 lots. The monthly evening sale has become a landmark of this small, attractive seaside town, which also boasts seven miles of flat sandy beaches and fine golf links. Among the lots are general household furniture and effects, including antiques. People have become wise to the value of goods, but auctions such as this are still good places to hunt down oddities, rarities, knick-knacks and memorabilia, or to pick up nearly new items at a fraction of the original price. The smaller 'table' items are sold first, with the better quality items and antiques generally kept until the end of the sale. One-and-a-half miles away at Highbridge, J H Palmer & Sons are also responsible for Monday cattle auctions.

BUYER'S PREMIUM: *10%*
SALES: *Monthly on last Thu of month at 6.00pm.*
VIEWING: *Day of sale from 9.00am.*
REFRESHMENTS: *None available on the premises.*
PARKING: *None available on the premises.*
STORAGE: *Yes*
TRANSPORTATION: *Yes*
SHIPPING: *Yes*

Crewkerne

BUYER'S PREMIUM: *10%*
SALES: *General: on Wed at 9.30am. Specialist: fortnightly on Thu at 11.00am.*
VIEWING: *General: day prior 10.00am-7.00pm, morning of sale from 9.00am. Specialist: Sat prior 9.30am-12.30pm, Tue prior 10.00am-7.00pm, Wed prior 10.00am-4.30pm, morning of sale from 9.00am.*
REFRESHMENTS: *Own café.*
PARKING: *Own car park.*
STORAGE: *Yes*
TRANSPORTATION: *Yes*
SHIPPING: *Yes*

LAWRENCE

South Street. Tel: (0460) 73041

800-1,000 lots. The saleroom is about three-quarters of a mile from the railway station. Lawrence is an independent company and provides a comprehensive auction service. In Saleroom 2 there are weekly Wednesday general sales of goods of all types, selling in the £25 or upwards price bracket. As the Lawrence brochure says, goods in this sale range from 'reproduction furniture through to silver pepperpots'.

Separate specialist sales are held on average twice a month on Thursdays, dealing with various categories such as English and Continental furniture, clocks and watches, paintings, silver, jewellery, porcelain, Eastern carpets, mechanical music, toys, books and many others. Some specialist categories occur more frequently than others: check with the auctioneers.

Dulverton

BUYER'S PREMIUM: *Nil*
SALES: *Monthly (except Dec) on last Fri of month at 10.30am.*
VIEWING: *Day prior 2.00pm-6.00pm, morning of sale from 9.00am.*
REFRESHMENTS: *Home-made available.*
PARKING: *Ample parking near by.*
STORAGE: *Yes*
TRANSPORTATION: *Yes*
SHIPPING: *Yes*

JOHN D FLEMING & CO

The Town Hall, Fore Street. Tel: (0398) 23597

400-500 lots. The Town Hall is next door to John D Fleming's estate agency office, in the centre of this quiet little country town which borders Exmoor. The monthly auction, established over 15 years ago by the present proprietor and auctioneer, is an individual sale taking much of its atmosphere from John Fleming's informal style. The 'Antique and Modern' sale includes china, silver, jewellery, electrical goods (all guaranteed by the auctioneer), general furniture and furnishings. Also here will be collectables, bygones, and miscellanea of all ages, including the odd motor vehicle. The better quality goods are offered for sale in the afternoon session, which begins after the 1.00pm-2.00pm lunch break. The auctions have an excellent reputation and have seen six world-record prices for antiques. It is taken for granted that lots may range in price from pence to many thousands of pounds.

Frome

BUYER'S PREMIUM: *Nil*
SALES: *Fortnightly on Wed at 11.00am.*
VIEWING: *Mon and Tue prior 9.00am-7.00pm, morning of sale from 9.00am.*
REFRESHMENTS: *Own café.*
PARKING: *Ample parking near by.*

DORES & REES

The Auction Rooms, 32 Vicarage Street. Tel: (0373) 62257

400-500 lots. This is a small, privately run, friendly sale, ideal for the dealer, private buyer or earnest collector. Frome is an attractive old market town. The Gothic-style saleroom, which was once a chapel, is at the rear of St John's Church, close to the centre. The fortnightly Wednesday sale is of antique and modern household furniture and effects, with a tremendous variation in the value and quality of the lots. Beautiful pieces of antique furniture, an oil painting, or a piece of valuable china or jewellery will be sold on the same day as a refrigerator, a cooker, a tatty dresser, a box full of children's toys and puzzles, various items of kitchen and garden equipment and other lesser quality goods. Prices reached in one sale can vary from anything from £1 to £4,000.

STORAGE: *Yes*
TRANSPORTATION: *Yes*
SHIPPING: *Yes*

GRIBBLE BOOTH & TAYLOR

Minehead

Mart Road Saleroom, Mart Road. Tel: (0643) 703646

500-600 lots. Minehead is the most westerly of the county's resorts, with splendid walks, sands and sheltered gardens. Gribble Booth & Taylor are members of Royal Life Estates, and associated companies hold auctions in Avon, Wiltshire, Dorset, Hampshire, with another Somerset auction at Wells. The saleroom is part of an industrial estate in the seafront area. A separate room is used to sell some 200 to 300 lots of 'smalls', and this is a must for anyone interested in ornaments, china, glass, porcelain and the like. The main room has a notable stock of modern and reproduction wardrobes, cabinets, dressing tables, cottage pine and genuine antiques. Kitchen and electrical equipment come towards the end of the sale, with gardening tools and equipment last of all.

BUYER'S PREMIUM: *Nil*
SALES: *Every three weeks on Thu at 10.30am.*
VIEWING: *Day prior 9.00am-5.00pm, day of sale from 9.00am.*
REFRESHMENTS: *Own café.*
PARKING: *Own car park.*
STORAGE: *Yes*
TRANSPORTATION: *Yes*
SHIPPING: *Yes*

COOPER & TANNER (NATIONWIDE ANGLIA)

Standerwick, near Frome

The Frome Market. Tel: (0373) 831010

500-600 lots. The market complex is one of the most up-to-date in the country, and lies on the A36 about three miles north-east of Frome. Within easy driving distance are the Bratton Downs, with a white horse carved into the chalk hillside, and the country seat and safari park of the Marquess of Bath at Longleat.

The weekly Wednesday sale is of livestock and 'deadstock' — timber, tools and similar goods. This is an ideal sale for the DIY enthusiast to attend. On the second Friday of the month there are sales of antique and modern furniture and general household effects.

Special sales in various categories also take place, at irregular intervals throughout the year. These could include garden tools and equipment, garden trees and shrubs, horses and tackle and so on.

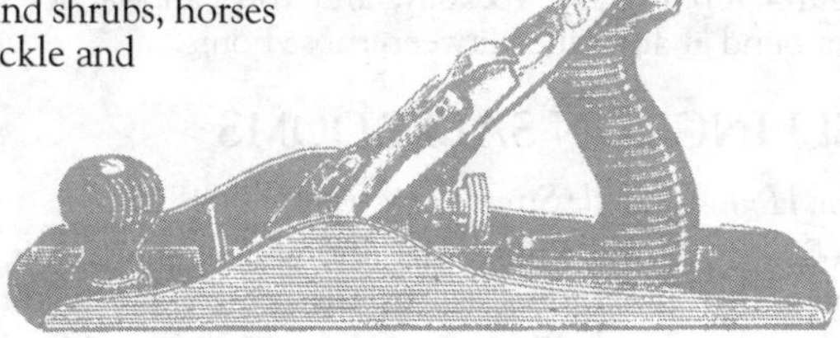

BUYER'S PREMIUM: *10%*
SALES: *Livestock and deadstock: weekly on Wed at 10.00am. General: monthly on second Fri of month at 11.00am. Special sales: at irregular intervals on Sat at 11.00am.*
VIEWING: *General: day prior 2.00pm-7.30pm. All: morning of sale.*
REFRESHMENTS: *Own café.*
PARKING: *Own car park.*
STORAGE: *Yes*
TRANSPORTATION: *Yes*
SHIPPING: *Yes*

Taunton

BUYER'S PREMIUM: *10%*
SALES: *General: every three weeks on Thu at 11.00am. Antiques: every four to six weeks on Thu at 11.00am.*
VIEWING: *General: day prior 2.00pm-4.00pm, morning of sale from 8.30am. Antiques: 10.00am-8.00pm, morning of sale from 8.30am.*
REFRESHMENTS: *Own café, general sale only.*
PARKING: *None available on the premises.*
STORAGE: *Yes*
TRANSPORTATION: *Yes*
SHIPPING: *Yes*

GREENSLADES

The Priory Saleroom, Winchester Street. Tel: (0823) 277121

500-600 lots. Taunton is the county town of Somerset and the bustling, prosperous centre of a thriving agricultural area. Market days are Tuesday and Saturday. Greenslades are well known in the area for their livestock sales, and they also hold two types of general auction in Taunton. Every three weeks they hire the Taunton Rugby Club, Priory Bridge Road, for a general sale of modern and shipping furniture and household effects. In addition, their own Priory Saleroom is used every four to six weeks for a sale of antiques and collectables. Many of the lots come from complete house clearances, so there is plenty of variety in age and character. The sales can be a treasure trove where you might find 43 pieces of Burleigh ware, a Victorian four-piece jug and bowl set, a Jacobean oak dresser or a modern three-piece lounge suite.

Greenslades are members of the Society of Fine Art Auctioneers.

Taunton

BUYER'S PREMIUM: *10%*
SALES: *General: twice a month on first and third Wed of month at 10.00am. Antiques: monthly on last Wed of month at 10.30am.*
VIEWING: *General: day prior 2.30pm-5.30pm, morning of sale from 9.00am. Antiques: 9.00am-8.00pm, morning of sale from 9.00am.*
REFRESHMENTS: *Own café.*
PARKING: *Own car park.*
STORAGE: *Yes*
TRANSPORTATION: *Yes*
SHIPPING: *Yes*

HUNTS

Magdalene House, Magdalene Street, Church Square.
Tel: (0823) 332525

900-1,000 lots. Hunts are partly responsible for the local livestock sales, but they also hold three interesting general and antique auctions per month in Taunton.

On the first and third Wednesdays of the month there are well-attended sales of general household furniture, effects and Victoriana, at the Market Hall Salerooms, Priory Bridge Road. Here you can bid for anything from a kitchen sink up to a five-piece bedroom suite, through electrical goods, china items, books and so on.

The other sale is held on the last Wednesday of the month at the Magdalene House saleroom opposite St Mary's Church, about three-quarters of a mile from Priory Bridge Road. This is an equally large affair, and is concerned with mixed antiques and collectables. The lots in this sale are just as unexpected and wide ranging, but are usually more valuable. Official viewing times are given here, but the saleroom is open from 9.00am-5.30pm every weekday, and you can wander in and look around at any time between those hours.

Wellington

BUYER'S PREMIUM: *10%*
SALES: *General: fortnightly*

WELLINGTON SALEROOMS

Clifton House, Mantle Street. Tel: (0823) 664815

400-600 lots. This is a busy, friendly, family-run auction. It was established over 20 years ago by the present proprietors, Ray and Maggie Cooper, who are helped on sale day by Mr Cooper's mother. The saleroom is an old Methodist chapel, a large, distinctive building on the town's main street. In the front a newly opened retail shop called Choice Gallery sells furniture and other goods on commission.

The fortnightly auctions are looked forward to by local people as social events. Friends cheerfully greet the Coopers and each other before wandering around the hall in small groups, discussing the lots. These range from general modern furniture through to collectables. Many of the local people will tell you proudly they have completely furnished and equipped their houses with articles bought at these sales. Every six weeks the general sale is followed by a special sale of antiques and collectables. For this sale the modern furniture is moved up into the first-floor saleroom. At other times it is sold in the downstairs saleroom.

on Tue at 11.00am. Antiques: every six weeks after general sale.
VIEWING: *Day prior 9.00am-8.00pm.*
REFRESHMENTS: *None available on the premises.*
PARKING: *None available on the premises.*
STORAGE: *Yes*
TRANSPORTATION: *Yes*
SHIPPING: *Yes*

SOUTH YORKSHIRE

WILLIAM H BROWN

Barnsley

See WILLIAM H BROWN, Doncaster, South Yorkshire

TUDOR AUCTION ROOMS

Carcroft

28 High Street. Tel: (0302) 725029

650-750 lots. Carcroft is just off the A1, and the saleroom is in the middle of town. George Allen runs the large and busy sale, which has been a popular local focal point for over 10 years. It used to be held on Sundays before falling foul of the Sunday trading laws. A typical sale will offer a large selection of antique furniture, including clocks, pictures, washstands, sideboards and display cabinets. Modern household furniture and goods will also be found, such as cookers, bedroom and lounge suites, televisions and all sorts of bric-à-brac. The selling starts with 'miscellaneous items', which vary a good deal because Tudor Auctions are the official auctioneers for various county courts. Then come general bric-à-brac, pottery, clocks, pictures and prints, electrical goods, and modern household furniture. The auction finishes with the antiques.

BUYER'S PREMIUM: *10%*
SALES: *Weekly on Sat at 11.00am.*
VIEWING: *Fri prior 4.00pm-7.00pm, day of sale from 9.00am.*
REFRESHMENTS: *Own café.*
PARKING: *None available on the premises.*
STORAGE: *Yes*
TRANSPORTATION: *Yes*
SHIPPING: *Yes*

WILLIAM H BROWN

Doncaster

28 Nether Hall Road. Tel: (0302) 367766

200-500 lots. William H Brown have two separate auctions in South Yorkshire, one in Barnsley and one in Doncaster.

The Barnsley sale is held on a Thursday at the Rockingham Welfare Hall, Hoyland Common, which is within 400 yards of

BUYER'S PREMIUM: *10%*
SALES: *Barnsley: monthly on Thu at 10.00am (except Aug and Dec). Doncaster: monthly on Tue at 10.30am (replaced at*

irregular intervals by antiques sale on Thu).
VIEWING: *Barnsley: day prior 5.30pm-8.00pm. Doncaster, general: day prior 10.00am-4.00pm. Doncaster, antiques: Mon prior 10.00am-4.00pm, Tue prior 10.00am-6.00pm.*
REFRESHMENTS: *Own café and van.*
PARKING: *Ample near by.*
STORAGE: *Yes*
TRANSPORTATION: *Yes*
SHIPPING: *Yes*

Junction 36 of the M1. This sale is organised from William H Brown's office at 11 Regent Street South, Barnsley, tel: (0226) 299221. It takes place every month except August and December, and is of general household furniture and effects. Typical sales have included Victorian and reproduction furniture, a wide selection of antiques, jewellery, porcelain, pottery, silver, brass, garden equipment and other goods.

William H Brown's Doncaster sale takes place monthly on Tuesday, and has goods of similar quality and variety. This Tuesday sale is replaced at irregular intervals by a special sale of antiques, which is always held on a Thursday.

Doncaster

DONCASTER AUCTION ROOMS

Queens Road. Tel: (0302) 367766

BUYER'S PREMIUM: *10%*
SALES: *Weekly on Thu at 6.30pm.*
VIEWING: *All week 10.00am-4.00pm.*
REFRESHMENTS: *Own café.*
PARKING: *Ample parking near by.*
STORAGE: *Yes*
TRANSPORTATION: *Yes*
SHIPPING: *Yes*

500-800 lots. This is a pleasant sale run by a husband-and-wife team. Part of the building housing the saleroom has been sectioned off as an antique centre, with a number of small units selling all kinds of antiques and bygones (open Monday-Saturday 10.00am-4.00pm). It is also possible to wander into the saleroom and look around at these times, but vendors are still bringing in goods for sale late in the week, and so the saleroom does not really fill up until close to the sale day. The selling starts with boxes of miscellaneous items, including crockery and linen. At 7.30pm collectables and smaller antiques come under the hammer, and then auctioning returns to miscellaneous items. Modern furniture and antiques bring the sale to a close.

Sheffield

A E DOWSE & SON

Cornwall Galleries, Scotland Street. Tel: (0742) 725858

BUYER'S PREMIUM: *5%*
SALES: *General: fortnightly on Tue at 11.00am. Antiques: monthly on Sat at 11.00am. Specialist: monthly on Sat at 11.00am. Fine art : quarterly on Mon at 12.00 noon.*
VIEWING: *General: morning of sale from 9.00am. Antiques and specialist: day prior 4.00pm-7.30pm, morning of sale from 9.30am. Fine art: day prior 2.00pm-6.00pm, morning of sale from 9.30am.*
REFRESHMENTS: *Own café.*
PARKING: *Ample near by.*
STORAGE: *Yes*
TRANSPORTATION: *Yes*
SHIPPING: *Yes*

400-500 lots. The large saleroom complex (over 6,000sq ft) is midway along Scotland Street. To get there from the city centre follow signs to Barnsley.

A E Dowse was founded in 1915 by a former mayor of Scunthorpe, and the auction is now run by the second and third generation of the Dowse family.

There are at least four sales per month here, in various categories. A general auction of shipping goods and modern furniture and effects is held every fortnight. In addition, there is a monthly auction of general antiques and collectors' items, and a separate monthly specialist auction, devoted to diecast, tinplate and collectors' toys, and stamps, coins, postcards and cigarette cards.

Finally there are quarterly auctions of fine art, antiques and related items.

EADON LOCKWOOD & RIDDLE

Sheffield

Western Saleroom, Crookes. Tel: (0742) 686294

400-450 lots. The company was established over 150 years ago and is a well-known landmark in this pleasant residential area of Sheffield. Just behind the saleroom, the Methodist church takes advantage of sale-day custom to provide home-made cakes and sandwiches, tea and coffee. The auction offers a wide range of good quality general furniture and other effects, such as carpets, domestic and ornamental china and glass, silver, jewellery and various knick-knacks. Twice a year in May or June and November or December, Eadon Lockwood & Riddle hold special antiques sales which are widely advertised and attract buyers from far afield.

BUYER'S PREMIUM: *10%*
SALES: *General: every three weeks on Fri at 10.00am. Antiques: twice a year in May/Jun and Nov/Dec on Wed at 10.00am.*
VIEWING: *Day prior 9.00am-5.00pm.*
REFRESHMENTS: *None available on the premises.*
PARKING: *Ample parking near by.*
STORAGE: *Yes*
TRANSPORTATION: *Yes*
SHIPPING: *Yes*

ELLIS, WILLIS & BECKETT

Sheffield

54 Campo Lane. Tel: (0742) 729667

300-400 lots. Campo Lane is in the city centre, backing on to the cathedral. Number 54 has an office front, but behind that are the ground and first-floor salerooms, which can become quite full on sale days. Included in the Thursday fortnightly sale is a wide selection of general household furniture and effects, which includes pictures and paintings, some excellent china, glassware, pewter, collectables, brass and so on. The firm are official auctioneers for the county courts, so the sales may include stock from bankrupt shops and other businesses. In the past, contents of a hairdressing equipment wholesalers have been sold, as have various bits of DIY equipment and car accessories.

Every quarter, but not in regular months, there are Wednesday evening sales of antiques. Most of the lots in this sale are goods which have been kept back from the general sales because of their quality.

BUYER'S PREMIUM: *Nil*
SALES: *General: fortnightly on Thu at 11.00am. Antiques: quarterly on Wed at 6.00pm (no fixed months).*
VIEWING: *General: day prior 1.30pm-3.30pm, day of sale from 10.30am. Antiques: day of sale from 10.30am.*
REFRESHMENTS: *None available on the premises.*
PARKING: *None available on the premises.*
STORAGE: *Yes*
TRANSPORTATION: *Yes*
SHIPPING: *Yes*

WILKINSON & BEIGHTON

Thurcroft

Woodhouse Green. Tel: (0709) 700005

500-600 lots. Thurcroft is about a two-minute drive from Junction 1 of the M18. The saleroom building is an old cinema on the main road of this quiet little Yorkshire town. Inside there are two separate salerooms — the majority of the auctions take place on the ground floor, but occasionally the second-floor saleroom is used to accommodate an extra large sale. This is one of the fastest-growing and one of the largest auction rooms in South Yorkshire, but it is a friendly place, with experts always available to give advice.

BUYER'S PREMIUM: *10%*
SALES: *Fortnightly on Mon at 11.00am (includes quarterly special antiques sale).*
VIEWING: *Day prior 11.00am-4.00pm.*
REFRESHMENTS: *Own café.*
PARKING: *Own car park.*
STORAGE: *Yes*
TRANSPORTATION: *Yes*
SHIPPING: *Yes*

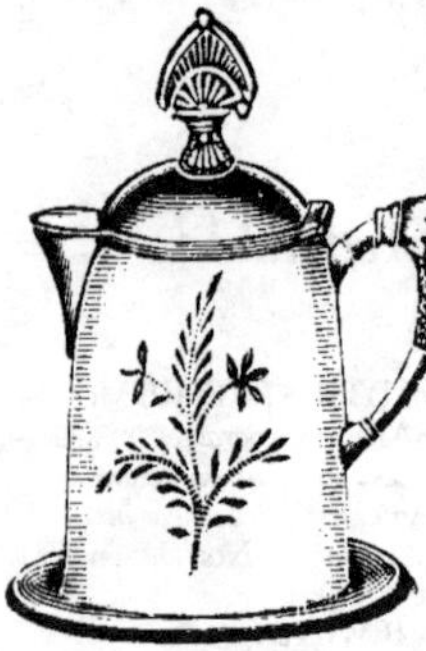

A sale of 'Antiques and Shipping Goods' is held once a fortnight, and includes a variety of furniture, pictures, china, porcelain and so on. Every quarter this sale is replaced by a special sale of fine antique furniture and *objets d'art*, and other goods of higher quality.

STAFFORDSHIRE

Hanley, near Stoke-on-Trent

BUYER'S PREMIUM: *Nil*
SALES: *Fortnightly on Tue at 10.00am or 11.00am depending on number of lots.*
VIEWING: *Sat prior 10.00am-2.00pm, day prior 10.00am-12.00 noon.*
REFRESHMENTS: *Vending machine.*
PARKING: *Own car park.*
STORAGE: *Yes*
TRANSPORTATION: *Yes*
SHIPPING: *Yes*

BUTTERS

Warner Street. Tel: (0782) 267752

400-500 lots. Hanley is a small and pleasant town, and its main claim to fame is that it was the birthplace of Arnold Bennett. Butters is an independent family concern established in 1856, and can be found in the centre of the town, just behind the museum and art gallery. The fortnightly sale alternates between general goods and general goods plus liquidated stock. In the past, the latter type of sale has included office equipment (desks, filing cabinets and typewriters), plumbing goods, kitchen units, motor cars and vans, and even a car ramp from a garage. Other sales of liquidated stock often take place on site, and these are worth enquiring about. The general-only sales start with bric-à-brac including china, paintings and silver, and then move on to furniture, finishing with domestic electrical appliances. Antique and better quality furniture are kept for a special section in the middle of the sale.

Hanley, near Stoke-on-Trent

BUYER'S PREMIUM: *10%*
SALES: *General: fortnightly on Mon at 10.00am. Special: every three months on Mon and Tue at 10.00 am (replaces general sale).*
VIEWING: *General: Fri prior 10.00am-4.00pm, Sat prior 9.00am-12.00 noon. Special: Thu prior 10.00am-7.00pm, Fri prior 10.00am-4.00pm.*
REFRESHMENTS: *None available on the premises.*
PARKING: *Ample near by.*
STORAGE: *Yes*
TRANSPORTATION: *Yes*
SHIPPING: *Yes*

LOUIS TAYLOR

10 Town Road. Tel: (0782) 260222

800-1,000 lots. The saleroom is opposite the Potteries Centre and has a fortnightly Monday sale of general household goods. There will usually be brass, china, glass and pictures, in addition to furniture of various types and ages, including antiques.

At three-monthly intervals the general sale is replaced by a special two-day sale which takes place over Monday and Tuesday. The special sales have a good reputation and are well attended by people from far afield. The first day of the sale is for porcelain and china, the second for paintings, silver, jewellery, glass and furniture. All the sales here have a comfortable atmosphere which should put at ease those new to bidding.

BURY & HILTON

Leek

Heritage Salerooms, Britannia Street. Tel: (0538) 373308

500-600 lots. This is a comprehensive sale in the heart of a beautiful Staffordshire town. The saleroom is a converted school, and is usually surrounded by cars on sale days. The auction starts outside with 50 or 60 lots which could include various types of bicycle, gardening equipment and other outdoor items. After those, selling continues inside with crockery and boxes of miscellaneous items, which are worth searching through. Next to be sold are cookers and other household appliances, followed by smaller items of furniture. The larger pieces of furniture (beds and so on) are sold last.

Twice a year, in April and October, the sale dates are arranged to coincide with school holidays.

Bury & Hilton also hold special fine art and antiques sales at Coronation Hall, Osmaston, near Ashbourne, Derbyshire. The hall is thatched, the village is beautiful, and there are some attractive pubs to visit near by. The sale is also fun because it is something of a social event for the entire village.

BUYER'S PREMIUM: *Nil*
SALES: *General: monthly on first Thu of month at 10.30am (except Jan). Fine art and antiques: twice a year in Apr and Oct on Thu at 11.00am.*
VIEWING: *General: Sat prior 10.00am-1.00pm, Wed prior 12.00 noon-3.00pm. Antiques: Tue prior 10.00am-9.00pm.*
REFRESHMENTS: *Own café.*
PARKING: *Own car park.*
STORAGE: *Yes*
TRANSPORTATION: *Yes*
SHIPPING: *Yes*

WINTERTONS LTD

Lichfield

Lichfield Auction Centre, Wood End Lane, Fradley.
Tel: (0543) 263256

1,000-1,500 lots. Wintertons Ltd have been auctioneers since 1864. Their sales are busy and efficient but not intimidating, despite the fact that at the antique and fine art auctions it is possible to buy a painting or piece of furniture worth many thousands of pounds. However, if your pockets do not run to that kind of money, it is also possible to walk away with a piece of silver or furniture after paying no more than £10-£20.

The fortnightly sales are of Victorian and general household furniture and effects, displayed to advantage in three large salerooms.

On the first day of the two-day antiques and fine art sales (held every two months), there are silver and plated items, jewellery, collectors' items and ceramics. After a 30-minute lunch break there is usually a sale of textiles, which might include Victorian or 1930s dresses, lace and so on, followed by coins, stamps and medals, ceramics and glass. On the second day, pictures are sold in the morning, followed by as many as 400 lots of furniture and furnishings in the afternoon.

BUYER'S PREMIUM: *10%*
SALES: *General: fortnightly on Thu at 10.30am. Antiques and fine art: every two months on Wed and Thu at 11.00am.*
VIEWING: *General: Wed prior 12.30pm-5.00pm. Antiques and fine art: Tue prior 1.30pm-7.00pm.*
REFRESHMENTS: *Own excellent restaurant.*
PARKING: *Own large car park.*
STORAGE: *Yes*
TRANSPORTATION: *Yes*
SHIPPING: *Yes*

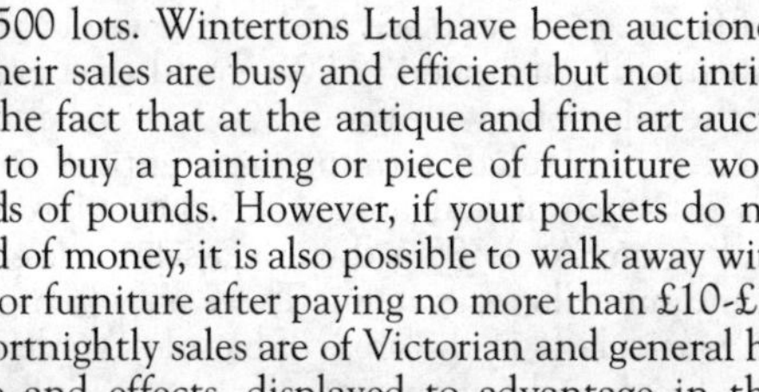

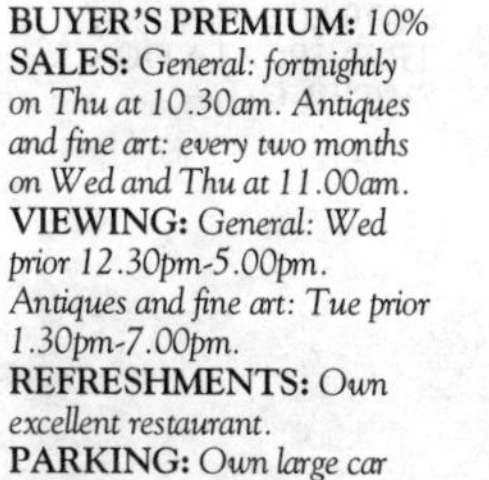

Newcastle-under-Lyme

BUYER'S PREMIUM: *Nil*
SALES: *About every two months on Thu at 5.30pm.*
VIEWING: *Day of sale from 2.30pm.*
REFRESHMENTS: *Own café.*
PARKING: *Own car park.*
STORAGE: *No*
TRANSPORTATION: *Yes*
SHIPPING: *No*

HEYWOODS

Newcastle Smithfield Market. Tel: (0782) 617343

400-500 lots. The sale takes place in one of the stock sheds used during the Monday livestock sales, for which the same company is responsible. The location adds to the atmosphere of informality which prevails in the sale. It is packed with local people, and porters and others are only too willing to offer an opinion on the lots. The sale usually offers a range of antique and Victorian furniture, besides general household furniture and effects, boxes of ornaments and crockery, bags of linen, good quality pine furniture, electrical goods and many other items. Occasionally there will be stock from businesses or shops that have gone bankrupt, which could mean a large number of clothes' rails from a factory, bundles of coat hangers or brand new clothes.

Penkridge

BUYER'S PREMIUM: *Nil*
SALES: *Weekly on Wed at 11.00am.*
VIEWING: *Day of sale from 8.00am.*
REFRESHMENTS: *Own café.*
PARKING: *Own car park.*
STORAGE: *No*
TRANSPORTATION: *Yes*
SHIPPING: *No*

SOUTH & STUBBS

Penkridge Market, Pinfold Lane. Tel: (078571) 4905

800-1,000 lots. This is an old-style country auction which makes a good day out for the family. While the sale is on, it is worth having a browse in the local market, where there is a wide range of stalls selling bric-à-brac and local crafts. There are several sections within the auction. The proceedings begin outside at 11.00am with the sale of garden produce. At 1.00pm the sale of farm eggs takes place, and is followed by the sale of poultry. Meanwhile, at around 12.00 noon, the general auction begins in the saleroom, with about 200 lots of better quality items. These could include furniture from antique to modern, as well as ornamental and domestic china, pictures, brass, pewter and so on. At 1.30pm there is a sale of lesser quality furniture and miscellaneous items. There are often good buys to be had, particularly in the areas of bicycles, gardening tools and builders' tools and equipment.

Stafford

BUYER'S PREMIUM: *Nil*
SALES: *Fortnightly on Thu at 9.45am.*
VIEWING: *Day prior 2.00pm-6.00pm.*
REFRESHMENTS: *Own café.*
PARKING: *None available on the premises.*
STORAGE: *No*
TRANSPORTATION: *Yes*
SHIPPING: *No*

HALL & LLOYD

The Saleroom, South Street. Tel: (0785) 58176

900-1,000 lots. The saleroom is a massive building situated close to the railway station. On sale day two auctions take place simultaneously, and buyers have to check what is being sold when and where. If you have come with a group, it is useful to split up and share the work. It all adds to the excitement of this independent, family-run sale, which has become a landmark in the area. The saleroom is open until 3.00pm the day before for vendors to bring in goods (for trade the saleroom is open earlier in the week as well). On the sale day, one of the two auctioneers starts by selling outside effects such as lawn mowers and gardening tools, while in another area the second auctioneer sells beds and bedding, including linen. When the outside effects have been sold, the auctioneer moves across to begin selling the lesser quality furniture. He stops about halfway through the lots to begin the sale of 'cabinet items' such as jewellery, porcelain, ornamental and domestic china, and brass. He then moves on to the better quality furniture, which may include some antiques, and in the mean time the other auctioneer will be completing the sale of lesser quality furniture. This auctioneer finishes the proceedings with electrical goods, which could include record players, videos and televisions.

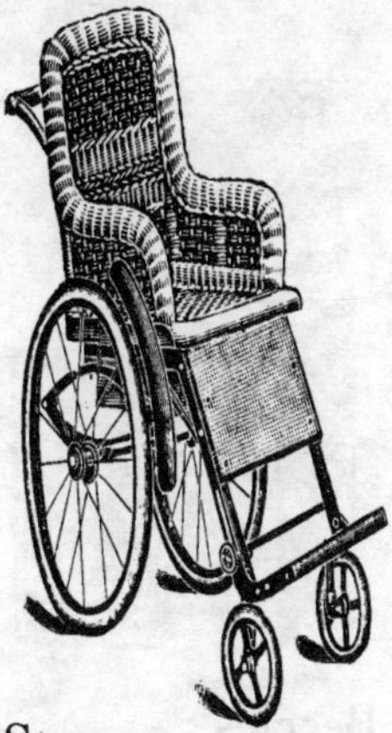

C TOMKINSON

Stone

The Smithfield, Mill Street. Tel: (0785) 813870

200-300 lots. This is a popular traditional-style country auction which is held every Thursday in the cattle market, in the sheep pens which are used for livestock sales on Mondays. The proceedings start with fresh farm and garden produce, and dressed poultry. At 12.00 noon the general sale commences. The lots are laid out in rows, and the auctioneer walks along them, followed by the crowd, selling each lot as he comes to it. This is a strictly cash only sale. Among the lots there will usually be household furniture, garden furniture and tools, and odd items such as motor car tyres, tins of nails, boxes of crockery, suitcases (perhaps full of toys) and other items. The sale is carried out with friendly banter, and those with patience and a willingness to search may well pick up something of interest.

The auctioneers also hold a large Monday sale of locally fed prime cattle, sheep and pigs, which are bought by butchers attending from a wide area.

BUYER'S PREMIUM: *Nil*
SALES: *General: weekly on Thu at 10.30am.*
VIEWING: *Morning of sale.*
REFRESHMENTS: *None available on the premises.*
PARKING: *Own car park.*
STORAGE: *No*
TRANSPORTATION: *No*
SHIPPING: *No*

BAGSHAWS AGRICULTURAL

Uttoxeter

17 High Street. Tel: (0889) 562811

500-600 lots. It is advisable to turn up early for this busy country auction, so as to have a thorough search through the lots before the sale starts. There is no predicting what will be among them, or the whereabouts in the sale of a particular item. This is a sale full of surprises, at which lots go for a few pounds or a few thousand pounds. The sale is held in the cattle market, in a yard surrounded by what used to be old stables (now used to store the sale goods). Perhaps 400 lots will be sold outside, and in among the lawn mowers and other outside effects there may well be pieces of high quality furniture. In a

BUYER'S PREMIUM: *Nil*
SALES: *Monthly on Fri at 11.00am.*
VIEWING: *Day of sale from 9.00am.*
REFRESHMENTS: *Available in town centre near by.*
PARKING: *In cattle market area.*
STORAGE: *Yes*
TRANSPORTATION: *Yes*
SHIPPING: *No*

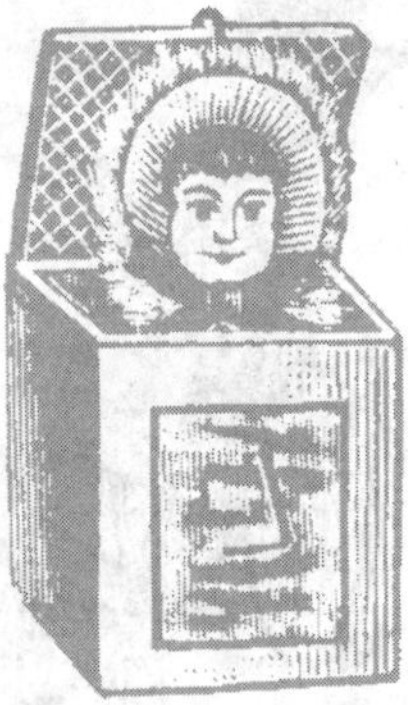

recent sale a Regency mahogany desk fetched £1,700, while the next lot, a roll of wire netting, was sold for £5. At another sale a desk brought in by a vendor on the back of a lorry (used normally to convey scrap metal) fetched over £800. Upstairs in the saleroom there will be another 200 lots or so. Some of them will be boxes of assorted items, which could include china and ornaments, and are worth rummaging through. A typical sale will also have jewellery, silver, brass, paintings, prints and other goods.

SUFFOLK

Beccles

DURRANTS

Beccles Auction Mart, Gresham Road.
Tel: (0502) 712122

BUYER'S PREMIUM: *Nil*
SALES: *Weekly on Fri at 10.30am.*
VIEWING: *Thu 9.00am-4.00pm.*
REFRESHMENTS: *Own café.*
PARKING: *Own car park.*
STORAGE: *Yes*
TRANSPORTATION: *No*
SHIPPING: *No*

800-1,000 lots. This is perhaps the largest auction in the area, and it is certainly one of the most interesting. At least one object always seems to fetch a four-figure sum, and at the same time a great many lots sell for under £5. The sale starts at 10.30am with good-quality Victorian and other furniture and effects. Items sold in this section of the auction in the past have included Regency mahogany dining chairs, antique oak elbow chairs, Victorian dining tables, mahogany and oak side tables, eight-day longcase clocks and flintlock pistols, as well as pottery and porcelain, and a large amount of Victorian bric-à-brac and miscellaneous items. These include things like gold jewellery and silver pocket watches. In contrast to this sale, a second sale starts at 12.30pm in the Old Sale Room, consisting of roughly 300 lots of modern and shipping furniture and miscellaneous effects. Outside at 1.30pm, a sale of outdoor items begins, for example bicycles, timber and other building equipment, gardening tools, electric and hand mowers. This is a good section of the sale for gardeners, as quite often a bundle of gardening tools, perhaps a spade, fork, hoe and rake, will all be included in one lot and sell for a very reasonable price.

Bury St Edmunds

HERITAGE AUCTIONS

The Village Hall, Great Barton.
Tel: (0953) 884369 and (0760) 440384

BUYER'S PREMIUM: *10%*
SALES: *Monthly on first Sun of month at 11.00am.*

500-600 lots. This is a cheerful but well-run Sunday auction. It takes place in the village hall, which is next to a playing field with swings and slides — useful for bored children. The three partners who run the auction encourage private buyers and have an excellent arrangement for transport, should a successful bid be made for any item too large to carry home on a roof rack. The sale includes a wide range of furniture, plus china, glass, silver and jewellery, pictures, clocks and other items, which tend to be more antique than modern. There are usually no electrical goods or television sets.

Great Barton is just east of Bury St Edmunds on the main road to Diss. The village hall is directly opposite the village's only petrol filling station. Whilst in the area, antique-hunters may be interested in the Risby Barn Antique Centre, which is open all day. It is in Risby, about five miles away on the other side of Bury St Edmunds.

VIEWING: *Sat prior 12.00 noon-5.00pm, morning of sale from 9.00am.*
REFRESHMENTS: *Light refreshments table in hall.*
PARKING: *Own car park.*
STORAGE: *No*
TRANSPORTATION: *Yes*
SHIPPING: *No*

LACY SCOTT

10 Risbygate Street. Tel: (0284) 763531

400-500 lots. Lacy Scott have been auctioneers since 1869. At the general Saturday auction you can expect to find a wide array of modern and antique furniture, porcelain, silver and brass, books and general bric-à-brac.

A quarterly three-day fine art sale is usually held in March, June, September and December. The sale begins on Monday at 10.30am with textiles, dolls, collectors' items, ceramics, glass, metalware and oriental works of art. There are up to 800 lots, with no break for lunch. The Tuesday of the sale is usually in two sessions. It starts at 2.00pm with 500 or so lots of jewellery, silver and plate. The second session begins at 6.30pm and consists of 200 or 300 lots of oil paintings, watercolours and prints. During the next two days the saleroom is set up for the Friday sale, which will include perhaps 200 or 300 lots of English and Continental furniture, mirrors, clocks, carpets and rugs.

There is also a quarterly specialist toy sale, generally held on a Saturday in February, May, August and November. The starting time varies according to the number of lots, but is usually 10.30am, with simultaneous auctions of Dinky toys in one part of the building and railway models in another.

Lacy Scott are also responsible for weekly Wednesday sales of cattle, pigs and poultry at Bury St Edmunds market, followed by motor vehicles at 12.30pm. Sheep sales are held in the nearby village of Ingham in July, August and September. Bury St Edmunds is a small town with expanding industries, but as these sales suggest, it still has the character of a country market town. There are many fine old buildings, for example the Town Hall (designed as a theatre by Robert Adam) and a Queen Anne house on Angel Hill, which now houses a collection of clocks.

Bury St Edmunds

BUYER'S PREMIUM: *10%. Toy sale: nil.*
SALES: *General: every two to three weeks on Sat at 9.30am. Fine art: quarterly in Mar, Jun, Sep and Dec, on Mon at 10.30am, Tue at 2.00pm, and Fri (times vary). Toys: quarterly in Feb, May, Aug, and Nov, on Sat at 10.30am (time depends on lots).*
VIEWING: *General: morning of sale from 8.00am. Fine art: for Mon and Tue, Fri prior 2.00pm; for Fri, Thu prior 4.00pm-8.00pm and morning of sale from 9.00am. Toys: Fri prior from 4.00pm-8.0pm.*
REFRESHMENTS: *Own café.*
PARKING: *Car park opposite.*
STORAGE: *Yes*
TRANSPORTATION: *Yes*
SHIPPING: *No*

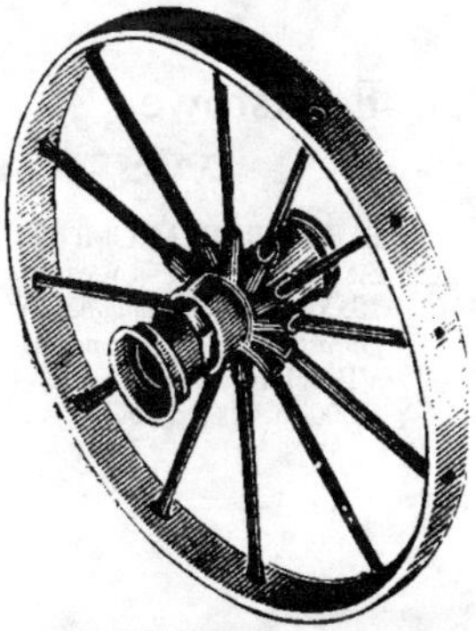

Clare

BUYER'S PREMIUM: *Nil*
SALES: *Every three weeks on Sat at 11.00am.*
VIEWING: *Fri prior 5.00pm-9.00pm, day of sale from 9.00am.*
REFRESHMENTS: *Excellent homemade refreshments sold to raise money for local charities.*
PARKING: *Council car park 500 yards away.*
STORAGE: *Yes*
TRANSPORTATION: *Yes*
SHIPPING: *Yes*

SUFFOLK SALES

The Saleroom, Church Street. Tel: (0787) 277993

500 lots. Before finding his forte as an auctioneer, Michael Dyson kept a smallholding in the nearby village of Poslingford. Over the ten years since the auction was started, it has become something of an institution and its reputation has spread through East Anglia. It is a fine country auction in the centre of a beautiful small Suffolk town. Opposite the saleroom is an adventure playground, a bonus for children. A typical sale will have good-quality general furniture, a wide selection of antiques, silver and silver plate, jewellery, china, bygones, collectables, old records and so on. A lot of pine and soft furnishings are sold, but there is very little electrical equipment, although the odd cooker may turn up now and then. Mr Dyson notes that many young people setting up home come to buy their furniture at his sales, and items like armchairs for re-upholstering are always popular. Bicycles can also be bought: people on holiday in the area sometimes buy one and then put it back in for auction at the end of their stay.

Felixstowe

BUYER'S PREMIUM: *Nil*
SALES: *Monthly on Wed at 10.00am.*
VIEWING: *Tue prior all day.*
REFRESHMENTS: *None available on the premises.*
PARKING: *Own car park.*
STORAGE: *Yes*
TRANSPORTATION: *Yes*
SHIPPING: *Yes*

BANNISTER & CO

Felixstowe Auction Rooms, 89 St Andrew Road.
Tel (0394) 282828

300-400 lots. Wednesdays are busy for the auction-goer in Suffolk: there are two monthly sales in Felixstowe, monthly sales at Woodbridge and Ipswich, and a fortnightly sale in Saxmundham. Care is taken so that the two Wednesday auctions in Felixstowe do not clash. Bannister & Co's sale is a good general auction with a wide mix of antique and modern household furniture and effects, plus china and crockery, silver, jewellery, glass, paintings and collectables. The saleroom is in easy walking distance of the railway station, and is also visited by overseas buyers who arrive at the ferry port. The town is an attractive Edwardian resort and an important container port.

Felixstowe

BUYER'S PREMIUM: *Nil*
SALES: *Monthly on Wed at 10.00am (includes antiques and fine art sale every other month).*
VIEWING: *Day prior 10.00am-4.00pm (and*

DIAMOND MILLS & CO

Orwell Hall, Orwell Road. Tel: (0394) 282281

300-400 lots. A lacquered press chest embossed with Oriental figures, a Victorian bow-front five-drawer chest, a marble-top washstand, a period wardrobe, five dining chairs, 112 pieces of Noritake china dinner and tea ware, mahogany boxes, porcelain, copper and brass, bedroom effects, double and single divans, mirror-backed sideboards, pine chests, collectables and a box of costume jewellery . . . these are a few examples of typical lots at this sale. Diamond Mills & Co run an efficient auction with computerised paying systems to cut down waiting. The auction is generally divided into Victorian, Edwardian, modern and general sections. Every other month the auction becomes an antiques and fine art sale.

6.00pm-7.30pm for antiques and fine art).
REFRESHMENTS: *Own café.*
PARKING: *Own car park.*
STORAGE: *Yes*
TRANSPORTATION: *Yes*
SHIPPING: *Yes*

WEBSTER AUCTIONEERS & VALUERS

Ipswich

13 Great Colman Street. Tel: (0473) 257491

500-700 lots. This is a good general auction in the centre of the town. A typical sale will include a selection of period and modern household furniture, but Webster in the main specialises in the sale of trade stocks, plant, machinery and vehicles, both commercial and private. Trade stocks range from groceries and jewellery, to engineering equipment and computers. So you can expect to find a mixture of goods catalogued — perhaps a rococo-style three-seater sofa, a dumper truck, industrial cleaning fluids, restaurant seating or a BMW. Selling ends at about 3.00pm.

Great Colman Street is in easy walking distance of Christchurch Park Museum and the Buttermarket, where the old dwelling called the Ancient House is now a wonderful bookshop, with low ceilings and many steps and stairs.

BUYER'S PREMIUM: *Nil.*
SALES: *Monthly on the first Wed of month at 10.00am.*
VIEWING: *Tue prior until 8.00pm.*
REFRESHMENTS: *Light refreshments sold.*
PARKING: *None available on the premises.*
STORAGE: *No*
TRANSPORTATION: *Yes*
SHIPPING: *No*

LOWESTOFT AUCTION ROOMS

Lowestoft

South Lowestoft Industrial Estate, Pin Bush Road.
Tel: (0502) 516209

400-500 lots. According to Mr Hailey, the auctioneer, 'anything can be bought at a Lowestoft Auction, from a cat box to a caravan'. The company moved into its new building on the south side of town in 1989. As well as fortnightly general sales, Lowestoft Auctions also hold car auctions on alternate Saturdays. They also operate a furniture removal company, so things can become hectic in the office. The removals side of the business is useful for buyers with a large piece of furniture to take home. The town is a fishing port, and many of the lots in the general sale have connections with fishing and boating. In addition, there is always a wide variety of furniture, silver and brass, paintings, crockery, cutlery, linen, bric-à-brac and so on, of all types and in all conditions. If time allows, take a walk around the harbour to see the fleet of trawlers, the kipper-curing houses and net-drying frames. Lowestoft kippers were once famous, and it is still possible to buy proper oak-smoked kippers here.

BUYER'S PREMIUM: *Nil*
SALES: *Fortnightly on Thu at 10.00am.*
VIEWING: *Wed prior 2.00pm-6.00pm.*
REFRESHMENTS: *Own café.*
PARKING: *Own car park.*
STORAGE: *Yes*
TRANSPORTATION: *Yes*
SHIPPING: *Yes*

Saxmundham

BUYER'S PREMIUM: *Nil*
SALES: *Fortnightly on Wed at 11.30am.*
VIEWING: *Tue prior 9.00am-4.00pm, morning of sale from 9.00am-11.30am.*
REFRESHMENTS: *None available on the premises.*
PARKING: *Limited free parking with additional paying parking.*
STORAGE: *No*
TRANSPORTATION: *Yes*
SHIPPING: *Yes*

FLICK & SON (WILLIAM H BROWN)

Saxmundham Saleroom. Tel: (0728) 603232

500-600 lots. Wednesday is market day in Saxmundham and is always busy, but the crowds double when Flick & Son hold their fortnightly sale. On auction days there is also a small antiques and crafts fair in the market hall, with some 15 or 16 stalls selling an interesting range of goods. The auction takes place in what used to be a bakery, and old ovens can still be seen at the rear of the hall.

The auction starts at 11.30am, in two sections. Outside is the sale of garden produce, vegetables, flowers and so on (but no livestock), which goes on until roughly 2.30pm. Meanwhile, the main auction is taking place inside the saleroom, where there will generally be furniture, brass, copperware, china, paintings, kitchenalia, books, jewellery, bric-à-brac and other items of all types and values. When this sale is over the auctioneer moves outside for the sale of outside effects, including for example bicycles, mowers, wire netting and carpenters' tools. The entire proceedings finish at around 3.00 to 3.30pm.

Southwold

BUYER'S PREMIUM: *Nil*
SALES: *Quarterly on Thu at 10.30am.*
VIEWING: *Wed prior 10.30am-4.00pm.*
REFRESHMENTS: *Own café.*
PARKING: *Plenty of parking near by.*
STORAGE: *Yes*
TRANSPORTATION: *Yes*
SHIPPING: *Yes*

H A ADNAMS

The Auction Room, St Edmund's Avenue. Tel: (0502) 723292

400-500 lots. This sale generally has a wide variety of lots, ranging in price from £1 for, box of bric-à-brac, the odd cup or two, or perhaps a child's puzzle, up to a five-figure sum for a piece of furniture or silverware. A typical sale will have antique and modern furniture, soft furnishings, bedroom effects, paintings, ceramics, copper and brass, dinner and tea services, clocks, books and plenty of miscellaneous items. The auction is a good adjunct to a near-perfect seaside town with fine cliffs, a long sandy beach, a little harbour and a wealth of handsome houses, many of them Georgian. St Edmund's Avenue is in the town centre, just off Pier Avenue, and the sale usually ends around 3.30 to 4.00pm.

Sudbury

BUYER'S PREMIUM: *10%*
SALES: *General: weekly on Thu at 1.30pm. Antiques and fine art: every two months on Wed at 10.30am.*
VIEWING: *General: morning of sale from 9.00am. Antiques and fine art: day prior*

WILLIAM H BROWN

Olivers Rooms, Burkitts Lane. Tel: (0787) 880305

200-300 lots. The saleroom's name comes from the 200-year-old firm of Olivers, which is now part of the William H Brown group. This is the fine art auction centre for W H Brown's South East region. Specialist sales of fine furniture, pictures, ceramics, glass, silver and plate, jewellery and *objets de vertu*, clocks, rugs and metalware are held regularly, and an annual programme of sales is available on request. Weekly sales of antique and household furniture and effects include china, brass, bric-à-brac, and outside effects.

This is one of the few smaller weekly auctions that produce a catalogue, or rather a sheet identifying the lots on offer. As vendors bring in articles right up to the day before the sale, this is no small feat. The auction takes place in a large, purpose-built saleroom about 200 yards from the market square. Thursday is also market day in Sudbury, so the town will be crowded. An antiques and fine art sale is also held here every two months. Close to the saleroom is the Thomas Gainsborough House Museum, the birthplace of the artist.

2.00pm-7.00pm, morning of sale from 9.00am.
REFRESHMENTS: *None available on the premises.*
PARKING: *Free public car parks.*
STORAGE: *No*
TRANSPORTATION: *Yes*
SHIPPING: *Yes*

ABBOTTS

Woodbridge

Abbotts Auction Rooms, Campsey Ashe. Tel: (0728) 746323

700-800 lots. This is one of the largest old-fashioned market auctions left in East Anglia, with the sale of cattle, sheep, pigs, produce, eggs and furniture all conducted by one firm. It is a treat to attend, and the population of this small, attractive village is easily trebled on sale days. There are three large salerooms in addition to the offices and store room on the premises. The proceedings begin with the sale of livestock at 10.30am. The first to go under the hammer are the pigs, and the auctioneer reaches the cattle at about noon. While this is going on, the general sale begins in Saleroom Two at 11.00am, and will usually include furniture in all states of repair, household effects, kitchenalia, brasses, collectors' items, boxes of bric-à-brac, china, ornaments and so on. At 11.30am, in yet another area, the sale of produce begins. All the selling is completed by around 4.30pm. There are also well-attended monthly antique sales, with a wide range of antique furniture, silver, pottery, pictures, jewellery and objets de vertu.

BUYER'S PREMIUM: *7½%*
SALES: *General: weekly on Mon at 11.00am. Antiques and fine art: monthly on Wed at 10.00am Mar to Oct, 11.00am Nov, Jan, Feb; no sale Dec.*
VIEWING: *General: Sat prior 9.00am-11.00am, morning of sale from 8.30am. Antiques and fine art: Mon prior 2.00pm-8.00pm, morning of sale from 8.30am.*
REFRESHMENTS: *Tea shop on site.*
PARKING: *Own very large car park.*
STORAGE: *Pre-sale short term.*
TRANSPORTATION: *Yes*
SHIPPING: *Yes*

NEAL SONS & FLETCHER

Woodbridge

Theatre Street Salerooms, Theatre Street. Tel: (03943) 2263

300-400 lots. Woodbridge is an attractive small town on the Deben Estuary, with small narrow streets and a long river front. The saleroom building was a theatre in Napoleonic times, became a school in Victorian times and then became a theatre again. It is worth a visit in its own right. The monthly general sale is a good-humoured, well-run catalogue auction, attended by some fine Suffolk characters. It usually has a good array of antique and modern furniture, soft furnishings, paintings, ceramics and collectables. The sale finishes around 2.30 to

BUYER'S PREMIUM: *Nil*
SALES: *General: monthly on Wed at 10.30am. Antiques and fine art: quarterly (no fixed months) on Wed and Thu at 10.30am.*
VIEWING: *General: day prior 2.30pm-4.30pm, 6.30pm-8.00pm. Antiques and fine art: 11.15am-4.30pm and 6.30pm-8.00pm.*

REFRESHMENTS: *None available on the premises.*
PARKING: *Own car park.*
STORAGE: *Yes*
TRANSPORTATION: *Yes*
SHIPPING: *Yes*

4.30pm. There are also quarterly two-day sales of antiques and fine art, which attract private buyers and dealers from all over the country. These sales are not held in a regular month, but there is usually one in each season.

SURREY

Godalming

BUYER'S PREMIUM: *10%*
SALES: *High Street: Wed at 11.00am, Thu at 10.30am; Bridge Street: 9.30am (first and third Sat of the month); Queen Street: Tue at 10.30am (monthly).*
VIEWING: *High Street: Sat prior, 9.00am-12.00 noon, Mon prior, 9.00am-7.00pm, Tue 9.00am-3.00pm; Bridge Street: day prior, 9.00am-7.00pm; Queen Street: Sat prior, 9.00am-12.00 noon, and day prior, 9.00am-5.00pm.*
REFRESHMENTS: *At High Street and Bridge Street only.*
PARKING: *Ample parking near by.*
STORAGE: *Yes*
TRANSPORTATION: *Yes*
SHIPPING: *Yes*

HAMPTONS FINE ART (incorporating MESSENGER MAY BAVERSTOCK)

93 High Street. Tel: (04868) 23567

400-500 lots. Hamptons hold sales at three different auction rooms in Godalming. The High Street auction room holds specialist sales on Wednesdays and Thursdays. These are given over to furniture, glass, china, collectables, jewellery, silver and so on one week, followed by pictures the following week and books the week after that. There are, however, gaps of five weeks between each cycle of specialist sales.

An interesting setting is provided by Hamptons' Bridge Street saleroom, which is situated in an old church. Here there are sales of Victoriana and 20th-century effects on the first and third Saturday of the month.

Hamptons also have a monthly sale of general items at their Queen Street saleroom, which includes anything from good Victorian furniture to washing machines and lawn mowers. It is possible to spend a wonderful day at one of these sales, and yet spend no more than a few pounds. Children are welcome.

Guildford

BUYER'S PREMIUM: *10%*
SALES: *On Tue at 10.30am, once every six to eight weeks.*
VIEWING: *Sat prior, 9.00am-12.00 noon. Day prior, 9.00am-5.00pm.*
REFRESHMENTS: *None available on the premises.*
PARKING: *None on the premises.*
STORAGE: *No*
TRANSPORTATION: *Yes*
SHIPPING: *Yes*

CLARKE GAMMON

Bedford Road. Tel: (0483) 66458

500-600 lots. Clarke Gammon describe themselves as 'independent auctioneers' and their sales, held once every six to eight weeks, are certainly rather up-market affairs, including antique furniture, antique and modern silver, oil and watercolour paintings, prints, metalware, English and Continental ceramics, clocks, Oriental carpets and books. A host of unusual and interesting items may be found among the lots described as 'bygones': carved African elephant book-ends, Victorian needlework boxes, coachmen's whips and wooden rocking horses, to name but a few. The auctioneers also sell jewellery and trinkets, porcelain figures, musical instruments of all kinds, photographic and optical items, and Victorian wheel barometers and thermometers.

PHILLIPS

Guildford

Millmead. Tel: (0483) 504030

300-400 lots. Phillips' saleroom is across the River Wey from the Yvonne Arnaud Theatre, and is part of a period, white-fronted building. Sales of antiques, later furniture and works of art are held monthly, and specialist sales of silver and jewellery take place throughout the year.

The lots in these rather up-market sales are described in more detail in the sales catalogues, which are sold at the reception desk to the left of the entrance and are also available by post.

BUYER'S PREMIUM: *10%*
SALES: *Monthly on Tue at 10.30am.*
VIEWING: *Sat prior, 9.00am-12.00 noon, day prior, 10.00am-7.00pm.*
REFRESHMENTS: *None available on the premises.*
PARKING: *Millbrook public car park.*
STORAGE: *No*
TRANSPORTATION: *Yes*
SHIPPING: *Yes*

SOUTH EAST MARTS

Guildford

Guildford Market, Slyfield Green. Tel: (0483) 573386

500-600 lots. Slyfield Green is an industrial complex on the Woking road, about two miles out of Guildford. There are good old-fashioned country-style auctions here twice a week on Tuesday and Wednesday. These take place in the open and are of general bric-à-brac. On the second and fourth Saturday of each month, under cover, there are sales of general household furniture and effects, including antiques.

The same company is also responsible for the Thursday weekly general auctions at Hailsham Market, Hailsham, East Sussex, tel: (0323) 844874, and the six-weekly Wednesday auction at the Sussex Auction Galleries, 59 Perrymount Road, Haywards Heath, West Sussex, tel: (0444) 414935. This Wednesday sale at Haywards Heath is of more valuable items: lots include antiques, fine art and collectables, and prices in the past have ranged from £5 to £28,000.

BUYER'S PREMIUM: *Guildford and Hailsham: nil. Haywards Heath: 10%*
SALES: *Guildford, bric-à-brac: twice weekly on Tue at 10.30am and Wed at 11.00am. Guildford, general: twice monthly on second and fourth Sat of month at 10.00am. Hailsham: weekly on Thu at 11.00am. Haywards Heath: every six weeks on Wed at 10.30am.*
VIEWING: *Guildford, bric-à-brac: during sale. Guildford, general: day prior 2.00pm-6.30pm, morning of sale from 8.30am. Hailsham: morning of sale from 8.00am. Haywards Heath: Mon and Tue prior 9.30am-4.30pm.*
REFRESHMENTS: *Guildford and Hailsham: own café. Haywards Heath: none available on the premises.*
PARKING: *Guildford and Hailsham: own car park. Haywards Heath: none available on the premises.*
STORAGE: *Yes*
TRANSPORTATION: *Yes*
SHIPPING: *Yes*

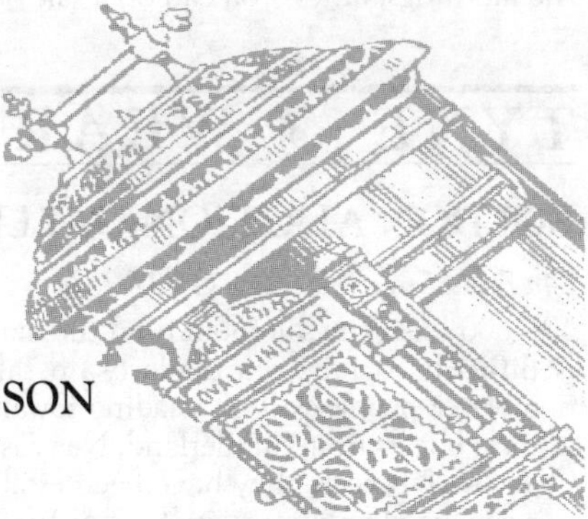

HOGG ROBINSON

Kingston upon Thames

74 London Road.
Tel: (081) 541 4139

400-600 lots. Hogg Robinson's large complex is close to the Cattle Market, a short distance away from Kingston's main

BUYER'S PREMIUM: *10%*
SALES: *Weekly on Thu*

(general sales of 20th-century items at 12.00 noon, antiques sales at 10.00am.)
VIEWING: *General: Day prior, 2.00pm-8.00pm and morning of sale from 9.00am; antiques: Tue prior, 2.00pm-8.00pm, Wed prior, 9.00am-5.00pm, and morning of sale from 9.00am.*
REFRESHMENTS: *Sometimes available.*
PARKING: *Limited available on the premises.*
STORAGE: *No*
TRANSPORTATION: *Yes*
SHIPPING: *Yes*

shopping precinct. Every week an auction takes place in one of the two salerooms here. The general sale of 20th-century items is held three times a month, and the sale of antiques and fine art once a month. The sale of 20th-century items has no categories; goods are allocated lot numbers and are sold in the order in which they arrive at the saleroom, rather than according to what they are.

In contrast, the monthly antiques sale has a formal pattern, and goods are sold by category. Furniture usually starts the bidding, followed by carpets, clocks, pictures, books, miscellaneous items, jewellery, silver and glass.

Catalogues are available for both sales.

Virginia Water

BUYER'S PREMIUM: *10%*
SALES: *Wed at 9.30am, once every five or six weeks.*
VIEWING: *Day prior, 9.00am-8.00pm.*
REFRESHMENTS: *None available on the premises.*
PARKING: *Large car park near by.*
STORAGE: *Yes*
TRANSPORTATION: *Yes*
SHIPPING: *Yes*

WENTWORTH AUCTION GALLERIES

21 Station Approach. Tel: (09904) 3711

600-700 lots. This saleroom is only a few minutes' walk away from the railway station, and is situated to the rear of some offices. Golfers may be more interested to know that it is only just over a mile from here to the famous Wentworth golf course. The proprietor of Wentworth's, Mr Richardson, takes part in the onerous task of auctioning lots on sale days. Since sales began here more than 23 years ago they have become more than just a place where people buy; many people come now just to talk and enjoy the atmosphere of general banter and friendship that exists here. The lots are usually of high quality and are varied, including jewellery, china, brass, silver, paintings, prints, and modern, antique and general household furniture. One important point to note if you wish to contact the auctioneers is that their telephone is manned only during the mornings, unless you call on a sale or viewing day.

TYNE & WEAR

Boldon

BUYER'S PREMIUM: *5%*
SALES: *Weekly on Wed at 10.00am (includes antiques sale about every two months).*
VIEWING: *Day prior 2.00pm-6.00pm.*
REFRESHMENTS: *None available on the premises.*
PARKING: *Ample near by.*

BOLDON AUCTION GALLERIES

24a Front Street. Tel: (091) 537 2630

500-600 lots. The saleroom is on the main road in Boldon and is difficult to miss, particularly on sale days when a great number of people will be heading towards it. The weekly sale attracts buyers from Sunderland, Newcastle and South Shields. Over the ten years they have been established, the sales have gained a good reputation in Tyne & Wear both for the friendly way in which they are conducted, and for the variety of interesting lots. The sales have a wide variety of goods: general household furniture and effects including reproduction and modern items, ornaments, kitchen and garden goods, bric-à-brac, toys, collectables, bygones and others. The cheaper miscellaneous items start the sale, and are followed by linen and furniture. About once in every two months the sale is devoted to better quality articles, including antiques, paintings and collectors' items. The pub opposite the saleroom is a pleasant place in which to wait for your lot to come up.

STORAGE: *Yes*
TRANSPORTATION: *Yes*
SHIPPING: *Yes*

ANDERSON & GARLAND

Crawcrook

See ANDERSON & GARLAND, Newcastle upon Tyne, Tyne and Wear

NORTH EASTERN AUCTIONEERS

Gateshead

Ellison Road, Dunston. Tel: (091) 460 0303

400-600 lots. The saleroom is a former garage. It is a large building lying a little way out of town, and is well signposted. A general sale is held here every Wednesday, and offers all sorts of household furniture, often with office furniture and equipment as well. North Eastern Auctioneers also hold periodic Saturday sales of police lost property and county court repossession items. The frequency of these sales varies, but may be as often as once a month, and the type of goods also varies enormously, from small items of jewellery to bicycles and three-piece suites.

In addition, every two months there are sales of catering equipment, including cookers, mixers, tables, butchers' equipment and other items. Other catering sales are held regularly at ten different sites in England and Scotland.

BUYER'S PREMIUM: *10%*
SALES: *General: weekly on Wed at 10.30am. Lost property, etc: periodically on Sat at 10.30am (no fixed dates). Catering: every two months on Mon at 4.00pm.*
VIEWING: *General and lost property: day of sale from 9.00am. Catering: day of sale from 2.00pm.*
REFRESHMENTS: *Own café.*
PARKING: *Own car park.*
STORAGE: *Yes*
TRANSPORTATION: *Yes*
SHIPPING: *Yes*

ANDERSON & GARLAND

Newcastle upon Tyne

Marlborough House, Marlborough Crescent. Tel: (091) 232 6278

300-700 lots. Anderson & Garland have been fine art auctioneers in the north of England since 1840. Their fine art sales take place every two months in the Marlborough House Saleroom, which is about 200 yards from the central railway station. Sales last four days, with each day concentrating on different categories. The first day will include about 300 lots of paintings, while on the second day there will be about 300 lots each of silver and jewellery. The third day is for collectors' items such as photographic equipment, bronzes, ivories, toys, models, needlework, coins, stamps and so on, with glass and

BUYER'S PREMIUM: *10%*
SALES: *Newcastle: every two months on Tue, Wed, Thu and Fri at 10.30am. Crawcrook: fortnightly on Thu at 9.30am.*
VIEWING: *Newcastle: Thu and Fri prior 10.00am-4.30pm, Sat prior 9.30am-12.30pm. Crawcrook: Tue prior 2.00pm-7.00pm, Wed prior 10.00am-4.00pm.*
REFRESHMENTS: *Newcastle: none available on*

the premises. Crawcrook: own café.
PARKING: *Ample parking near by.*
STORAGE: *Yes*
TRANSPORTATION: *Yes*
SHIPPING: *Yes*

porcelain in the afternoon. Finally, on the fourth day, around 250 to 300 lots of furniture and some 20 to 30 lots of Oriental rugs and carpets are sold. The firm has a second saleroom at Pattinsons Rooms, Kepier Chare, Crawcrook, tel: (091) 413 8348, where there are fortnightly sales of Victorian and general furnishings and effects.

Newcastle upon Tyne

BUYER'S PREMIUM: *10%*
SALES: *General: weekly on Tue and Wed at 9.30am. Antiques: every six weeks on Thu at 10.00am.*
VIEWING: *General: Mon 10.00am-5.00pm, Tue (for Wed sale) 9.00am-4.00pm. Antiques: day prior 9.00am-2.30pm.*
REFRESHMENTS: *Vending machine.*
PARKING: *Ample parking near by.*
STORAGE: *No*
TRANSPORTATION: *Yes*
SHIPPING: *Yes*

THOMAS N MILLER

18-26 Gallowgate. Tel: (091) 232 5617

400-600 lots. The spacious saleroom complex is in the city centre opposite St James's Park (Newcastle United's football stadium). This popular auction was established in 1902 and proudly boasts that it has furnished and equipped many a local household. Almost everything you might need is on sale, from lounge and bedroom suites and televisions to cutlery, cut-glass bowls and jewellery. Two sales are held every week, in a large room which is divided for the sales. On Tuesday the auction is of smaller lots such as domestic and ornamental china, kitchen items, cutlery, small electrical goods, glass, brass and so on. The Wednesday sale includes furniture of all periods and better quality small items, usually of a higher value than the lots available at the Tuesday sale. In addition, a special catalogued sale of antiques and fine art is held every six weeks on a Thursday.

Whitley Bay

BUYER'S PREMIUM: *5%*
SALES: *General: weekly on Thu at 10.15am. Antiques: about every two months on Mon at 1.00pm.*
VIEWING: *General: day prior 10.30am-4.30pm. Antiques: Fri prior 2.00pm-5.00pm, Sat prior 9.00am-12.00 noon.*
REFRESHMENTS: *None available on the premises.*
PARKING: *None available on the premises.*
STORAGE: *Yes*
TRANSPORTATION: *Yes*
SHIPPING: *Yes*

J C FEATONBY

234/236 Park View. Tel: (091) 252 2601

400-500 lots. Whitley Bay is one of the most popular seaside resorts on the north-east coast, with a sandy beach and a long and breezy promenade. Surprisingly, not many of the visitors to the town find their way to J C Featonby's saleroom, even though the weekly Thursday sale is a pleasant way to pass part of the day.

The large, purpose-built saleroom is full of 'good-to-browse-through' items, from knick-knacks to English wooden furniture dating from the first half of the century. A wide range of tables and chairs, 1930s dressing tables, period wardrobes and cabinets can usually be found.

In the morning the smaller items are auctioned off, including curtains and gardening tools and equipment. This part of the sale usually goes on until 1.00pm, when there is a break for lunch. At 2.00pm the auctioning begins again with the sale of the furniture. About every two months J C Featonby hold a special auction of antiques, paintings and fine art.

WARWICKSHIRE

BELLCOURT AUCTIONS

69 High Street. Tel: (0789) 772611

300-400 lots. Bidford is an attractive, traditional village with a lovely fifteenth-century bridge over the river, and an unusual church with wonderful stained glass. Both are well worth a visit should you have time between making bids at Bellcourt's very busy and friendly family-run auctions. The Tuesday sales are of antique furniture, silver, plated ware, jewellery, oil paintings, watercolours, prints, pottery, glass, Oriental ceramics and works of art, including rugs, dolls and clocks. The Thursday sales concentrate on more general household furniture and effects such as electrical goods, kitchenalia, bedroom suites and lounge suites, as well as smaller items: ornaments, lamps, silver plate, carpets and rugs. Now and then, larger outdoor items are sold under the cover of a lean-to outside the main saleroom, and when these are being sold, they are usually at the start of the sale. The saleroom used to be a billiard room in the early Victorian house. Nowadays the areas of the house which are not used either for storage or as offices are occupied by John Homer and his family, who organise the sales.

Bidford-on-Avon

BUYER'S PREMIUM: *10%*
SALES: *Weekly on Tue and Thu at 7.00pm.*
VIEWING: *Day of sale from 9.30am.*
REFRESHMENTS: *Vending machine in saleroom.*
PARKING: *Own car park in grounds, also parking in street.*
STORAGE: *Yes*
TRANSPORTATION: *Yes*
SHIPPING: *Yes*

A B AUCTIONS

Unit 13, Paynes Lane Industrial Estate. Tel: (0788) 536362

300-400 lots. When you are looking for the saleroom, an excellent landmark is the tall chimneystack belonging to the Rugby Cement Company, which is next to the saleroom and can be seen clearly from as far away as the M6. However, do not be put off by the location, for Rugby (best known for its public school, immortalised by Thomas Hughes in *Tom Brown's Schooldays*) is surrounded by many beautiful villages.

At AB Auctions there is a rich variety of goods on sale, and a friendly atmosphere prevails on sale days. It is usually not long before someone comes up to ask your opinion about one lot or another. The Saturday sale comprises modern household furniture and effects, including lounge and bedroom suites, pine, wall units, carpets, mirrors, automatic washing machines, ornaments, lamps, brass items, copper and bric-à-brac. There are also some outside effects, such as garden ornaments and tools, mowers and bicycles. Outside effects usually begin the auction. The Monday evening sale comprises antiques and fine art.

Rugby

BUYER'S PREMIUM: *50p (lots up to £10), £1 (£10-£20), £2 (£20-£50), 5% (£50 and over).*
SALES: *General: weekly on Sat at 1.00pm. Antiques and fine art: weekly on Mon at 7.00pm.*
VIEWING: *General: day of sale from 9.30am. Antiques: day of sale from 2.30pm.*
REFRESHMENTS: *Own café.*
PARKING: *Allowed on road.*
STORAGE: *Yes*
TRANSPORTATION: *Yes*
SHIPPING: *Yes*

Rugby

BUYER'S PREMIUM: *10%*
SALES: *Weekly on Mon at 10.00am.*
VIEWING: *Day of sale from 8.00am.*
REFRESHMENTS: *Own café.*
PARKING: *Public car park opposite.*
STORAGE: *Yes*
TRANSPORTATION: *Yes*
SHIPPING: *Yes*

RUGBY SALEROOMS LTD

20 Little Church Street. Tel: (0788) 542367

300-450 lots. This is a family-owned and run saleroom, with Mr M Seaman taking charge of the selling and Mrs Seaman looking after the mountain of paperwork involved in a busy auction. Many of the staff have been with the firm for years, having joined as teenagers. The atmosphere is friendly and informal, and should not intimidate those new to auction-going. The range of goods is wide — lots in the past have included a stuffed elephant, a live horse and 1,000 bunches of flowers from a local smallholding — but more usually the sale has furniture from antique to modern, including pine dressers, beds and mattresses, bookcases, tables and upholstered furnishings, paintings, silver, jewellery, clocks and so on. Typical items sold here include an Art Nouveau oak smoker's cabinet, Mappin & Webb hallmarked rat-tail cutlery, diamond rings, gold bracelets and lady's cocktail watches.

Stratford-upon-Avon

BUYER'S PREMIUM: *10%*
SALES: *Fortnightly on Sat at 10.30am.*
VIEWING: *Day prior 2.00pm-5.00pm*
REFRESHMENTS: *Own café.*
PARKING: *Own car park.*
STORAGE: *Yes*
TRANSPORTATION: *Yes*
SHIPPING: *Yes*

PHILLIPS BROTHERS

The Saleroom, Bearley Road, Snitterfield. Tel: (0789) 731114

600-700 lots. Snitterfield is a charming village four miles north of Stratford-upon-Avon, and has associations with both Shakespeare and Charles II. If time allows, drag yourself away from the auction to see the font and carved scroll work in the church, which is only a few steps from the saleroom.

Phillips Brothers hold a large and interesting general sale of household furniture and effects, which covers a huge range of items. Every two months or so the sale will include perhaps 100 lots from the police — these will be unclaimed lost property or 'detained property', whose owner cannot be determined. Anything can turn up in this part of the sale: tyres, tools and tarpaulins from lorries, jewellery, rings, watches and household items.

Twice a year, in no regular month, the general sale is taken over completely by police lost property. Once a quarter, again not at regular intervals, the general sale is run simultaneously with a horse tackle sale. For those buying large and heavy objects, the saleroom has large double doors at the back, and cars and vans can drive right in to load up.

Tiddington

BUYER'S PREMIUM: *10%*
SALES: *Antiques: monthly on Fri at 11.00am. Pictures:*

BIGWOOD AUCTIONEERS LTD

The Old School. Tel: (0789) 69415

300-700 lots. As well as monthly sales of antique and reproduction furniture and effects, a range of specialist auctions is held here. A sale of oils, watercolours and drawings takes place once a month, with quarterly sales of fine and inexpensive wines and spirits, and three sales a year of books, prints and maps.

The antique and reproduction sale has a wide variety of items. This makes Bigwood Auctioneers particularly interesting, as there are always some surprises. For instance, a Regency mahogany bow-fronted chest and a 1920s wind-up gramophone might well stand next to a stripped pine table or a grand piano. On a small table you might find a Chinese rectangular 18th-century teapot standing next to one in the form of a 1950s sports car.

The premises used to be an old school, and depending on the size of the sale, one or both salerooms will be used. Situated in the main street of this quiet village, the building has a distinctive clock tower and is difficult to miss.

monthly on Fri at 11.00am. Wines and spirits: quarterly in Mar, Jun, Sep and Dec on Thu at 6.00pm. Books, prints and maps: three times a year on Fri at 11.00am (dates vary).
VIEWING: *Antiques, pictures and books, prints and maps: Wed prior 9.00am-5.30am, Thu prior 9.00am-7.00pm, morning of sale from 9.00am. Wines and spirits: day of sale from 9.00am.*
REFRESHMENTS: *Coffee only.*
PARKING: *To front and rear of saleroom.*
STORAGE: *Yes*
TRANSPORTATION: *Yes*
SHIPPING: *Yes*

WEST MIDLANDS

BIDDLE & WEBB

Birmingham

Ladywood Middleway. Tel: (021) 455 8042

300-400 lots. Biddle & Webb have been holding auctions in Birmingham for almost as long as anyone can remember. The saleroom is a tall, prominent brick building bearing Biddle & Webb signs, on the same road as the Birmingham Children's Hospital. Two weekly sales and three monthly sales are held here. Every Tuesday there are auctions of 'semi antiques', which means Edwardian and Victorian furniture and collectables. Every Wednesday there is an auction of general modern furniture and effects, including electrical goods and kitchen items, china, bric-à-brac, gardening tools and equipment, and other items, usually on the inexpensive side.

The monthly sales are devoted to (1) fine art; (2) antique furniture, china, metalware and so on; (3) silver, gold, jewellery and coins. Periodical sales of lost and unclaimed property are also held on behalf of West Midlands Police and Gatwick Airport.

BUYER'S PREMIUM: *Nil*
SALES: *Semi antiques: weekly on Tue at 10.30am. General: weekly on Wed at 10.30am. Fine art: monthly on first Fri of month. Antique furniture etc: monthly on second Fri of month. Silver, gold, etc: monthly on fourth Fri of month. All monthly sales start at 11.00am.*
VIEWING: *General and semi antiques: Sat prior 9.00am-12.00 noon, Mon and Tue prior 9.00am-5.00pm. Fine art and antiques: Mon-Thu 10.00am-4.00pm. Silver, gold, etc: Tue-Thu prior 10.00am-4.00pm.*
REFRESHMENTS: *Own café.*
PARKING: *Ample parking near by.*
STORAGE: *Yes*
TRANSPORTATION: *Yes*
SHIPPING: *Yes*

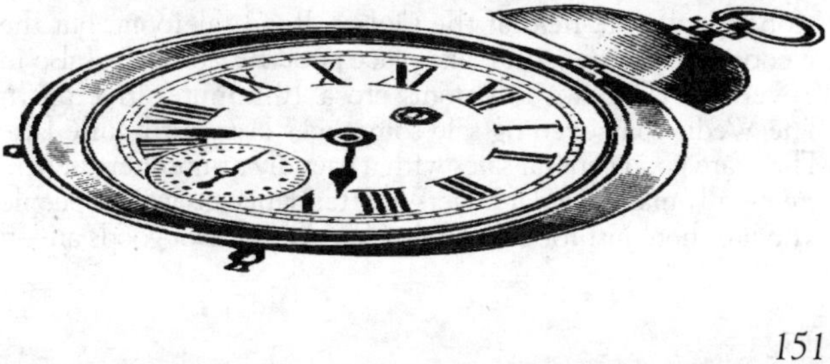

Birmingham

BUYER'S PREMIUM: *Nil*
SALES: *General: weekly on Tue at 10.30am. Unclaimed goods: monthly on Mon at 10.00am (usually last Mon of month).*
VIEWING: *General: Sat prior 9.00am-11.45am, Mon prior 8.30am-5.00pm. Unclaimed goods: during sale.*
REFRESHMENTS: *Van selling snacks.*
PARKING: *Ample parking near by.*
STORAGE: *Yes*
TRANSPORTATION: *Yes*
SHIPPING: *Yes*

RONALD E CLARE

70 Park Street, Digbeth. Tel: (021) 643 0226

400-500 lots. The salerooms are part of a modern building extending to over 15,000 square feet on two levels, which are used alternately. It stands behind the company offices, and has a loading bay. All the items you might expect can be found here — antique, modern and reproduction furniture, electrical items, bric-à-brac, ceramics, glass, paintings and carpets — but the sale also includes the occasional car or commercial vehicle, pieces of machinery, office furniture and shop stock. Stamps and books can also be found. During one auction it was possible to bid for lots as varied as a Royal Doulton teacup and saucer, and a fork lift truck. The prices vary too, from as little as a couple of pounds to many thousands.

Once a month, usually on the last Monday, there is a sale of unclaimed goods from the Post Office and parcel carriers, running to some 500-600 lots. Periodical sales are also held of collectors' items, diecast models and fashion.

Coventry

BUYER'S PREMIUM: *10%*
SALES: *Weekly on Wed at 10.00am.*
VIEWING: *Day prior 9.00am-4.30pm, day of sale from 9.00am.*
REFRESHMENTS: *Hot drinks only.*
PARKING: *Public car parks adjoining.*
STORAGE: *Yes*
TRANSPORTATION: *Yes*
SHIPPING: *Yes*

COVENTRY AUCTION CENTRE

3 Queen Victoria Road. Tel: (0203) 223377

300-400 lots. Coventry is one of England's most ancient cities, but the old city centre was almost completely destroyed in a fierce air raid in November 1940. Coventry Auction centre is on the opposite side of the city to the cathedral, and has been established over 40 years. Smaller items start the weekly sale. These may include brass fire dogs, ebony clocks, antique telescopes, or crockery. The sale usually continues with an assortment of bicycles, toys, books, colour television sets, electrical goods of all types, and arts and crafts. At the end there is usually furniture of all types, ranging from modern, self-assembly pieces to high quality Victorian and antique items.

There are other sales at irregular intervals, on behalf of liquidators and the local courts.

Coventry

BUYER'S PREMIUM: *50p a lot.*
SALES: *Weekly on Mon at 11.00am and Wed at 7.00pm.*
VIEWING: *Mon sale: Sat prior 9.30am-5.30pm, day of sale 9.00am-11.00am. Wed sale: day of sale from 9.00am.*
REFRESHMENTS: *Own café.*

HORIZON AUCTIONS

Gulson Road (behind UBM). Tel: (0203) 22000

1,000-1,200 lots (Mondays), 250-300 lots (Wednesdays). Monday sales are held at the Gulson Road saleroom, but the Wednesday evening sales take place at 80 Broad Street (also in Coventry). The two salerooms are a 10-minute drive apart. The Wednesday evening sale sometimes lasts until quite late. These are good general sales with a friendly atmosphere. There are usually many regular buyers in attendance, as well as people who are there just for curiosity's sake. All types of goods are on offer: Victorian, Edwardian, modern and reproduction furniture, ceramics, glass, metalware, ornaments, jewellery and electrical goods among other things.

PARKING: *Own car park.*
STORAGE: *Yes*
TRANSPORTATION: *Yes*
SHIPPING: *Yes*

Knowle, near Solihull

PHILLIPS

The Old House, Station Road. Tel: (0564) 776151

250-400 lots. This is a branch of Phillips London, who have 34 salerooms spread over Britain and branches in Europe and North America. However, one need not be intimidated by their reputation: often provincial branches of big firms like this have simply absorbed long-established local companies without spoiling the old friendly atmosphere. The prices range from £30 to £30,000-£40,000. The Old House is on the Dorridge turn-off from the A41 Solihull to Warwick road, and is an attractive brick and timber building which was originally a 17th-century farmhouse. The sales cover a wide range of items, from fine furniture, Victoriana, and silver, to paintings, ceramics and books.

BUYER'S PREMIUM: *10%*
SALES: *Weekly on Wed at 11.00am (occasionally also 2.00pm).*
VIEWING: *Sat 9.30am-12.30pm, Mon 9.00am-5.00pm, Tue 9.00am-7.00pm.*
REFRESHMENTS: *On sale day.*
PARKING: *Limited, but three public car parks near by.*
STORAGE: *No*
TRANSPORTATION: *Yes*
SHIPPING: *Yes*

Wolverhampton

G A FINE ARTS AND CHATTELS

The Waterloo Road Saleroom, 3 Waterloo Road.
Tel: (0902) 771511

400-500 lots. The saleroom is close to Beatties, the locally famous department store, and also near the Wolverhampton Wanderers football ground. The fortnightly sales are of general household effects and furniture, miscellaneous items, bric-à-brac, kitchen goods, domestic and ornamental china and so on. Every six to eight weeks there is a two-day sale on Thursday and Friday, with around 800 lots of antiques and fine art. The Thursday session is mainly for smaller items such as china, pottery and glass, while the Friday is devoted to furniture and paintings. Past sales have included 19th-century French longcase clocks, pieces by Lalique such as a clock, vase and reading lamp, glazed pottery by John Piper, candlesticks, bisque dolls, William IV tea and coffee services, 18th-century mahogany side tables and Queen Anne walnut writing tables.

BUYER'S PREMIUM: *5%*
SALES: *General: fortnightly on Thu at 11.00am. Antiques: every six to eight weeks on Thu and Fri at 10.00am.*
VIEWING: *General: day prior 10.00am-4.00pm. Antiques: day prior 10.00am-4.00pm, 6.00pm-8.00pm.*
REFRESHMENTS: *Own café.*
PARKING: *None available on the premises.*
STORAGE: *Yes*
TRANSPORTATION: *Yes*
SHIPPING: *Yes*

WEST SUSSEX

Billingshurst

SOTHEBY'S

Summers Place. Tel: (0403) 783933

700-1,000 lots. Summers Place is Britain's largest provincial saleroom, and with an average of two sales a day for four days a week it must also be one of the busiest. The setting is 37 acres

BUYER'S PREMIUM: *10%*
SALES: *On average two per day Mon to Thu, at 10.00am or 10.30am, and again at*

1.00pm or 2.00pm.
VIEWING: *Mon to Fri 9.30am-4.30pm, Sat 9.30am-12.30pm, occasionally Sun 2.30pm-5.00pm. Lots are on view two days prior to sale.*
REFRESHMENTS: *Own restaurant.*
PARKING: *Own car park.*
STORAGE: *Yes*
TRANSPORTATION: *Yes*
SHIPPING: *Yes*

of gardens and fields. Morning and afternoon sales are held from Monday to Thursday, and the reception counters and salerooms are open from Monday to Friday all day, plus Saturday morning and occasionally Sunday afternoon as well. The specialist sale categories include antique and decorative furniture, silver and plate, oil paintings and watercolours, portrait miniatures, Old Masters, dolls, toys, teddy bears, garden statuary, metalwork, textiles, prints and maps, Oriental carpets and rugs, military vehicles and militaria. Past lots have included gentlemen's pocket watches, a Vickers Carden Loyd tractor, a 1930s military supply vehicle with the appearance of a tank, a George III paperwork tea caddy and a World War II Jeep.

Note: Do not be put off by the imposing entrance to the saleroom. As the Sotheby's sign clearly states, visitors are welcome.

Chichester

BUYER'S PREMIUM: *10%*
SALES: *Monthly on Thu (day can vary) at 10.00am (includes fine art and antiques sale about five times a year).*
VIEWING: *Sat prior 9.00am-12.00 noon, day prior 10.00am-4.30pm.*
REFRESHMENTS: *None available on the premises.*
PARKING: *Pay and display car park.*
STORAGE: *Yes*
TRANSPORTATION: *Yes*
SHIPPING: *Yes*

PHILLIPS

Baffins Hall, Baffins Lane. Tel: (0243) 787548

300-400 lots. Chichester was one of the earliest sites in Britain to be occupied by the Romans, who called it *Regnum*. Phillips' saleroom is just off East Street, which has some fine old houses and is in the town centre. The regular monthly sales are called 'General Furnishing Sales' and could include antique, modern and reproduction furniture, pictures, ceramics, Oriental and European works of art, jewellery, silver and plate, and other categories. The day of the sale can vary, but is usually Thursday. Periodically, perhaps five times a year, the general sale is replaced by a special fine art and antiques sale. This may occasionally spread over Wednesday and Thursday.

Chichester

BUYER'S PREMIUM: *10%*
SALES: *Monthly on last Fri of month at 10.30am.*
VIEWING: *Day prior 10.00am-4.00pm, morning of sale from 9.00am.*
REFRESHMENTS: *None available on the premises.*
PARKING: *Own car park.*
STORAGE: *Yes*
TRANSPORTATION: *Yes*
SHIPPING: *Yes*

STRIDE & SON AUCTIONEERS

Southdown House, St John's Street. Tel: (0243) 780207

700-800 lots. This family-run firm was started over 100 years ago by the great-grandfather of the present proprietor, Mr N J Stride. The saleroom is a large, flint building opposite the cattle market. Livestock sales take place at the latter on Wednesday; also on Wednesday, and on Saturday, too, there is a general market with stalls selling antiques, bric-à-brac and local crafts. Stride & Son's sale is held on the last Friday of the month, and is of general household furniture and effects, including antiques, paintings, silver, china and jewellery of all values. The lots could sell for anything from £5 up to £14,000, so it is always interesting. For the first half-hour or so, various items such as bicycles, gardening tools and equipment and lesser quality furniture are sold outside. At around 11.00am the auction moves into the main saleroom. It is organised so that the better quality lots appear as the sale progresses.

SUMMERLEY AUCTION ROOM

Felpham, near Bognor Regis

90 Limmer Lane. Tel: (0243) 821212

400-500 lots. The saleroom is a converted flint barn in the heart of this beautiful Saxon village. The barn is easy to find once you have found the village, and on sale days all the traffic seems to be heading in that direction. Sale day is rather like a social event, and there will be plenty of cars and trailers parked outside. The proprietors, Stephen and Sheila Sergeant, employ an auctioneer to conduct the selling, which is run in a friendly, unhurried manner. All sorts of things may be in the sale, but you can usually expect three-piece suites, upholstered furniture, garden furniture, beds, tables, desks, ornaments, mirrors, plenty of china, silver, photograph albums, interesting bric-à-brac and miscellaneous items. Among it all there will usually be a sprinkling of good antiques and pictures, and it is the latter — oils, watercolours, and prints — that finish the sale. This is a sale to suit most needs and pockets, and the lovely countryside makes a visit a wonderful day out.

BUYER'S PREMIUM: *10%*
SALES: *Monthly on last Sat of month at 10.30am.*
VIEWING: *Thu prior 9.30am-5.00pm, Fri prior 9.30am-8.00pm.*
REFRESHMENTS: *Own café.*
PARKING: *Ample parking near by.*
STORAGE: *Yes*
TRANSPORTATION: *Yes*
SHIPPING: *Yes*

SOUTH EAST MARTS

Hayward's Heath

See SOUTH EAST MARTS, Guildford, Surrey

KING & CHASEMORE

Midhurst

Bepton Road Saleroom. Tel: (9073081) 2456

300-350 lots. Midhurst is an attractive town, close to Cowdray House and its polo ground. Bepton Road is a continuation of the town's main road, and the saleroom is easy to spot — it has been converted from the old Ebenezer Chapel. The sales are called fine art and antiques sales, and on the whole live up to their name. The lots are usually of high quality and they tend not to sell for less than £20. The average is around £100, and prices go as far as £10,000. The atmosphere remains informal though, thanks to the exuberant personality of Mr E Lintott, who conducts most of the bidding.

BUYER'S PREMIUM: *10%*
SALES: *On average every six weeks on Thu at 11.00am.*
VIEWING: *Tue and Wed prior 10.00am-12.00noon, 2.00pm-4.00pm.*
REFRESHMENTS: *None available on the premises.*
PARKING: *Grange Road public car park.*
STORAGE: *No*
TRANSPORTATION: *Yes*
SHIPPING: *Yes*

DENHAMS

Warnham, near Horsham

Horsham Auction Galleries, Warnham. Tel: (0403) 55699

600-900 lots. The Horsham Auction Galleries are on the A24, two miles north of Horsham, just outside the tiny picturesque village of Warnham. The galleries are a huge building, next to

BUYER'S PREMIUM: *10%*
SALES: *Antiques and fine art: monthly on third Wed of month at 10.00am. General: monthly*

on first Wed of month at 10.00am.
VIEWING: *Sat prior 9.00am-12.00 noon, Tue prior 10.00am-4.00pm (antiques until 7.00pm).*
REFRESHMENTS: *Own café.*
PARKING: *Own car park.*
STORAGE: *Yes*
TRANSPORTATION: *Yes*
SHIPPING: *Yes*

a large conference centre and hotel but in a rural setting — you may see chickens wandering around the parking area. The most important sale is that of antiques and fine art, held on the third Wednesday of the month, which usually includes antique furniture, silver, jewellery, European and Oriental ceramics, pictures, prints, clocks, Persian rugs and various collectors' items. The firm also holds a secondary general sale of lower value goods, including general household furniture and household effects.

Worthing

R H ELLIS & SON

44 High Street. Tel: (0903) 38999

BUYER'S PREMIUM: *8%*
SALES: *General: twice a month on Mon at 10.00am. Antiques: once a month on Mon at 10.00am. Special: once a quarter on Mon at 10.00am.*
VIEWING: *Fri prior 9.00am-1.00pm, 2.15pm-5.00pm, Sat prior 9.00am-1.00pm, 2.00pm-4.00pm.*
REFRESHMENTS: *None available on the premises.*
PARKING: *Public car park opposite.*
STORAGE: *Yes*
TRANSPORTATION: *Yes*
SHIPPING: *Yes*

400-500 lots. This independent, family-owned and run company was established over 50 years ago and is very much a local landmark. The saleroom is next to the company's office in a converted cottage, close to the centre of the popular seaside resort. There are three sales per month, one of antiques and two of general modern household furniture and effects. The general sales typically include a mixture of lounge and dining room suites, domestic and other electrical equipment, and kitchen and gardening items. The antiques sales include good quality Victorian and Edwardian furniture, porcelain, domestic and ornamental china and so on, as well as earlier antiques.

Special sales are held once a quarter, usually in addition to the three regular monthly sales, and offer silver, jewellery, paintings, Oriental rugs and other good quality items.

WEST YORKSHIRE

Bradford

JOHN H RABY & SON

21 St Mary's Road. Tel: (0274) 491121

BUYER'S PREMIUM: *Nil*
SALES: *Weekly on Thu at 10.30am (includes antiques sale once a month).*
VIEWING: *Day prior 10.00am-4.00pm.*
REFRESHMENTS: *Own café.*
PARKING: *Own car park.*
STORAGE: *Short duration only.*
TRANSPORTATION: *Yes*
SHIPPING: *No*

300-400 lots. There are two St Mary's Roads in Bradford. This one is about two miles north of the city centre and close to the great Lister Mill (postal district Bradford 8). The saleroom is a converted Sunday School. It has been the setting for the weekly sale for the past 20 years, although the company responsible was established well before that, in 1914. The weekly sales are of general household furniture and effects, and miscellanea. There is often a large amount of 'shipping furniture', which can be particularly good value. Once a month the general sale is replaced by a sale of antiques. Both sales have a wide range of articles, both in type and value, with possibilities for both the fleamarket-goer and the international dealer.

THRIPPLETON & BISHOP

Bradford

Southend Hall, Tickhill Street. Tel: (0274) 734963

200-400 lots. This is the place to come for antique or pre-1930s furniture, collectables, small silver items or jewellery. The fortnightly sales take place in the evening, in what was once a church hall, about half a mile from the city centre and just off the A647 Leeds Road. There are two types of sale, held alternately: the first type is for antique and pre-1930s furniture only, and the second type has furniture, plus a full range of collectables, small silver items, jewellery, bric-à-brac, porcelain, paintings and so on. Because of the extra number of lots, this sale begins half-an-hour earlier, with smaller items taking up the first hour of the auction. All the lots are well laid out and easy to view, and browsing is good fun. The furniture could include mahogany, oak and walnut, bedroom, dining and occasional pieces; and there could be desks, bureaux and chairs, or pine furniture for stripping.

BUYER'S PREMIUM: *Nil*
SALES: *Fortnightly on Thu. Antique and pre-1930s furniture: 6.30pm. Antique and pre-1930s furniture plus other items: 6.00pm. Sales alternate.*
VIEWING: *Day prior 9.30am-5.00pm, day of sale from 9.30am.*
REFRESHMENTS: *Own café.*
PARKING: *Own car park.*
STORAGE: *Yes*
TRANSPORTATION: *Yes*
SHIPPING: *Yes*

EDDISONS AUCTIONS

Hebden Bridge

See EDDISONS AUCTIONS, Huddersfield, West Yorkshire

EDDISONS AUCTIONS

Huddersfield

4-6 High Street. Tel: (0484) 533151

450-500 lots. The saleroom is a large, interesting building with plenty of gargoyles outside and a big saleroom with a lofty ceiling inside. It is prominent in the town centre and is only five doors away from the town hall. The building has been an auction house since 1844 but was designed for horse auctions, which explains the wide passages and corridors. About every two to three weeks, depending on how quickly the lots come in, there is a sale of general household furniture and effects, which can be very rewarding. This sale is replaced every quarter by a special catalogued sale of antiques, which starts at 11.00am.

Another branch of the firm is responsible for regular Tuesday fortnightly sales which take place at 35 West End, Hebden Bridge, Yorkshire, tel: (0422) 842007. These are of Victorian and later furniture, china and miscellanea.

Eddisons are also involved in on-site auctions, very often of liquidated stock.

BUYER'S PREMIUM: *Antiques sales: 10%. Others: nil*
SALES: *General: every two to three weeks on Wed at 10.30am (replaced quarterly by antiques sale starting at 11.00am). Hebden Bridge: fortnightly on Tue at 1.00pm.*
VIEWING: *Huddersfield: day prior 9.30am-4.30pm. Hebden Bridge: Sat prior 10.00am-4.00pm, Mon 10.00am-1.00pm.*
REFRESHMENTS: *cafés and sandwich bars near by.*
PARKING: *None available on premises.*
STORAGE: *No*
TRANSPORTATION: *Yes*
SHIPPING: *Yes*

WHITWORTHS

Huddersfield

32/34 Wood Street. Tel: (0484) 427467

300-350 lots. The saleroom is a 19th-century building in the centre of town, close to the Classical-style railway station. This

BUYER'S PREMIUM: *10%*
SALES: *About every six weeks*

on Fri at 12.00 noon.
VIEWING: *Wed and Thu prior 10.00am-4.00pm.*
REFRESHMENTS: *None available on the premises.*
PARKING: *None available on the premises.*
STORAGE: *Yes*
TRANSPORTATION: *Yes*
SHIPPING: *Yes*

is a typical independently run local sale, which has gained a loyal following with both buyers and vendors over the years. Sales are held about every six weeks, and are looked forward to by local people, many of whom will pop in at least briefly during their lunch time. A typical sale will have a comprehensive range of high-class household furnishings and antiques. There will often be bankruptcy or liquidated stock, with some police lost property and jewellery.

Ilkley

ANDREW HARTLEY FINE ARTS

Victoria Hall, Little Lane. Tel: (0943) 816363

600-900 lots. The saleroom is a building of character, which was once a theatre with baths underneath (the baths are still there, but covered over). It is close to the town's only set of traffic lights. The busy and entertaining weekly sale is packed with Victorian, Edwardian, and later furniture, plus a wide range of other goods. Every two months, this general sale is replaced by one of antiques and fine art, which may last two days depending on the number of lots. The firm also holds special sales of toys and games, twice a year in March and October; and other specialist sales are held at irregular intervals. Past categories have included wine and paintings.

BUYER'S PREMIUM: *5%*
SALES: *General: weekly on Wed at 10.00am (replaced by antiques sale every two months). Toys: twice a year in Mar and Oct on Sat at 1.30pm. Other specialist: at irregular intervals.*
VIEWING: *General: day prior 10.00am-7.00pm. Antiques: Sat prior 9.30am-12.30pm, Mon and Tue prior 9.30am-4.30pm. All sales: morning of sale from 9.15am.*
REFRESHMENTS: *None available on the premises.*
PARKING: *Ample parking near by.*
STORAGE: *Yes*
TRANSPORTATION: *Yes*
SHIPPING: *Yes*

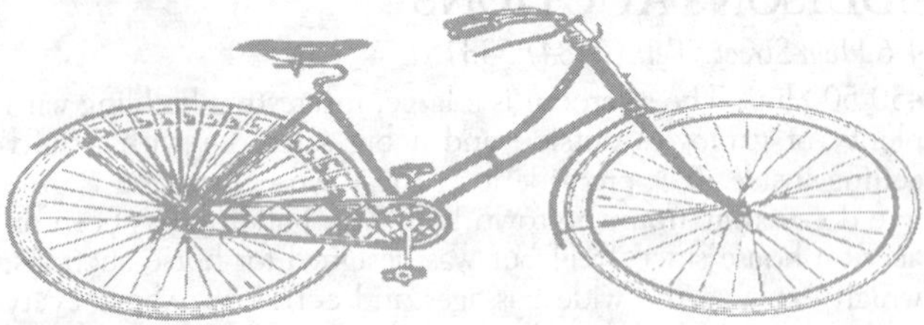

Leeds

IMPERIAL

3/5 Cross Chapel Street, Headingly. Tel: (0532) 752664

1,000 lots. Imperial holds specialist sales of stamps, postcards, coins, medals, ephemera, cigarette cards and similar collectables at the Methodist church hall, Chapel Street, Leeds 6. They have a well-deserved reputation for these sales and receive postal bids from all over the world — sometimes as much as 95 per cent of the bidding will be by post. The lots are on view for three weeks before the sale. Viewers can just walk in during normal office hours; or an appointment can be made for viewing at other times. On the day of the sale lots are on view at the church hall.

BUYER'S PREMIUM: *£1 per lot.*
SALES: *Every six weeks on Sat at 3.00pm.*
VIEWING: *Three weeks prior at Imperial's office, Mon-Fri 9.00am-5.00pm (other times by appointment), day of sale at church hall from 10.00am.*
REFRESHMENTS: *Available on sale day.*
PARKING: *Own car park.*
STORAGE: *Yes*
TRANSPORTATION: *Yes*
SHIPPING: *Yes*

HARRY WARD & SON

Leeds

2 St Peter's Buildings, York Street. Tel: (0532) 455425

800-900 lots. This independent family-run business has been established in Leeds for over 100 years. The saleroom is near the Play House Theatre and the main bus station. It can be chaotic at times, because goods to be auctioned are being delivered all the time, sometimes even during a sale. The goods in the Wednesday sale are sold on behalf of loss adjusters and trustees, 'under county court instructions' and in similar circumstances, so the range and type of lots is enormous. There are smaller items such as cameras, jewellery, ornaments and so on, and also brand new larger articles, such as linen baskets, sofabeds, bathroom suites and garden furniture. A typical sale might have food mixers and vacuum cleaners, office stationery, desks and typewriters, or perhaps new sheepskin coats.

The Friday sale is of general household furniture and effects, and is usually divided into morning and afternoon sessions, with a break for lunch from 1.30pm to 2.00pm. This sale often includes the complete contents of a house, which means everything from the cruet set to the bedroom suite, television and garden mower. In the morning smaller items are sold, such as china, glass, silver, paintings, and bric-à-brac. The afternoon is given over to furniture, followed by carpets and rugs at 3.00pm.

BUYER'S PREMIUM: *Nil*
SALES: *Twice weekly on Wed and Fri at 10.30am.*
VIEWING: *Morning of sale from 9.00am.*
REFRESHMENTS: *Own café.*
PARKING: *Quarry Hill car park.*
STORAGE: *Yes*
TRANSPORTATION: *Yes*
SHIPPING: *Yes*

WHARF SALEROOM

Leeds

Canal Wharf, Water Lane. Tel: (0532) 434464

300-400 lots. The saleroom has been converted from an old grain warehouse, and stands on the canal bank. It has a loading bay (unused) directly on to the canal, so people with children need to be cautious. Any auction house which conducts two large sales per week must at times look a little chaotic, and this one is no exception. The company was established in 1923, in a building half a minute away from the present saleroom, and the sale has been a landmark in Leeds ever since. Many elderly people at the present sales proudly boast of having furnished and equipped an entire house from purchases made here.

The Wharf auctions are a wonderful mix of cheap and expensive goods. Valuable lots and antiques are put into the same sale as the rest, so there is never any telling what the value of the next lot will be. An old chest of drawers could be sold for £2 while the very next item could bring a hush over the saleroom as the bids quickly rise to a couple of thousand pounds. The Tuesday evening sale is for smaller

BUYER'S PREMIUM: *Nil*
SALES: *Twice weekly on Tue (small items) and Wed (large items) at 7.00pm.*
VIEWING: *Day of sale from 4.00pm.*
REFRESHMENTS: *None available on the premises.*
PARKING: *Own car park.*
STORAGE: *No*
TRANSPORTATION: *Yes*
SHIPPING: *Yes*

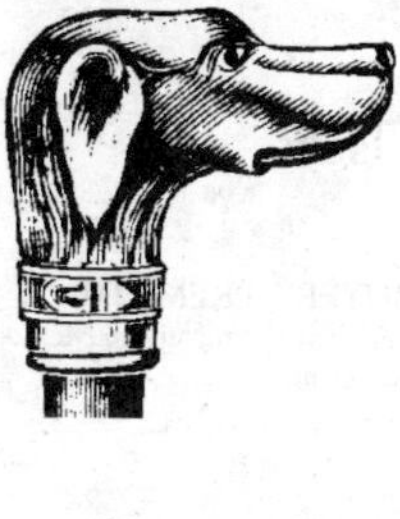

items such as china, glass, silver, jewellery and collectors' items. The Wednesday evening sale is for larger items, including electrical goods and furniture from antique to modern.

Lepton, near Huddersfield

BUYER'S PREMIUM: *Nil*
SALES: *Weekly on Tue at 6.30pm.*
VIEWING: *Day of sale from 4.00pm.*
REFRESHMENTS: *Own café.*
PARKING: *Own car park.*
STORAGE: *Yes*
TRANSPORTATION: *Yes*
SHIPPING: *Yes*

BASIL KENNY

Thornes Farm, Knotty Lane. Tel: (0484) 603933

300-400 lots. Those looking for an unusual item of furniture or an original present will have fun browsing and bidding here. The auction is four miles out of Huddersfield, about 400 yards off the main road to Wakefield. The saleroom is a marvellous 15th-century cruck barn, which is still part of a farm. Typically the lots will include clocks, pictures, embroidered linen and antiquities of all sorts, and there is usually a large amount of porcelain and good quality Victorian furniture. Vendors are paid in cash on sale day, which adds to the excitement and bustle and gives successful bidders a chance to meet the previous owners of their purchases. Ideally this means that buyers can find out the history of the piece and any little quirks it might have. One buyer, for instance, was told that his newly acquired longcase clock would only work if it was wound up slowly at 4.00am.

New Mill

BUYER'S PREMIUM: *Nil*
SALES: *Every three weeks on Fri at 2.00pm.*
VIEWING: *Wed prior 7.00pm-9.00pm, Thu prior 2.00pm-9.00pm, day of sale from 12.00 noon.*
REFRESHMENTS: *None available on the premises.*
PARKING: *None available on the premises.*
STORAGE: *Yes*
TRANSPORTATION: *Yes*
SHIPPING: *Yes*

WM SYKES & SON

Old School Room, Sude Hill. Tel: (0484) 683543

400-450 lots. This pleasant little village is about two miles from Holmfirth, and tucked away inside it is an Aladdin's cave of treasure. Anyone engaged in furnishing or restoring an old house, or looking for an unusual gift, will find plenty to interest them among the doors, old brass taps, jewellery, bygones, cameras, lamps, silver and brass which regularly appear at the sales. In the centre of the old school hall and crammed on to tables, you will find a large selection of ornamental china, glass, brass, kitchen china, cutlery, collectables, toys, and so on, plus jewellery in cabinets. The auctioning starts with linens and then moves on to the large items of second-hand furniture, which are set around the edge of the hall. These range from new self-assembly kits to Victorian, cottage pine, and antique.

Ossett

BUYER'S PREMIUM: *Nil*
SALES: *Fortnightly on Mon at 10.00am.*

CHAS W HARRISON & SON

Ashfield House, Illingworth Street. Tel: (0924) 279005

500-600 lots. It is easy to find the saleroom in Ossett, because of the number of people heading in that direction. Lots are put into the fortnightly Monday sales on instructions from liquidators, the county courts, the Sheriff's office and others, and they can include almost anything. Examples from past sales are the entire contents of a mini supermarket (including the stocks of tinned and packet foods), computer equipment and car accessories, the entire contents of a carpet shop, hi-fi and electrical components, light and sound equipment, sewing machinery, garage accessories and office furniture, and the more usual antiques and general household furniture. Motor vehicles, caravanettes and caravans are always sold at 1.00pm prompt, and can be inspected in the yard.

The company is also responsible for many on-site auctions. These sales occur throughout the year and are sometimes very interesting.

VIEWING: *Sat prior 9.30am-1.30pm.*
REFRESHMENTS: *None available on the premises.*
PARKING: *Free public car park adjacent.*
STORAGE: *No*
TRANSPORTATION: *Yes*
SHIPPING: *No*

DEWSBURY AUCTIONS

629 Huddersfield Road. Tel: (0924) 461210

600-700 lots. The proprietors of the sale are Mr and Mrs William Crow, who also own the retail furniture shop in front of the saleroom. The twice-weekly sales make an entertaining day out, with lots ranging from furniture to livestock. Children are not encouraged however — they are allowed to attend the yard sales but not the general indoor auctions. The premises are said to be haunted, and a ghost can often be heard walking the full length of the first floor. Ex-mail order goods are prominent in the sale, including brass, ornaments, clothing, furniture and other items.

The Saturday sale starts with 'deadstock', which means bundles of wood, DIY equipment, lawn mowers, bicycles and motor bikes. This part of the sale goes on for two to two-and-a-half hours. At 1.00pm the sale of poultry, rabbits, pigeons, hens and various other livestock starts, followed at 2.30pm by the general sale.

The Tuesday afternoon sale has fewer lots and there are usually fewer prospective buyers, so things may go a little cheaper. On the last Tuesday of the month the auction is moved to 6.30pm, and becomes a catalogued sale for better quality items.

Ravensthorpe

BUYER'S PREMIUM: *Nil*
SALES: *Twice weekly on Sat at 11.00am and Tue at 1.30pm (6.30pm on last Tue of month for better quality items).*
VIEWING: *Day of sale from 8.30am (12.00 noon for evening sale).*
REFRESHMENTS: *Café across road.*
PARKING: *Queen Street public car park.*
STORAGE: *No*
TRANSPORTATION: *No*
SHIPPING: *No*

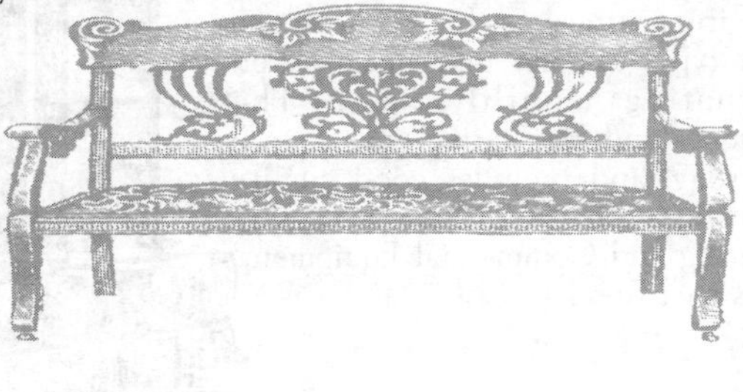

WILTSHIRE

Salisbury

BUYER'S PREMIUM: *10%*
SALES: *Shutter sale: fortnightly on Fri at 9.30am. Antiques: monthly on Thu at 10.00am. Specialist sales: three times a year at irregular intervals, on Mon at 10.30am.*
VIEWING: *Shutter sale and antiques: Tue and Wed prior, 10.00am-4.30pm. Specialist sales: Thu and Fri prior, 10.00am-4.30pm, Sat prior 10.00am-12.00 noon.*
REFRESHMENTS: *None available on the premises.*
PARKING: *Public car park on other side of the river.*
STORAGE: *Yes*
TRANSPORTATION: *Yes*
SHIPPING: *Yes*

WOOLLEY & WALLIS

Salisbury Salerooms, Castle Street. Tel: (0722) 411422

500-700 lots. The fortnightly Friday sales go under the title of 'Shutter sales'. These are sales of all types of household furniture and effects: items such as beds, tables, chairs, various boxes containing bric-à-brac, and sundries. A pine door with leaded panels was offered at one recent sale, together with, among other things, a Victorian oak and brass letterbox, a Chesterfield settee, eight Chippendale design dining chairs, two pairs of skis, a skateboard and a shopping trolley! (The last three items were sold on behalf of the Wiltshire Constabulary.) Lists with a description of the sale goods are placed strategically around the saleroom.

The monthly Thursday sales are of antique furniture. In addition, there are specialist sales of paintings and watercolours, European ceramics and glass, Oriental ceramics and works of art, silver, jewellery, *objets de vertu*, Eastern carpets and rugs, and books and prints.

Established for more than 100 years, these sales have real atmosphere. The auctioneers produce an attractive newspaper on a monthly basis, giving future sale dates, past sale prices and some business gossip.

Swindon

BUYER'S PREMIUM: *10%*
SALES: *General: fortnightly on Sat at 10.30am. Antiques and Decorative: every two months on Thu at 10.30am. Catering and Commercial: every two months on Tue at 10.30am (alternate months to antiques).*
VIEWING: *Day prior 10.00am-6.00pm, morning of sale from 9.00am.*
REFRESHMENTS: *Own café.*
PARKING: *The Planks public car park.*
STORAGE: *Yes*
TRANSPORTATION: *Yes*
SHIPPING: *Yes*

ALLEN & HARRIS WITH OSMOND TRICKS

The Planks, Old Town. Tel: (0793) 615915

500-600 lots. Swindon became a boom town when the Great Western Railway was built, and today its railway museum and railway village are interesting to visit. Allen & Harris with Osmond Tricks is a member of Royal Life Estates, and there are associated sales in Avon, Somerset, Dorset and Hampshire. The fortnightly sales at Swindon are of general household items and effects, including some interesting lots. In addition, two other types of sales take place on an alternating monthly basis. The 'Antiques and Decorative' sale is on a Thursday, and includes good quality antiques, china and so on. The 'Catering and Commercial Equipment' sale is on a Tuesday.

• LONDON •

London is unrivalled for sheer number of auction rooms, and in Sotheby's, Christie's, Phillips and Bonhams it has some of the most famous auctioneers in the world. In these salerooms, auctions take place most days of the week, with a staggering variety of objects coming under the hammer: from sculpture to egg cups, arms and armour, books, works of art, jewellery, silver, costumes and textiles, stamps and many other goods, which may be sold for a few pounds or for millions. Entrance to all auctions is free, and the reputation of the salerooms should not put anyone off visiting them. The sales are exciting, and viewing the lots can be as informative as visiting a museum, because the goods are often of high quality, and may be famous examples of their kind.

As with all the auctions in this book, always check with the saleroom before making any journey, as sale days and viewing times can vary.

BONHAMS

Montpelier Street, SW7
Tel: (071) 584 9161

Ring the telephone number above for up-to-the-minute sale listings, with dates and times.

BUYER'S PREMIUM: *10%*
SALES: *Most weekdays.*
VIEWING: *Mon 8.45am-7.00pm, Tue to Fri 8.45am-6.00pm, Sun 12.00 noon-5.00pm.*
UNDERGROUND: *Knightsbridge*
BUSES: *9, 14, 52, 73, 74*

CHRISTIE'S

8 King Street, St James's, SW1
Tel: (071) 839 9060

BUYER'S PREMIUM: *10%*
SALES: *Most weekdays.*
VIEWING: *Mon to Fri 9.00am-4.00pm.*
UNDERGROUND: *Green Park*
BUSES: *9, 11, 14, 73*

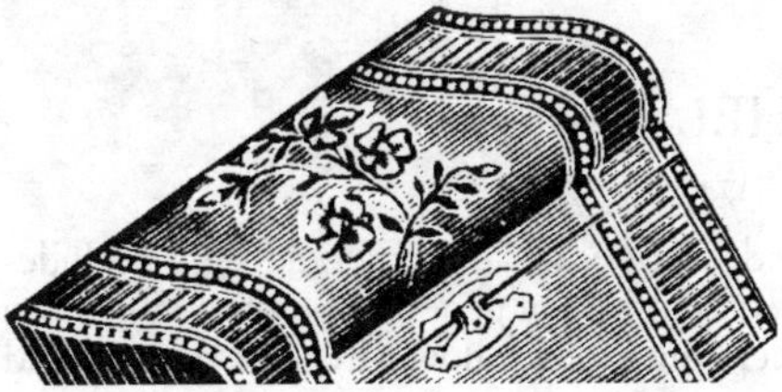

PHILLIPS

101 New Bond Street, W1
Tel: (071) 629 6602

For details of all the week's sales, telephone the 24-hour recorded information service on (071) 495 6912. Affiliated to Phillips is Glendining's, tel: (071) 493 2445, which specialises exclusively in sales of coins and medals, usually on Wednesdays.

BUYER'S PREMIUM: *10%*
SALES: *Most weekdays.*
VIEWING: *Mon to Fri 8.30am-5.00pm, Sat 8.30am-12.00 noon, Sun 2.00pm-5.00pm.*
UNDERGROUND: *Bond Street*
BUSES: *7, 8, 10, 12, 25, 73, 88*

SOTHEBY'S

34-35 New Bond Street, W1
Tel: (071) 493 8080

For details of forthcoming auctions, ring the 24-hour recorded information line on (071) 409 2686.

BUYER'S PREMIUM: *10%*
SALES: *Most weekdays.*
VIEWING: *Mon to Fri 9.00am-4.30pm, Sun 12.00 noon-4.00pm.*
UNDERGROUND: *Bond Street*
BUSES: *7, 8, 10, 25, 73, 503*

OTHER LONDON AUCTIONS

In addition to the four famous auction houses, there are many others with regular general and specialist sales. A selection is given here, with details of other London salerooms that are owned by Bonham's, Christie's and Phillips.

Contrary to what you might expect, prices in London auctions are not necessarily higher than those in country sales. The tradition of shopping at a local auction has rather been lost in London, and fewer private buyers attend the sales. Settings may not always be as attractive as those of sales held regionally, but London auctions have their own atmosphere and can be just as rewarding for buyers and browsers alike. All the following London auctions offer advice on storage, transportation and shipping.

W5

ACADEMY AUCTIONEERS & VALUERS

Northcote House, Northcote Avenue, Ealing
Tel: (081) 579 7466

BUYER'S PREMIUM: *10%*
SALES: *Monthly, usually Tue and Wed at 2.30pm.*
VIEWING: *Mon 2.30pm-9.00pm, morning of sale from 9.30am.*
UNDERGROUND/BR: *Ealing Broadway*
BUSES: *65, 207*

1,000-1,300 lots. This is a good local auction with a high standard of lots. People who buy at West End auctions can often be found searching around these salerooms. The auctions are normally held over two days. Tuesdays are devoted to Oriental items, European ceramics and works of art, textiles and decorative arts, followed by pictures at around 7.15pm. The Wednesday sale starts with silver and silver plate, works of art, jewellery and watches and clocks. Furniture, carpets and mirrors from around 6.30pm.

EC1

BLOOMSBURY BOOK AUCTIONS

3-4 Hardwick Street (off Rosebery Avenue)
Tel: (071) 833 2636/7 and (071) 636 1945

BUYER'S PREMIUM: *10%*
SALES: *Fortnightly on Thu at 1.00pm, 11.00am and 2.00pm.*
VIEWING: *Tue prior 9.30am- 5.30pm, Wed prior 9.30am-8.00pm, morning of sale from 9.30am.*
UNDERGROUND: *Angel*
BUSES: *19, 38, 153, 171, 171A*

400-500 lots. These are specialist fortnightly sales of printed books, including antiquarian books, manuscripts, prints and drawings, first and limited editions, periodicals, autograph letters, music, maps and atlases.

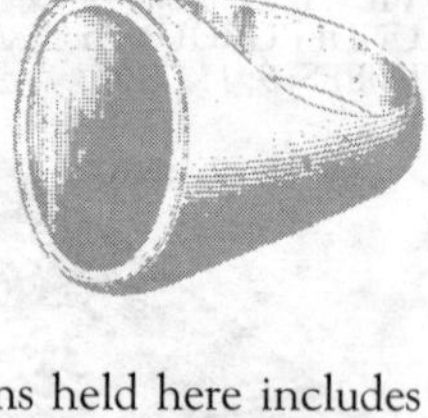

SW10

BONHAMS CHELSEA

65-9 Lots Road. Tel: (071) 351 7111

BUYER'S PREMIUM: *10%*
SALES: *Three or four a week at 10.30am and 2.00pm.*

200-300 lots. The wide variety of auctions held here includes an excellent weekly Tuesday sale of general household furniture and furnishings. Other categories follow a regular pattern and include silver and silver plate, jewellery, porcelain, works of art, pictures, prints, tribal art, books, garden furniture and architectural fittings. There are also collectors' sales, which in the past have included automobilia, cameras, scientific and musical instruments, juke boxes, gaming machines, toys and dolls, militaria, erotica, tiles, textiles and cigarette cards. There is a public car park next to the saleroom.

VIEWING: *Mon to Fri 8.45am-5.00pm (Mon 7.00pm), Sat and Sun 10.00am-1.00pm.*
UNDERGROUND: *Sloane Square (not near)*
BUSES: *11, 22*

CHRISTIE'S SOUTH KENSINGTON — SW7

85 Old Brompton Road. Tel: (071) 581 7611

2,000-3,000 lots. A variety of auctions is held every week, and there are often two sales a day. Categories include British, Continental and Oriental ceramics, costumes and textiles, old, modern and costume jewellery, silver, carpets, paintings, sculpture, printed books, clocks and wine. A popular and well-attended sale of furniture is held every Wednesday at 1.00pm.

BUYER'S PREMIUM: *10%*
SALES: *Most weekdays at 10.30am, 1.00pm, 2.00pm or 5.00pm (times vary).*
VIEWING: *Mon 9.00am-7.30pm, Tue to Fri 9.00am-5.00pm, Sat 10.00am-1.00pm.*
UNDERGROUND: *South Kensington*
BUSES: *14, 30, 45, 49, 74, C3*

DOWELL LLOYD & CO — SW15

118 Putney Bridge Road. Tel: (081) 788 7777

500-1,000 lots. The saleroom covers over 16,000sq ft, and a series of interesting sales is held here. Every other Saturday sees a sale of general household furniture, effects and miscellaneous items, including pictures, carpets, porcelain, domestic and ornamental china, and so on, with many antiques. In the alternate weeks, the Thursday is devoted to 'Police Lost Property', which can include almost anything but usually features radios, tools, and always plenty of bicycles. Finally a sale of jewellery is held every Tuesday.

BUYER'S PREMIUM: *10% (jewellery 5%, nil for police artefacts)*
SALES: *General: fortnightly on Sat at 9.30am. Jewellery: Weekly on Tue at 9.30am (Wed if Mon is a Bank Holiday). Police Lost Property: fortnightly on Thu at 9.30am (alternate weeks to general sale).*
VIEWING: *General and lost property: day prior 9.00am-7.30pm. Jewellery: day prior 9.00am-5.00pm.*
UNDERGROUND: *Putney Bridge or East Putney*
BUSES: *14, 22, 74, 220*

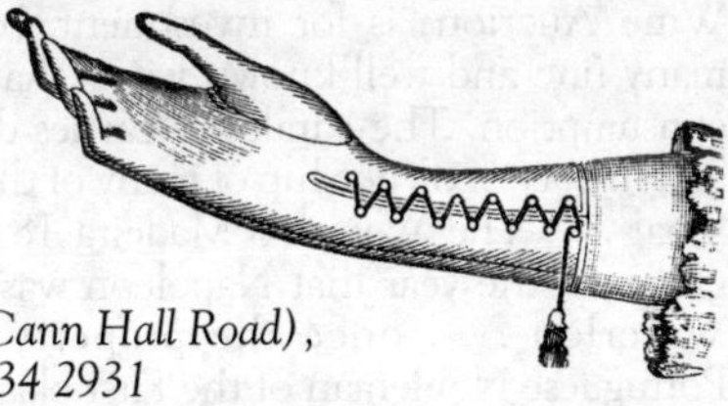

FORREST & CO — E11

79/85 Cobbold Road (off Cann Hall Road), Leytonstone. Tel: (081) 534 2931

400-500 lots. The saleroom is close to the grass and trees of Wanstead Flats. Forrest & Co are official auctioneers for various county courts, liquidators, and Customs and Excise, so the sales often include the most amazing mix of goods. There might be food, soft drinks and alcohol, cars and forklift trucks, televisions, stereo recorders and computers, brand new men's, women's, and children's clothing, Pierre Cardin stockings and disposable

BUYER'S PREMIUM: *10%*
SALES: *Fortnightly on Thu at 11.00am.*
VIEWING: *Day prior 10.00am-5.00pm.*
BRITISH RAIL: *Forest Gate*
UNDERGROUND: *Leyton*
BUSES: *58, 162*

nappies, full-size snooker tables, garage or office equipment, antique furniture or brand new suites, plus other household furniture and general effects. A truly comprehensive auction.

WC2

STANLEY GIBBONS AUCTIONS LTD

399 Strand. Tel: (071) 836 84444

BUYER'S PREMIUM: *15%*
SALES: *Monthly on Thu or on Thu and Fri at 2.00pm (no auctions usually in Jul and Aug).*
VIEWING: *Two or three days prior to sale 10.00am-4.00pm, morning of sale 10.00am-12.00 noon.*
UNDERGROUND: *Charing Cross or Covent Garden.*
BUSES: *1, 1A, 4, 56, 9, 11, 13, 15, 23, 68, 77, 77A, 155, 170*

300-2,000 lots. Stanley Gibbons is one of the most famous names in stamps, and has been serving collectors worldwide since 1856. A vast range of specialist auctions is held here, and virtually all the world's top collectors are notified of them. Many of the sales are over two days. The comfortable saleroom is situated above 'The World's Largest Stamp Shop' (opposite the Savoy Hotel), which is open six days a week and contains an unrivalled stock of stamps. Staff are always on hand to answer any queries; the auction department is open on weekdays only.

EC1

HATTON GARDEN AUCTIONS

36 Hatton Garden. Tel: (071) 242 6452

BUYER'S PREMIUM: *10%*
SALES: *Weekly on Thu at 1.30pm.*
VIEWING: *Mon to Fri 9.00am-4.00pm.*
UNDERGROUND: *Chancery Lane or Farringdon*
BUSES: *22, 501, 28*

100 lots. This is a small, friendly lunchtime auction set in the heart of London's diamond and jewellery trading district. The sale is of antique and modern jewellery and silver, and may include domestic and ornamental china. Selling is often over within an hour, so be there on time.

SE7

INTERNATIONAL WINE AUCTIONS

40 Victoria Way. Tel: (081) 293 4992

BUYER'S PREMIUM: *10%*
SALES: *Every two months on Tue at 10.30am.*
VIEWING: *None*
UNDERGROUND: *Embankment, Charing Cross*
BUSES: *Any to Trafalgar Square. Commonwealth House in Northumberland Avenue is five minutes' walk away (no buses pass down Northumberland Avenue).*

600-700 lots. The majority of the wine sold by International Wine Auctions is for investment, but the sales also include many fine and well-known wines that are ready for immediate consumption. The catalogue carries descriptions of the origins and history of ownership of many of the wines sold, for example, 'Boal . . . The Waterloo Madeira 1815 . . . made from grapes grown in the year that Napoleon was defeated at the Battle of Waterloo . . . once the property of Count Cunavial, a Portuguese Nobleman of the First class . . .' The labels attached to the bottles are described as well, ranging from 'perfect condition' to 'slightly worn and stained' or even 'badly damaged and covered with clear adhesive tape'. The wines are kept in the company's warehouse in south-east London, but sales take place at Commonwealth House, Northumberland Avenue, London WC2, tel: (071) 930 6733, on sale day only — otherwise ring the number above. Shipping can be arranged if necessary.

MAYFAIR AUCTIONS

SE17

7 Dartford Street. Tel: (071) 703 1984

300-400 lots. Dartford Street is just off the Walworth Road, a busy cosmopolitan shopping area well known for the colourful East Street market. The weekly evening auctions include a mix of general household furniture and effects of all periods from antique and modern, including silver and gold, jewellery, domestic and ornamental china, porcelain, pictures, clocks and watches, carpets and pictures.

BUYER'S PREMIUM: *£1 per lot.*
SALES: *Weekly on Thu at 6.00pm.*
VIEWING: *Day of sale from 10.00am.*
UNDERGROUND: *Elephant and Castle or Kennington*
BUSES: *12, 35, 42, 45, 53, 63, 68, 171, 184, 188*

THOMAS MOORE AUCTIONEERS

SE10

217-19 Greenwich High Road. Tel: (081) 858 7848

200-300 lots. The saleroom is in the heart of Greenwich, in easy reach of the Royal Observatory. The auctions are well attended and typically include china, glass, furniture and effects, paintings, prints, porcelain, silver, jewellery, books, postcards, stamps, coins and so on. Most of the lots are from the Victorian, Georgian and Regency periods, and there will very seldom be anything dating from after 1940.

BUYER'S PREMIUM: *10%*
SALES: *Weekly on Thu at 10.00am.*
VIEWING: *Day prior 2.00pm-8.00pm.*
BRITISH RAIL: *Greenwich or Maze Hill*
BUSES: *108B, 177, 180, 185, 188*

PHILLIPS MARYLEBONE

See PHILLIPS WEST TWO, London W2

PHILLIPS WEST TWO

W2

10 Salem Road. Tel: (071) 229 9090

400-500 lots. Salem Road is behind Whiteley's shopping precinct in Bayswater. There are two sales each week, a general auction of antique and modern furniture and porcelain on Thursday, and a collectors' sale on Wednesday in various categories such as postcards, film and theatre memorabilia, toys, sporting items, tribal art, textiles and so on.

A sale of oil paintings, watercolours and prints is held every Friday at Phillips Marylebone, Hayes Place, Lisson Grove, NW1, tel: (071) 723 2647.

BUYER'S PREMIUM: *10%*
SALES: *Phillips West Two: collectors' items weekly on Wed at 12.00 noon, furniture weekly on Thu at 10.00am. Phillips Marylebone: pictures weekly on Fri at 11.00am.*
VIEWING: *Day prior 9.00am-7.00pm, day of sale from 9.00am.*
UNDERGROUND: *Phillips West Two: Bayswater. Phillips Marylebone: Marylebone*
BUSES: *Phillips West Two: 12, 88. Phillips Marylebone: 13, 82, 159*

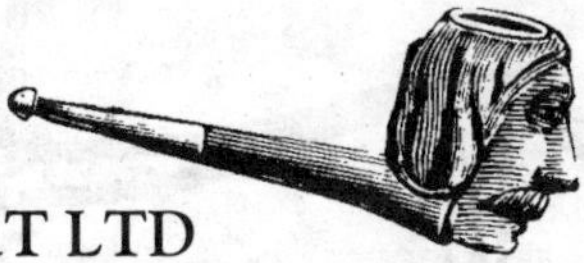

ROSEBERY'S FINE ART LTD

SE19

The Old Railway Booking Hall, Crystal Palace Station Road. Tel: (081) 778 4024

300-400 lots. The saleroom is close to the Crystal Palace National Sports Centre, and is part of the British Rail station.

BUYER'S PREMIUM: *10%*
SALES: *General: monthly on*

Sat at 12.00 noon. Antiques: monthly on last Wed of month at 12.00 noon.
VIEWING: *Day prior 10.00am-8.00pm.*
BRITISH RAIL: *Crystal Palace*
BUSES: *12, 35, 40, 42, 68, 171, 176, 184, P3*

Two sales are held each month, and both are well attended. The Saturday general sale is usually near the beginning of the month, and a sale of antiques is held on the last Wednesday.

N11

SOUTHGATE AUCTION ROOMS

Munro House, Munro Drive, Cline Road, New Southgate. Tel: (081) 886 7888

BUYER'S PREMIUM: *10%*
SALES: *Weekly on Thu at 6.30pm.*
VIEWING: *Day of sale from 9.00am.*
UNDERGROUND: *Bounds Green*
BUSES: *221*

500-600 lots. This is a weekly sale of general household furniture and effects, with miscellaneous items of all periods from modern to antique. The first 200 lots are usually smaller items of silver and gold, jewellery, watches, brooches and the like. They will usually be followed by beds, lounge suites, tables, electrical goods, linen, paintings, china and so on. This is strictly a cash only sale, and no cheques or credit cards will be accepted. Successful bidders must make at least part payment in cash before leaving the saleroom, and have until noon on Saturday to complete the price.

SW6

A WELLESLEY BRISCOE & PARTNERS

The Warehouse, Roxby Place. Tel: (071) 381 8558

BUYER'S PREMIUM: *Nil*
SALES: *Normally weekly on Sun at 11.30am.*
VIEWING: *One hour prior to sale.*
UNDERGROUND: *Earls Court*
BUSES: *30, 31, 74, C3*

100 lots. Specialist sales of Oriental carpets, textiles and tapestries are held here. They come from all the important Oriental weaving centres, and include antiques, silks and nomadic items. Before selling, the auctioneer talks about the area each carpet comes from, and explains the different weaving methods used and the meaning of the patterns that are woven into the rugs. To save time, prospective buyers can ask for any lot to be brought forward and auctioned out of sequence. The sale is usually completed by around 1.30pm. Roxby Place is off the Old Brompton Road, and there is usually plenty of parking space.

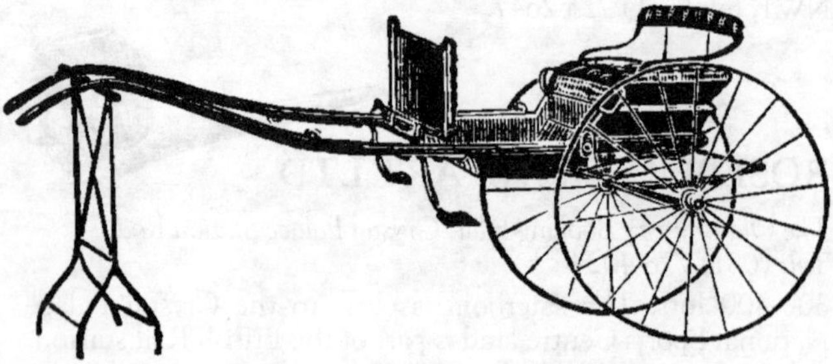

• WALES •

CLWYD

MAYNARDS

33 Abergele Road. Tel: (0492) 534430

250-450 lots. The saleroom is on the main road running through this attractive modern seaside resort. Maynards is a family-run business, set up seven years ago by June Pender and her husband after over 20 years in the antiques trade. June Pender takes her turn on the auctioneering rostrum, and does her best to create an unintimidating atmosphere in the saleroom. A good cross-section of goods can be found, including furniture, china (ornamental and domestic), silver, glass, pictures and other household effects, and endless miscellaneous items.

Once a month the sale turns into either an antiques sale or a collector's sale. The latter is usually a 'cabinet sale' of smaller items, such as pieces of good quality domestic or ornamental china, silver, brass, old toys, memorabilia and bygones, gold, jewellery and so on. A great many buyers take the goods they have bought to sell on stalls at fairs, which are plentiful in this area.

Colwyn Bay

BUYER'S PREMIUM: *6% lots over £100. Other lots nil.*
SALES: *Weekly (occasionally fortnightly) on Tue at 10.30am (includes a monthly antiques or collector's sale).*
VIEWING: *Day prior 11.00am-4.00pm, morning of sale.*
REFRESHMENTS: *None available on the premises.*
PARKING: *On road, or public car park a few minutes' walk away.*
STORAGE: *Yes*
TRANSPORTATION: *Yes*
SHIPPING: *Yes*

DODDS PROPERTY WORLD

Victoria Auction Galleries, Chester Street. Tel: (0352) 2552

300-500 lots. Bidders must plan their time at this busy, friendly sale. The main sale begins at 10.30am, and while it is still going on, the sale of outside effects begins at 1.00pm outside. This part of the sale could include cars, trailers, bicycles, building equipment, wheelbarrows and other gardening equipment, chainsaws, timber and so on. It usually goes on for an hour or so. Meanwhile, the main part of the auction begins with electrical goods such as washing machines, dishwashers, spin dryers, cookers and fridges, followed by table items including china (both domestic and ornamental), glass, lamps, books, clocks and so on. The sale finishes with various items of furniture of all grades — some of the pieces may be antiques while others will be almost new. The goods vary in quality, which adds to the interest.

Periodically throughout the year there are evening sales of antiques, which replace the normal Wednesday sale and are at no regular intervals.

Special carpet sales are held quarterly on the first Wednesday of December, March, June and September. These offer good bargains in new Axminster carpets.

Mold

BUYER'S PREMIUM: *Nil*
SALES: *General: weekly on Wed at 10.30am (except on antique and carpet sale days). Antiques: at irregular intervals on Wed at 5.45pm. Carpets: quarterly on first Wed of Dec, Mar, Jun and Sep at 6.00pm.*
VIEWING: *Day prior 9.30am-1.00pm, 2.00pm-4.30pm. Carpet sales: also 5.30pm-7.30pm.*
REFRESHMENTS: *Refreshments adjacent.*
PARKING: *Own car park.*
STORAGE: *Yes*
TRANSPORTATION: *Yes*
SHIPPING: *Yes*

Wrexham

SETH HUGHES & SON

12-15 George's Crescent. Tel: (0978) 265123

BUYER'S PREMIUM: *Nil*
SALES: *Thu at 1.00pm (includes antiques and fine art sale about every three months).*
VIEWING: *Day prior 9.00am-1.00pm, 2.00pm-5.00pm.*
REFRESHMENTS: *None available on the premises.*
PARKING: *Multi-storey car park near by.*
STORAGE: *Yes*
TRANSPORTATION: *Yes*
SHIPPING: *Yes*

250-300 lots. Seth Hughes & Son was established in 1875 and has enjoyed three generations of family involvement. The large showroom-type window in front of the saleroom displays articles to be sold in forthcoming sales. Lots are displayed to their best advantage, cleaned and polished and set out with plenty of room to view, and the proprietors, Mr and Mrs Dan Evans, are on hand to offer advice if needed.

The general sale follows no particular order, and usually contains a wide selection of household furniture and effects, ornaments, bric-à-brac and so on. About every three months an antiques and fine art sale replaces the general sale, with articles such as silver, porcelain, furniture and paintings sold in groups.

DYFED

Aberaeron

EVANS BROS

See EVANS BROS, Llanybydder, Dyfed

Carmarthen

JOHN FRANCIS

See SPENCERS, Ross-on-Wye, Hereford & Worcester

Carmarthen

JONES EVANS & CO

St Mary Auction Mart, 2 St Mary Street. Tel: (0267) 236502

BUYER'S PREMIUM: *Nil*
SALES: *Monthly on Wed at 10.30am (includes periodic antiques sales).*
VIEWING: *Mon and Tue prior 9.00am-1.00pm, 2.00pm-5.00pm, morning of sale from 9.00am.*
REFRESHMENTS: *Available at periodic antiques sales only.*
PARKING: *Town centre car park.*
STORAGE: *Yes*
TRANSPORTATION: *Yes*
SHIPPING: *Yes*

300-350 lots. This sale is held monthly and tends to have items of Welsh interest, with Welsh bygones among the general household furniture, antiques, craft work, electrical goods, bicycles and so on. The lots are not sold in categories: first a table might be sold, then the box of china underneath it, followed by a painting, a Royal Doulton tea cup, a set of six dessert plates, a pottery vase, an assortment of coins and military badges, a dinner service, a swivel desk chair and a chest of drawers. This helps to keep buyers in the saleroom for the duration of the auction. Periodically the general sale is replaced by a special antiques sale, but selling and viewing times remain the same.

Kidwelly

CASTLE AUCTION MART

Unit 4, Station Road. Tel: (0554) 891256

BUYER'S PREMIUM: *10%*
SALES: *Weekly on Mon at*

400-500 lots. This is a family-run auction, whose reputation has increased year by year since it was begun by Leslie and Jean

Treharne in the mid 1980s. According to Mrs Treharne, 'Local auctions are not only a good way to buy but also an excellent way of making money out of goods cluttering up your home. We're as happy to sell one item for a vendor as a dozen.' The saleroom is centrally located by the railway station, and there is generally a comprehensive range of good and lesser quality furniture and effects. In addition there are often antiques, jewellery, silver, paintings, stamps, coins, cars, vans, boats, caravans and motorbikes. Vehicles are sometimes sold outside, but there are large double doors at the rear of the saleroom to allow the odd single vehicle inside.

10.30am.
VIEWING: *Day of sale from 9.00am.*
REFRESHMENTS: *Day of sale only.*
PARKING: *Own car park.*
STORAGE: *Yes*
TRANSPORTATION: *Yes*
SHIPPING: *Yes*

GRAHAM H EVANS

Kilgetty

The Auction Sales Centre, The Market Place.
Tel: (0834) 811151
800-900 lots. There is a good friendly atmosphere about this sale. Newcomers are greeted with a welcoming nod, and locals seem genuinely pleased to see strangers taking an interest in their auction. The sale is generally full of good bargains, with electrical goods, china, teacups, dinner services, teapots, glass, beautiful old-fashioned ornaments (the type that grandmother had above her fireplace), collectables, craft items, and gardening, farming and kitchen bygones, in addition to all sorts of furniture in a wide range of periods.

The sale of motor vehicles and trailers begins outside at 3.30pm. This part of the sale brings in a new set of potential buyers. Once a year, usually in April or May but always on a Saturday at 12.00 noon, there is a special sale of boats, boating equipment and boat paraphernalia. This sale has gained a good reputation over the years, and buyers from all over Wales and England regularly attend.

BUYER'S PREMIUM: *Nil*
SALES: *Fortnightly on second and last Sat of month at 10.30am (general) and 3.30pm (motor vehicle).*
VIEWING: *Day prior 4.00pm-7.00pm, morning of sale from 9.00am.*
REFRESHMENTS: *Own café.*
PARKING: *Own car park.*
STORAGE: *Yes*
TRANSPORTATION: *Yes*
SHIPPING: *Yes*

EVANS BROS

Lampeter

See EVANS BROS, Llanybydder, Dyfed

JOHN WATKINS & CO

Llanbadarn Fawr

The Church Hall. Tel: (0970) 612464
400-600 lots. Llanbadarn Fawr is a pleasant old village just inland of Aberystwyth on the A44. The church hall is hired for the three days it takes to prepare a one-day sale. Mrs E A Watkins, who runs the company with her husband, shares the auctioneering with David Evans. The auction will start with perhaps 200-250 lots of 'smalls' which are set out on the table in the front of the hall. These might include whole or part tea and dinner sets, teapots, jugs, plates and dishes of all sorts,

BUYER'S PREMIUM: *Nil*
SALES: *About every three weeks (approx 18 sales a year) on Wed at 10.00am (includes an antiques sale about every three months, starting at 10.30am).*
VIEWING: *Day prior 4.00pm-6.00pm, day of sale from 9.00am.*

REFRESHMENTS: *Not available on the premises but available near by.*
PARKING: *Own car parking area.*
STORAGE: *Yes*
TRANSPORTATION: *Yes*
SHIPPING: *Yes*

silver cutlery, sets of silver spoons and silver-mounted brushes, brass candlesticks and horse brasses, and innumerable miscellaneous items — ornaments, books, photograph albums and so on. The sale also includes good quality furniture and general household effects of all types and values. House clearances sometimes result in television sets, washing machines, dishwashers and the like appearing in the sale.

Every three months or so the general sale is replaced by an antiques sale, which starts at 10.30am and includes 400-600 lots thought to be too good to put into the usual sale.

Llandeilo

JONES & LLEWELYN

The Llandeilo Auction Rooms, 21 New Road. Tel: (0558) 823430

BUYER'S PREMIUM: *General: nil. Antiques sales: 10%*
SALES: *General: every third week on Sat at 10.00am. Antiques: four times a year (one per season) on Tue, times vary.*
VIEWING: *General: day prior 2.00pm-6.00pm, morning of sale. Antiques: Sun and Mon prior 2.00pm-6.00pm, morning of sale.*
REFRESHMENTS: *Own café.*
PARKING: *Own car park.*
STORAGE: *Yes*
TRANSPORTATION: *Yes*
SHIPPING: *Yes*

500-600 lots. Mr Richard Llewelyn started in the business in this historic little market town over 40 years ago, and is still conducting the sales. Over the years these have become one of the town's attractions, and many visitors put them high up on their list of activities. There are two sale galleries. Gallery A is on the first floor, and is used in the general Saturday sale for better quality furniture and 'smalls', such as brass, china, glass, porcelain and pictures. There are often as many as 40 lots of oil paintings, watercolours and drawings, and there is also usually a great deal of Doulton china. Gallery B is for larger items such as electrical goods, kitchenalia, gardening tools and equipment, cottage and shipping furniture — 1930s and 1940s pieces, which may be particularly good value for money.

While the general sales will contain some antiques, the 500 or so lots at the seasonal antiques sales are of higher quality, including furniture, pictures, ceramics, silver, jewellery and other items. Antiques sales are held four times a year, on a Tuesday in spring, summer, autumn and winter. There are no fixed months for these sales, and they may be during the day or evening. The antiques sales are eagerly anticipated, not only by local people but by buyers from all over Wales and England.

Llanelli

LLANELLI AUCTION MART

Unit 4, Cambrian Works, Cambrian Street. Tel: (0554) 771938

BUYER'S PREMIUM: *Up to £100: 10%. Over £100: 5%*
SALES: *Weekly on Tue at 11.00am.*
VIEWING: *Mon prior 3.00pm-5.00pm, day of sale from 9.00am.*
REFRESHMENTS: *Own café.*

300-400 lots. The saleroom is in the area of town known as 'Seaside', and a comfortable, friendly atmosphere prevails. The auction is popular with both locals and holidaymakers, perhaps because of the variety of lots. A typical sale might have lounge, dining and bedroom suites, dressing tables, chests of drawers, wash-stands, display cabinets and kitchen cabinets, corner cupboards and bedsteds, and a good range of china — part or whole Crown Derby sets, various fruit bowls, a Staffordshire coffee service, chamber pots and bone china — plus wall clocks, mirrors, pictures, electrical appliances, carpets, mowers, cycles and a wealth of bric-à-brac.

PARKING: *Own car park.*
STORAGE: *Yes*
TRANSPORTATION: *Yes*
SHIPPING: *Yes*

EVANS BROS

Mart Offices. Tel: (0570) 480444

Evans Bros hold interesting country auctions in various parts of Wales, selling a wide range of antique and modern furniture, china, glass, pictures, bygones, local craft items and so on. The main sale locations are the Mart Offices in Llanybydder (500-600 lots); the Memorial Hall, South Road, Aberaeron (300-400 lots); and Victorian Hall, Bryn Road, Lampeter (up to 600-700 lots).

Llanybydder

BUYER'S PREMIUM: *Nil*
SALES: *Llanybydder: monthly on Sat at 10.30am. Aberaeron: monthly on Wed at 11.00am. Lampeter: every eight to ten weeks on Sat at 11.00am.*
VIEWING: *Llanybydder: day prior 9.00am-12.00 noon, 1.00pm-4.30pm. Aberaeron: day prior 3.00pm-6.00pm. All: day of sale from 9.00am.*
REFRESHMENTS: *Llanybydder: van selling snacks. Aberaeron and Lampeter: own cafés.*
PARKING: *None available on the premises.*
STORAGE: *No*
TRANSPORTATION: *Yes*
SHIPPING: *Yes*

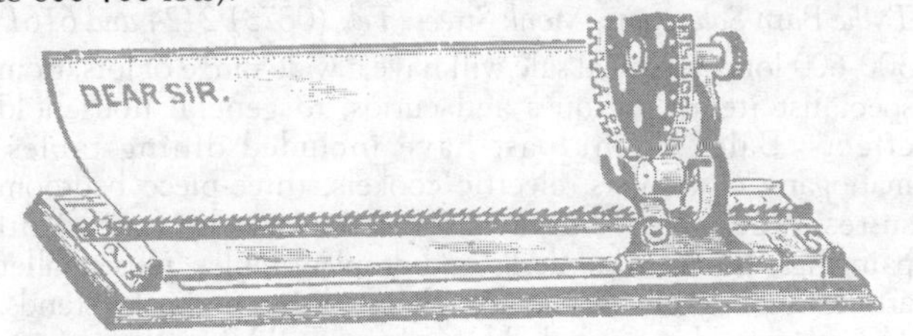

PAINE & THOMAS

Hafren Hall, Station Road. Tel: (0267) 235330

300-350 lots. St Clears is not far from the coast, and holidaymakers swell the numbers in the saleroom during the summer. The monthly sale held here by Paine & Thomas consists of household furniture and effects; including some antiques, outdoor effects such as bicycles, and Welsh bygones and craft items.

St Clears

BUYER'S PREMIUM: *Nil*
SALES: *General: monthly on Sat at 10.30am.*
VIEWING: *Day prior 9.00am-5.00pm.*
REFRESHMENTS: *Own café.*
PARKING: *Own car park.*
STORAGE: *Yes*
TRANSPORTATION: *Yes*
SHIPPING: *Yes*

GWENT

CORNERSTONE RENNIES

The Market Hall. Tel: (0873) 2327

800-1,000 lots. The Market Hall is in the main street in Abergavenny, and has a distinctive green spire. It is also the home of a Friday produce market and of the Halifax Property Services' general sale. The Cornerstone Rennie sale takes place on the third Thursday of the month (except in January),

Abergavenny

BUYER'S PREMIUM: *Nil*
SALES: *Abergavenny: monthly (except Jan) on third Thu of month at 10.30am. Monmouth: every six to eight weeks on Thu at 11.00am.*

VIEWING: *Abergavenny: morning of sale from 9.00am. Monmouth: Tue prior 12.00 noon-4.00pm, morning of sale from 9.00am (closed day prior).*
REFRESHMENTS: *Abergavenny: café in hall.*
PARKING: *Abergavenny: at rear of hall.*
STORAGE: *Yes*
TRANSPORTATION: *Yes*
SHIPPING: *Yes*

and includes general household furniture and effects, such as sitting room, dining room and bedroom suites, garden equipment, electrical goods, televisions, china, crockery, bicycles and so on.

The same firm also holds a sale of antiques and fine art every six to eight weeks, at the Nelson Rooms, Glendower Street, Monmouth. This will usually have some 700-800 lots of furniture, porcelain, pottery, glassware, silver and silver plate, paintings (usually a lot — perhaps as many as 100), clocks, old musical instruments and other good quality articles. The saleroom is on two floors, with the main selling area upstairs. This sale goes on all day and finishes at around 6.00pm.

Abergavenny

WILLIAM EVANS & CO

Tythe Barn Salerooms, Monk Street. Tel: (0873) 2424 and 6161

BUYER'S PREMIUM: *Nil*
SALES: *About every two months on last Thu of month at 11.00am.*
VIEWING: *Day prior 2.00pm-6.00pm, morning of sale from 9.00am.*
REFRESHMENTS: *None available on the premises.*
PARKING: *None available on the premises.*
STORAGE: *No*
TRANSPORTATION: *Yes*
SHIPPING: *Yes*

300-600 lots. A typical sale will have a wide range of lots, from specialist items, antiques and curios, to general household effects. Sales in the past have included dining tables, mahogany chiffoniers, electric cookers, three-piece bedroom suites, sideboards, bureaux, brass bedsteads, framed oil paintings, Indian rugs, desks and dropleaf tables, plus smaller articles such as cheese moulds, cheese dishes and cake stands. The more modern household articles are sold first, then pieces from the 'smalls' tables, and then furniture and carpets. The best items are kept until last.

Abergavenny

HALIFAX PROPERTY SERVICES (MONTAGUE HARRIS & CO)

The Market Hall. Tel: (0873) 5141

BUYER'S PREMIUM: *Nil*
SALES: *Abergavenny: monthly on last Thu of month at 10.30am. Brecon: about eight times a year on Wed at 12.00 noon (includes some antiques sales).*
VIEWING: *Abergavenny: day prior 4.30pm-6.00pm, morning of sale. Brecon: day prior 12.00 noon-6.00pm, morning of sale. Both: morning of sale.*
REFRESHMENTS: *Abergavenny: own café in hall.*
PARKING: *Abergavenny: at rear of hall. Brecon: hotel car park.*
STORAGE: *Yes*
TRANSPORTATION: *Yes*
SHIPPING: *Yes*

600-700 lots. The Market Hall is something of a landmark in Abergavenny, and its green spire is visible from all parts of town. On Fridays it is the home of a very busy produce market, and it is also the location of the Cornerstone Rennie general sale, which has similar lots. A typical sale will include general household furniture and effects, china, porcelain, motor parts and a wide range of miscellaneous items. Vendors can bring in their goods on the previous Wednesday, when the busy preparation begins. Larger items are sold in an annexe known as The Square. Buyers must pay for every purchase in cash, at the completion of each successful bid.

The firm also has an office at the Bulwark Chambers in Brecon, tel: (0874) 3452, which holds eight or so interesting auctions a year at the Wellington Hotel in Brecon. There are no set months to these sales but they always occur on a Wednesday, and include around five general and three antiques sales, with some 300-400 lots in each. Worth enquiring about if you are in the area.

CORNERSTONE RENNIES

Monmouth

See CORNERSTONE RENNIES, Abergavenny, Gwent

GRAHAM DANIEL TRINITY AUCTIONS

Newport

Trinity Hall, Temple Street. Tel: (0633) 251906

300-400 lots. This sale has the friendly atmosphere of a traditional country auction, even though it is a comparative newcomer, having been in existence for only a few years. Mr Daniel worked in the haulage business in Bristol before arriving in this busy town and setting up the auction with his wife Audrey, who deals with the mound of clerical work.

The sale includes a wide range of household furniture and effects, plus miscellaneous items of all types and values. Lesser quality items are sold at the start and end of the sale, sandwiching the better goods, but within those categories, lots are sold in the order in which they arrive at the saleroom. A fridge-freezer could follow an Art Nouveau stripped and waxed bookcase and a Victorian pine kitchen table, and be followed in turn by a pine dresser. There is generally a good deal of jewellery, such as gold pendants, Victorian gold diamond set rings, antique brooches and the like. Graham Daniel is official auctioneer to the local constabulary, so expect among other things a great number of bicycles.

The saleroom is open every day of the week for viewing, and members of the public are welcome to pop in, which many do on their way home from work or during a shopping expedition. A friendly and informal atmosphere prevails, which should set at ease those new to auctions.

BUYER'S PREMIUM: *10%*
SALES: *Weekly on Thu at 10.00am.*
VIEWING: *Daily 9.30am-5.30pm.*
REFRESHMENTS: *Own café.*
PARKING: *Car park directly opposite.*
STORAGE: *Yes*
TRANSPORTATION: *Yes*
SHIPPING: *Yes*

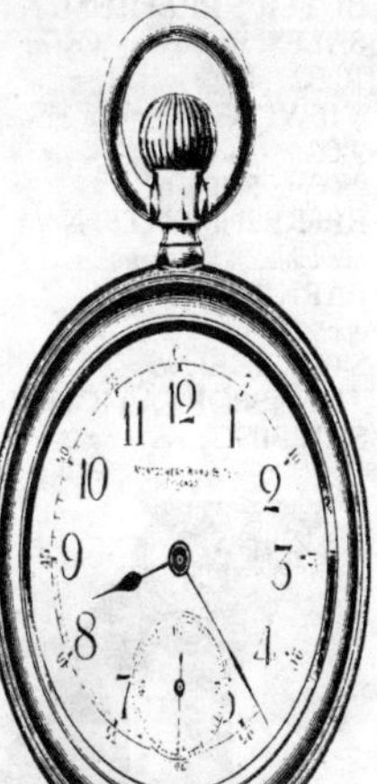

GWYNEDD

MORGAN EVANS & CO LTD

Anglesey

The Anglesey Chattel Auctioneers, The Saleroom, Cattle Market, Gaerwen. Tel: (0248) 77582

400-500 lots. The Cattle Market is on a loop road at the back of the village, about quarter of a mile off the A5 Menai Bridge-Holyhead road. There are weekly livestock sales here, and motor auctions on the first and third Thursday of the month. There is also an annual Christmas sale of dressed poultry.

BUYER'S PREMIUM: *Nil*
SALES: *General: fortnightly on Wed at 10.30am. Antiques: at irregular intervals about 17 times a year on Wed at 10.30am. Motor auctions: first and third Thu of the month at 6.00pm. Dressed poultry:*

annual on last Wed before Christmas at 11.00am.
VIEWING: *General: Mon prior 2.00pm-5.00pm. Antiques: Mon prior 10.00am-12.30pm, 2.00pm-5.00pm, morning of sale from 9.00am. Motor auctions: day of sale from 4.00pm. Dressed poultry: morning of sale from 9.00am.*
REFRESHMENTS: *Licensed bar and restaurant.*
PARKING: *Own car park.*
STORAGE: *Yes*
TRANSPORTATION: *Yes*
SHIPPING: *Yes*

Morgan Evans & Co's fortnightly general sale is held in Saleroom 2, and includes general household furniture and effects. The firm also holds antique and fine art sales about 17 times a year in Saleroom 1, which is heated, with seating for up to 150 and a good amplification system. This saleroom also has an adjoining licensed bar and small restaurant. Typical lots might include Victorian chests, 'grandmother' clocks, Edwardian jardinières, pine tables, large mirrors, jewellery, paintings and prints, and china, plus collectables — old wirelesses, old toys, militaria, Art Nouveau, Art Deco and the like. There is always a lunch break between 1.00pm and 1.30pm on antiques sale days (not for the general sale).

Llandudno

BALL & BOYD

The Auction Rooms, Back Madoc Street.
Tel: (0492) 77239 and 77230

BUYER'S PREMIUM: *Nil*
SALES: *Weekly on Wed at 10.00am.*
VIEWING: *Day prior 9.00am-1.00pm, 2.00pm-5.30pm.*
REFRESHMENTS: *None available on the premises.*
PARKING: *Car park opposite.*
STORAGE: *No*
TRANSPORTATION: *Yes*
SHIPPING: *Yes*

900-1,000 lots. The saleroom is centrally located near the Town Hall and opposite one of the largest car parks in Llandudno. The car park is used by the auctioneers for the sale of cars, caravans, trailers, boats and other vehicles. These are sold off during the afternoon when the auctioneer, followed by those who are interested, nips across from the saleroom — an additional touch of interest in an already entertaining and busy sale.

It starts at 10.00am with the goods which are laid out on the tables: bric-à-brac, odd pieces of china, ornaments, lamps, electric fires, gas fires and so on. When these have all gone, the tables themselves are sold. After that there is a lunch break, usually from around 1.00pm to 2.00pm. The sale of furniture starts at 2.00pm and ranges from antique to nearly new, in all sorts of conditions: bedroom, lounge and dining suites, chairs, settees, dressers, pine, mahogany and so on. At 3.00pm, it is time for the sale of vehicles mentioned above, and at the same time, inside, the sale of better quality 'smalls' (small items) begins.

In the meantime, at odd times throughout the day, about 200-250 unnumbered lots are sold. These are called 'A' lots and are all small items — jewellery, silver, mechanical toys and other articles which could be slipped into an unscrupulous pocket if displayed.

This is a family-run business, established for over 36 years. The sale is usually interesting, and there are some good bargains to be had. Add to that the fact that Llandudno is an attractive resort, and you have an excellent day out for the family.

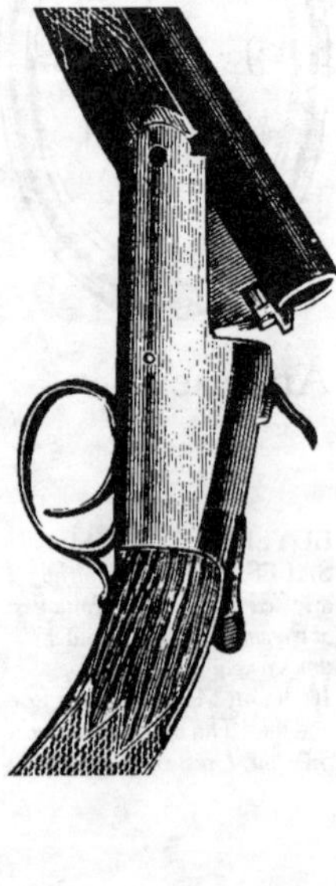

MID GLAMORGAN

PONTYPRIDD SALEROOMS & AUCTION MART

Pontypridd

39a Cefn Lane, Glynoch. Tel: (0443) 403764

400-450 lots. Mr V J Hobbs, the proprietor of this sale, declares it 'the best-run auction in South Wales', and he may not be far wrong. Mr Hobbs worked for the previous owner of the firm for over 30 years, and 'liked the business so much he bought the company'. The sale includes household furniture and effects, china, glass, pictures, jewellery, bicycles, electrical goods, bygones, craft items and many other goods, mostly of middling value but with some antiques. The lots are attractively displayed — ornaments and crockery, for example, will be neatly set out on one of the dressers or sideboards in the sale. Cheaper items are sold first, followed by jewellery, which is always sold at 12.30pm. At the completion of the jewellery sale and up until 2.00pm, the better quality items will be sold. After those, the sale finishes as it started, with cheaper lots.

BUYER'S PREMIUM: *10%*
SALES: *Fortnightly on Wed at 10.00am.*
VIEWING: *Day prior 2.00pm-7.00pm, morning of sale from 9.00am.*
REFRESHMENTS: *Own café.*
PARKING: *Own car park planned.*
STORAGE: *No*
TRANSPORTATION: *Yes*
SHIPPING: *No*

POWYS

HALIFAX PROPERTY SERVICES LTD (MONTAGUE HARRIS & CO)

Brecon

See HALIFAX PROPERTY SERVICES LTD, Abergavenny, Gwent

F H SUNDERLAND & CO

Brecon

See F H SUNDERLAND & CO, Talgarth, Powys

F H SUNDERLAND & CO

Talgarth

Talgarth Market. Tel: (0874) 42261

300-400 lots. Talgarth is about eight miles north-east of Brecon, and is an ideal centre for those in search of fine scenery. Near by are Cwm-trappe (a wooded dell) and the Pwll-y-wrach Falls on the River Enig; and for a slice of authentic local life there is F H Sunderland's sale at Talgarth Market.

It takes place in the market shed used the previous Friday for livestock sales. There is a wide variety of lots, and their quality also varies enormously. Among the furniture, it might be

BUYER'S PREMIUM: *Nil*
SALES: *Talgarth: About every six weeks on Tue at 12.00 noon. Brecon: at irregular intervals on Tue or Wed at 12.00 noon.*
VIEWING: *Talgarth: morning of sale from 9.30am. Brecon: day prior 9.30am-5.30pm.*
REFRESHMENTS: *None available on the premises.*

PARKING: *Talgarth: by the market.*
STORAGE: *Yes*
TRANSPORTATION: *Yes*
SHIPPING: *Yes*

possible to buy a beautiful set of dining chairs or a Windsor chair in perfect condition, or a painted pine dressing table with a broken leg. On the 'smalls' table, a box containing nearly-new cheap mugs might stand alongside a Royal Doulton jug in perfect condition.

F H Sunderland & Co also hold periodic sales of special antiques at Bishops Meadow Motel, Hay Road, Brecon. There is no fixed interval between these sales, which occur only when enough lots of sufficient quality have been gathered. They are always held midweek, however, and are well worth attending as they usually offer bargains in all areas of antiques — paintings, china, silver, collectables and so on.

Welshpool

HARRY RAY & CO

The Town Hall. Tel: (0938) 552555

BUYER'S PREMIUM: *Nil*
SALES: *Fortnightly on Fri at 10.00am.*
VIEWING: *Day prior 1.30pm-5.00pm.*
REFRESHMENTS: *None available on the premises.*
PARKING: *Town centre car park.*
STORAGE: *Yes*
TRANSPORTATION: *Yes*
SHIPPING: *Yes*

500-600 lots. The town hall is in the centre of Welshpool, and with its large clock on top it is difficult to miss. This sale is all a country auction should be: not just a good place to pick up a piece of furniture or garden tool, but also a place where local people meet friends and exchange gossip. The sale is informal, friendly, and offers the possibility of picking up all sorts of goods. It starts outside with items such as ladders, wheelbarrows, lesser-value furniture and even parts of furniture, gardening tools and equipment, building equipment, perhaps the odd door or window frame or bath suite, and boxes of odd bits. If a lot fails to attract a bidder it is added to the next lot, so one successful bid could find you the proud owner of a box of assorted household items, an old wardrobe, a car tyre and a couple of suitcases full of books.

There are three auctioneers to keep things moving, and the sale moves inside without a break, for china, ornaments and other better quality small articles. Also in this section is furniture of a wide range of types and values — modern, old or reproduction, pine, chests of drawers, suites for the bedroom, living room and dining room, chairs and so on, with bargains to be had in all departments.

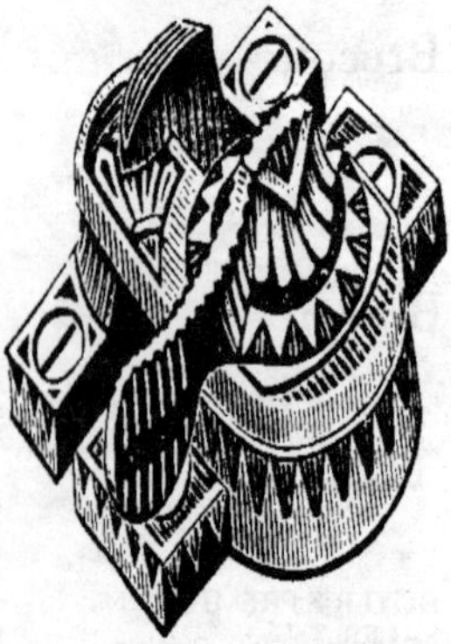

SOUTH GLAMORGAN

Cardiff

PHILLIPS

10 Westgate Street. Tel: (0222) 396453

BUYER'S PREMIUM: *10%*
SALES: *On Wed at 11.00am, twice monthly.*

300-400 lots. This saleroom, which is just down the road from Cardiff castle, holds sales specialising as much as possible in country furniture, particularly Welsh country furniture and other items with Welsh connections, including porcelain. Here there are two auctions a month: one of Victorian and later furniture and effects, and one of antiques, at which furniture, silver, ceramics, and paintings are sold among other things. The sale of Victorian and later furniture and effects usually consists of good quality, inexpensive lots.

VIEWING: *Mon prior, 9.00am-5.00pm, Tue prior, 9.00am-6.30pm. Antiques also Sat prior, 9.00am-12.00 noon. Morning of sale from 9.00am.*
REFRESHMENTS: *None available on the premises.*
PARKING: *Available at Westgate Street public car park*

WEST GLAMORGAN

THOMAS, EDWARDS & ANTHONY MORRIS

Neath

The Croft Salerooms, Croft Road. Tel: (0639) 639541

300-400 lots. This is one of those Welsh sales where everyone who enters the saleroom is acknowledged, whether known or not, and where someone can usually tell you about prices fetched in previous sales. Many of the articles are desirable, and many have clearly come from houses where they have been well looked after: the furniture has the deep shine that comes from generations of caring owners, and the ornaments and vases are often old and interesting, if not necessarily 'antique'. Brass items abound, and as a rule fetch good prices: your neighbour in the saleroom may tut-tut the hammer price of a set of brass fire irons, but it is likely to be only a fraction of what it might fetch in a shop.

In contrast to the general sale, the same firm holds catering equipment sales every three months, which are interesting for the private buyer as well as for catering professionals. This latter sale takes place five minutes' walk away from Croft Road, in the cattle market. Periodic sales are also held at the cattle market on behalf of the Sherriff's Office and bailiffs (distrained equipment), and the police (lost property). These sales are also held on a Tuesday.

BUYER'S PREMIUM: *Nil*
SALES: *General: about every six weeks on Tue at 1.00pm. Catering equipment: every three months on Tue at 11.00am. Distrained/Lost Property: irregular intervals on Tue, usually at 11.00am.*
VIEWING: *General and Distrained/Lost Property: day prior 2.30pm-4.30pm, morning of sale from 10.30am. Catering equipment: day prior 2.00pm-4.30pm, morning of sale from 9.00am.*
REFRESHMENTS: *Available at the cattle market.*
PARKING: *None available on the premises.*
STORAGE: *Yes*
TRANSPORTATION: *Yes*
SHIPPING: *Yes*

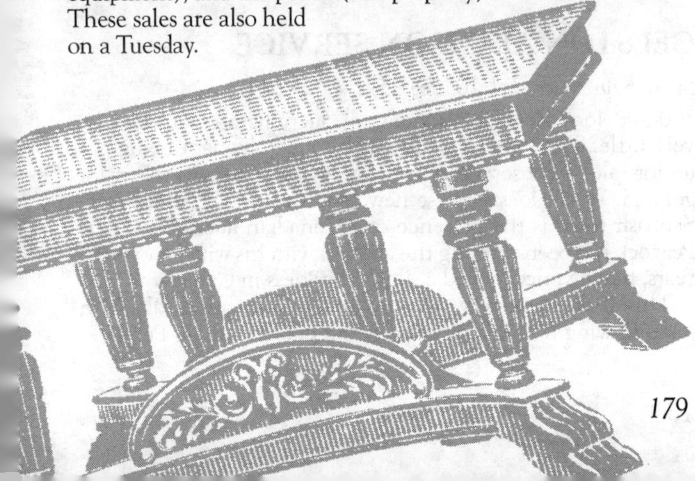

• SCOTLAND •

BORDERS

Hawick

LAWRIE & SYMINGTON

See LAWRIE & SYMINGTON, Peebles, Borders

Peebles

LAWRIE & SYMINGTON

Peebles Market, South Parks, Caledonian Road.
Tel: (0555) 2281

BUYER'S PREMIUM: *Nil*
SALES: *Peebles: monthly on Wed at 10.30am. Hawick: monthly on Tue at 6.00pm.*
VIEWING: *Peebles: Sun prior 12.00 noon-4.00pm, Tue prior 9.00am-4.00pm. Hawick: Mon prior 10.00am-4.00pm, day of sale from 10.00am.*
REFRESHMENTS: *Peebles: none available on the premises. Hawick: own café.*
PARKING: *Ample parking near by.*
STORAGE: *Yes*
TRANSPORTATION: *Yes*
SHIPPING: *Yes*

700-800 lots. This is a good general sale, held in the market which from July to February is also busy with sheep sales. At times during the auction there will be two sales taking place. Selling starts at 10.30am in one of the sheds, when the bidding for perhaps as many as 500 lots of smaller items gets under way. This sale often carries on past 1.00pm, which is when the general sale of furniture begins. The latter usually has 300 lots or so, set out in two sheds.

The same company conducts monthly Tuesday evening sales at the Auction Mart, Weensland Road, Hawick, tel: (0450) 73261. These are of good quality general household furniture and effects, and the number of lots is restricted to 400. Both sales contain a wide variety of articles, with lots regularly selling from as little as £1.

DUMFRIES & GALLOWAY

Annan

THOMSON, RODDICK & LAURIE

See THOMSON, RODDICK & LAURIE, Dumfries, Dumfries & Galloway

Castle Douglas

GELSTON AUCTION SERVICE

St Andrew Street. Tel: (0556) 3591

BUYER'S PREMIUM: *Nil*
SALES: *Weekly on Fri at 6.00pm.*
VIEWING: *Day of sale from 1.00pm.*
REFRESHMENTS: *None available on the premises.*
PARKING: *Free parking on street.*
STORAGE: *No*
TRANSPORTATION: *Yes*
SHIPPING: *Yes*

300-500 lots. Regular attenders of auctions are surprised by very little. The sight of a full-sized stuffed elephant being put up for sale, a conservatory or even an aeroplane, is taken for granted. What does surprise newcomers to this beautiful little Scottish town is the presence of a Canadian auctioneer. Bert Peacock has been running the auction with his wife for over 10 years, having once owned a similar business in Canada.

This is really a very friendly and light-hearted sale with jokes flowing to and fro between the public and Mr Peacock.

Indeed it is suspected that many of the people come solely for an evening's entertainment. The sale contains a wide range of general furniture and household effects, as well as antiques. The saleroom is just by the town's only cinema, so it is easy to find. Another way is to follow the general direction of the crowd from about 5.30pm on Fridays.

Castle Douglas

WALLETS MART PLC

Newmarket Street. Tel: (0556) 2381

500-600 lots. Castle Douglas is a clean and attractive little place at the north end of Carlingwark Loch. It is surrounded by some picturesque and popular villages, and it is from houses in these that the majority of goods offered up for auction come, with vendors bringing in their goods up to the Wednesday previous to the sale.

The auction itself is held in the cattle market. There are no general furniture sales from August to December, as this is when the auctioneers are busiest with livestock sales. Buyers at the general sale follow the auctioneer from the rings to the byres. Everything is sold: baths, kitchen sinks, old taps, lengths of copper piping or planks of wood. In addition there is furniture of all types and of all values. There is usually plenty of china and crockery, with the number of cups in the tea sets often matching the number of saucers — not a common occurrence at country auctions, as anyone who frequents them will know.

BUYER'S PREMIUM: *Nil*
SALES: *Periodically on Fri at 10.30am. (General sales Dec to Jul only.)*
VIEWING: *Thu prior 8.00am-5.00pm.*
REFRESHMENTS: *None available on the premises.*
PARKING: *Own car park.*
STORAGE: *No*
TRANSPORTATION: *No*
SHIPPING: *No*

Dumfries

JOHN GIBSON & SON

2 Irving Street. Tel: (0387) 53670

300-400 lots. Anyone interested in Robbie Burns will need no introduction to Dumfries. The poet is buried in St Michael's churchyard, and Burns' House, Burns' Street, was his home from 1793 until his death in 1796. It is now a museum.

John Gibson & Son is not quite so old, but has been a well-respected firm since 1820. It is an efficient, family-run business which regularly draws buyers and vendors from all over Dumfries and Galloway. The saleroom, at one time a church, is a popular weekly hunting ground for bargain seekers and browsers, packed as it is with a good selection of modern, antique and reproduction furniture, as well as bric-à-brac, Victoriana, ornaments, china and so on. Any cars or boats, or other large objects, are sold in the garage, which is near the saleroom. There is always a break for lunch between 12.00 noon and 12.30pm. The morning sale contains smaller, cheap household goods such as kettles, pots, pans and small furniture

BUYER'S PREMIUM: *Nil*
SALES: *Weekly on Thu at 10.30am.*
VIEWING: *Day prior 10.00am-4.00pm.*
REFRESHMENTS: *None available on the premises.*
PARKING: *Public car park in Queensbury Street.*
STORAGE: *Yes*
TRANSPORTATION: *Yes*
SHIPPING: *No*

(including dining chairs and coffee tables), while the afternoon session is for the larger items.

Dumfries

BUYER'S PREMIUM: *10%*
SALES: *Antiques: five times a year on Tue at 10.45am. Shotguns etc.: twice a year, usually Jul and Dec on Mon and Tue at 6.00pm. General (Annan): monthly on Tue at 10.30am.*
VIEWING: *Antiques and shotguns etc.: day prior 4.30pm-7.45pm, morning of sale from 9.00am, except fishing tackle: day of sale 4.30pm-5.45pm. General (Annan): day prior 2.00pm-4.00pm, morning of sale from 9.00am.*
REFRESHMENTS: *Own cafés.*
PARKING: *Own car parks.*
STORAGE: *Yes*
TRANSPORTATION: *Yes*
SHIPPING: *Yes*

THOMSON, RODDICK & LAURIE

60 Whitesands. Tel: (0387) 55366

400-500 lots. Thomson, Roddick & Laurie, established in 1880, conduct an extensive range of auctions, including specialist collector's sales, in Scotland and in Carlisle, Wigton and Brampton in England. In Dumfries they hold five major catalogue sales a year, at Loreburn Hall, Newall Terrace. Included are 18th- and 19th-century furniture, silver, metalware, ceramics, glass, jewellery, pictures, prints, collector's items and good reproduction furniture.

In addition there are two major sales of shotguns, firearms and accessories, usually in July and December. Each of these sales covers two evenings, and also includes militaria and sporting prints (Monday) and fishing rods, reels and tackle (Tuesday).

The same firm holds regular and well-attended monthly sales of general household furniture and effects and various miscellaneous items, at 20 Murray Street, Annan, tel: (04612) 2575.

Lockerbie

BUYER'S PREMIUM: *Nil*
SALES: *Fortnightly on Tue at 10.00am.*
VIEWING: *Sat prior 9.30am-12.30pm, Mon prior 9.30am-12.00 noon and 1.30pm-5.00pm.*
REFRESHMENTS: *None available on the premises.*
PARKING: *None available on the premises.*
STORAGE: *Yes*
TRANSPORTATION: *Yes*
SHIPPING: *Yes*

R LOVE

Old Mart Salerooms, Victoria Road. Tel: (05762) 2554

300-400 lots. Lockerbie is a small market town, rediscovering normality after the terrible air disaster of 1988. The saleroom is just off the attractive main street behind the King's Arms Hotel, and is a whitewashed, listed building with exposed beams inside. The sale of general household furniture and effects includes outdoor items, antiques and Victorian items and bric-à-brac. Selling starts with lesser quality bric-à-brac, such as pots and pans, individual pieces of china, books and other small miscellaneous items. Household furniture finishes the morning sale. A break for lunch is followed by the sale of better-quality furniture, carpets and rugs, paintings, prints and jewellery, brass, ironware and better quality china.

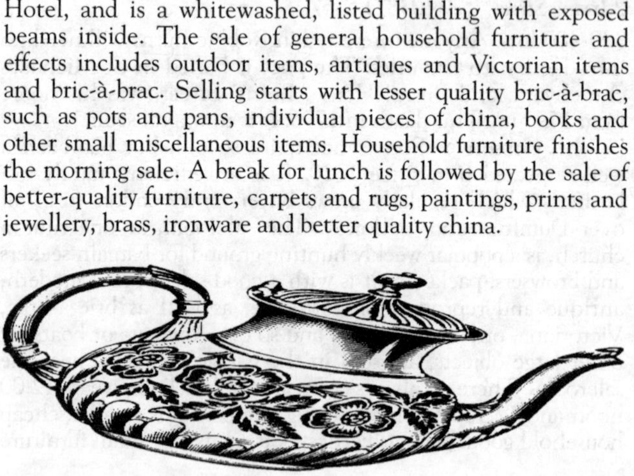

FIFE

DUNFERMLINE AUCTION CO (FIFE) LTD

Dunfermline

Loch Street, Townhill. Tel: (0383) 727434

300-500 lots. Dunfermline is most famous for the magnificent abbey church in which Robert the Bruce was buried. The weekly auction is held in a compact first-floor saleroom with a café on the ground floor. Many a happy hour can be passed browsing through the large variety of furniture, household bric-à-brac and collectors' pieces gathered here. The auctioneer's stand is usually surrounded by a large and noisy crowd exchanging banter even when the auctioneer is selling. Some of the crowd come from nearby offices and shops; others make a visit to the auction part of the weekly shopping expedition. For range and variety the auction is difficult to beat. Many of the lots come as part of complete house clearances, and there will usually be ornamental and domestic china, brass, paintings, pictures, silver, jewellery and furniture of all types. A special sale of antiques is held in place of the general sale every five or six weeks.

BUYER'S PREMIUM: *10%*
SALES: *Weekly on Tue at 11.00am (including antiques sale every five or six weeks).*
VIEWING: *Sat 8.30am-12.30pm, Mon 8.30am-5.30pm, morning of sale.*
REFRESHMENTS: *Café on ground floor.*
PARKING: *Own car park.*
STORAGE: *Yes*
TRANSPORTATION: *Yes*
SHIPPING: *Yes*

LADYBANK AUCTION MARKET

Ladybank

Kinloch Street. Tel: (0337) 30488

500-600 lots. Ladybank is small and the saleroom is easy to find. It stands in Kinloch Street, which runs parallel to the main street. This is an interesting sale which always includes antiques as well as general household furniture and effects — sitting room, dining room and bedroom suites, tables and chairs, garden equipment, cookers, refrigerators and other electrical equipment, bicycles, crockery, parts of or whole tea and dinner sets, ornaments, silver and paintings. Amongst these there may be watercolours, many of them showing local scenes.

BUYER'S PREMIUM: *5%*
SALES: *Weekly on Fri at 6.00pm.*
VIEWING: *Day prior 2.00pm-9.00pm, day of sale all day.*
REFRESHMENTS: *Usually a café van outside.*
PARKING: *Car park opposite.*
STORAGE: *Yes*
TRANSPORTATION: *Yes*
SHIPPING: *Yes*

ROBERT DOWIE

Leven

Station Road. Tel: (0333) 23438

600-800 lots. Leven is a beautiful, clean Scottish town at the western end of the bay of Largo. It is a favourite resort with Edinburgh folk, particularly for fishing and for golf at the Lundin links. It is a shock in this setting to enter the saleroom and hear the very English accent of Mr Vernon J Prangnell-O'Neill as he conducts the auction, although he too is Scottish. Mr Prangnell-O'Neill used to work for Phillips,

BUYER'S PREMIUM: *10%*
SALES: *Fortnightly on Thu at 11.00am (includes specialist antique and fine art sale every two months).*
VIEWING: *General: day prior 2.00pm-5.00pm. Antiques and fine art: day prior 10.00am- 5.00pm.*

REFRESHMENTS: *Own tea bar with home baking.*
PARKING: *Free parking on street.*
STORAGE: *Yes*
TRANSPORTATION: *Yes*
SHIPPING: *Yes*

Fine Art Auctioneers, and has worked in the auction and antique business all over Europe and North America. He runs a very pleasant and friendly auction of general household furniture and effects. The lots are of particularly high quality, even the electrical goods, and there are beautiful china tea and dinner sets, bedroom and dining room suites and so on. Every second month the sale becomes a specialist antique and fine art sale, including jewellery, silver, glass, 18th-century and Edwardian furniture, Persian rugs and the like.

St Andrews

MACGREGOR AUCTIONS

56 Largo Road. Tel: (0334) 72431

BUYER'S PREMIUM: *Nil*
SALES: *Fortnightly on Fri at 10.30am (includes antiques and fine art sale every three months).*
VIEWING: *Thu prior 9.00am-7.00pm.*
REFRESHMENTS: *None available on the premises.*
PARKING: *Own car park.*
STORAGE: *Yes*
TRANSPORTATION: *Yes*
SHIPPING: *Yes*

500-700 lots. St Andrews is best known for its university, and for golf. The Royal and Ancient Club here is the recognised authority on the game, which has spread throughout the world from Scotland. There is a golf club factory near to MacGregor Auctions. Since Mrs S Edwards took over the firm in 1983, it has enjoyed increasing popularity not only locally, but with buyers from all over Britain and, indeed, abroad. The excellent fortnightly Friday sale includes a wide selection of general household furniture and effects in addition to china, silver, crockery, cutlery, ornaments and the like.

Every three months the Friday sale becomes an antiques and fine art sale, which often includes articles withdrawn from the general sale because of their quality. Due to the amount of work involved in preparing this sale (setting out, listing and preparing the catalogue), the previous fortnightly general sale is often cancelled. Telephone before travelling any distance, to check that an auction is taking place.

GRAMPIAN

Aberdeen

ABERDEEN & NORTHERN MARTS LTD

Furniture Sale Hall, Cattofield Terrace. Tel: (0224) 481331

BUYER'S PREMIUM: *Nil*
SALES: *Weekly on Tue at 1.00pm.*
VIEWING: *Day of sale from 9.00am.*
REFRESHMENTS: *Own café.*
PARKING: *Own car park.*
STORAGE: *Yes*
TRANSPORTATION: *Yes*
SHIPPING: *Yes*

300-400 lots. The saleroom is in the Kittybrewster area of the town. The very day after the weekly sale, vendors start to bring in lots for the next week's sale. Items might include lounge, bedroom and dining room suites, dressers, card tables, veneered fold-over tables, overmantle mirrors, occasional tables, plated cutlery, dinner canteens, silver, china and glass, ornaments, paintings, Scottish bygones and local crafts, kitchenalia, books, puzzles, children's toys, gardening tools and equipment, electrical goods of all kinds including televisions, and bicycles.

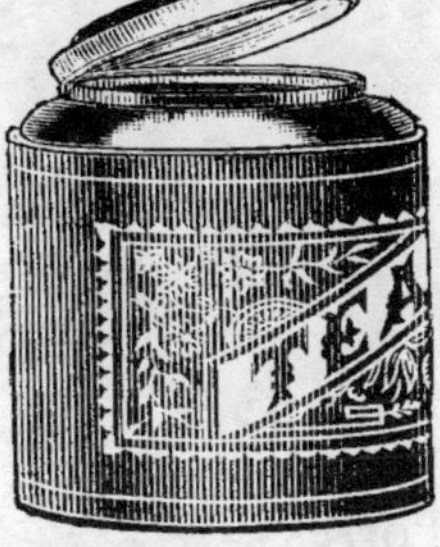

As in most good Scottish sales, almost anything could come up for auction. The goods will vary greatly in condition and value, and a careful search through the lots will generally reveal plenty of bargains. This is not an auction to frighten the new auction-goer, as the saleroom is full of humour and friendliness.

JOHN MILNE

9 North Silver Street. Tel: (0224) 639336

400-500 lots. Aberdeen is an ancient cathedral and university city, a popular seaside resort and a port busy with fishing and North Sea oil activity. This auction has been part of the Aberdeen scene for over 100 years, and has been run by the Milne family for the whole of that time. It is presently under the stewardship of Robert Milne. Being one of the largest auctions in North East Scotland, it regularly draws in buyers and vendors from all over the region, and much further afield.

Number 9 North Silver Street is a traditional Aberdeen granite building and stands opposite the music hall. Inside there are two large salerooms, one used for the current week's sale and the other being prepared for the next. There is usually a good mix of antique, modern and reproduction furniture and household effects, in addition to silver, pottery, jewellery, glass, pictures and the like. The sale starts with these small items, and at 12.00 noon moves on to the sale of furniture, finishing at around 2.00pm depending on the number of lots.

Aberdeen

BUYER'S PREMIUM: *10%*
SALES: *Weekly on Wed at 10.00am.*
VIEWING: *Day prior 10.00am-7.00pm.*
REFRESHMENTS: *None available on the premises.*
PARKING: *Metered parking in street or Golden Square Centre car park.*
STORAGE: *Yes*
TRANSPORTATION: *Yes*
SHIPPING: *Yes*

CLUNY AUCTION

8-9 Cluny Terrace. Tel: (0542) 33318

400-500 lots. Buckie is an attractive little fishing port with an interesting harbour. The saleroom is just a little way from the main street, past the Thistle Bar. It is a stone and mortar building which Mrs B Ferguson, who runs the auction with her husband, remembers being a saleroom when she was a little girl. It later had several other uses, until Mr and Mrs Ferguson saw the need for a country auction in this part of Scotland and started up in the late 1980s. The sale has increased in popularity each year since. Mrs Ferguson claims to have been surprised at first by the number of young folk setting up home who come to buy. 'But when you consider the quality of the older furniture and compare it with what can be bought new today for the same money, it shows how many young couples have an eye for a good bargain.' The saleroom is L-shaped and the rostrum is surrounded by tables containing interesting lots of smaller items, such as all kinds of china, porcelain, jewellery

Buckie

BUYER'S PREMIUM: *Nil*
SALES: *Fortnightly on Thu at 6.15pm (including antiques sale three or four times a year).*
VIEWING: *Day prior 2.00pm-8.00pm, morning of sale from 10.00am.*
REFRESHMENTS: *Own light refreshments.*
PARKING: *Ample space near by.*
STORAGE: *Yes*
TRANSPORTATION: *Yes*
SHIPPING: *Yes*

and so on. Furniture is placed around the room, and some at the back is wheeled forward on trolleys for selling. Three or four times a year the sale becomes a special sale of antiques, but selling and viewing times remain the same.

Forres

BUYER'S PREMIUM: *Nil*
SALES: *General: fortnightly on Thu at 6.15pm (except on antiques sale days). Antiques and fine art: occasionally on Thu at 10.30am.*
VIEWING: *Day prior 9.30am-12.00 noon and 2.00pm-5.00pm.*
REFRESHMENTS: *Cafés near by.*
PARKING: *Ample free street parking.*
STORAGE: *No*
TRANSPORTATION: *Yes*
SHIPPING: *Yes*

HAMILTON AUCTION MARTS PLC

Tylers Street. Tel: (0309) 72422

200-300 lots. Forres is an impressive little town on the eastern bank of the Findhorn, with a population of just over 5,000. It is a popular resort with sportsmen and tourists, the former for the salmon and trout fishing, the latter for the wonderful scenery and balmy climate. The saleroom is an impressive listed building at the west end of the town, and was at one time a mart for sheep, pigs and cattle. It is now solely used for the general auction. Quite a number of local people as well as visitors attend the sale, popping in on their way home from work perhaps, to see what's up for grabs. There is usually a fine mixture, ranging from Scottish tin baths to beautifully cared-for antiques. Occasionally, special daytime sales of antiques and fine art are held, instead of an evening general sale.

HIGHLAND

Dingwall

BUYER'S PREMIUM: *Nil*
SALES: *Weekly on Fri at 5.00pm.*
VIEWING: *Day prior 8.30am-5.00pm, day of sale.*
REFRESHMENTS: *None available on the premises.*
PARKING: *Own car park.*
STORAGE: *No*
TRANSPORTATION: *Yes*
SHIPPING: *No*

FRASERS AUCTION ROOMS

15 Tulloch Street. Tel: (0349) 63252

300-400 lots. Dingwall is a small town with a beautiful old church and cross. It is a little off the tourist map, and is perhaps best known by outsiders for its proximity to Strathpeffer, just over five miles away at the foot of Ben Wyvis, in some of the finest scenery in the Highlands. Those taking the trouble to find their way to Frasers Auction Rooms are in for a treat, because there is a real flavour of Scotland here. Perhaps as many as two-thirds to three-quarters of the people who attend the sale turn up week after week. Many of them attend not only to buy but also to meet up with friends, catch up with local gossip and chat over local events. As is the case with most Scottish sales, there is always a surprising and interesting range of articles, including furniture of all types, conditions and values. There will also be local bygones, which will usually be interesting, and also crockery, jewellery, silver, books and so on.

LOTHIAN

PHILLIPS SCOTLAND

Edinburgh

65 George Street. Tel: (031) 225 2266

100-200 lots. Phillips have two salerooms in Scotland, in which over 140 sales are held every year. In the large Edinburgh saleroom, which is diagonally opposite the Assembly Rooms, there are fortnightly general sales of furniture, pictures, ceramics and so on, with a weekly specialist sale on Friday (occasionally on other days as well). The specialist sales come under headings such as 'Antique Furniture, Clocks, Rugs, Works of Art', 'Oil Paintings', 'Silver', 'Oriental Ceramics and Works of Art', 'Ceramics and Glass', 'Watercolours and Prints', 'Jewellery', 'Books', 'Textiles, Dolls and Costumes', 'Decorative Arts', and 'Arms and Armour'.

An annual specialist sale of golfing memorabilia is arranged by Phillips at either their Edinburgh or Glasgow Salerooms to coincide with the Open Golf Championship.

BUYER'S PREMIUM: *10%*
SALES: *General: fortnightly on Thu at 11.00am. Specialist: weekly on Fri at 11.00am (sometimes more often). Golfing memorabilia: annually in Jul on a Tue (times and locations vary).*
VIEWING: *General: day prior 9.30am-4.30pm. Specialist: two days prior, 9.30am-4.30pm. Golfing memorabilia: day prior, 9.30am-4.30pm.*
REFRESHMENTS: *None available on the premises.*
PARKING: *None available on the premises.*
STORAGE: *Yes*
TRANSPORTATION: *Yes*
SHIPPING: *Yes*

SCOTTISH HOUSE AUCTIONS

Edinburgh

5 Loaning Road, Unit 8c, Restairig. Tel: (031) 659 6634

400-450 lots. This busy and popular saleroom is in the suburb of Leith, the port of Edinburgh. A landmark to look out for is the Meadowbank Sports Centre. The fortnightly sale attracts a great deal of attention, all the more so during the summer when the Edinburgh Festival is on. In addition to the usual array of household effects there is often brand new furniture, which makes the sale particularly popular with young people setting up home. A considerable amount of office furniture and equipment is usually available here too, as are older furniture and antiques.

BUYER'S PREMIUM: *10%*
SALES: *Fortnightly on Wed at 6.00pm.*
VIEWING: *Mon and Tue prior 11.00am-8.00pm, morning of sale from 11.00am.*
REFRESHMENTS: *None available on the premises.*
PARKING: *Ample parking near by.*
STORAGE: *Yes*
TRANSPORTATION: *Yes*
SHIPPING: *Yes*

WEST END AUCTIONS

Edinburgh

248 Morrison Street. Tel: (031) 229 6124

300-350 lots. This is a typically friendly weekly sale, with porters, auctioneers and clerks going about their business but always ready to answer queries. People attend the auction for the atmosphere as well as to bid. The numbers are often swelled by foreign visitors, especially Australians, who are clearly intrigued by the assorted three-piece lounge suites, old records, antique earrings, brooches and other lots selling at 100 an hour.

BUYER'S PREMIUM: *Nil*
SALES: *Weekly on Thu at 6.30pm.*
VIEWING: *Wed prior 9.00am-7.00pm, day of sale from 9.00am.*
REFRESHMENTS: *Own café.*
PARKING: *Public car park opposite.*
STORAGE: *No*
TRANSPORTATION: *Yes*
SHIPPING: *Yes*

Haddington

BUYER'S PREMIUM: *Nil*
SALES: *Quarterly in Mar, Jun, Sep and Dec. General: Tue, Wed and Thu at 10.30am. Antiques: following Thu at 1.30pm.*
VIEWING: *General: morning of sale from 8.00am. Antiques: day prior 2.00pm-4.00pm, 7.00pm-9.00pm.*
REFRESHMENTS: *None available on the premises.*
PARKING: *Ample parking near by.*
STORAGE: *Yes*
TRANSPORTATION: *Yes*
SHIPPING: *Yes*

LESLIE & LESLIE

77 Market Street. Tel: (062082) 2241

400-500 lots. Haddington is a well-preserved town about 17 miles from Edinburgh on the A1. Market Street is between the two main streets in the town centre. Here Leslie & Leslie hold large, busy sales in March, June, September and December. Each sale lasts three days — Tuesday, Wednesday and Thursday — and begins at 10.30am each day. Lots include modern and shipping furniture, household effects such as electrical goods, mirrors, china and bric-à-brac. There could be some antiques, but these will probably be in need of attention. The best items are kept for the special antiques sale on the following Thursday. This sale will include paintings, china, silver, brass and so on.

ORKNEY

Kirkwall

BUYER'S PREMIUM: *Nil*
SALES: *Monthly on Wed at 10.30am.*
VIEWING: *Day prior 2.00pm-5.00pm, morning of sale.*
REFRESHMENTS: *Own café.*
PARKING: *Car park direcly opposite.*
STORAGE: *Yes*
TRANSPORTATION: *Yes*
SHIPPING: *Yes*

KIRKWALL AUCTION MART

44 Junction Road. Tel: (0856) 2520

250-300 lots. Kirkwall is one of the largest towns in the Orkneys. It has narrow streets and houses with thick walls and small windows, suited to a stormy climate and perhaps reflecting Norwegian origins. Kirkwall Auction Mart is close to the landmark of St Magnus Cathedral. Like most Scottish sales, especially those in remoter places, this one has a special atmosphere which is, no doubt, due to the local way of life. Everybody is acknowledged on entering the saleroom, whether known or not, with a brief nod of the head by those present. Most of the buyers seem to know each other, and occasionally a bidder will shake his head and shout, 'Oh, let old William have it!' There is no particular order of sale. Lots come up as they have been brought in by vendors, and there is a wide range of furniture, often locally crafted. There will also be jewellery, china, silver and miscellaneous items from a myriad of different backgrounds.

Stromness

BUYER'S PREMIUM: *Nil*
SALES: *Monthly on Fri at 10.30am.*

WEST MAINLAND MART LTD

Ferry Road. Tel: (0856) 850288

300-400 lots. Ferry Road is known to some as North End Road, but once you are in Stromness it is difficult to miss the market complex. A livestock market is held on Wednesday in the same saleroom as the monthly Friday sale of general household furniture and effects, and a good deal of activity goes into clearing the place up. As at Kirkwall, the sale generally includes several items of good quality furniture. Smaller items, although not perhaps antiques, are often old and lovingly cared for by generations of owners. Typical items include vases, ornaments, china, silver and photograph frames with original pictures. Good buys are often to be had; like the Kirkwall sale, this one seems to be looked forward to as a social event as much as anything else.

VIEWING: *Day prior 2.00pm-5.00pm.*
REFRESHMENTS: *None available on the premises.*
PARKING: *Own car park.*
STORAGE: *No*
TRANSPORTATION: *Yes*
SHIPPING: *No*

SHETLAND

SHETLAND MARTS LTD

Lerwick

33 South Road. Tel: (0595) 2369

200-300 lots. Lerwick is a busy, cosmopolitan town and its capacious harbour is often crowded with vessels from many nations. Because the auctioneers are preoccupied with livestock sales during the second half of the year, the general auctions are only held from December through to June.

The sales are attended mostly by locals, perhaps because visitors come to these pleasant islands for reasons other than buying at auction. Some remarkable, rare and interesting pieces turn up at these auctions from time to time, perhaps for this very reason.

BUYER'S PREMIUM: *Nil*
SALES: *Dec to Jun, monthly on Wed at 2.00pm.*
VIEWING: *Day prior, 6.00pm-8.00pm.*
REFRESHMENTS: *None available on the premises.*
PARKING: *Own car park.*
STORAGE: *No*
TRANSPORTATION: *Yes*
SHIPPING: *Yes*

STRATHCLYDE

THOMAS R CALLAN

Ayr

22 Smith Street. Tel: (0292) 267681

700-750 lots. Smith Street is in the centre of Ayr, opposite the railway station and next to the Burns statue. Burns was born just two miles way in Alloway, in a small thatched cottage which can be visited. Thomas R Callan's saleroom has been a landmark in Ayr since it was started by the father of the present owner, Mr D Callan, in 1933, and recently a third-generation Callan became involved in the firm. The sale contains a wide and interesting range of goods of all values and in all conditions.

Selling starts with small items such as boxes of bric-à-brac, pots and pans, silver, tea and dinner sets, glass, jewellery,

BUYER'S PREMIUM: *Nil*
SALES: *Weekly on Thu at 10.30am.*
VIEWING: *Day prior 8.00am-5.00pm.*
REFRESHMENTS: *None available on the premises.*
PARKING: *Own car park.*
STORAGE: *Yes*
TRANSPORTATION: *Yes*
SHIPPING: *Yes*

ornaments, collectables and the like. There is a break between roughly 1.30pm and 2.00pm, when the sale of furniture begins, and the sale ends at around 4.45pm. Every six weeks or so the general sale becomes a sale of antiques, including articles withdrawn from the general sale because of their value. Selling and viewing times remain the same.

Ayr

BUYER'S PREMIUM: *Nil*
SALES: *General: weekly on Tue at 10.00am. Semi antiques: monthly on first Fri of month at 10.00am. Antiques and fine art: every two/three months on Fri at 10.00am.*
VIEWING: *General: day prior 10.00am-4.30pm. Semi antiques: day prior 10.00am-4.30pm. Antiques and fine art: day prior 10.00am-8.00pm.*
REFRESHMENTS: *None available on the premises, but available near by.*
PARKING: *Public car park near by.*
STORAGE: *No*
TRANSPORTATION: *Yes*
SHIPPING: *Yes*

SANDGATE AUCTIONS

58A Sandgate/42 Fort Street. Tel: (0292) 263263

600-800 lots. The saleroom has two addresses, one for the back, one for the front, but both give access. The building itself is an old church. The main sale area is very large, and the auctioneer, Mr W D Grant, stands in what used to be the pulpit. There are three main sales. Two are held in the saleroom and the other in one of the local hotels.

The weekly Tuesday sale is of general household furniture and effects, and includes china, kitchenalia, electrical goods and the like. On the first Friday of the month there is a sale of what they call 'semi antiques', which usually means 1900s-1960s items. There are usually around 300-400 lots in this sale, which includes inexpensive jewellery and Victorian bric-à-brac.

Every two or three months, usually on a Friday, there is an antiques and fine art sale, which takes place in a local hotel — not always the same one. There may be as many as 800 lots in this sale.

Biggar

BUYER'S PREMIUM: *Nil*
SALES: *Monthly on Mon at 10.30am.*
VIEWING: *Fri prior 1.00pm-4.00pm, morning of sale.*
REFRESHMENTS: *Drinks machine.*
PARKING: *On street (no meters).*
STORAGE: *Yes*
TRANSPORTATION: *Yes*
SHIPPING: *No*

BIGGAR AUCTION MARKET

South Back Road. Tel: (0899) 20002

600-700 lots. Perhaps the reason why many Scottish auctions are so colourful is that the general furniture and household effects sales often take place in the same buildings as the livestock sales. The lots are set out in the rings and byres which not long ago were used to show and sell livestock. The same auctioneer stands in the box from which he sells cattle, and the buyers have the same determined look as their farming counterparts. Here the small items are sold from within the ring first.

Boxes containing varied miscellaneous items are set out on tables, with the better quality items set apart in their own display. The sale moves to the back for electrical goods such as vacuum cleaners, washing machines, spin driers and the like, plus bicycles, linen and carpets. The sale of larger items of furniture begins at 2.30pm after a break.

CHRISTIE'S SCOTLAND

Glasgow

164-166 Bath Street. Tel: (041) 332 8134

100-200 lots. Do not be intimidated by the famous name. You will not be landed with a multi-million pound Van Gogh painting by an inadvertant twitch of the eye. The prices reached here can be quite modest, and in some of the sales a few lots will sell for under £30. Even if you don't expect to buy, a visit enables you to see valuable paintings and rare antiques that you might otherwise never get close to.

The frequency of sales varies. There are usually two or more specialist sales a week, and categories include pictures, furniture and works of art, books and prints, clocks and scientific instruments, ceramics, toys and dolls, silver, jewellery and much more besides.

BUYER'S PREMIUM: *10%*
SALES: *Usually two or three times a week on Tue, Wed, and Thu at 11.00am (may vary).*
VIEWING: *Two days prior 10.00am-4.00pm or 7.00pm.*
REFRESHMENTS: *None available on the premises.*
PARKING: *Sauchiehall Street car park.*
STORAGE: *Yes*
TRANSPORTATION: *Yes*
SHIPPING: *Yes*

ARTHUR E COLLINS & SON LTD

Glasgow

114 Trongate. Tel: (041) 552 0489

100-250 lots. Trongate is a busy thoroughfare which has changed a great deal since the days when Burns, Sir Walter Scott, Adam Smith and other great men walked down it. The old Glasgow Cross, at the junction of Trongate, Saltmarket and Gallowgate, is perhaps the best landmark to look for. The saleroom is comparatively small, and easily filled by the 50 or 60 people who attend most sales.

The weekly Tuesday and Thursday sales contain around 200-250 lots of jewellery, which are unredeemed pawnbroker pledges. The quality varies considerably, and lots will fetch anything from £5 to £1,500. The weekly Wednesday sale usually includes some 150-180 lots of antique, modern or reproduction furniture, but will occasionally be given over to electrical goods. The items in this sale, as in the jewellery sales, will be unredeemed pawnbroker pledges, including televisions, radios, videos, shavers, and, sets of golf clubs. Lots are sold at the rate of some 120 an hour, so it is important not to arrive late.

BUYER'S PREMIUM: *Nil*
SALES: *Jewellery: weekly on Tue and Thu at 1.30pm. Furniture: weekly on Wed at 1.30pm (occasionally replaced by electrical goods).*
VIEWING: *Day of sale 9.00am-12.00 noon.*
REFRESHMENTS: *None available on the premises.*
PARKING: *King Street car park.*
STORAGE: *Yes*
TRANSPORTATION: *Yes*
SHIPPING: *No*

GREAT WESTERN AUCTIONS

Glasgow

1 Bothwell Lane Kelvin Bridge. Tel: (041) 339 3290

600-700 lots. There are two Bothwell Lanes in Glasgow. It is important to check that you have the right one: it lies off Glasgow Street. This is one of the most friendly sales I have ever attended. It is run by the rare combination of a mother and daughter team, and since Anita Manning and her daughter Lala took over in January 1989, the sale has enjoyed a

BUYER'S PREMIUM: *10%*
SALES: *Fortnightly on Sat at 11.00am.*
VIEWING: *Day prior 11.00am-7.30pm, morning of sale from 9.00am.*
REFRESHMENTS: *Own café.*

PARKING: *Kelvin Bridge underground car park.*
STORAGE: *No*
TRANSPORTATION: *Yes*
SHIPPING: *No*

growing reputation. Private buyers find the friendly atmosphere helpful, and as an additional aid to buyers Anita Manning has produced an informative leaflet which is freely available round the saleroom. It sets out the background to the auction and gives tips on how to bid.

Each sale contains a wide mix of antique and modern furniture, jewellery, silver, ceramics and so on, and a notable number of paintings, watercolours, drawings and prints. There may be as many as 150 hung round the wall, making Great Western Auctions one of the largest non-specialist sellers of pictures in Scotland, if not the largest. The auction starts briskly with the sale of perhaps 150 or so lots of jewellery, silver, silver plate and so on. The paintings, watercolours, drawings and prints are then sold from the walls, and in the early afternoon the furniture and household items are sold.

Glasgow

KERR & McALISTER

Queens Park Auction Hall, 140 Niddrie Road.
Tel: (041) 423 4271

BUYER'S PREMIUM: *Nil*
SALES: *Weekly on Thu at 6.30pm.*
VIEWING: *Wed and Thu 9.30am-4.30pm.*
REFRESHMENTS: *None available on the premises.*
PARKING: *Free parking on street.*
STORAGE: *Yes*
TRANSPORTATION: *Yes*
SHIPPING: *Yes*

350-400 lots. Niddrie Road is on the south side of the city in rather a quiet area. Quiet, that is, except for Thursday evenings, when it seems to come to life with people walking with that determined gait so typical of bargain hunters. The 5,000sq ft of saleroom allow buyers plenty of space for studying the lots. Buyers are rarely disappointed, as there is always a wide range of lots, covering all periods and dates, from high quality antiques to modern items — an elm and ash-stick Windsor chair, a washing machine, a Wedgwood meat dish or a Caucasian carpet, a television, or a William Henry Earp watercolour. Small items such as pieces of jewellery and silver may be kept in the 'smalls cabinet'. Ask one of the staff to unlock it if you wish to look at something more closely.

Glasgow

ROBT McTEAR & CO (AUCTIONEERS) LTD

Royal Exchange Saleroom, 6 North Court, St Vincent Place.
Tel: (041) 221 4456

BUYER'S PREMIUM: *10%*
SALES: *Antiques: weekly on Fri at 10.30am. General (Otago Lane): weekly on Wed at 6.00pm.*
VIEWING: *Antiques: Day prior: 10.00am-4.00pm. General (Otago Lane): day of sale, 10.00am-5.00pm.*
REFRESHMENTS: *None available on the premises.*

400-500 lots. Robt McTear & Co hold two regular weekly sales. The sale of antiques and paintings is held on Friday mornings, in the Royal Exhange Saleroom, right in the centre of the city just 100 yards or so from busy George Square. Selling starts with around 50 or 60 lots of jewellery. Next to be sold is silver and silver plate, porcelain and china, and paintings. The sale finishes with furniture.

At the smaller saleroom at 30 Otago Lane, which is at the west side of the city in the Kelvin Bridge area, there are

Wednesday evening sales of general household furniture and effects. There could be some antiques, or valuable items of china and jewellery at this sale. Lots are auctioned at the rate of 85 to 100 per hour.

Both sales are well attended and friendly. They offer excellent buys in a great variety of areas, and there should be something at one of the sales to suit all tastes and pockets.

PARKING: *None available on the premises.*
STORAGE: *Yes*
TRANSPORTATION: *Yes*
SHIPPING: *Yes*

PHILLIPS, SCOTLAND

Glasgow

207 Bath Street. Tel: (041) 221 8377

This is one of two Phillips salerooms in Scotland. The Glasgow saleroom has monthly general sales of furniture, pictures, ceramics, silver and jewellery. There are also regular specialist sales under headings like 'Fine Jewellery', 'Pianos and Furniture', 'Decorative Arts' and 'Scottish Contemporary Art'. Each July a particularly well-attended three-day sale is held, of fine oil paintings, ceramics, silver, jewellery, fine furniture, clocks, rugs and works of art.

BUYER'S PREMIUM: *10%*
SALES: *General: monthly on Tue at 11.00am. Specialist: about ten throughout the year. Fine art and antiques three-day sale: annually in Jul at 11.00am.*
VIEWING: *General: Sat prior 9.30am-12.00 noon. Mon prior 9.30am-4.30pm. Specialist and annual three-day: two days prior 9.30am-4.30pm.*
REFRESHMENTS: *None available on the premises.*
PARKING: *None available on the premises.*
STORAGE: *Yes*
TRANSPORTATION: *Yes*
SHIPPING: *Yes*

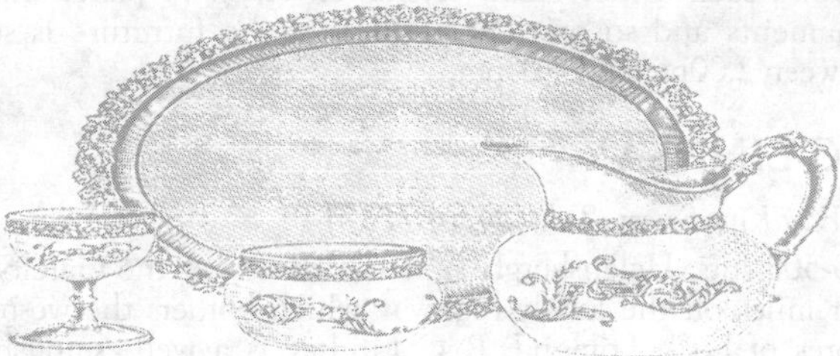

D B LORAINE

Greenock

26 West Stewart Street. Tel: (0475) 23150

400-500 lots. This is an enormous saleroom and it needs to be: very often as many as 500 people will attend. When the doors open at 9.00am there is usually a rush to grab one of the 50 or so seats available. The sale's popularity may be explained by the fact that it is the only one in this corner of Scotland. The nearest alternative is Robert Paterson and Son in Paisley, which is 18 or so miles away. Another reason could be the friendly atmosphere and the efficiency of the auctioneers; the firm has been going since 1921 and all the staff have long records of employment with the company. The sale starts with smaller items such as china, crockery, ornaments, silver and lamps, then moves on to televisions, washing machines, fridges and spin dryers. Furniture and carpets are sold last. There is a good mix of quality and types of goods. Prices are variable, but there are usually good bargains to be had.

BUYER'S PREMIUM: *10%*
SALES: *Weekly on Wed at 10.00am.*
VIEWING: *Mon, Tue and Thu 9.00am-4.00pm, Fri 9.00am-1.00pm.*
REFRESHMENTS: *None available on the premises.*
PARKING: *Multi-storey car park 100 yards away.*
STORAGE: *No*
TRANSPORTATION: *Yes*
SHIPPING: *Yes*

Hamilton

BUYER'S PREMIUM: *10%*
SALES: *General: weekly on Mon at 10.00am. Antiques and fine art: quarterly on third Thu of Feb, May, Aug and Nov at 10.00am.*
VIEWING: *General: Fri prior 4.00pm-6.00pm. Antiques and fine art: day prior 4.00pm-6.00pm.*
REFRESHMENTS: *Own café.*
PARKING: *Own car park at rear.*
STORAGE: *No*
TRANSPORTATION: *Yes*
SHIPPING: *Yes*

L S SMILLIE & SONS LTD

Lower Auchingramon Road. Tel: (0698) 282007

400-500 lots. Hamilton is 11 miles south-east of Glasgow, a little to the west of the M74 motorway at the junction of the A74 road and the road which travels through Strathaven to Ayr and Stranraer. The lack of a street number is explained by the fact that the saleroom takes up half the street and is an unmistakable fine old stone building. There are two regular sales. The weekly Monday sale is of general household furniture and effects, and there is a quarterly sale of antiques and fine art, held on the third Thursday of February, May, August and November. Both attract buyers from all over Scotland and from England, Germany, Ireland and North America. The quarterly sale usually has around 500-800 lots. The Monday sale consists of furniture and carpets, china, glass, silver, silver plate, and also electrical goods such as televisions and washing machines. Furniture is sold between 10.00am and 12.00 noon. Between 1.00pm and 2.00pm there is the sale of 'smalls', such as porcelain, crystal, silver, silver plate, china, ornaments and so on. The residue of the furniture is sold between 2.00pm and 4.00pm.

Helensburgh

BUYER'S PREMIUM: *10%*
SALES: *Monthly on Fri at 11.00am.*
VIEWING: *Wed and Thu prior 10.00am-1.00pm, 2.30-5.00pm.*
REFRESHMENTS: *None available on the premises.*
PARKING: *Railway station car park near by.*
STORAGE: *Yes*
TRANSPORTATION: *Yes*
SHIPPING: *Yes*

R C LINDSAY

31 East King Street. Tel: (0436) 72314

400-500 lots. Helensburgh is at the mouth of the Gareloch, four miles off the lovely highway which borders the western shores of Loch Lomond. R C Lindsay is a well-established Scottish auction house which was founded in 1863. Angela Reid, the present auctioneer (one of the few female auctioners in Britain), runs an interesting sale with a good mix of modern and antique lots. It is popular with dealers and increasingly with private buyers, probably because they never know what to expect: lots have ranged from a 1980s fridge to an 18th-century child's rocking cradle. The auction starts in the back room with the electrical items and household goods. There is a break for lunch at around 12.30pm. Selling recommences at 1.00pm in the main room, with the better quality lots.

Kilmun

BUYER'S PREMIUM: *10%*
SALES: *Monthly on Sat at 11.00am.*
VIEWING: *Fri prior 2.00pm-7.00pm.*

W CUNNINGHAM

Kilmun Hall. Tel: (0369) 4102

400-500 lots. Kilmun village is a popular summer resort, sheltered from the north winds by Kilmun Hill. Dunoon is just seven miles away, and the road from there to Kilmun runs along the western side of Holy Loch. One of the most pleasant ways to make the journey is to take a boat. The presence of US military bases near by explains the number of Americans who attend most sales. There are plenty of small items to interest them as souvenirs: silver spoons and sets of cutlery, or items of jewellery and china. Dinner and tea services are also popular, and fun items such as a 1920s biscuit barrel or a Victorian novelty teapot will create a lot of interest. Fine items of furniture, longcase clocks, sideboards and full sets of dining chairs can be found, but will always attract keen bidding.

REFRESHMENTS: *Own café.*
PARKING: *Street parking permitted.*
STORAGE: *Yes*
TRANSPORTATION: *Yes*
SHIPPING: *Yes*

UNITED AUCTIONS (WESTERN) LTD

Oban

West Highland Auction Mart, Lochside Street. Tel: (0631) 62233

200-400 lots. Oban has a population of around 7,000 people and is a very pleasant, clean little town with plenty of opportunities for sea or salmon and trout fishing. Not far from the saleroom, a pleasant walk along Lochside Street and down Argyll Square will lead you to Oban Bay. There is no general sale during October, as that is when the auctioneers are busiest with livestock sales, which take place in the same building. In the summer months though, between April and August, perhaps for the sake of summer visitors, every effort is made for the sale to be held twice a month. Lots are numbered and typewritten lists with descriptions are produced for each sale, at the princely price (at the time of writing) of 5p.

Large items are sold first from the rear of the hall, but otherwise there is no particular order — items are sold in the order in which they have arrived at the saleroom. Tables are set up to hold smaller items such as crockery, tea and dinner sets, silver, ornaments, cutlery and bundles of linen. Quite often the number of lots in the sale will double because a small hotel has closed and is selling its effects.

BUYER'S PREMIUM: *Nil*
SALES: *Monthly (except Oct) on Sat at 10.30am. Often twice a month from Apr to Aug.*
VIEWING: *Morning of sale.*
REFRESHMENTS: *None available on the premises.*
PARKING: *Lochavullin car park opposite.*
STORAGE: *Yes*
TRANSPORTATION: *Yes*
SHIPPING: *Yes*

ROBERT PATERSON & SON

Paisley

8 Orchard Street. Tel: (041) 889 2435

1,000-1,300 lots. Paisley is known the world over as a centre of thread manufacture. It is an interesting blend of the old and new, and its parish church is the restored part of a 12th-century abbey. Robert Paterson & Son's premises are to be found two minutes away from Paisley Cross, in a late Victorian construction built by the great-grandfather of the present auctioneer, Andrew Paterson, whose son Robert has joined the firm. That makes five generations of family involvement — the boast is that this is the oldest family auctioneering firm still selling in Scotland.

A large new saleroom was added at the back of the building

BUYER'S PREMIUM: *10%*
SALES: *Fortnightly on Tue at 10.30am (alternate general and catalogued sales).*
VIEWING: *Day prior 9.00am-5.00pm.*
REFRESHMENTS: *None available on the premises.*
PARKING: *Own small car park.*
STORAGE: *Yes*
TRANSPORTATION: *Yes*
SHIPPING: *Yes*

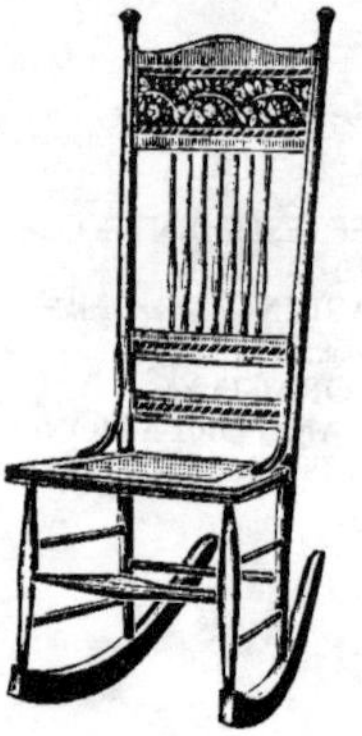

in 1976. Here, the general sale begins with silver and jewellery, and then moves on to electro-plate and furniture. Everything stops at 12.30pm for a sale of pictures, books and Paisley shawls. Prices vary from £5 to possibly £30,000. Alternate sale days are devoted to specialist catalogued sales of antiques and paintings.

TAYSIDE

Alyth

BUYER'S PREMIUM: *Nil*
SALES: *Weekly on Mon at 6.00pm (alternately at Alyth and Blairgowrie).*
VIEWING: *Day of sale from 2.00pm.*
REFRESHMENTS: *None available on the premises.*
PARKING: *Ample space at both salerooms.*
STORAGE: *Yes*
TRANSPORTATION: *Yes*
SHIPPING: *Yes*

J & J HOWE

24 Commercial Street. Tel: (08283) 2594

400-500 lots. The sale alternates on a weekly basis with J & J Howe's second saleroom just five miles away at 30 Reform Street, Blairgowrie, tel: (0250) 2361. The Alyth (pronounced ail-lith) saleroom is directly opposite the town's main square; the one at Blairgowrie is a short distance from the town centre.

J & J Howe is a long-established, traditional Scottish country auction with many buyers regularly attending both sales. Some of them come partly to meet friends, and stay to chat until Mr McNaughton, the auctioneer, turns them out, usually long after the sale has finished. Both sales have the same routine and the same wide range and variety of lots. They start with small items such as china, ornaments, silver and jewellery, which are set out on tables round the rostrum, and then move on to furniture and other large items which are placed around the walls. About every two months the sale at Blairgowrie is devoted to better quality furniture and effects.

Blairgowrie

J & J HOWE

See J & J HOWE, Alyth, Tayside

Crieff

BUYER'S PREMIUM: *10%*
SALES: *Fortnightly on Wed at 11.00am (includes antique and fine art sale about every quarter).*
VIEWING: *Day prior 8.00am-5.00pm, morning of sale from 8.00am.*
REFRESHMENTS: *None available on the premises.*
PARKING: *Town centre car park.*

WM NEIL & SON (CRIEFF) LTD

22 Galvelmore Street. Tel: (0764) 3276

500-600 lots. Crieff claims to be the most picturesquely situated hill town of Scotland, and is very popular as a health resort as well as for fishing, mountaineering and golf — the Gleneagles golfing centre with its three courses is only nine miles away.

The immediate impression visitors have at this sale is of the neatness and cleanness of the lots. Everything looks as though it has been washed or polished before being set out. Two spacious salerooms give the prospective buyer plenty of room to study the lots, a luxury not afforded by all salerooms. The auctioneer takes bids as he walks around the hall, stopping to stand on a stool at various points so he can see everyone. He starts the selling with perhaps 100 lots of linen, before moving on to furniture and general household effects, crockery, ornaments, jewellery, pictures, prints and so on. There is usually enough of a mixture of antique and modern to interest every type of buyer.

About every quarter (though sometimes less often), Wm Neil & Son hold special, well-attended antique and fine art sales, instead of their general sale.

STORAGE: *Yes*
TRANSPORTATION: *Yes*
SHIPPING: *Yes*

ROBERT CURR & DEWAR

Ward Road. Tel: (0382) 24185

400-500 lots. Robert Curr & Dewar is a family firm started in 1862 by an uncle of the grandfather of the present owner, whose son has entered the firm as well. Ward Road is in the centre of Dundee, a short walk from the Tay Road Bridge, and the single-storey saleroom building is almost opposite the main Post Office.

There are two salerooms, with three furniture storerooms at the back. The sales are good-humoured, well-run affairs. On Fridays there are sales of general household furniture, including modern and reproduction, and other household effects such as televisions, washing machines and other electrical goods, bicycles, china and sundry household items. The monthly Wednesday sale concentrates on antiques, fine art and associated lots.

Dundee

BUYER'S PREMIUM: *Nil*
SALES: *General: weekly on Fri at 12.00 noon. Antiques and fine art: monthly on Wed at 12.00 noon.*
VIEWING: *Day prior 2.00pm-7.00pm, morning of sale.*
REFRESHMENTS: *None available on the premises.*
PARKING: *Multi-storey car park one block away.*
STORAGE: *Yes*
TRANSPORTATION: *Yes*
SHIPPING: *Yes*

B L FENTON & SON

84 Victoria Road. Tel: (0382) 26227

300-400 lots. Dundee is a delight for the auction-goer — it is only a short walk from this sale to Robert Curr & Dewar's salerooms, and at West Port there is Marshal & Johnston's fortnightly sale.

B L Fenton & Son's weekly sale is of general household furniture and effects. Roughly every two months the general sale is replaced by a special antiques sale at 6 Forebank Road. Times are the same as for the general sale, but viewing hours may be extended, depending on the number of lots. The system of numbering lots may cause confusion: all items brought in by one vendor are given the same number, but they are not all sold at the same time. This makes it doubly important to note exactly what you want to bid for as well as its number. Failure to do so could mean going home with a set of lined curtains instead of a porcelain jardinière.

Dundee

BUYER'S PREMIUM: *Nil*
SALES: *Weekly on Thu at 10.00am (includes antiques sale about every two months at 6 Forebank Road).*
VIEWING: *Day prior 1.00pm-4.30pm (may be extended for antiques sale).*
REFRESHMENTS: *None available on the premises.*
PARKING: *None available on the premises.*
STORAGE: *No*
TRANSPORTATION: *Yes*
SHIPPING: *Yes*

Dundee

BUYER'S PREMIUM: *Nil*
SALES: *Fortnightly on Wed at 11.00am.*
VIEWING: *Day prior 9.30am-4.30pm.*
REFRESHMENTS: *None available on the premises.*
PARKING: *South Tay Street car park.*
STORAGE: *No*
TRANSPORTATION: *Yes*
SHIPPING: *Yes*

MARSHALL & JOHNSTON

7 Blinshall Street. Tel: (0382) 24931

500-1,000 lots. The three Dundee sales described in this book are within 15 minutes' drive of each other. Marshall & Johnston's auctions have been in existence since 1850. The saleroom is a most attractive old church, with the bulk of the auction taking place on the ground floor. When there is a particularly large number of lots, the basement is also used and the sale is continued to the next day (starting time 12.00 noon). Auctioneer Mr Ian Low starts his sale with smaller items such as china, porcelain, brass, glass, silver, ornaments, mirrors and pictures, including watercolours, drawings, prints and miniatures. The sale of jewellery starts at about 1.00pm, and is followed by a half-hour break. The sale of furniture, carpets and linen begins at 2.00pm or 2.30pm, depending on the number of lots. There is usually a wide range, including Victorian, modern and reproduction items, stripped and painted pine, dining room and bedroom suites, and so on.

Forfar

BUYER'S PREMIUM: *Nil*
SALES: *Monthly on Fri at 6.00pm.*
VIEWING: *Day prior 8.00am-5.00pm, day of sale.*
REFRESHMENTS: *None available on the premises.*
PARKING: *Own small car park.*
STORAGE: *Yes*
TRANSPORTATION: *Yes*
SHIPPING: *Yes*

DOIGS

Chapel Street. Tel: (0307) 62201

400-500 lots. Four generations of the Doig family have been involved in this auctioneering firm since 1888. Mr James Doig's grandfather began the company by selling goods outside the houses of vendors, setting the lots out in the garden or street. Today part of the sale may be conducted outside in summer when the weather is good, but mostly it takes place under cover in a large, former jute factory in the centre of town. There is something to interest dealers, private buyers and browsers here: a Victorian walnut davenport, an Edwardian salon suite, a mahogany chair and other good quality pieces (some of which may need restoration) may be found alongside various items of silver, pottery, electrical goods and gardening tools, as well as kitchenalia and collectables — perhaps an early Singer sewing machine or a collection of early telephone switchboards and handsets.

Montrose

BUYER'S PREMIUM: *10%*
SALES: *General: fortnightly on Sat at 10.30am. Specialist: monthly on Fri at 7.00pm.*
VIEWING: *General: day prior 2.00pm-5.00pm, day of sale from 9.00am. Specialist:*

TAYLORS AUCTION ROOMS

11 Panmure Row. Tel: (0674) 72775

2,000 lots. Situated opposite the Montrose Academy in the centre of Montrose, Taylors is one of the largest regular sales in Tayside and perhaps in Scotland, drawing buyers and vendors from all over the region. To get through the vast number of lots at most of the fortnightly auctions, three separate sales take place. Two start at 10.30am. One is in the Panmure Row saleroom and includes smaller items such as china, glass, porcelain, lamps, ornaments, bric-à-brac, collectables, bygones and so on. At the same time lesser quality furniture is sold directly opposite in the main saleroom, Bow Butts. When both these sales are completed, which is usually in the early afternoon, the auctioning of better quality furniture begins in the Bow Butts saleroom and continues until around 6.00pm. Also at Bow Butts, there are monthly specialist sales on Friday evenings, in categories such as jewellery, paintings, textiles and linen, garden furniture, books and so on.

day prior 2.00pm-5.00pm, 6.00pm-8.00pm.
REFRESHMENTS: *Caravan selling snacks.*
PARKING: *None available on the premises.*
STORAGE: *Yes*
TRANSPORTATION: *Yes*
SHIPPING: *Yes*

LINDSAY BURNS & CO LTD

Perth

6 King Street. Tel: (0738) 33888

900-1,000 lots. The auction room is a short walk from the railway station, along Leonard Street. The landmark to look out for is the saleroom building itself: a beautiful Georgian former church, standing out among the terraced houses which surround it. The fortnightly sale is one of many attractions in this attractive and ancient city, and typically will include Victoriana, glass, china, ornaments, jewellery, linen, *objets d'art* and Scottish bygones, as well as modern and antique furniture. One of the reasons why so many private buyers are regulars, and why holidaymakers return so often, is no doubt the presence of Mrs Elspeth Burns, who makes sure that everything runs smoothly. Special antique and fine art auctions are held four times a year in place of the general sale.

BUYER'S PREMIUM: *General: Nil. Antiques sales: 10%*
SALES: *Fortnightly on Thu at 10.30am (includes antiques and fine art sale about every three months).*
VIEWING: *General: day prior 9.00am-5.00pm. Antiques: day prior 9.00am-6.00pm.*
REFRESHMENTS: *None available on the premises.*
PARKING: *Own car park.*
STORAGE: *Yes*
TRANSPORTATION: *Yes*
SHIPPING: *Yes*

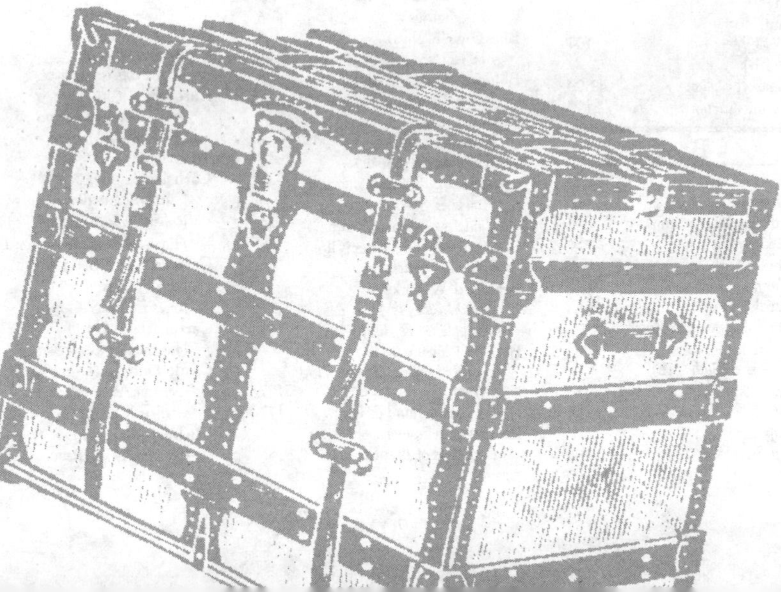

• INDEX •

A

B

C

• INDEX •

T

U

V

W

• READER RECOMMENDATIONS •

We realise that there are many interesting auctions and that we may not have included your own favourite, so we would be very grateful to hear of any saleroom where you have found any particularly interesting or unusual items.

Please send your report forms to:
The Automobile Association
Special Projects (TCA)
AA Publishing
Fanum House
Basingstoke
Hants RG21 2EA

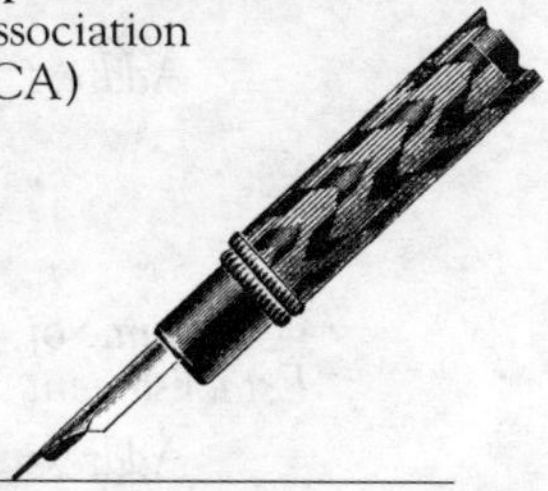

Your Name : ______________________________

Address : ______________________________

____

Name of Establishment : ______________________________

____

Address : ______________________________

____

Your Comments : ______________________________

____

____

____

____

____

____

____

____

Your Name

Address

Name of Establishment

Address

Your Comments

Your Name

Address

Name of Establishment

Address

Your Comments

Your Name

Address

Name of Establishment

Address

Your Comments

Your Name

Address

Name of Establishment

Address

Your Comments

Your Name ______________________

Address ______________________

____

Name of Establishment ______________________

Address ______________________

____

Your Comments ______________________

____

____

Your Name ______________________

Address ______________________

____

Name of Establishment ______________________

Address ______________________

____

Your Comments ______________________

____

____

____